Politicized Enforcement in Argentina

Countries throughout the world have passed regulations that promise protection for workers and the environment, but violations of these policies are more common than compliance. All too often, limitations of state capacity and political will intertwine, hindering enforcement. Why do states enforce regulations in some places, and in some industries, but not in others? In *Politicized Enforcement in Argentina*, Amengual develops a framework for analyzing enforcement in middle-income and developing countries, showing how informal linkages between state officials and groups within society allow officials to gain the operational resources and political support necessary for enforcement. This analysis builds on state-society approaches in comparative politics, but in contrast to theories that emphasize state autonomy, it focuses on key differences in the way states are porous to political influence.

Matthew Amengual is an assistant professor at the Massachusetts Institute of Technology in the MIT Sloan School of Management. He is affiliated with the Institute for Work and Employment Research and the Sustainability Initiative. His research on labor and environmental politics has been published in *Politics & Society*, *World Development*, *Industrial and Labor Relations Review*, and *Desarrollo Económico*.

Politicized Enforcement in Argentina

Labor and Environmental Regulation

MATTHEW AMENGUAL
Massachusetts Institute of Technology

CAMBRIDGE
UNIVERSITY PRESS

32 Avenue of the Americas, New York, NY 10013–2473, USA

Cambridge University Press is part of the University of Cambridge.

It furthers the University's mission by disseminating knowledge in the pursuit of education, learning, and research at the highest international levels of excellence.

www.cambridge.org
Information on this title: www.cambridge.org/9781107135833

© Matthew Amengual, 2016

This publication is in copyright. Subject to statutory exception and to the provisions of relevant collective licensing agreements, no reproduction of any part may take place without the written permission of Cambridge University Press.

First published 2016

A catalog record for this publication is available from the British Library.

Library of Congress Cataloging-in-Publication Data
Names: Amengual, Matthew, author.
Title: Politicized enforcement in Argentina : labor and environmental regulation / Matthew Amengual.
Description: New York, NY : Cambridge University Press, [2016]
Identifiers: LCCN 2015042011 | ISBN 9781107135833 (Hardback)
Subjects: LCSH: Administrative agencies–Argentina. | Environmental agencies–Argentina. | Labor laws and legislation–Argentina. | Labor policy–Argentina. | Environmental law–Argentina. | Environmental policy–Argentina–Citizen participation. | Industrial laws and legislation–Argentina. | Industrial policy–Argentina. | BISAC: POLITICAL SCIENCE / Government / General.
Classification: LCC JL2031 .A75 2016 | DDC 331.12/0420982–dc23 LC record available at http://lccn.loc.gov/2015042011

ISBN 978-1-107-13583-3 Hardback

Cambridge University Press has no responsibility for the persistence or accuracy of URLs for external or third-party Internet Web sites referred to in this publication and does not guarantee that any content on such Web sites is, or will remain, accurate or appropriate.

Contents

Acknowledgments		*page* vii
1	Introduction: the challenge of enforcement	1
2	Explaining enforcement of labor and environmental regulations	16
PART I LABOR REGULATION		
3	Labor regulation in Argentina	51
4	Enforcement with unions in the driver's seat	73
5	State-driven and co-produced enforcement in labor regulation	112
PART II ENVIRONMENTAL REGULATION		
6	Chaotic environmental regulation in Argentina	147
7	Putting out fires in Santa Fe and Córdoba	168
8	Pollution in the "Garden of the Republic"	190
PART III CONCLUSION		
9	Conclusion	219
Appendix: List of Interviews in Argentina		241
Works Cited		251
Index		267

Acknowledgments

This work was born out of a set of conversations that began for me at MIT in 2005, when a group of graduate students and faculty became intensely interested in the role of regulation in development. The gap between the promise of policies and actual practices on the ground drew our attention to the regulators who are charged with implementation on a day to day basis. We read broadly, debated intensively, and traveled to learn firsthand what was happening inside bureaucracies, firms, and societal organizations involved with regulation. We periodically reconvened at MIT to share our findings from the world and debate how regulation works, as well as ways to improve its practice. I learned a tremendous amount from my friends, mentors who were part of these discussions, and from the rich literature on regulation and states. Yet, when I set off to Argentina in 2008, the theoretical toolkit that I brought with me was, in many ways, terribly inadequate. I chose to study Argentina, in part, because I believed that I would find differences in the organization of the state bureaucracies that could account for variance in the ways regulations were implemented. The regulatory bureaucracies I encountered, however, were all far removed from the Weberian ideal-types highlighted in the literature. As a result, dominant theories were of little guidance for understanding what I encountered on the ground. The puzzle became to understand how and why seemingly flawed bureaucracies sometimes enforced regulations and sometimes did not. In searching for an answer, I needed to build upon the literature that had informed my thinking so deeply and develop a new set of tools to make sense of aspects of regulatory politics that had been otherwise hidden. Through the lens of the Argentine cases, this book is my attempt to offer a new way of thinking about the way politicized states enforce the rules of the game. By doing so, my hope is to not only shed some light on what drives different actions by states that had been otherwise homogenized, but also to reveal the possibilities and constraints of regulation that had been obscured.

viii *Acknowledgments*

In the process of writing this book, I incurred many debts. They began with my dissertation committee, who have left a huge mark on my work. Suzanne Berger patiently helped me cut through the haze to identify the contours of a theory when I could not. Steve Levitsky's careful reading and insightful suggestions immeasurably improved my work, and he provided an example of detailed field research and theoretical development to which I aspired. Mike Piore's characteristically stimulating ideas shaped my research agenda and constantly encouraged me to recognize what was truly surprising about my findings. While all members of my committee helped me tremendously, Rick Locke played an outsized role in all stages of this project. He has been a continual mentor from the inception of this work to its publication, and has demonstrated by example what it means to be a scholar committed to generating and diffusing knowledge that is rigorous and relevant.

A large part of the work I did on this project took place in Argentina. The funding I used to conduct fieldwork was provided by a grant from the MIT Center for International Studies and from the International Dissertation Research Fellowship Program of the Social Science Research Council, with funds provided by the Andrew W. Mellon Foundation. In Argentina, I was fortunate to gain insights, direction, and support from a number of colleagues and friends, including Sebastian Etchemendy, Carla Giacomuzzi, Adriana Marshall, Bárbara Medwid, Lucas Ronconi, and Cecilia Senén-Gonzalez. While conducting interviews, I often felt like a traveling salesman with nothing to sell, trying to convince people to help me when I could offer very little in return. It is no exaggeration to say that this book would not have been possible without the hundreds of people who sat down with me and shared their stories. Along the way, there were a few who helped me gain access at key moments, including José Luis Blasco, María Eugenia Di Paola, Ariel Carbajal, Alfredo Montalván, Guillermo Alonso Navone, Carlos Aníbel Rodríguez, Jorge Sappia, Omar Hugo Sereno, and José Luis Yacanto. I am greatly indebted to all of them. I am also grateful to those who worked with me on the research in Indonesia that helped shed some comparative light on the Argentine cases, especially Laura Chirot, Mohamad Anis Agung Nugroho, and Achmed Hasan.

Luckily, I had ample support in the difficult task of taking in the complicated world and forming it into this book from a broad community of scholars. I am especially grateful to: Salo Coslovsky, Kristin Fabbe, Janice Fine, Tom Kochan, Jason Jackson, Gabi Kruks-Wisner, Alisha Holland, Akshay Mangla, Roberto Pires, Susan Silbey, Ben Ross Schneider, Andrew Schrank, David Weil, and Adam Ziegfeld. Their advice and encouragement made this work immeasurably stronger. I greatly appreciate the scholars who read a complete draft at my workshop: Patrick Heller, Margaret Levi, Marcus Kurtz, Margaret Keck, Alison Post, and Richard Snyder. I also thank Anna Katsavos, for helping make sure the ideas in this book are clearly expressed. Finally, I acknowledge the *Industrial and Labor Relations Review* and *Politics & Society* for publishing articles out of this project and for permission to use the material in this book.

Acknowledgments   ix

While much of the last ten years was spent thinking about regulation in Argentina and elsewhere, a lot happened outside of the narrow world of research for which I am deeply grateful. For my parents, Ann and Randy, who laid the foundation for my scholarship and continually supported me to make my work possible. For the arrival of Luca, our *piccolino,* whose *vuoi giocare con me?* helped me focus on what really matters. And most of all for Monica, who has been an intellectual partner throughout this project. Busy with her own work, she nevertheless endured seemingly endless conversation about the bureaucrats, labor leaders, environmentalists, and managers who fascinated me. *Grazie.*

1

Introduction

The challenge of enforcement

A labor inspector, flanked by a union leader, rang the doorbell of an industrial laundry hidden in a residential neighborhood of the city of Córdoba, Argentina, to conduct a routine check of working conditions. When they entered, they found the building was so damp that water had accumulated on the ceiling and was raining back down on the dozen workers who moved sheets and towels in and out of large machines. The inspector explained to the workshop supervisor how the lack of ventilation had created hazards, and informed the supervisor that officials who specialize in health and safety would conduct a follow-up investigation to ensure that conditions improved. Meanwhile, the union leader gathered information from workers about pay, hours, and benefits. Conducting brief interviews with workers, the union leader compared worker responses to the requirements of labor law and the collective bargaining agreement.[1] This particular industrial laundry was given thirty days to comply with a variety of standards before it would be fined or possibly shut down. In this case, officials from the state regulatory bureaucracy worked closely with the union to ensure that these workers benefited from the rights specified in labor laws, including being paid their full wage and having the opportunity to be included in the social welfare system.

Although Córdoba's labor inspectorate was riddled with features that are generally understood to undermine regulation – officials hired by virtue of their political connections instead of merit, uncompetitive salaries for public sector workers, conflicts of interest, and a shortage of resources – this inspector had helped workers in similar laundries recover thousands of pesos in back pay and gain legally mandated protections. Not all workers in Córdoba, however, benefited from inspections. There were pervasive violations of basic standards

---

[1] I directly observed this inspection during fieldwork in 2008.

in the brick-kilns scattered outside the province's capital city, some resulting in the deaths of children on worksites. Labor inspectors, however, repeatedly failed to take substantive action. Consequently, workers in this industry continued to have their wages stolen, to be exposed to unsafe working conditions, and to be left out of social welfare institutions.

Similar unevenness in enforcement is also evident in the control of pollution from industry. In the province of Santa Fe, an industrial food-processing plant continually blanketed the community with noxious air pollution. Safety lapses in the plant resulted in explosions that were uncomfortably close to a residential area. People living near the plant had increased rates of respiratory diseases and worried that a large-scale industrial accident would tear through their neighborhood. In response to their complaints, regulators from the provincial environmental agency worked with the plant to install pollution control technologies. Regulators also served as intermediaries between the plant and the community, facilitating a negotiated process by which the plant could come into compliance. Similar to Córdoba, the regulatory bureaucracy in Santa Fe lacked most of the features generally associated with capable states – officials were patronage employees, were not insulated from political interference, and had an extreme lack of resources. Yet, as a result of enforcement, community leaders said the incidence of respiratory diseases declined, and plant managers said that they do not have to worry about disruptive protests. While this particular community benefited from environmental protection, nearby agro-industrial plants (under the same regulatory laws and jurisdiction) continued to pollute with impunity. State regulators did little in these cases to ensure that policies have tangible effects, and the communities around these plants continued to live with high levels of contamination.

In the 1990s in the neighboring province of Tucumán, environmental regulations were largely not enforced. Officials took samples of water pollution from sugar mills producing ethanol and found contaminants at levels more than one hundred times the legal limits. Until 2003, there were few, if any, steps taken either to punish violators or to enable firms to comply. Efforts to improve compliance increased gradually, and by 2008 the local environmental agency began a far-reaching campaign to enforce regulations. Officials enforced regulations even in places where community groups did not immediately mobilize. The resulting action led to more than fifty million dollars in investments by the industry to reduce pollution. This substantial increase in enforcement is puzzling because politicians remained ambivalent about environmental protection, and Tucumán had a substantially lower level of economic development compared to that of Santa Fe (where enforcement did not increase). Moreover, in Tucumán regulators achieved broad enforcement without forming a traditionally strong bureaucracy. Instead, the province hired officials with preexisting ties to the industry and gave them short-term contracts with few career prospects within the state bureaucracy – organizational features that left the agency open to political interference.

Uneven states and weak institutions

Why do states enforce regulations in some places, and in some industries, and not in others? How can states that lack many of the features considered necessary for state capacity – such as meritocratic and politically insulated bureaucracies – enforce regulations? The answer to this puzzle, I argue, lies in recognizing that even porous states have informal structures that allow some societal organizations to influence the bureaucracy and deflect other organizations. I do not contradict the claim that forming strong bureaucracies can help advance enforcement. Rather, I argue that the different ways in which states are porous to political influence can determine how enforcement occurs. In places where these structures allow pro-enforcement groups to form linkages with officials, these groups are able to influence state action and to provide resources to officials. Under these conditions, enforcement can become possible, even when regulatory agencies have not undertaken conventional reforms to become politically autonomous bureaucracies.

Building on this insight, we can account for differences of enforcement by examining the way the structures of linkages between state and society interact with resources inside the state apparatus. Furthermore, we are able to gain insights into a broader set of questions related to institutional weaknesses and to the functioning of states that depart from the strong state ideal-type that is pervasive in the literature. In the following sections, I introduce the problems of uneven enforcement and weak institutions, outline dominant approaches to account for differences in enforcement, and provide an initial elaboration of an alternative theory (developed in detail in Chapter 2). The remainder of this introduction situates the problem of enforcement in the two policy areas that are the subject of the analysis – labor and environmental regulation – and outlines the plan of the book.

UNEVEN STATES AND WEAK INSTITUTIONS

Unevenness in state responses to regulatory violations is an issue not only in Argentina. The gap between promised protections of regulations and the realities on the ground is all too evident in many countries and industries. In Bangladesh, for example, the horrific Rana Plaza factory collapse in 2013 that claimed the lives of more than 1,000 workers might have been prevented if government regulators enforced basic safety codes.[2] In China, air pollution levels, which are consistently double of China's own legal standards, have been tied to widespread declines in life expectancy and have become a political issue. While there is enforcement of policies meant to reduce pollution in China, such enforcement varies tremendously across regions and municipalities.[3] Even countries with ample resources often fail to identify and mitigate violations.

---

[2] Jim Yardley, "Garment Trade Wields Power in Bangladesh," *New York Times*, 7/24/2013
[3] Van Lo Rooij, Benjamin, and Carlos Wing-Hung 2010; Chen, Ebenstein, Greenstone, and Li 2013

A survey of workers in low-wage industries in three major cities of the United States found that more than a quarter of the workers were paid less than the minimum wage and three-quarters were underpaid for overtime.[4] Most of these violations go undiscovered and uncorrected by regulators. Yet, in some cases in the United States, regulators have taken far-reaching action to protect workers from labor standards violations. A partnership between janitorial workers and regulators in Los Angeles, for example, recovered millions of dollars in back pay for workers and brought thousands of jobs into the formal sector.[5] A similar story can be found in environmental regulation in the United States; enforcement rigor varies by community poverty levels, resulting in inequalities in the *de facto* protections afforded by environmental policies.[6]

The illustrations above are cases of variation in state responses to violations of rules that are meant to structure the way the economy and society function. The uneven character of state enforcement of legislated rules, however, is pervasive across a wide variety of issue areas. An analysis of intellectual property protections in China, for instance, found substantial disparities in the quality of enforcement. While China does, at times, take steps to protect intellectual property, the process is fraught with politics and is often not effective.[7] Studies of immigration administration in the United States and Germany have also shown stark variation in the way the deportation laws are enforced, with informal processes influencing which migrants are removed from the country and which are given clemency.[8] Similarly, researchers have found systematic differences in the judicial responses to police killings in Latin America; police who violate rights of citizens are only sometimes held into account.[9] Finally, a study of street vendors in Colombia, Peru, and Chile found pervasive, but not universal, nonenforcement of laws governing public space. In these countries, some politicians used "forbearance" as a strategy for subsidizing their poor constituents (and thereby maintaining electoral support).[10] These examples from diverse policy areas and polities illustrate the breadth of the phenomenon in which violations of basic laws are widespread, and the parts of the state charged with enforcement act in a highly uneven fashion, selectively applying the rules.

Unevenness in enforcement has tremendous implications. For individuals, enforcement can make the difference between health, prosperity, life, and death. At a broader level, enforcement plays a key role in the way institutions function. It has long been established that institutions matter profoundly in the ways societies and economies function, but the presence of formal institutions is only loosely connected to actual behaviors in much of the world.[11] In all of

---

[4] Bernhardt, Milkman, Theodore, Hackathorn, Auer, DeFiilippis, González, Narro, Perelshteyn, Polson, and Spiller 2010. On the broader enforcement challenge in the United States, see: Weil 2014

[5] Fine and Gordon 2010   [6] Konisky 2009   [7] Dimitrov 2009   [8] Ellermann 2009

[9] Brinks 2008   [10] Holland 2015   [11] O'Donnell 1993; Levitsky and Murillo 2013

Uneven states and weak institutions

the examples above, whether dealing with intellectual property, immigration, labor standards, or environmental pollution, rules that were meant to structure social relations broke down to varying degrees. When the state apparatus does respond to violations in basic rules with enforcement, weak institutions can become "activated," and rules that were previously ignored can have a substantial impact.[12] As such, enforcement often plays a key role in mediating the relationship between formal rules and actual practices. Thus, to develop a more complete understanding of the way institutions function in much of the world, we must explain enforcement.

Explaining enforcement

What explains variation in enforcement? This is the central question of this book. In the broadest sense, there are many factors at play – including the level of economic development of the country, the degree of the breakdown in institutional order, and the historical legacies of state development. Yet, even within these structural conditions, there is puzzling variation in enforcement. For example, an analysis of labor regulation using firm-level data from seventy two developing and middle-income countries found only a very weak correlation between country wealth and the probability of a firm being inspected.[13] Thus, the focus of this book is to explain the politics of enforcement within societies. Such variation has tremendous practical implications because it determines who gains the benefits (or pays the costs) of policies that have already been selected. Moreover, accounting for this variation provides an opportunity for theoretical development in the functioning of uneven states and weak institutions.

There are broadly two sets of explanations that can account for enforcement. On the one hand, scholars analyze state capacity, contrasting "strong" and "autonomous" states with those that are "fractured," "flailing," and "weak." Drawing on a long theoretical tradition, the central argument is that the quality of the state apparatus determines outcomes. The most common form of analysis focuses on a single task (many studies, for instance, focus on industrial development) and explains distinct outcomes based on the degree of state capacity.[14] Thus, the expectation is that variation in state action should be determined by the quality of the state apparatus; places that have bureaucracies characterized by meritocracy, political insulation, and rationality (i.e., approximating the Weberian ideal) should perform better than those that lack these features. An extension of this theory holds that in order to be effective, states also need to have close ties to society.[15] Yet, even in many state-society approaches, "coherent" bureaucracies are treated as a necessary condition for

---

[12] Levitsky and Murillo 2013   [13] Almeida and Ronconi 2012
[14] For example: Evans and Rauch 1999; Kohli 2004   [15] Evans 1995

6   *Introduction: the challenge of enforcement*

capacity. The policy implication for this line of argument is that the best and, in many ways, the only solution to improving enforcement is to reform bureaucracies to make them more closely approximate the ideal.

On the other hand, researchers often point to political control as key for explaining the behavior of the state apparatus. Whether or not the state takes actions toward any particular goal hinges on which groups gain power and become the "principals" that direct the state's "agents" in various bureaucracies. The role of the state bureaucracy, according to this model, is to respond to political signals from principals and to adjust its action accordingly. Political support is fundamental; even if the state has the capacity to enforce rules, enforcement may not occur when those in power stand to gain from violations of the rules.[16] Thus, the key causal factors are the preferences of political principals and their ability to use various levers of control, such as budgets and appointments, over the bureaucracy.

In many ways, these accounts of differences in state action are radically different from one another. Statist approaches tend to deemphasize politics by focusing our attention on the agency of officials who are insulated from self-interested players outside the state and who have organizational incentives to pursue programmatic objectives. By contrast, political approaches deemphasize agency within the state and highlight the role of political winners and losers in directing subordinates. Despite these differences, both sets of theories hold a set of common commitments: first, states must have internal coherence (e.g., they must have bureaucracies that are meritocratic and hierarchical) and, second, politics takes place primarily outside the state apparatus (either in the creation of the autonomous and strong state, or in the realm of formal institutions of external bureaucratic control). While the role of coherence in the statist perspective is obvious, coherence is no less important in principal-agent approaches. If the bureaucracy is subject to influence or weakness in internal organization, it cannot reliably respond to signals by formal external principals.[17] Such bureaucracies are common in "politicized" states that are weakly institutionalized in the sense that there is a high degree of fluidity in the way power is exercised outside of formal hierarchies.[18] All states are politicized to some extent, but they vary on the degree of direct influence that groups can assert outside of formal channels. Highly politicized states are often characterized by widespread patronage, corruption, or weak hierarchical control. Under conditions of substantial politicization, dominant theories posit that there is insufficient internal coherence of the bureaucracy for either state autonomy or formal external control to function. Both sets of theories described above expect that such political interference within the state apparatus will only undermine enforcement of laws and prevent the activation of institutions.

[16] Berliner, Greenleaf, Lake, and Noveck 2015   [17] Huber and McCarty 2004
[18] Chalmers 1977

Uneven states and weak institutions 7

This theoretical expectation renders the actions of many states puzzling, including the examples from Argentina described above. Enforcement occurred in these cases despite the fact that the bureaucracies lacked all basic features of internal coherence – officials were patronage hires, and direct interference in the bureaucracy that diluted the command of political principals was the norm. Differences in enforcement cannot be accounted for simply by virtue of a combination of political support and a state's approximation to coherence. This puzzle is found not only in Argentine regulation; states around the world act in highly uneven ways that are not reducible to differences in average levels of capacity or political support.

Argument in brief: an alternative explanation of enforcement

This book advances an alternative explanation for variation in state action to enforce basic laws through a study of labor and environmental regulation. Unlike the theories summarized above, the account of state action does not hinge on bureaucratic coherence. Instead, building on insights from research on state-society relations, a central claim in this study is that, to explain variation, it is necessary to examine the ways informal structures that make the state porous to society influence the way state bureaucrats generate resources for enforcement. Not all states are politicized in the same way; informal avenues for political access may privilege some actors over others. By unpacking both the varied role of political influence inside the state as well as the way politics interacts with the operational aspects of administration, it becomes possible to understand puzzling differences in state enforcement. In brief, the argument makes three analytical claims.

First, combinations of state-society linkages and administrative resources within the state apparatus are crucial for explaining enforcement. Linkages consist of routinized processes of consultation and agreements that facilitate direct interaction between officials and organizations in society that have interests in enforcement (e.g., unions in labor regulation, community groups in environmental regulation). Linkages structure access to the politicized state, determining which groups can influence and operationally support officials, and which groups cannot (even when there are no functioning formal institutions governing access to the state). These structures are both political and operational because groups in society can exercise power to influence outcomes of state action while simultaneously providing material support and information about social conditions. For example, in the description of the inspection at the beginning of this chapter, the union leader both helped the inspector collect information and advocated for application of regulations that would benefit his members (importantly, business leaders did not have the same access to the inspector).

For enforcement, linkages are particularly important. When bureaucrats have linkages with societal groups that have capabilities for, and interest in, enforcement, regulators can better access information about violations that is diffused throughout society and often purposefully hidden. Moreover, regulators may not have a clear interest in enforcement, either due to corruption or to political resistance by powerful groups that stand to lose from state intervention. Linkages with groups that have interests allied with policy goals enable the state to undertake certain tasks against these strong headwinds, even when the organizational features of the state apparatus are insufficient to counter this resistance.

The ultimate influence of linkages is contingent on levels of administrative resources. Distinct from the political insulation of the bureaucracy, the degree of administrative resources is crucial in determining the state's contribution to the operational tasks of enforcement. Bureaucracies that have little or no administrative resources will leverage linkages with allied groups differently from bureaucracies with ample resources (as described below). In sum, to explain enforcement we must examine combinations of linkage structures and administrative resources.

Second, I propose a conceptual typology of distinct patterns of enforcement. The typology allows us to move beyond thinking about broad averages of "strong" or "weak" states and shift to understanding differences in the ways that states are uneven. The key differences across the patterns of enforcement are the triggers of state action, as well as the determinants of intensity and distribution of enforcement. The first type is *society-dependent enforcement,* which has three attributes: enforcement is triggered by the demands of linked-groups outside of the state apparatus; the intensity of enforcement is determined by the resources societal groups have to offer state officials; and the distribution of enforcement closely matches the distribution of power among societal organizations that have linkages with the state. While enforcement is made possible through societal action, it has real limits – most notably it is focused on relatively narrow segments of the economy and can empower groups to pursue interests that only partially overlap with the objectives of policy. I expect society-dependent enforcement to occur when regulators lack administrative resources but have linkages with groups that seek enforcement.

By contrast, when there are greater levels of administrative resources internal to the state as well as linkages between regulators and allies in society, bureaucrats can use societal resources strategically to supplement the state. This combination leads to a pattern of *co-produced enforcement.*[19] In this pattern, particular instances of enforcement are triggered both by societal groups and bureaucrats. As a result, co-produced enforcement has greater breadth than society-dependent enforcement and does not simply follow the distribution of resources in society. Additionally, the intensity of enforcement should be particularly high as the capabilities of the allied societal groups are combined with resources in state bureaucracies.

---

[19] On co-production, see: Ostrom 1996

Uneven states and weak institutions 9

These two patterns differ from the only pattern generally recognized in the literature: *state-driven enforcement*, which is allocated by formalized planning processes within the bureaucracy and which entails mobilization only of capabilities internal to the state. This pattern obtains when there are few linkages between officials and allies in civil society, but where there are administrative resources. In this pattern, intensity is determined completely by the resources internal to the state apparatus. Therefore, our expectations converge on those in the literature – political support from principals and organizational coherence within the state are necessary for enforcement.

These three patterns of enforcement are not self-reinforcing equilibria. Nor are they institutionalized in the proper sense of the term. Rather, they are underpinned by particular combinations of state-society linkages and administrative resources that shift over time. In the third part of the argument, I propose a hypothesis for transitions among these patterns that recasts political control theories and highlights the way linkages with pro-enforcement groups can be used as imperfect substitutes for investments in administrative resources. Congruent with standard political control theories, I argue that interests, preferences, and partisan alignments of those appointed to run bureaucracies influence state action. In contrast to theses theories, in the context of highly politicized states, the results of political support from "above" are contingent on the existence of groups in society that have resources to make enforcement happen on the ground. Thus, political principals indirectly promote (or reduce) enforcement through interventions in the bureaucracy that open up the opportunities for linkage formation. In other words, political leaders do not directly determine where enforcement takes place, but instead they influence which groups are able to support enforcement.

As such, political leaders who support enforcement potentially have a choice between allowing linkages to form or allocating scarce resources to augment the administrative resources of the state. Thus, under certain conditions, politicians have the opportunity to use linkage formation in order to avoid allocating scarce resources to an agency that entails budgetary cost (money that could be allocated elsewhere). In these cases, support for enforcement should translate into the society-dependent pattern. All things being equal, investment in administrative resources is more likely to occur under two sets of political conditions. One condition is the combination of political support for enforcement with a set of preexisting political alliances that block linkage formation. For instance, the organizations in society that have resources to help with enforcement may be in a coalition with political opponents, making linkage formation with these groups intractable. In these cases, I expect increases in political support for enforcement to lead to transitions from the society-dependent to the state-driven pattern. Second, ties with specific societal groups might not be able to quell a broad conflict. As a result, investments in administrative resources become necessary to respond to political demands, even if linkages are politically attractive to leaders of bureaucracies. Therefore, in these conditions, co-produced enforcement should be the result. In sum, I recast political control theories to parse out the diverse outcomes of political support for enforcement. In doing so, I highlight the relationship *between* linkages and administrative resources, identifying the conditions under which political demands for state action will translate into one, or the other, or both.[20]

Scope conditions

What are the scope conditions of this argument? First, I expect the theory to hold where there are at least some societal organizations that have interests broadly aligned with specific policy goals. If groups that support a policy have been completely decimated (or have never existed in any form), there is little reason to think pro-enforcement interests will ever be powerful enough to form linkages with state officials. Second, while all states have some unevenness, the full range of patterns described above occur in states with medium levels of resources (that is, those that are not completely failing and those that do not have overwhelmingly strong bureaucracies and potentially unlimited resources) that constitute the majority of countries throughout the world. These scope conditions explicitly exclude countries with absolutely no resources to enforce policies; in these cases, the state apparatus is less important and only societal power determines outcomes. In addition, I expect the dynamics described above to be most evident in places with highly politicized states; where states are highly impervious and all influence is formalized, linkages will simply not form.

Third, I expect this argument to function for policies that are politically contested and that involve large numbers of transactions as well as high levels of discretion during implementation.[21] In other words, this theory applies to the part of the state apparatus responsible for maintaining institutions constituted by complex sets of rules that may (or may not) be followed in a broadly distributed population. In addition to labor and pollution regulation, this set of policies includes intellectual property rights, immigration control, and natural resource management. In all of these issues, there are some groups that mobilize for, and others that mobilize against, implementation. Under such contestation, the various ways in which the state is porous to society will play a role in determining which groups prevail. While the focus of this book is on regulation,

---

[20] This relationship is substantially different to the one that has been theorized in contexts of bureaucratic autonomy. For example, Carpenter's study of bureaucracies in the United States found that ties between officials and civil society organizations could enhance autonomy and resources inside the state. This relationship was contingent, however, on the officials having strong reputations and demonstrated capacity – conditions that are absent in much of the world. See: Carpenter 2001

[21] These policies can be described as "discretionary" and "transaction intensive." See: Pritchett and Woolcock 2004

Uneven states and weak institutions

I do not expect this theory to describe the way certain forms of economic regulation without the same structure, such as utility regulation, function.[22] In these cases, the number of transactions is relatively small and the state can easily enforce policies with very few operational resources.

Main contributions

First, this book develops a way of understanding unevenness in state action in the context of weak institutions. All states are politicized in ways that depart from the ideal-typical Weberian form. Despite the differences among them, these states tend to be homogenized in the literature and are compared with "strong" states instead of with one another. By contrast, I show how variation in the ways that states are politicized has real implications for the functioning of the institutions that have profound effects on economies and societies. In doing so, this book breaks new ground by reorienting the study of states from questions of how they might reform in Weberian ways and toward building a conceptual apparatus to explain the patterns of uneven actions in states that are "flawed."[23] This finding travels well beyond enforcing regulations to a wide range of policy areas, such as the delivery of basic services, in which there are competing interests and porous states.

Second, a key insight from this analysis is that enforcement to strengthen institutions is often contingent upon *whether* and *how* officials mobilize resources outside the state. Thus, this book provides a way to understand when and how weak institutions are activated and, therefore, influence key social and economic outcomes. However, unlike dominant state-society approaches, the analysis does not divide connections between state and society into mutually exclusive categories – politically motivated (rent-seeking or particularistic) and cooperative (public-good generating). Nor does it depend on states having autonomous bureaucracies. Instead, it breaks down the bright distinction between particularistic and productive state-society ties by introducing a third category of ties that involve both political expediency and a real extension of capacity to implement a policy toward a specific end. In doing so, this analysis solves a central theoretical limitation in many state-society approaches that, by emphasizing the apolitical nature of relationships between societal groups and officials, have difficulty accounting for the formation of state-society ties. Moreover, it integrates political theories of state behavior with state-society approaches, thus unifying disparate traditions of inquiry.[24]

---

[22] On utility regulation and privatization, see: Murillo 2009; Post 2014

[23] Others have also gone down this path, notably: Schneider 1991; Darden 2008.

[24] A similar approach is taken in Huber 2007, whose analysis provides a way of looking at bureaucracies that is both administrative and political, but does not engage with the broader comparative politics literature on state-society relations and capacity.

12   *Introduction: the challenge of enforcement*

LABOR AND ENVIRONMENTAL REGULATION

This book analyzes uneven state responses to institutional weakness through an analysis of two policy areas, labor and environmental (specifically pollution) regulation. At their core, these policies embed the market in society and protect people and natural systems from complete commodification.[25] While they are highly contested, often by economic interests that stand to have increases in short-term costs imposed on them by regulations, practically all countries have passed labor and environmental laws of one sort or another. The political economy of creating and reforming regulations has been the subject of intense study in political science. For instance, debates about labor regulation in Latin America in the early 2000s have focused almost entirely on the intense battles over labor law reform. Many scholars of Latin American labor politics rightly justify their focus on the laws as important because, following the work of Collier and Collier, these laws are the locus of intense "political battles" that result in highly visible outcomes.[26] But all recognize that selecting laws is just the beginning, not the end, of politics.

Indeed, in much of the world there is a tremendous gap between regulations on the books and practices in the economy. Returning to the Latin American labor example, many countries in the region inherited, and maintained, highly protective labor laws, but half of the workers in the region are in the "informal" sector and do not benefit from many protections.[27] Similarly, in the early 2000s, labor organizations in Indonesia won a series of legal reforms that built upon on the legacies of the Sukarno period and augmented worker protections, but these policies largely have not been applied to the majority of workers who have informal jobs.[28] Even in other countries, where legislative action is relatively new, compliance is often weak. China, for example, has recently adopted a burst of new environmental laws and, as of 2010, had a total of at least 29 national laws and more than one thousand regulations. Still, there remains "an extraordinary gap between the written law and how the law works in practice."[29] In the same fashion, new labor laws in China have had varied impacts on employment relations.[30] The group of countries that share the basic characteristics of protective regulatory laws and weak compliance is truly massive, encompassing most middle-income and developing countries. Despite the widespread recognition in the indeterminacy of merely passing laws, much less attention has been paid to the politics of enforcing regulations that are on the books in these parts of the world. This book joins recent studies in beginning to fill this important gap in the literature.[31]

---

[25] Polanyi 2001   [26] Collier and Collier 1979   [27] ILO 2008
[28] Caraway 2004; ILO 2013a   [29] Stern 2013 p. 42. See also: Stalley 2010
[30] Kuruvilla, Lee, and Gallagher 2011
[31] In recent years, there have been some notable exceptions on which this book builds: Anner 2008; Piore and Schrank 2008a; Pires 2008; Schrank 2009; Ronconi 2010; Coslovsky 2011; Coslovsky, Pires, and Silbey 2011; Kuruvilla, Lee, and Gallagher 2011; Pires 2011

Labor and environmental regulation 13

The features of these two issue areas that make enforcement such a wicked problem also make them a rich terrain for theoretical development. First, since institutional weaknesses are pervasive and states do not always respond, there is ample variation in the dependent variable of interest across multiple industries, regions, and bureaucracies. Second, enforcement of labor and environmental regulations is a difficult task for all states. These types of regulations have technical and legal attributes, they apply to a large number of firms that are spread throughout the society, and enforcement often involves negotiation and continued contestation by parties with different interests.[32] Third, there are polarized interests that compete over implementation of these policies that bring contestation into sharp relief. In this way, labor and environmental regulation are different from development objectives that have been at the heart of the statist literature, such as economic growth (where most groups agree on the objective of growth, but disagree on how to achieve it). By examining the way the state undertakes a task that has considerable headwind, we have the opportunity to gain new insights into state capacity and institutional weakness.

Finally, pairing an analysis of labor and environmental regulation in Argentina provides the opportunity to examine policies that involve similar sets of action by states, yet have extremely different organizations of interests and forms of political contestation. On the one hand, labor politics in Argentina involves corporatist unions that are historically strong and heavily involved in partisan politics. On the other hand, environmental politics involves community and professional organizations that are pluralistic, nonpartisan, and that historically have not been strong. Thus, studying these two sets of issues together allows for comparisons that, first, can rule out alternative explanations that arise from the specific forms of interest group organization and, second, can also unpack the different ways in which states are politicized.

In addition to the opportunity for theoretical development, these policy areas are important because they have concrete consequences on people's lives and the functioning of economies and societies. When regulations are not enforced, workers are cheated out of legally mandated benefits, pollution is not mitigated, and firms have few incentives to invest in sustainable practices. Ultimately, weak regulatory institutions hinder sustainable and just development. Debates over solutions to labor and environmental standards have been clouded by a widespread pessimism about the possibilities for enforcement in much of the world. This pessimism is due partly to the way these debates have drawn on standard notions of state strength and therefore have not been able to recognize the full range of outcomes that can occur where these conditions do not obtain. There appear to be few possibilities for enforcement because the reforms necessary to create politically insulated and operationally self-sufficient regulatory agencies are, in the short-term, out of reach. This book illuminates

---

[32] Coslovsky, Pires, and Silbey 2011

alternative pathways to enforcing labor and environmental regulations that have been missed in dominant debates. In addition to reforming the bureaucracy and circumventing the state by developing "private"[33] regulatory regimes, I show there are opportunities for enforcement in alliances between officials and societal organizations, even in places where there have not been reforms to the state or international pressure to improve standards. Although these alternative pathways to enforcement are fragile and depend on continual political support, they are important avenues for improving standards in much of the world.

PLAN OF THE BOOK

The remainder of this book is separated into three parts and a conclusion. In Chapter 2, I further develop the theory introduced here with the specific application to labor and environmental regulation. I contrast this theory with leading arguments for regulatory enforcement from the literature. In addition, I articulate a strategy to conceptualize and measure differences in the intensity of enforcement across cases. The chapter ends by detailing the methodological approach used in this book, which analyzes subnational variation in labor and environmental regulation in Argentina. A subnational approach is particularly well-suited to studying uneven states. By going down to the level of local regulatory agencies, it is possible to detect variation in state enforcement action that is often overlooked in more macro-level approaches. Argentine labor and environmental regulation constitute a particularly useful context for analyzing variation in enforcement. In many ways, Argentina is typical because it has protective regulations on the books, high levels of noncompliance, and politicized state bureaucracies charged with enforcement. Moreover, unlike many countries that have been the subjects of studies of regulation, Argentina has not received intense international attention from activists pressuring the government to enforce.[34] Yet, within this context, there are tremendous differences across regions, industries, and policy areas that provide an opportunity to assess the ability of competing theories to explain variations in enforcement.

The book is then divided into Parts 2 and 3, which respectively analyze labor and environmental regulation. Each Part begins with an overview of the policy area in Argentina, situating the cases that follow. Although the Parts are separated by issue for readers who primarily have interest in one of the two policy areas, the chapters are organized around the theoretical puzzles at hand. In Chapters 4 and 6, I analyze cases of society-dependent enforcement in

---

[33] Vogel 2008; Locke 2013

[34] On labor, see comparisons between Argentina and Central American cases, with an emphasis on domestic politics in the former: Murillo and Schrank 2005; Anner 2011. In environment, I join the work of Hochstetler and Keck 2007 who have emphasized the importance of domestic environmental politics.

Plan of the book 15

provinces that have highly politicized bureaucracies with extremely limited resources for regulating labor practices (Córdoba and Tucumán) and environmental standards (Córdoba and Santa Fe). These cases show that, contrary to state capacity approaches, enforcement is possible even in highly flawed bureaucracies. In these chapters I describe the way the structures of linkages that connect bureaucrats with organizations in society make enforcement possible and shape the way it is allocated in the economy. In these cases, I also account for prevalence of society-dependent enforcement, first by examining the combinations of linkages and administrative resources, and second by exploring the politics that underlie linkage formation and the lack of investment in administrative resources. The four cases exhibit a variety of political and economic conditions, including levels of economic development, relative strength of interest groups in favor of (or against) enforcement, and levels of political competition; yet, these cases broadly converge on the same pattern of enforcement (at certain points of time). To explain this similar outcome, I show how linkages were used as a substitute for investments in administrative resources.

Chapters 5 and 7 analyze cases of changing patterns of enforcement in labor (Federal Capital and Santa Fe) and environmental (Tucumán) regulation. In all three cases, investment in administrative resources within the bureaucracy enables enforcement that goes well beyond the society-dependent pattern. I analyze the politics that lead to the allocation of resources to these bureaucracies, but not always to administrative reform. In two cases, the Federal Capital (labor) and Tucumán (environment), resources inside the state were combined with ties to pro-enforcement societal groups. These cases reveal the dynamics of co-produced enforcement, which resulted in high levels of enforcement that were sustained over a period of time in highly problematic industries. Just as in the previous pair of chapters, the political and economic conditions across these cases vary tremendously. Yet these cases all exhibited political barriers to linkages being used as a substitute for administrative resources. By tracing the process of changes in the bureaucracies, I show how this dynamic of blocked substitution created the conditions for investment in administrative resources. The book concludes by returning to the problem of state unevenness and enforcement. Using evidence from Vietnam, the United States, and Indonesia, the conclusion probes the limits of the scope conditions and brings the Argentine cases into sharper comparative context.

2

Explaining enforcement of labor and environmental regulations

This chapter presents a theory to explain variation in enforcement. The first steps in this analysis are to unpack what enforcement means in practice and to develop a measurement strategy for the policy areas at hand. Labor and environmental regulations set standards constraining the actions of firms and establish rights for workers and communities. They are an essential part of the set of policies states adopt in order to embed the market in society.[1] In labor policy, these standards include minimum wages, benefits, severance pay, and health and safety requirements.[2] Environmental pollution standards include limitations on discharges to the air, water, and soil, as well as a number of process standards for pollution management and treatment. Violations either deny, or threaten to deny, the rights of workers to enjoy basic protections, and preclude people from living in a safe and clean environment.

Enforcement is about the state's role in ensuring that firms meet their obligations, rights are respected, and institutions are strong. Researchers have shown that enforcement does influence compliance in a wide variety of settings. Consider evidence from labor regulation. Analyses of health and safety regulation in the United States have found "a strong link" between enforcement and compliance.[3] One recent study of California's Division of Occupational Health and Safety exploited randomly conducted inspections to identify the impact of an inspection. The analysis revealed that inspections resulted in a

---

[1] Polanyi 2001

[2] This study focuses mainly on direct regulation of individual, not collective, labor rights. While the two certainly overlap in practice, in Argentina individual rights are regulated by labor inspectors in the provinces, and the federal Ministry of Labor is responsible for overseeing unions more generally; the subjects of the empirical analysis of this book are the provincial regulators who are involved in most of the everyday tasks of enforcement.

[3] Weil 1996

16

Labor and environmental regulations

9.4% reduction in injuries and a 26% reduction in medical costs. In addition, the study did not find any evidence of reduced employment or firm survival.[4] Such results are not limited to research in industrialized countries. In Brazil, research on labor inspection found that enforcement reduced accidents in the auto-parts industry, formalized workers, and reduced deaths in fireworks manufacturing.[5] A study of labor inspection in Argentina found that increases in the number of inspectors resulted in improved compliance with social security, overtime, and wage regulations.[6] Overall, the message from this literature is clear: enforcement can influence overall rates of compliance.

In addition, enforcement can be important to individuals, even when it fails to shift the overall level of compliance in the economy. Take the example of a worker who went to inspectors in the Dominican Republic because she believed she was denied a job due to her union activity.[7] The inspectors neutralized the problem by putting pressure on her former employer not to slander her and helped the worker find a new job. This action did not address the broad problem of blacklisting workers, but it had a concrete impact on the life of a particular worker who secured employment. These small actions that help workers who lack power are an important attribute of enforcement, even when they do not meet the stronger test of shifting overall levels of compliance.

How should enforcement be conceptualized and measured? For many analysts, enforcement primarily occurs through deterrence; the higher the probability of detection and the greater the penalties, the more likely it is that rational firms will choose to comply.[8] Closer examination of regulation in practice, however, reveals that while deterrence is important, it only encapsulates a small portion of what regulators do.[9] In addition to monitoring and penalizing, additional tools include instructing firms on how to comply,[10] appealing to firms' normative or identity commitments,[11] conciliating conflict among actors,[12] or using some combination of these actions.[13] Seen in this light, it becomes clear that enforcement is much more than the simple application of previously chosen policies and the creation of incentives for firms to comply. Rather, enforcement is a multifaceted process, involving continual political contestation that seeks to alter patterns of behavior in society and the economy.[14]

While recognizing the complexities of regulation in practice, it is helpful for analytic purposes to distill enforcement into a stylized process in order to

---

[4] Levine, Toffel, and Johnson 2012   [5] Pires 2008   [6] Ronconi 2010
[7] Amengual 2010   [8] Becker 1968   [9] See: Coslovsky, Pires, and Silbey 2011
[10] Piore and Schrank 2008a   [11] Kelman 1981; Lee 2008   [12] Hawkins 1984
[13] Kagan and Scholz 1984; Scholz 1991; Ayres and Braithwaite 1992; Hunter and Waterman 1992; Hawkins 2002; May 2004; Gunningham, Thorton, and Kagan 2005; May 2005; Fiorino 2006; Pires 2008; Coslovsky 2009; Locke, Amengual, and Mangla 2009
[14] For a more elaborate treatments of the pragmatic nature of regulation, see: Coslovsky, Pires, and Silbey 2011

better specify the types of resources bureaucrats need. First, regulatory bureaucracies need information about compliance and noncompliance in an economic sector. This information can be gathered actively, by sending inspectors out to firms, or passively, by waiting for individuals and civil society organizations to bring the information to the state. Second, bureaucracies need to be able to process the information and craft a response that creates incentives for firms to comply and enables them to respond to those incentives. Third, bureaucracies need to be able to resist efforts to block enforcement by organized interests that may bear the immediate costs of regulations. Contrasted with firm owners or managers for whom regulations can impose costs or constraints, the beneficiaries of regulations are generally diffuse (as in environmental protection) or in a position of weakness (as in labor protection). Therefore, state agencies need some way to go against the power imbalance.[15] If any one of these three capabilities is disrupted or blocked, enforcement will be reduced.

Building on this analysis, we can develop a strategy for operationalizing and measuring levels of enforcement. Most studies tend either to eschew measuring levels of enforcement altogether (e.g., opting only for comparison of enforcement styles) or to use a small set of quantitative indicators of enforcement (e.g., number of inspectors to estimate enforcement intensity).[16] Both approaches are problematic. Focusing only on enforcement styles (e.g., whether regulators use penalties or instruction) ignores the question of *how much* action regulators take in the first place. This oversight is significant because, as described above, one of the major problems in regulation is that enforcement does not occur. Using only a small number of quantifiable indicators, which are often not contextualized, leaves out much of what regulators do in practice and can result in tremendous measurement error (e.g., giving comprehensive inspections the same weight as superficial ones).

In contrast to both of these approaches, I use a wide variety of data sources (e.g., number of inspections and first-hand accounts of their quality) to construct context-sensitive measures of relative enforcement levels.[17] And to provide clarity in comparisons among many cases, I create a simple spectrum (outlined in Table 2.1) that gives precise operationalization of low, medium, and high levels of enforcement. This scale is insensitive to *why* the state is enforcing regulations in any particular case. All triggers are treated the same, ranging from a union leader who has a conflict with a manager, to a firm that wants to gain an advantage over its competitor, to a neighborhood group that has a problem with pollution, to a bureaucratic decision based on a technical analysis of an industry. The benefit of this approach is that it treats

---

[15] Wilson 1980

[16] For the strategy approach, see: Piore and Schrank 2008a; McAllister 2010. For the broad indicator approach, see: Anker, Chernyshev, Egger, Mehran, and Ritter 2002; Almeida and Carneiero 2005; Marshall 2007; Kus 2010; Ronconi 2010

[17] Adcock and Collier 2001

Explaining enforcement

TABLE 2.1 *Levels of Enforcement*

Level of Enforcement		Definition	Observable Indicators
Low ▲ ⋮	Low level of enforcement	Enforcement is rare, and regulators allow violations to occur widely without crafting a response	• Regulators generate very little information, if any, about violations • There are few inspections • Penalties are not credible and/or regulators do not take steps to help firms comply
⋮	Medium level of enforcement	Enforcement occurs consistently, and regulators resolve violations on a case-by-case basis	• Regulators generate a steady flow of information about violations • There are routine inspections • Responses to violations sometimes include penalties or instruction
⋮ ▼ High	High level of enforcement	Enforcement is intense and systematic; regulators go beyond case-by-case resolution and take broad steps to create the conditions for higher rates of compliance	• Regulators systematically and actively generate information about violations • There are strategically targeted inspections • Responses to violations combine credible penalties with other tools (e.g., pedagogy or publicity)

the act of enforcement separately from the motivations for enforcement, allowing the two concepts to be analyzed independently.

EXPLAINING ENFORCEMENT

Why do states undertake these actions to enforce regulations in some cases but not in others? At issue are the actions of regulatory bureaucracies in response to violations of regulations. An explanation for enforcement needs to address two sets of factors: political support and state capacity. On the one hand, political support among those in power is often presented as a key determinant of whether or not a government is willing to enforce regulations. Pro-enforcement groups battle against businesses (either individual violators, entire industries, or both) over the way policies are implemented. On the other hand, the capacity of the state bureaucracy to undertake the complex tasks of enforcement is equally important because without capacity, political willingness becomes moot. Ultimately, political support and state capacity are intertwined – support for implementation may, in some circumstances, lead to reform of enforcement agencies, and, conversely, the prospects of the state being able to implement policy may influence the efforts of interest groups in their clashes over regulatory reform.

This analysis focuses on the meso-level – above the details of individual street-level agents and below the politics of legislative reform – in order to gain the greatest traction on the often hidden politics of enforcement. It begins by analyzing the debates in the literature and identifying the key hypotheses to explain enforcement. The review presents the two dominant alternative arguments – the politics of enforcement and state capacity – and identifies the space for a new contribution. The third section outlines my argument and shows how it builds on, and departs from, previous approaches.

Political support

There are a number of political factors emphasized in the literature. First, political support for enforcement can be influenced by economic forces that pit social and environmental protection more or less directly against short-term economic interests. Broadly speaking, enforcing regulations in industries that are especially cost-sensitive, labor-intensive, or natural resource-intensive should be most costly to politicians because they will garner the most intense pressure from businesses that stand to lose from regulations. For example, when labor-intensive garment industries compete on low wages, businesses have an interest in blocking enforcement of a variety of regulations that might increase labor costs. Moreover, workers and communities may fear losing jobs and may not support enforcement, even if it affords them protections. And when unemployment and informality are high, there might be surplus labor that weakens the bargaining power of workers and communities, making them less likely to push for enforcement.[18] Under these conditions, costs to politicians for enforcement are increased.[19]

One specific economic variable that merits special attention is trade, which can place deregulatory pressures on governments. At a national level, for example, when countries face trade competitors that have weak regulatory standards, politicians have been shown to roll back implementation of

---

[18] Economic crises amplify these forces, so we can expect to have less enforcement during a crisis. For a general analysis of these dynamics, see: Mosley 2008; Ronconi 2012

[19] Businesses can be interested in capturing regulators to protect themselves against competitors, which could under very specific conditions lead to support for enforcement. This alternative dynamic, which is often absent in protective regulation outside of the Organisation for Economic Co-operation and Development (OECD), will be explored in more detail in the chapters that follow.

Explaining enforcement

environmental regulations controlling pollution.[20] At the industry level, sectors that are exposed to global competition are likely to be sensitive to production costs and, therefore, inspire more political resistance to enforcement.[21] And, individual firms that compete in international markets based on low-cost production stand to lose if regulations are enforced. Not all forms of trade, however, are equal; researchers have shown that subcontracting by multi-nationals can erode labor enforcement and standards, while foreign direct investment can improve them.[22] Similarly, global integration can have a positive effect on environmental performance through the diffusion of practices or through firms meeting the higher standards in order to have access to markets.[23] Economic processes that improve standards should augment compliance in a number of firms and, consequently, reduce the political costs of enforcement. Ultimately, the hypothesis that derives from this line of argument is that political support for enforcement should be influenced by economic structures that make short-term economic goals conflict more or less directly with worker and environmental protection.

Second, organization and mobilization among groups that are in favor, or against, regulation can influence enforcement levels. Business organizations are often assumed to be against regulation. Business opposition is expected to be most potent in concentrated industries (i.e., a few number of large firms) and when firms are well organized to put collective pressure on politicians.[24] By contrast, environmental and labor groups may generate political support for enforcement. Environmental groups can draw attention to regulatory issues, can initiate legal actions, and can disrupt economic activities through protests. Mobilization to support for environmental protection by civil society organizations has been shown to trigger enforcement in a wide range of contexts.[25] In China, for example, community pressure was associated with regulators issuing more substantial sanctions and greater fines.[26] And, in Brazil, popular protest helped give political support for implementing regulations in the heavily polluted Cubatão, thereby substantially improving compliance.[27] Environmental groups have been found to be most effective when they have international connections, as they can leverage these connections to gain key resources and augment pressure on the state.[28] The hypothesis that derives from this line of argument is that environmental groups with greater resources are expected to generate more political support for enforcement.

In labor politics, unions have been shown to wield influence in regulatory policies and to influence enforcement.[29] For instance, in the 1980s and 1990s

---

[20] Cao and Prakash 2012   [21] Chan and Ross 2003
[22] Mosley 2010 has an extensive review of this literature.
[23] Vogel 1995; Garcia-Johnson 2000; Gallagher 2009   [24] Etchemendy 2011
[25] Steinberg 2001; O'Rourke 2004a; Van Rooij, Fryxell, Lo, and Wang 2013
[26] Van Lo Rooij, Benjamin and Carlos Wing-Hung 2010   [27] Lemos 1998
[28] Keck and Sikkink 1998; Steinberg 2001   [29] Weil 1991

in Latin America, there were a variety of economic, ideological, and international pressures to deregulate labor markets. Deregulatory reforms, however, were blocked in many cases by unions.[30] Although it is not simple to measure the strength of unions, labor power is often operationalized through the size of the membership (and overall density) and the degree of centralization. Studies have shown that union strength is amplified when the partisan allies of labor unions are in power. Specifically, Murillo argues that when partisan alliances between unions and political parties are combined with political uncertainty, there is a greater likelihood of pro-labor reform.[31] Examining a sample of Latin American countries, she finds that when labor-linked parties are in power, regulatory reforms are three times more likely to occur than are deregulatory reforms. The mechanisms behind this relationship help shed light on the way unions influence political support for regulation. Murillo argues that "as uncertainty rises, politicians care about keeping their traditional labor allies if the latter can provide not just marginal votes but also political resources and activists that are crucial in retaining and recovering electoral support."[32] In sum, the relative strength of unions and their positions in the governing coalition can be expected to influence political support for enforcing labor regulations.

This analysis of union relationships with political parties brings us to a third key factor that might influence political support for enforcement: the ideology of political leaders. In labor politics, for example, Mosley theorizes that left-oriented parties protect their core constituencies even in the face of economic pressures; her quantitative analysis of cross-national variation in labor standards supports the link between left-leaning parties and worker protection.[33] Cross-national studies have shown that combinations of political representation of labor and state capacity best account for variance in labor rights.[34] In Latin America, research has shown that left-leaning governments tend to increase the size and output of labor inspectorates.[35] In environmental regulation, however, ideology is often less of an issue in middle-income and developing countries.[36] While there are many "green" parties in advanced industrial countries, there are few parties outside of these countries that have explicit environmental platforms (and that have come to power). The expectation, therefore, is that left-leaning parties should support labor enforcement, but environmental enforcement should not be influenced by the ideology of those in power.

In sum, there is a series of hypotheses derived from the literature regarding political support for regulation. These three main factors – (1) potential

---

[30] Madrid 2003; Cook 2007

[31] Etchemendy and Palermo 1998; Murillo 2005; Murillo and Schrank 2005

[32] Murillo 2005 p. 444   [33] Mosley 2008; Mosley 2010. See also: Ronconi 2012

[34] Berliner, Greenleaf, Lake, and Noveck 2015   [35] Ronconi 2012

[36] Indeed, Cao and Prakash 2012 p. 69 test the role of ideology in cross-national regression of *de jure* environmental regulation and find no effect.

Explaining enforcement

economic costs of enforcement; (2) relative strength of environmental, labor, and business organizations; and (3) ideology of political parties – give us an important starting point for explaining variation in enforcement. These arguments all highlight the role of social organizations outside of the state in determining enforcement of regulations. Moving from political support to action by regulators is, however, not a simple proposition.[37] How do these forces translate into enforcement? Here, there is less certainty in the literature. On the one hand, the literature on political control over regulatory agencies has shown that various "principals" influence "agents" bureaucracies.[38] On the other hand, bureaucrats can also be impervious to external control, especially when bureaucracies lack capacity.[39] The next section turns to the problem of state capacity.

State capacity for enforcement

The capacity of states actually to enforce regulations is an equally important factor influencing variation in enforcement. Quite simply, states without the capabilities necessary for enforcement will fail, no matter political willingness. While the bureaucratic apparatus does not encompass the totality of state capacity, regulatory agencies are the central key actors in enforcement. Indeed, many accounts of failure to protect workers and the environment often stress the absence of capable regulators.[40] For example, one recent work argues, "even if Lesotho wanted to enforce its laws and improve working conditions, it is hardly in a position to do so" due to its "impoverished, weak, and unstable" government institutions.[41] Lesotho is hardly an exception in its weak labor inspectorate; the International Labor Organization's (ILO) recent report on labor inspection voiced concern about the "severe strains" that scarce resources have placed on the "professionalism, independence, and impartiality of inspectors."[42] Similarly, in environmental regulation, another recent work argues that throughout the developing world "regulatory agencies that are charged with implementing and enforcing environmental laws are chronically underfunded and understaffed."[43] Another study of environmental regulation

---

[37] Pressman and Wildavsky 1973

[38] See, for example: McCubbins and Schwartz 1984; Moe 1985; McCubbins, Noll, and Weingast 1987; Scholz, Twombly, and Headrick 1991; Carpenter 1996

[39] Huber and McCarty 2004

[40] On labor, see: Castillo 1999; Jatobá 2002; Inter-American Development Bank 2004; Bensusán 2007; Cooney 2007; Bernhardt, McGrath, and DeFilippis 2008; Anner 2008. On environment, see: World Bank 1995; Dasgupta 2000; Carruthers 2001; VanDeveer and Dabelko 2001; O'Rourke 2002; Inter-American Development Bank 2002; McAllister 2008; Henry 2010; McAllister, Van Rooij, and Kagan 2010

[41] Seidman 2009   [42] ILO 2006c p. 4

[43] McAllister 2008 p. 1. In labor regulation, the problem is just as evident in Latin America. See: Bensusán 2006

in Chile points to bureaucratic structures that promote "agency capture" and prevent the implementation of environmental policies.[44] Similarly, one substantial constraint on enforcement in China has been, according to a series of studies, local governments that protect economic interests against the demands of the central government in both labor and environmental regulation.[45] Overall, the logic of these arguments holds that bureaucratic flaws constitute one of the central reasons regulations are rarely enforced, especially in middle-income and developing countries.

By contrast, instances of successful enforcement have been explained by virtue of capable state regulatory bureaucracies and the types of strategies that they adopt.[46] A set of new and important studies have shown how reform of regulatory agencies is possible in countries that have struggled to augment state capacity for enforcement. In Brazil, for instance, successful enforcement of environmental regulations is often driven by the prosecutors of the *Ministério Público*, who are "politically independent" and governed by professional norms.[47] The *Ministério Público* has many organizational features that contrast it with the agencies described previously; officials are selected through a rigorous and competitive exam, have competitive salaries, are systematically socialized into the organization, and have rewarding, long-term careers. Improvements in enforcement have also been tied to reforms of regulatory agencies. For instance, in the Dominican Republic, workers were left unprotected by the weak inspectorate inherited from the Trujillo era until the late 1990s, when there was a far-reaching reform in the inspectorate.[48] Many of the elements of the reform are mirror images of the problems that scholars claim plague most regulatory agencies: merit-based hiring with minimum standards for education (all new inspectors were lawyers), salaries that are competitive with the private sector, civil service protection, and promising career prospects. The argument follows that the adoption of these practices was fundamental for improving enforcement.

The theoretical underpinnings of many of these arguments take, as a starting point, elements identified by Weber's classic analysis of bureaucracy.[49] First, the bureaucracy should be meritocratic – officials should be recruited through

---

[44] Carruthers and Rodriguez 2009

[45] Kuruvilla, Lee, and Gallagher 2011; Van Rooij, Fryxell, Lo, and Wang 2013

[46] For example, see: Piore and Schrank 2008a; Schrank 2009; Pires 2011; Weil 2014

[47] See: McAllister 2008; Coslovsky 2009; McAllister 2010. In Brazil, labor regulation offers another example. The Brazilian labor inspectorate developed a bureaucracy of highly trained professionals with strong civil service protection, who, by virtue of the strength of their organization, have been able to effectively enforce labor regulations in many instances. See: Pires 2008; Pires 2009

[48] Frundt 1998; Schrank 2009

[49] Gerth and Mills 1946. For an example of this approach, see: Kiser and Schneider 1994; Rauch and Evans 2000; Henderson, Hulme, Jalilian, and Phillips 2007. For other standards by which bureaucracies are judged, see: Schneider and Heredia 2003

Explaining enforcement

competitive exams and have minimum levels of education. Second, officials should also have long-term career prospects for advancement and be protected from arbitrary firing. Third, officials should be dedicated employees of the state (without having outside employment that can potentially conflict with their official duties), and office holding should not be a source of personal rents. Fourth, Weberian bureaucracies should be governed by abstract, rational, hierarchical rules that reinforce vertical relations and make subordinates responsive to the instructions of their superiors. Beyond Weberian prescriptions, scholars also argue that bureaucracies can, and should, have additional sources of cohesion (at times in contradiction to hierarchical relations and formal rules), which include professional norms and strong organizational cultures.[50] Working in concert, the elements described here give officials strong incentives against corruption, insulate agents from political interference, and enable them to undertake complex operational tasks.

The role of these bureaucratic structures in the literature points to two separate ways in which the organization of regulatory agencies might influence enforcement. On the one hand, regulatory agencies need internal coherence to respond to political signals from their external principals. Quite simply, bureaucracies that cannot direct their agents or that lack resources will not reliably respond to political demands.[51] Put another way, external political control is limited by the degree to which there is hierarchical control within the bureaucracy.[52] Therefore, the principal-agent theories that are dominant in studies of bureaucratic politics in the United States largely do not apply to places with bureaucracies that lack internal coherence.

On the other hand, when there is extensive organizational coherence, professional regulators can become "autonomous" in a fuller sense; that is, they can be politically insulated and able to resist powerful interests.[53] In these cases, autonomous regulatory agencies with officials who are dedicated to the goals of the policy can take enforcement actions even when immediate political support is lacking.[54] These two arguments in the literature are, in many ways, not mutually compatible – ability to respond to political demands and insulation from politics are two very different mechanisms for policy implementation. Nevertheless, both sets of arguments hold that there is a positive relationship between coherence and enforcement and, in turn, suggest one clear hypothesis: in the absence of Weberian bureaucratic features, enforcement is highly *unlikely* due to a combination of capture, corruption, and operational deficiencies.

---

[50] Wilson 1968; Van Maanen 1973; DiLulio 1994; Kaufman 2006; Piore and Schrank 2008a. These are similar to the "non-bureaucratic foundations of bureaucratic functioning" of Rueschemeyer and Evans 1985 p. 59 and organizational models for explaining bureaucratic performance, see: Brehm and Gates 1993; Brehm and Gates 1997

[51] Geddes 1994; Huber and McCarty 2004   [52] Brehm and Gates 1997

[53] For instance: Huber 2007; McAllister 2008; Schrank 2013   [54] Wood 1988; Carpenter 2010

In addition to these "internal" characteristics, theories of state capacity have pointed to the importance of states being further strengthened through ties with society (i.e., "external" components of capacity).[55] Rather than acting on society from afar, officials work with societal organization to produce policy outputs.[56] Ties with society create a myriad of benefits, including providing information about social and economic conditions to which state officials have little direct access. According to dominant approaches, ties with society are virtuous *only* when there is an internally coherent bureaucracy (i.e., one with the Weberian features described previously). Peter Evans, who has been a leading advocate for thick ties between state and society, argues that bureaucratic "coherence ... [is] an *essential precondition* for the state's effective participation in external networks" because "without autonomy, the distinction between embeddedness and capture disappears."[57]

Prevailing theoretical approaches create a dichotomy between politically motivated ties between society and porous states (that are equated with rent-seeking or capture) and productive ties with societal organizations that do not unduly influence the state.[58] As such, the political actions by societal organizations to hold the state accountable are permissible, as long as the state then utilizes technical or universalistic criteria for implementing policy. Otherwise, the state becomes porous to political interference, particularistic in its application of rules, and reverts to having features that scholars identify as leading to failure. In sum, this literature suggests that close ties between societal groups enhance capacity, and thus enforcement, only when there are internally coherent bureaucracies.

What are the politics of making regulatory agencies more capable? While there is a large literature on the long-run macro processes of state formation and capacity,[59] for the purpose of explaining the variation in enforcement that is only imperfectly bound by such macro-processes, the most relevant theories are those that explain short- to medium-run changes in capacity.[60] Prominent comparative politics accounts of the politics of state capacity treat reform as a

---

[55] Evans 1995   [56] Evans 1995; Evans 1996; Lam 1996; Ostrom 1996; Tendler 1997

[57] Evans 1995 p. 50, 59

[58] At times in the literature these ties appear to be wholly technical, but in other treatments they involve negotiation. A sharp line, however, is drawn separating "embedded autonomy" from "embedded particularism." In the latter case, there are no universalistic rules that govern the use of power, rather case-to-case application depending on the circumstance. See: Herring 1999

[59] For example, see: Tilly 1992. For a recent contribution to this research (and a review of the main theoretical debates), see: Kurtz 2013

[60] With the primacy of autonomy, explanations for the generation of state capacity have been highly unbalanced toward the internal components (e.g., bureaucratic coherence) at the expense of examining ties to society. A similar argument was made in: Soifer and vom Hau 2008. There are, of course, exceptions. Heller 1999, for instance, argues that class mobilization was key to state-society ties in Kerala. Another is Montero 2001, who offers an account of the political determinants of "synergy."

Explaining enforcement

collective action problem, wherein the central tension is between the benefits of administrative reform and the particularistic gains that politicians can realize from patronage.[61] This approach has led to explanations for state capacity that hinge on the ways in which political competition can foster long-term strategies by elites, and thereby incentivizing elites to invest in bureaucratic reforms that are public goods and have long-term benefits.[62] Politicians with interests in decreasing political influence in the state apparatus are likely to improve state capacity by making bureaucracies more approximate the Weberian ideal. Thus, these studies provide one final hypothesis for consideration: state capacity (and therefore capacity for enforcement as well) should be enhanced when there is robust competition between political parties.

In sum, a review of the extant literature generates a number of specific expectations regarding when states should be able to enforce regulations. (1) Enforcement is unlikely when bureaucracies lack the features of internal coherence necessary for autonomy, largely because they will be unable operationally to deliver on the demands of legitimate political principals and will be captured by business. Thus, variation in enforcement may be explained by the degree to which regulatory agencies gain specific features, such as civil service protection, that move them closer to the ideal. (2) Ties between state and society are important but only when matched with an autonomous bureaucracy. In effect, this hypothesis reinforces the importance of internal coherence. (3) Reforms to the state that enhance capacity derive from collective action that gives politicians incentives for depoliticizing the state.

Limitations of dominant approaches

While studies both of the political support and state capacity traditions provide an important starting point for understanding the prospects of enforcement, they leave a number of unanswered questions. First, while building a Weberian state may help enforcement, there is variation in enforcement even without state autonomy. Explanations that depend on autonomy effectively homogenize all imperfect bureaucracies. By emphasizing approximation to the Weberian ideal, they offer little guidance for understanding the tremendous variation among states that fail to meet the characteristics of internal coherence. And by treating politicization as homogenous across states, these theories exclude a host of mechanisms that involve particularism *and* enable states to act in ways that are consistent with policy goals. Therefore, standard theories are largely incomplete and cannot fully account for important variation.

Researchers have begun, once again, to challenge the primacy of the Weberian organizations of state. A study of the famed South Korean developmental

---

[61] Schneider and Heredia 2003

[62] For different theories in this family of argument, see: Geddes 1994; Haggard 1997; O'Dwyer 2004; Grzymala-Busse 2007

state has found, for instance, that there was particularistic hiring to maintain political support as well as extensive use of informal social ties to enhance implementation.[63] Thus, one of the bureaucracies that is credited with leading industrialization was not nearly as insulated from politics as is often presumed. Focusing on a state with a much different legacy, research on graft, using both a case study of the Ukraine and cross-national evidence, found that corruption and graft can be institutionalized to reinforce hierarchies and give states the capacity to undertake basic tasks, such as collecting taxes and maintaining public order.[64] These studies suggest that we need not only to study the dynamics of depoliticizing states and the benefits of Weberian bureaucracies, but also to understand systematically the differences among politicized states.

Second, the ways in which politics influences enforcement in places with flawed bureaucracies have been largely unexplored. The predominant way of studying political influence is through principal-agent models. These models, however, require a coherent bureaucracy to transmit the demands of political principals. When hierarchical control within the state is weak, leaders are unable to direct the front-line officials who undertake the everyday tasks of enforcement.[65] Supporting this view, a recent study of political control models demonstrated that when bureaucracies lack capacity, the basic principles of the literature on bureaucratic control do not hold. Under conditions of low capacity, politicians have difficulty inducing action, and bureaucrats have fewer incentives to comply with legislative mandates.[66] Few alternatives have been proposed for countries that fall outside the scope conditions of principal-agent models or accounts based on dedicated, insulated bureaucrats.

Third, and related, by dividing connections between state and society into mutually exclusive categories – politically motivated (rent-seeking or particularistic) and cooperative (public good generating) – these theories have difficulty accounting for the formation of state-society ties. As a result, even though ties between the state and society are a crucial factor for generating state capacity in many formulations, there have been very few attempts to identify the possible source of such ties and how the process of their formation influences regulatory politics. These shortcomings have left a substantively important and, theoretically crucial, unexplained aspect of the politics of state capacity and enforcement.

---

[63] Ha and Kang 2011

[64] Darden 2008. Also see Berenson 2010 on social service provision in Poland and Russia

[65] Wilson 1968; Brehm and Gates 1997

[66] Huber and McCarty 2004. Congruently, one of the few studies that directly takes on the problem of political control of the bureaucracy in Argentina, found that political control by congress of tax administration was weak due to widespread corruption among officials in the bureaucracy. See: Eaton 2003

AN ALTERNATIVE EXPLANATION FOR ENFORCEMENT

This book develops an alternative explanation for enforcement that builds on, but substantially modifies, the theories described previously. As previewed in the introduction, this account does not depend on bureaucratic coherence. The explanation for enforcement advanced in this book has two main parts. First, it identifies two key factors that influence enforcement – politically motivated linkages that bureaucrats have with societal organizations that support enforcement, and resources internal to the bureaucracy – and examines their political underpinnings. As these two variables shift, the expectation is that there will be changes in the where enforcement takes place. Second, this book offers an explanation for distinct patterns of enforcement based on the interactions of these two factors. In doing so, it clarifies the workings of uneven states and recasts the hypotheses about political support and state capacity, identifying the dynamics of interaction of main actors involved in regulation – state officials, pro-enforcement groups, businesses, and political leaders – in places with weak institutions.

Linkages

One key factor influencing regulators' ability to undertake the key tasks involved in enforcement is the structure of state-society linkages, which consist of routinized processes of consultation and agreements that facilitate direct interaction between regulators and societal organizations that favor enforcement. Porous states have formal and informal structures that allow some societal organizations to access bureaucracies while deflecting others. These informal structures vary across parts of the state apparatus, affecting where societal organizations are able to influence state action directly and have the opportunity to provide operational resources to extend the reach of the state. All things equal, enforcement will be augmented when regulators have linkages with groups that have interests and capabilities aligned with regulatory objectives.

Linkages play a central role in determining whether or not regulators can undertake the key tasks of enforcement described at the beginning of this chapter. First, linkages augment the flow of information about violations, essential for enforcement, into the bureaucracy. For instance, surveillance by a neighborhood organization can extend the monitoring capabilities of regulators.[67] This mechanism has been documented in multiple cases in the United States; in Louisiana and California, community groups used inexpensive technologies to sample air pollution and to solve the problem of officials

---

[67] For examples of this from the United States, Vietnam, and Brazil, see: Lemos 1998; O'Rourke 2004a

arriving after the dispersion of released chemicals.[68] Similarly, unions and workers' centers have been shown to improve enforcement by independently gathering information and transmitting it to regulators.[69] Second, linkages can facilitate the sharing of material resources that bureaucrats need in order to respond to violations. For instance, in many places there have been routinized practices of unions providing transportation for labor inspectors.

Both information and operational support from groups in society can enable regulators to take the necessary steps for enforcement, but only if regulators have access to these resources. Linkages play a decisive role because without routinized ties, mobilizing these resources becomes much more costly and may simply be blocked. In these circumstances, bureaucrats are left on their own, and enforcement is reduced. For instance, even if unions have cars that they can put at the disposal of labor inspectors, without linkages these resources are likely to be out of reach. In many countries there are scores of groups that have information and resources to potentially help regulators, but these latent resources cannot always be utilized for lack of linkages. In sum, the ultimate effect of the existence of a labor or environmental group in a particular community is to a large degree contingent on the linkages that the group has with regulators.

In addition to information and material resources, linkages between bureaucrats and societal organizations can render political support for enforcement potent. Officials often have multiple, competing motivations; some may be truly committed to the mission of their organization,[70] while others may be indifferent at best and corrupt at worst. Those who do not enjoy civil service protection and can be fired or transferred for political reasons have little choice but to be highly attentive to the power structures around them. Firms that violate regulations have the opportunity to influence bureaucrats and are often more powerful than the beneficiaries of enforcement.[71] This is why the literature strongly suggests that in the absence of bureaucratic coherence, violators with political and economic resources will prevail and block enforcement.

The structure of linkages, however, can alter the constellation of groups that can penetrate the state directly and influence officials. Some organizations can provide political resources that push and enable bureaucrats to overcome resistance to enforcement, either from outside groups blocking action or from officials who stand to gain personally from not enforcing regulations. Linkages are important because if bureaucrats lack ties to groups that are broadly in

---

[68] O'Rourke and Macey 2003

[69] Weil 1991; Fine and Gordon 2010; Morantz 2013. This is the case even in transnational regulation: Oka 2015

[70] DiLulio 1994

[71] In labor regulation, workers who are the beneficiaries of enforcement often have a seat at the table, but have relatively little power to influence the regulatory process without the support of unions or an organization.

An alternative explanation for enforcement

favor of enforcement, it will be more difficult for this support to lead to action (and therefore more likely that groups opposing enforcement or internal inertia will prevail). Conversely, when pro-enforcement groups can easily cross the porous boundaries of the bureaucracy, enforcement becomes more likely (all things equal). When linkages are strong enough to allow for robust strategic alliances between regulators and pro-enforcement groups, enforcement should be possible, even when businesses are well organized and wield substantial economic power. The expectation, therefore, is that the political power of individual firms is *not* decisive in determining levels of enforcement, even without a coherent bureaucracy. Instead, the structures of linkages is an intermediary between the distribution of political power and the actions of officials.

This argument contrasts to theories that equate all political interference with capture by capital, and therefore no enforcement. It is consistent, however, with some prescriptions of formal regulatory processes. For example, Ayres and Braithwaite argue that public interest groups should "guard the guardians" in regulatory implementation and be formally empowered to participate in, and influence, the enforcement process.[72] Empirical analyses support claims that formal pro-enforcement organizations can augment the rigor of enforcement. Studies of regulators in the United States have, for example, shown that the average time an inspector spends in a workplace increases when there is a union present.[73] Building on these approaches, my argument holds that *informal* processes can have a similar impact when politicization weakens the formal rules of access to the state.

By admitting the political nature of linkages, it now becomes possible to offer an explanation for the short-term changes in state-society ties that goes beyond common approaches in the literature. Scholars who have emphasized the creation of strong ties between bureaucrats and groups in society often focus on macro-historical processes that embed states or the agency of officials with strong reputations (and considerable autonomy) in building alliances.[74] Neither of these structural factors can account for the fluid processes of linkage formation in contexts without bureaucratic autonomy. Instead, in these contexts, linkages come about when there is a group that can provide operational support for enforcement *and* further the political interests of the appointed heads of the bureaucracy. Therefore, to understand linkage formation, we must analyze the strategic relationships between political appointees (that nominally control regulatory bureaucracies) and organized groups.

There are a number of mechanisms through which linkage formation becomes attractive to political heads of bureaucracies. First, coalitions between elected officials and societal organizations provide the basis for partisan exchange between political support and access to the state. For example, in labor politics, alliances between unions and labor-based parties can form the

---

[72] Ayres and Braithwaite 1992   [73] Weil 1991   [74] Evans 1995; Carpenter 2001

basis of linkage formation between labor inspections and unions. Second, when pro-regulation groups mobilize and circumvent regulatory institutions by taking conflict into the streets and the courts, officials may seek to channel demands into the regulatory system to reduce conflict. For instance, environmental organizations that credibly threaten to blockade or sue a polluting factory can become viable partners for officials seeking to implement regulations. In these instances, societal groups can play a multilevel game, leveraging differences across levels of government to achieve their ends. Where municipal officials are not aligned with state-level (or provincial) officials, for instance, the former can be used to pressure the latter. Similarly, national-level government, such as federal prosecutors, can be used to pressure the state-level officials. The politics of linkage formation play out differently depending on the particular interests and structure of the appointed officials; yet, they all share one key characteristic: contestation is over not only responding to political pressure by allocating resources, but also over allowing groups into the state apparatus. As will be described in more detail below, this difference allows for multiple responses to pressure by groups seeking more enforcement (e.g., create linkages or invest resources in the regulatory bureaucracy) that result in varied outcomes.

The dual role of linkages – informally shaping the arena of politics within the state and influencing technical operation of the state – differentiates the concept from the apolitical way state-society ties are treated in the literature on statist development. Reintroducing politics, however, leads to one strong objection to this line of argument – that enforcement through linkages is simply a relabeling of regulatory capture. Despite its ubiquity in policy debates, regulatory capture tends to be ill-defined and often is used as a pejorative label for regulatory outcomes that one dislikes, making it more useful rhetorically than for careful analysis. Precisely in response to the shortcomings of the common use of the term, Carpenter and Moss have recently argued for a clearer definition of capture as a "process by which regulation, in law or application, is consistently or repeatedly directed away from the public interest and toward the interest of the regulated industry [or other interest group], by the intent of the industry [or interest group] itself."[75] They hold that to make a claim that there is capture, one has to have a clear view of the public interest and how a group intentionally pushes regulation to depart from it. Using this definition, enforcement through linkages is related to capture in that it involves political influence. It is substantially different, however, because it makes no claims about the public good. Rather, enforcement through linkages can be seen as victory for a set of pro-regulation groups in the implementation phase. In some cases such a victory might align with the public good and in others it might not (just as is the case with all regulatory politics). In contexts in which there are

---

[75] Carpenter and Moss 2013

An alternative explanation for enforcement

widespread violations of regulations, however, political influence encouraging some enforcement will likely overlap with policy objectives broadly compared with the counterfactual of no state response to institutional breakdowns.[76]

As a result of its uncertain relationship with the public good, enforcement through linkages has limits compared with ideal-typical programmatic implementation. Bureaucrats can be linked with one set of groups in a way that crowds out other groups, and civil society organizations do not categorically work toward socially beneficial outcomes that are consistent with the rule of law.[77] Ultimately, the character of enforcement depends on through groups advocating for it. If dominant groups are, for instance, community organizations driven by "not-in-my-backyard" motivations, their political influence will most likely result in enforcement that is focused only on businesses operating near mobilized communities. Similarly, if narrowly focused unions are dominant, then enforcement will tend to occur in ways that reflect the interests of the union leaders (e.g., create a benefit for members, strengthen the union's position in negotiations, or create opportunities to solicit bribes). Moreover, if groups do not find it in their interest to engage the state in enforcement, those that they nominally represent will not benefit from interventions by regulators.

Not all societal organizations, however, have such narrow interests; some are more public regarding.[78] When regulators have linkages with these organizations, we expect there to be greater opportunity for broader enforcement. In any case, with interests of societal organizations directly reflected in the enforcement process, there will be a departure from an administratively rational approach. Notwithstanding this departure from the ideal-type, in places with flawed regulatory bureaucracies, linkages to groups that are in favor of enforcement (even those with a particularistic interest) have the potential to make the difference between almost no enforcement and substantial levels of enforcement.

Administrative resources

The way regulators use their ties to society depends on resources internal to the state. In particular, taking into account the administrative resources of the bureaucracy – which depend on the staff, materials (cars, computers, etc.) – is crucial for explaining patterns of enforcement. Administrative resources influence two enforcement tasks – gathering information and crafting a response to

---

[76] Thus, enforcement through linkages involves an outcome akin to pro-regulatory groups winning legislative battles that may or may not be in the public interest (only with a focus on the implementation phase).

[77] Berman 1997

[78] In this analysis, I treat these differences as exogenous. For an explanation of why some social organizations take actions that are not in their narrow interest, see: Ahlquist and Levi 2013

34 *Labor and environmental regulations*

violations.[79] The first, and quite basic, component of administrative resources is the staff. Simply stated, a bureaucracy with only a handful of inspectors will be more constrained in its ability to gather information about violations *on its own* than one with many inspectors. Regulators may still be able to gather information but will likely have no choice but to do so by working with civil society organizations or by receiving individual complaints. Second, bureaucracies need basic material resources to function. In regulatory agencies, the weak point is almost always transportation, which tends to have a high cost relative to other inputs. In Honduras, for instance, labor inspectors without access to cars depended on workers to pay for taxi fare in order to inspect the factory.[80] These types of constraints are typical in labor inspectorates throughout the developing world.[81] Such resources, or lack thereof, directly influence the operating abilities of the bureaucracies. At the extreme, a bureaucracy with absolutely *no resources* will be unable to enforce regulations – quite simply the agency will become irrelevant and societal forces will completely dominate. But administrative resources do not have a simple, direct effect on levels of enforcement because bureaucracies can combine their resources with those of civil society organizations.[82]

The central conceptual difference between administrative resources and bureaucratic autonomy is that having administrative resources does not necessarily enable bureaucracies to resist political pressure. For example, the number of inspectors can make a tremendous difference in the prospects for enforcement, but there is no reason that the size of the bureaucracy should mechanically relate to autonomy.[83] Table 2.2 contains a set of

[79] Administrative resources can influence only two of the three tasks, not resisting efforts to block enforcement, because administrative resources do not include autonomy.

[80] Source: Author interviews with labor inspectors in Honduras in 2006

[81] See: Frundt 1998; ILO 2006a

[82] We would not expect a bureaucracy that had absolute no staff to be able to enforce regulations, or any other policy. For example, a large city with one police officer would not get very far in prosecuting crime. However, the threshold for administrative capacity is not very high. For instance, the United States Equal Employment Opportunity Commission in the 1960s had only thirty investigators to enforce Title VII of the 1964 Civil Rights Act. This is a very low level of administrative capacity, yet in this case, low levels of administrative capacity were combined with pressure from society that rendered it sufficient for enforcement. Pedriana and Stryker 2004

[83] On the one hand, some studies of the state use growth in the size of the bureaucracy as an indicator of politicization, therefore, evidence of a *decline* in capacity of the state to implement policies. Presumably because a bigger bureaucracy means more patronage. For example, a study of patronage in Argentina specifically uses the size of provincial bureaucracies as an indicator of patronage, rather than of autonomy. See: Remmer 2007. See also: Grzymala-Busse 2003 p. 1126. On the other hand, researchers that emphasize autonomy often do not incorporate discussions of the size of bureaucracies. For instance, Evans and Rauch (1999) study of economic effect of bureaucratic quality uses a number of indicators to measure the "Weberianess" of the bureaucracy, but they only focus on the core of the bureaucracy and, therefore, do not include any measure of its actual size. This measurement strategy does make sense if the main worry is

An alternative explanation for enforcement

TABLE 2.2 *Indicators of Administrative Resources and Bureaucratic Autonomy*

Indicator	Administrative Resources	Bureaucratic Autonomy
Civil service protection		✓
Exclusive employment for state		✓
Meritocratic recruiting		✓
Long-term career prospects		✓
High salaries	✓	✓
Large staff	✓	
Material resources (cars, computers, etc.)	✓	
Short-term capabilities	✓	

indicators for administrative resources and autonomy to illustrate how the two concepts are operationalized.

Differentiating administrative resources from autonomy also helps specify the political conditions under which investments in the internal components of capacity might occur. By privileging autonomy, dominant theories treat the politics of capacity as a collective action problem characterized by generalized benefits of reform that are shared by all and individualized costs to those who must forgo patronage. The move toward examining administrative resources as a key internal element of state capacity makes it possible to identify alternative dynamics that include politically motivated investments in the bureaucracy.

Increases in administrative resources come in response to mobilization by groups demanding enforcement, rather than through a generalized process of collective action toward depoliticized reform. This dynamic is largely congruent with the political control theory, and holds that partisanship, ideology, and the degree of mobilization of pro-enforcement groups should lead to increases in administrative resources. Cross-national empirical analysis supports this argument – changes in the number of labor inspectors per capita in Latin America found that there tend to be increases when left-leaning parties are in power.[84]

The politics of investment in administrative resources, however, become most clear when it is seen jointly with the politics of linkage formation. All things equal, when bureaucrats can respond to demands for policy implementation solely by forming linkages, scarce resources do not have to be allocated to augment administrative resources. When there are isolated demands for enforcement, for example, regulators may be able to respond to them on a piecemeal basis by building linkages. Thus, I expect that in these circumstances, political support for enforcement will not translate readily into more administrative

politicization. After all, bureaucrats with resources might even be better to capture than bureaucrats who are limited in their operational abilities.

[84] Ronconi 2012

36   *Labor and environmental regulations*

TABLE 2.3 *Stylized Argument in Brief*

	Weak Linkages	Strong Linkages
Low levels of resources	No enforcement	Society-dependent enforcement
High levels of resources	State-driven enforcement	Co-produced enforcement

resources. Under certain conditions, however, linkages are not politically viable substitutes for internal resources. For instance, organizations in society that have the resources may be in coalition with the political opponents, an alliance that can block the possibility of linkage formation. Alternatively, ties with specific societal groups might not be able to quell a broad conflict. As a result, investments in administrative resources become necessary to respond to political demands.

Patterns of enforcement

Combining internal and external components of state capacity with linkages generates an explanation for variation in patterns of enforcement. These patterns are not self-reinforcing equilibria. Rather, they are contingent on the political underpinnings of linkages and resources described above that make enforcement possible for a period of time while the conditions hold. There are transitions among these patterns of enforcement and, as expected in contexts of institutional weakness, instability over time. By organizing the patterns in a typology, we are able to gain more analytical traction on important differences in the way the state is uneven in its enforcement.

When linkages between officials and pro-enforcement groups are weak and there are ample administrative resources, our expectations align with those from the literature. In these cases, enforcement is *state-driven* and determined by the preferences of political principals and organizational quality of the bureaucracy. Business and pro-regulation groups will largely compete *outside* of the state apparatus for influence. Officials will not have substantial access to resources and information, nor will they get punctual political support of organized pro-enforcement groups through informal channels. Augmenting the autonomy of the regulatory agency and providing more support from formal political principals are the standard ways by which enforcement can be increased in this pattern. In addition, however, there are two alternate routes to enforcement that result in different patterns of state action.

When regulators have low levels of administrative resources but the structure of linkages allows pro-enforcement groups to have preferential access to the state, officials will generate enforcement capacity by drawing on the resources of society. The result will be *society-dependent* enforcement, in which

An alternative explanation for enforcement

the capabilities and interests of societal organizations that have strong linkages with bureaucrats are decisive for enforcement. When linked organizations are well equipped to generate information about violations, can help formulate a response, and are strong partners against political interference, enforcement is likely to occur at a medium level. The expectation is that the distribution of business power should be less important in determining enforcement levels; once pro-enforcement groups have strong linkages with regulators, there should be enforcement, even in industries with comparative high levels of structural power (e.g., command of economic resources and coherent business organization). In this pattern, the role of political principals who support enforcement is primarily through the promotion of linkages.

Leveraging the authority of the state apparatus allows for enforcement to have more force than if societal organization were acting alone. With low levels of administrative resources, however, bureaucrats have little choice but to enforce only where there is social mobilization. In effect, bureaucrats are dependent on society, and action by linked civil society organizations is a necessary condition for enforcement to occur in any particular case. As a consequence, society-dependent enforcement is likely to be limited in scope, leaving out economic sectors or communities where linked civil society organizations have few resources (or where there are no organizations at all). Its character will also depend on the particular nature of the societal groups pushing for enforcement (e.g., some being partisan, some being more public-regarding).[85] Moreover, if regulators have no linkages with civil society organizations that can help them in any particular case, they simply will not enforce, no matter the social, economic, or political conditions. In other words, society-dependent regulation results in highly uneven enforcement that follows a very specific pattern based on the landscape of linked organizations in civil society.[86] For this reason, in these cases, the structure of linkages is decisive.

By contrast, when administrative resources are greater, regulators are less dependent on societal groups. In these circumstances, linkages between state and society result in high intensity *co-produced enforcement*. In these cases, linkages facilitate bureaucrats' use of societal resources. Some barriers to enforcement – such as the lack of capacity for monitoring compliance – can be overcome by drawing on partners in civil society. Other barriers, such as resistance by organized interests, can be diminished by giving greater access to the state to those civil society groups that share the objective of enforcement. Co-production is most likely when linked civil society organizations are

---

[85] The varying interests of these groups make the pattern not reducible regulatory capture. Political influence of pro-enforcement groups may or may not advance the public interest, depending on the groups involved and the context in which enforcement takes place.

[86] Silbey makes a similar argument about the organization of enforcement around responses to consumer complaints. See: Silbey 1984

public-regarding and encourage the state to take actions that the groups will not be directly involved in. And when the bureaucracy has high levels of administrative resources, regulators can shift resources to places where civil society groups are weak so that enforcement goes beyond the immediate demands of the strongest groups. These are the chief differences between society-dependent and co-produced enforcement. Bureaucracies with high levels of administrative resources are not completely dependent on linked civil society organizations; therefore, action by civil society organizations is *not* a necessary condition in any particular instance. For there to be co-produced enforcement, there should be evidence of bureaucrats taking action in places where there has been no material support by linked civil society organizations. Yet, unlike state-driven enforcement, civil society organizations play a substantial role in generating resources to extend the state's capabilities and directly influence the choice of enforcement targets.

Revisions of main hypotheses from the literature

This analysis suggests a series of revisions to the hypotheses that are dominant in the literature. First, enforcement should occur in places and industries where there are linkages between pro-enforcement civil society organizations and state regulators, even if the regulators lack autonomy. Thus, instead of bureaucratic incoherence allowing only business to capture regulators and block enforcement, linkages can allow pro-enforcement groups to serve as countervailing forces within politicized states. Second, and related, increases in administrative resources should make enforcement more likely, even if the increases are not accompanied by Weberian reforms. Therefore, the state should have the possibility of undertaking tasks to respond to institutional weakness without the state needing to become Weberian. These two claims suggest broad opportunities for improving the enforcement of basic norms in a much wider range of contexts than current theory would predict. Third, without internal coherence, pro-enforcement organizations should augment state action *only* when these groups have linkages with regulators. Thus, we should not expect there to be a simple relationship between the distribution of power in society and enforcement; instead, this relationship should be mediated by informal structures of linkages and levels of administrative resources.

Note that these hypotheses do not imply that Weberian reforms, economic structures, societal mobilization, or ideology of ruling parties are unimportant. Rather, they suggest that there is a set of relationships between key variables, such as politically motivated linkages, and enforcement that have been obscured in the dominant debates. By developing a new account of enforcement, it is possible to explain a wide range of variation and to identify alternative pathways toward strengthening regulatory institutions. Moreover, it is possible to better understand the politics of state unevenness.

METHODS – A SUBNATIONAL APPROACH

The central objective of this book is to develop a further understanding of the politics of uneven state responses in the face of violations of basic legislated rules. Due to the challenges of identifying causal processes, contrasting comparable cases, and measuring key variables, studying this phenomenon requires highly detailed evidence. This section describes the subnational approach employed in this book and the particular attributes of labor and environmental regulation in Argentina that provide the opportunity to build and refine theories applicable to a broad range of countries.[87] The strength of this methodological approach comes from combining cross- and within-case analysis.[88] Within-case analysis allows us to determine whether or not specific factors are causally related to enforcement, while the comparative cases provide opportunities to probe the conditions under which these processes obtain.

Regulatory politics in Argentina

Regulatory politics in Argentina in the post-crisis period combines a series of elements that make it well suited for the study of enforcement. First, there were, at a broad level, sets of laws and rules that could be used to regulate certain practices in the economy. In fact, there was a broad push toward adopting policies to enhance the regulatory role of the state. Once the so-called poster child of economic liberalization, Argentina dismantled many of the state's regulatory functions in the 1990s. However, following the economic crisis in 2001, there was an explicit rejection of free-market policies, a shift that intensified under the presidencies of Néstor Kirchner and Cristina Fernández de Kirchner. The era of neoliberal dominance clearly came to an end in Argentina, ushering a newfound push to control the market. Labor unions rebounded and took the offensive, and the environmental movement reached a milestone with its first major march on the Plaza de Mayo. National-level political change brought with it a number of reinforced regulatory laws, including the General Environmental Law and the labor law reform in 2004.[89] Thus, there were strengthened regulatory laws on the books, decided by legislative action, that offered protections to workers and the environment.

Second, the rules on the books were far from self-enforcing, thus leaving ample room for the state to enforce. The economic crisis and years of state

---

[87] In doing so, it joins a set of studies that have used Argentine experiences to speak to larger theories in comparative politics. See: Levitsky and Murillo 2005

[88] Goertz and Mahoney 2012

[89] Most of the changes in legal frameworks have been national in scope. The vast majority of labor laws and collective bargaining agreements cover the entire country, with provinces only making slight adjustments with their own laws and agreements. Similarly, all provinces are required to meet minimum standards of environmental protection, and provinces can only pass laws that "complement" national legislation.

retreat resulted historically high rates of regulatory violations. For example, one main indicator of noncompliance with labor law is the percentage of workers who are unregistered (these workers often lack most labor law protections). The portion of unregistered workers historically has been relatively low in Argentina. Unlike countries that have never had a formality in the labor market, in Argentina widespread compliance in much of the labor market is something that many people who have been working in regulation can remember firsthand. But violations of basic labor laws increased substantially during the 1990s, and informality reached a peak of nearly 50% following the crisis.[90] Consequently, although the laws were changed to strengthen protections for workers in 2004, nearly half the workforce was left out. Environmental regulations were also rife with violations, with the practices of many industries not even approximating the requirements of legislation.[91] In this context there was a clear role for enforcement in making laws matter.

Third, as a middle-income country with more than twenty years of democratic rule, Argentina has resources that could potentially be mobilized to implement regulations. Enforcement, however, had to work through political institutions that are weak (meaning that the rules of the game frequently change and there is a high degree of discretion in the way rules are applied).[92] Overall, Argentina is widely perceived to have below average regulatory quality, government effectiveness, control of corruption, and bureaucratic quality.[93] Institutional weaknesses have been rife throughout the political system, including inside the state apparatus. Broadly, the Argentine bureaucracy has been described as having a core civil service that is largely unresponsive to political principals, as well as a "parallel bureaucracy" made of employees on short-term contracts whose positions exist at the whim of political leaders.[94] Moreover, the bureaucracy has been characterized as unstable, experiencing frequent shifts in structure and being impervious to reform.[95] Thus, this is a context from which we can learn about the politics of enforcement amidst the types of constraints that are prevalent in many countries that have less than ideal bureaucracies.

---

[90] Source: Data from the federal Ministry of Labor and Social Security, calculated based on national household surveys in urban areas

[91] There are not equivalent data for environmental violations, but it appears that in many provinces environmental regulators faced a situation in which the great majority of firms violated pollution limits. For example, in 2003, nearly every major industrial site in Tucumán grossly violated water pollution control laws, effectively depriving residents of the province (and neighboring provinces) of their right to a clean environment. For a broader view, and a discussion of the limitations of data, see: Di Paola 2002b

[92] Levitsky and Murillo 2005

[93] For example, the World Bank's Governance Indicators (2009) place Argentina in the 37th percentile in control of corruption, 45th in government effectiveness, 23rd in regulatory quality, and 29th in rule of law. Evans and Rauch's (1999) data place Argentina 31 out of 36 countries in "Weberianess."

[94] Spiller and Tommasi 2007   [95] Rinne 2003

Methods – a subnational approach

In sum, at a broad level, Argentina is a context where there was a push toward establishing and reaffirming new formal rules for the labor market and pollution control; yet, the state structures that were charged to enforce these rules were highly politicized. Beneath the national-level challenges in Argentina, there was widespread variation in a series of relevant variables. Although most labor and environmental regulations are national (and thus applied to the entire country), provincial governments with substantial independence from the national government had the bulk of the responsibility for enforcing the rules.[96] As will be described in the next section, the broad variation at the provincial level within the country makes Argentina particularly useful for studying the politics of enforcement.

Subnational approach

This book takes a subnational approach and analyzes variation in enforcement within Argentina because this method has a series of advantages over cross-national comparisons. To begin, working at the subnational level allows us to observe the causal processes that are hypothesized by alternative theories.[97] If the standard political control processes are at work, we should be able to observe bureaucrats responding to signals from their principals on the hierarchy of the state apparatus as they make decisions about where to enforce. If the autonomy of Weberian bureaucrats causes enforcement, we should be able to observe instances of political influence being thwarted by civil service protection and organizational norms, as well as instances of internal bureaucratic planning processes determining where enforcement takes place. Finally, if direct influence of societal organizations is driving enforcement, we should be able to trace enforcement to sequences of action by which organizations utilize informal yet routinized access to the state to contribute resources and political support that made action possible. These causal processes occur in and around local offices of the bureaucracies that are tasked with enforcement, thus making local offices the key locus of analysis.

A subnational approach also provides crucial advantages in measurement of both explanatory and dependent variables. One particularly problematic variable is bureaucratic quality. In large-N cross-national analyses, researchers often draw on perception-based indicators of bureaucratic quality, but such datasets have been shown to be biased and unreliable.[98] Even if these measures validly capture the "average" level of bureaucratic quality in a particular

---

[96] Jurisdictions are partially shared and contested, as in the recent push by the national Ministry of Labor to take a greater role in inspection, but the provincial governments still command the most important enforcement agencies. On the question of Argentine federalism and the autonomy of provinces, see: Jones, Sanguinetti, and Tommasi 2000; De Luca, Jones, and Inés Tula 2002; Eaton 2004; Gibson 2005

[97] Mahoney and Thelen 2010   [98] Kurtz and Schrank 2007

country, using whole-country data can introduce additional biases. Gingerich's study of civil servants in national-level bureaucracies in Chile, Bolivia, and Brazil illustrates this problem well.[99] He conducted a survey of more than 2,000 people working in government bureaucracies to assess the levels of politicization across 30 bureaucracies. These data reveal that there are greater differences within, rather than across, states. Comparisons of similar agencies across countries, such as central banks and customs agencies, reveal that in many cases national-level reputations cannot predict which agency in the comparison set will have the most Weberian features. Thus, we might wrongly code one country as having a weaker environmental regulatory agency than another because its overall bureaucratic quality is lower. This research in many ways understates the problem of whole-nation bias because it focuses entirely on the central government. Once subnational differences across regions are included, the degree of within-country variation should increase geometrically, especially in federal or decentralized countries. To avoid these problems of measurement, it is necessary to examine subnational variation in state action through an analysis at the subnational level with reference to particular sets of policies.[100]

At the local level, we can also directly measure differences in informal contacts between state and society. Linkages between bureaucrats and civil society organizations are often distinct for each industry, and, at times, for each community. Tsai's work on the ties between local government officials and village organizations in China, for instance, illustrates tremendous differences at the local levels in state-society relations.[101] The same phenomenon occurs in labor politics; an inspectorate might establish strong linkages with one union but not with another. Simply taking some average of linkages would miss important variation. In addition, when analyzing specific civil society organizations, we can identify the kinds of resources they have to offer the state (e.g., whether or not they have cars or people who can gather information) and determine if these resources were, in fact, mobilized for enforcement. Therefore, the strength and function of linkages is best measured by assessing the ties between specific organizations and the bureaucracy at the micro, not macro, level.[102]

Working at the subnational level also provides advantages in measurement of the dependent variable of interest. One of the main difficulties in studying enforcement is the paucity of data – one cannot simply examine the text of the law, as is often the practice in studies of regulatory reform. Quantitative indicators, such as number of inspections and fines, often are not available or are unreliable, especially in places where bureaucracies lack resources. Moreover, using raw numbers without putting them in context risks serious

---

[99] Gingerich 2012   [100] Snyder 2001b   [101] Tsai 2007

[102] This strategy gets past some of the "empirical lag" in studies of state-society relations. Schneider 1998.

Methods – a subnational approach

measurement biases. Counts of inspections, for instance, do not capture their quality. By examining the actions of specific bureaucracies in particular parts of society, it is possible to use accounts from the actors involved to construct a more complete assessment of relative levels of enforcement and of changes over time. Moreover, the central unit of analysis for measuring enforcement levels in this book is enforcement of a policy, in an industry, in a jurisdiction, at a specific time. At this level, it is possible to precisely identify variation in enforcement as it relates to key political processes.

In addition to improving measurement, working at the subnational level allows us to exploit multiple dimensions of variation – jurisdiction, issue area, industry, and time – without substantially varying macro-structural conditions. Given the range of competing explanations, it is particularly useful to compare enforcement across a range of 1) economic conditions that may influence the political costs and benefits of enforcement, 2) degrees of organization and mobilization of interest groups, 3) partisan and ideological commitments of elected officials, 4) the approximation of state bureaucracies to the Weberian ideal, as well as 5) the structures of linkages, and 6) levels of administrative resources in the bureaucracy. The empirical chapters focus on four, of the twenty-four, Argentine provinces – Córdoba, the Federal Capital, Santa Fe, and Tucumán – that were selected to create an array of cases that vary on these potential explanatory variables. These four provinces share some basic structural conditions; they all have diversified economies that include industrial sectors, and they all faced serious labor and environmental challenges. Two provinces – Córdoba and Santa Fe – are broadly similar in terms of factors that are often used to explain regulatory enforcement, such as the level of socio-economic development, economic structures, and partisan competition. The other two provinces – the Federal Capital and Tucumán – vary considerably between each other, and in contrast with Córdoba and Santa Fe, across all of these dimensions.

Using this set of provinces, we are able to examine whether variation in enforcement, both across provinces and over time, is explained by differences in the components of state capacity that are emphasized in the literature, such as civil service protection and political insulation. For example, some provinces augmented the levels of administrative resources in a particular regulatory bureaucracy without undertaking reforms in the quality of the bureaucracy (e.g., improving civil service protection). These changes provide a direct way to untangle the impacts of organizational features of the bureaucracy that promote coherence from the levels of administrative resources.

Also, examining variation both within and across provinces will allow us to assess whether enforcement levels can be explained directly by the political power of pro-enforcement groups, business groups, or partisan politicians. Changes in enforcement over time are particularly useful because they allow us to see whether these shifts co-vary with the power of a particular group. For instance, we can see whether increases in enforcement of labor regulation in a particular industry are related to increases in the capabilities of unions or other pro-enforcement groups, or vice versa. The potential strength of different groups can be assessed independent of enforcement outcomes by examining the size of their membership, their organizational resources, and their ability to win unrelated political battles (such as appointments in government agencies or subsidies).

Contrasts among industries in the same location are also helpful. The expectation from the literature is that those industries that are highly organized and sensitive to the potential costs of regulation should be interested and able to block it. If industries that export, for example, were the subject of greater enforcement than those that are more protected, we can conclude that the economic costs of enforcement (as they translate into political support) were not decisive. Therefore, I specifically selected industries that are more exposed global markets (e.g., metal manufacturing, garment production, citrus) and those that are not (e.g., construction and sugar). This approach is similar to the one Murillo takes in contrasting industries in nontradable public services with tradable sectors.[103]

By examining differences across and within provinces, we can also see the extent to which variation in structural conditions, such as the level of economic development, or the degree of violations of social norms (e.g., violations of labor law) may be influencing enforcement. Average income in the provinces included ranged from $3,062 a year in Tucumán, to $8,475 in the Federal Capital.[104] If economic development largely explains enforcement, for instance, levels should be much lower across all areas of Tucumán than in the Federal Capital. Furthermore, if the bureaucracy is largely responding to the degree of violations (as is assumed in some of the economics literature[105]), enforcement should correspond to violations. Across provinces and over time there were different frequencies of violations. Even within the same province, some industries had comparative high levels of compliance, while others were operating almost entirely outside of the rules. When there are substantial departures from the expected relationship between structural conditions and enforcement, it becomes possible to eliminate these alternative structural explanations and judge the main alternatives described previously.

One final dimension of variation utilized in this book, policy area, merits special attention. The analysis of two policy areas that involve similar tasks of implementation, but have extremely different politics, breaks with the tradition in comparative politics to examine one policy area or industry in multiple locations.[106] By examining one industry or policy, scholars gain the ability to make controlled comparisons. In this study, we are able to compare a single policy area (labor or environmental regulation) across subnational jurisdictions

---

[103] Murillo 2001   [104] In U.S. dollars. Source: Ministerio de Economía y Finanzas Públicas
[105] See the cites in Ronconi 2010   [106] See, for example: Evans 1995; Snyder 2001a; Post 2014

Methods – a subnational approach

and over time, but we gain additional dimension by including two different policy areas. These areas are comparable because the technical tasks of enforcement are held largely constant; in both issue areas officials inspect, penalize, and take steps to enable firms to comply with a set of rules.

Yet, especially in the Argentine context, the differences between these two policies are stark in ways that are helpful for exploring the validity of the argument advanced in this book and contrasting it with alternatives. A central concern is whether the dynamics of linkages and administrative resources are merely the product of a particular type of social or political structure. On the one hand, it could be that linkages become important only in such contexts of strong unions and corporatist and partisan politics. On the other hand, the role of linkages might be important only in issues with more independent societal groups that are not attached to any particular party or dependent on the state for organizational resources (the "inducements" in corporatist systems[107]).

Analyzing these two issue areas in Argentina provides an opportunity to compare policy areas with these very different features. Labor politics has been at the center of Argentine politics for nearly one hundred years. Societal organizations in labor are dominated by highly corporatist unions that hold a monopoly of representation for workers in each particular industry and province. The unions are hierarchically organized into large federations. While there have been some challenges by more social movement-oriented organizations, these efforts have not displaced unions.[108] In addition, labor unions are highly involved in partisan politics and have historically been aligned with one party (the Peronist PJ). Comparatively, Argentine labor unions are among the strongest in the region. In sum, labor politics is corporatist, partisan, and has a long historical legacy and extremely strong interest groups. Environmental politics is a much different affair in Argentina. The contemporary form of environmental organizations was established only after the return to democracy in the 1980s. Environmental groups are highly unstructured, both formally in the way they are legally incorporated and informally in their networks of relations with one another. No major political party has any partisan alliance with these groups, and environmental issues are largely nonpartisan. Argentine environmental organizations are not particularly strong by comparative standards and are certainly weaker than their counterparts in the labor movement. Finally, there is no strong historical legacy of environmental politics, allowing for fluidity in the types of strategies and alliances different actors can pursue.

With these differences, we can examine whether or not patterns of state action were derived from the position of interest groups, be it in terms of their political strength, or history, or partisan alliances. If this is the case, we should not expect to find similar patterns of enforcement across these two issue areas. The strength of labor unions and their partisan allies should lead to a pattern

---

[107] Collier and Collier 1979   [108] Etchemendy and Collier 2007

of enforcement that is highly different from that in environmental regulation. Yet, if the theory can account for variation in enforcement across both policy areas, this result suggests that enforcement patterns derive from more general variables. Such a result would also suggest that the findings are generalizable beyond the particulars of either labor or environmental politics of Argentina.

Data

The data used in the analysis were collected during sixteen months of field research in Argentina in 2008 and 2009. The primary source of data is more than 260 in-depth interviews that I conducted (a list of which is included in the appendix).[109] In each province, I interviewed: officials who could account for how the bureaucracies are organized and how enforcement occurs (current and past heads of regulatory bureaucracies, street-level bureaucrats); representatives of groups that both contest and observe enforcement (labor union leaders, industry association representatives, leaders of environmental organizations, leaders of neighborhood organizations); and politicians potentially capable of exerting influence on the regulatory bureaucracies.[110] These interviews provided firsthand accounts of interactions between the state and diverse organizations in society, as well as accounts of enforcement in practice. They allowed me to go beyond rough measures of state capacity, such as counts of inspectors, and to assess the way resources inside the state combined with those that lie outside of the bureaucracy. For labor regulation, I complement the in-depth interviews with an original 69-point written survey of 166 labor inspectors in six provinces.[111] The survey allows for statistical tests of some of the findings from the in-depth interviews and expands the geographic coverage of the analysis beyond the four main provinces.

To supplement these data, for each province I systematically searched local newspaper archives.[112] These searches produced thousands of media reports that made it possible to construct accounts of provincial politics and to triangulate interview data. I also gathered documentary evidence – including internal audits, databases, and reports – from regulatory bureaucracies and provincial

---

[109] The interviews lasted between twenty minutes and more than four hours. The majority of them (189) were recorded and transcribed.

[110] During this time, I was also often able to directly observe regulation in practice. On three occasions, I was able to join labor inspectors in the field, spending the day with them while they inspected worksites. On other occasions, I sat in on meetings between government officials and firms, as well as meetings among labor unions.

[111] The survey will be described in more detail in Chapter 3.

[112] The primary newspaper archives I employed are: Córdoba: *La Voz Del Interior, La Mañana de Córdoba*; Federal Capital: *Clarín, La Nación, Página/12*; Tucumán: *La Gaceta de Tucumán*; Santa Fe: *La Capital, El Litoral*. I searched these archives for keywords, including the names of the regulatory agencies, the names of key officials, and phrases related to regulation (e.g., "environment" and "labor inspector").

Conclusion 47

governments. Finally, I used a variety of national micro-data that provided an additional way to measure key variables.[113] When put together, these multiple sources of data provide a way to measure both enforcement and competing explanatory variables at a fine-grained level.

CONCLUSION

To recapitulate, I achieved four objectives in this chapter to advance the analysis of enforcement. First, I developed a way to operationalize the concept of enforcement that allows for comparisons across cases. This approach enables us to look beyond aggregate indicators that are often used to code differences across industries and geographies. Second, I reviewed dominant approaches to explaining differences in enforcement that emphasize either political will or state capacity. While these theories provide an important starting point for analysis, they have a series of limitations. Most importantly, they tend to separate politics from administration, and they do not offer a way of analyzing differences across states apart from approximation to the Weberian ideal. Third, I developed an alternative theory of enforcement that is built around combinations of linkages and administrative resources. This theory clarifies the ways in which politics interacts with state structures under conditions of weak institutions. What matters is not just which groups are strong or the presence of Weberian organizational features inside the states, but whether groups develop routinized linkages to officials and whether those officials have their own resources to mobilize. Based on combinations of linkages and administrative resources, I developed a typology of ideal-typical patterns of enforcement that provide a way of understanding variations in uneven state action. Finally, I described the research strategy employed in this book. In Parts I and II, I turn to empirical analysis of the Argentine cases that provide an opportunity to contrast the ability of competing theories of enforcement to account for variation.

---

[113] Such as rates of labor violations from the Permanent Household Survey (*Encuesta Permanente de Hogares*)

PART I

LABOR REGULATION

3

Labor regulation in Argentina

The period after the financial crisis of 2001 in Argentina was an era of rapid economic growth and of increasing state intervention in markets. President Néstor Kirchner's labor law reform restored many of the protections that had been removed in the neoliberal period. The new law, for example, mandated severance pay of one month for each year a worker was employed and restored *ultractividad*, a practice, advocated by unions, that kept collective bargaining agreements in place until a new agreement could be reached. Kirchner's Minister of Labor, Carlos Tomada, claimed that his administration would "recuperate the capacity of the state to govern" the labor market.[1] In addition, unions rebounded in strength, asserting power through strikes and repeatedly winning wage increases.[2] It appeared that the pieces were in place for robust political support of labor regulations, at least at the national level. Yet, noncompliance with labor laws hit historically high levels in the aftermath of the financial crisis, making the task of delivering on the promises of labor law extremely difficult. The coalition that supported labor law could not simply be replicated for enforcement because the sets of interests and the institutional arena in which contestation over enforced occurred were distinct.

This chapter explores the institutional, partisan, and interest group context of regulatory politics during the post-crisis period (2003–2009) that is the focus of this book. By doing so, this chapter accomplishes three goals. First, while enforcement politics occurs mainly in the provinces, it takes place within a broader set of national-level political and social processes. This chapter identifies the key groups of political actors – the labor-based Peronist party, unions, business associations – whose relative power and relationships the literature

---

[1] Tomada, Carlos. "La recuperación del trabajo y de sus instituciones rectoras," *Revista de Trabajo No. 4*, Ministerio de Trabajo y Seguridad Social, Buenos Aires, 2007 p. 76
[2] Etchemendy and Collier 2007

suggests should influence enforcement. In addition, the chapter describes the decentralized structure of labor administration and the broad variation across provinces. By doing so, it maps the general arguments about enforcement, outlined in Chapter 2, to the Argentine labor case. Second, the chapter describes the features of the Argentine cases necessary for locating them in the broader comparative context, both cross-nationally and in contrast with environmental politics (that will be made explicit in Part 3). In particular, I highlight three attributes of the Argentine context: 1) relatively strong laws but widespread noncompliance; 2) that strong unions had a historical partisan alliance with the *Partido Justicialista* (PJ); and 3) comparatively weak business organizations.

Finally, I undertake a preliminary evaluation of competing explanations for enforcement by examining a cross-section of provincial inspectorates. Given the importance of the alliance between the PJ and labor unions in national-level struggles of labor-regulatory reform, the analysis focuses on the relationship between politicians who might support enforcement and characteristics of the labor inspectorates. The results show that there are systematic differences between governors of different parties, but differences across provincial labor inspectorates do not map onto dominant notions of state capacity. Instead of being correlated with better-resourced and more coherent inspectorates, partisanship is related to differences in inspector-union linkages. The chapter ends by previewing the case studies of enforcement in the subsequent chapters.

STRONG LAWS, WEAK COMPLIANCE

By comparative standards, Argentine labor law historically has been relatively protective of workers, but compliance has been weak. Argentina established its first labor laws that prohibited factory work on Sundays and limited excessive work hours as early as 1905.[3] A lasting foundation for labor law was not laid, however, until the ascent of Perón in 1943 to Secretary of Labor, and later to president.[4] Specifically, Perón expanded workers' rights considerably by passing laws that provided for paid vacations, limited work hours, restricted firing, and severance pay. Overall, his actions were credited with improving working conditions and increasing wages for a broad swath of workers.[5] These labor laws applied to the entire nation, and, since then, such regulations have been primarily under the jurisdiction of the federal government.[6]

The basic template of labor laws established by Perón, for the most part, persisted in Argentina despite periods of intense turbulence and multiple suspensions during military rule.[7] Between 1983 and 2004, for example, many

---

[3] Vasquez Vialard and Julio Navarro 1990   [4] Collier and Collier 2002
[5] Doyon 1975; Buchanan 1985; James 1988; Torre 1989
[6] Provinces can adopt their own laws, but they only make marginal alterations to national laws.
[7] Murillo 2001

Strong laws, weak compliance 53

proposals designed to weaken the position of workers were either blocked or short-lived. When presidents attempted to change labor law, they encountered stiff union-led resistance. Alfonsín (Radical Civil Union, UCR), for instance, faced a series of thirteen general strikes during his administration. Labor organizations defeated most regulatory reform proposals during his presidency.[8] Although unions muted their mobilization against the deregulatory policies of Menem's (PJ) first administration (1989–1995), by the end of his second term (1995–1999) organized labor had fought hard to win many worker protections that had been lost. Under President De la Rua (Alianza, 1999–2001), a deregulatory labor reform bill was passed, but the legislative process was mired with corruption. By the time the turbulent period of reforms ended and the economy began to recover in 2004, most legal protections for workers had been restored.[9]

Continuity in formal institutions did not, however, mean continuity in practices in the labor market. Instead, a considerable disconnect between the legal rules and the practices in the labor market grew during the 1980s and 1990s, eventually peaking in the early 2000s in the wake of the financial crisis. One of the main indicators of labor law compliance, and the one that is most often used by officials in Argentina, is the percentage of workers unregistered with social security (*en negro*). Workers who are unregistered are less likely to benefit from most labor regulations, including: being paid salaries that comply with provisions in collective bargaining agreements; enjoying legally mandated benefits (e.g., vacation time); receiving legally mandated severance pay; and working in safe conditions. An official at the federal Ministry of Labor summed up the differences between registered and unregistered workers, stating: "We have two universes: the universe of formal labor in which we are almost first world, and informal work in which we are practically Bangladesh."[10] In 1990, household surveys found that approximately 25% of workers were unregistered. This number grew dramatically, reaching 36% by 1997, and 44% in 2002 during the economic crisis, after which the percentage decreased (although it has not returned to the 1990 levels).[11] These changes signified a tremendous decline in the portion of employment relations that were effectively structured by labor regulations. In addition to declines in compliance with individual worker protections, collective labor market institutions, such as wage bargaining, also broke down.[12]

---

[8] Cook 2007
[9] The politics of labor law reforms in this period have been described in detail in the literature. See: Etchemendy and Palermo 1998; Cook 1998; Etchemendy 2001; Murillo 2001; Etchemendy 2004; Murillo 2005; Murillo and Schrank 2005; Cook 2007
[10] Interview: B53, Senior Official, Ministry of Labor, Employment and Social Security, Buenos Aires, 9/4/2008
[11] Source: Ministerio de Trabajo, Empleo, y Seguridad Social
[12] Etchemendy and Collier 2007

54   *Labor regulation in Argentina*

In sum, Argentine labor regulations were marked by a strong gap between protective laws and the realities of many workers. This disconnect was typical of labor politics in much of Latin America, and, indeed, in much of the world. While some countries have not passed laws that are protective of workers, most countries have protective laws on the books that are not implemented.[13] Even during the period of far-reaching market reforms in Latin America, protective labor laws were kept in place, but, overall, the informal sector accounted for approximately half of all workers.[14] In Mexico, for instance, the core principles of a labor law adopted in 1931 have remained largely intact, but high levels of informality were evidence of substantial institutional weaknesses (43% of urban workers were informal in 2005).[15] In Brazil, the labor law that was inherited from Getulio Vargas in the 1940s remained largely intact with changes only at the "margins," but there were substantial *de facto* changes and broad institutional weakness (e.g., 49% of urban workers were informal in 2005).[16]

This form of institutional weakness has been attributed to politicians using nonenforcement as an "under-the-radar means of abandoning the status quo without publicly acknowledging a major policy reversal."[17] In addition, shifts in the political and economic structures can undermine the relevance of labor laws that remained "ossified" due to the high political cost of formal reforms (relative to the political costs of nonenforcement).[18] Thus, the Argentine case bears strong resemblance to a more general phenomenon of countries with strong laws on the books and widespread noncompliance.[19] In all of these contexts, "activation" through enforcement plays a central role in how institutions function. Before turning to enforcement structures, we must first examine the major political actors involved in labor regulation.

UNIONS, BUSINESSES, AND PARTISAN POLITICS

Contestation over labor regulations involves organized labor, political parties, and the business organizations. In the Argentine case, labor politics in the post-crisis period was marked by strong unions with partisan alliance to the PJ. This particular political structure had its origins in the period of labor incorporation. During this time, Perón used his position as Secretary of Labor to strengthen and control labor unions. While in 1943 approximately 20% of urban workers were organized, by 1953, 43% of all salaried workers were in a union; in absolute numbers, total union membership increased from 520,000 to 2.3 million between 1946 and 1951.[20] Unions were structured in a highly

---

[13] Burgess 2010   [14] Lora 2001; Bensusán 2006; ILO 2006b   [15] ILO 2006b; Cook 2007
[16] French 2004; ILO 2006b; Coslovsky, Pires, and Bignami 2013
[17] Levitsky and Murillo 2013
[18] This process has been described in the United States context. Estlund 2002
[19] For an attempt to measure this gap globally, see Stallings 2010   [20] James 1988 pp. 9–10

Unions, businesses, and partisan politics

centralized, corporatist fashion. The principal elements of this corporatist structure included: the designation of only one legally recognized union that could collectively bargain for each economic sector; collective bargaining agreements that would cover all workers in the sector, regardless of whether or not they are in a union; and empowering the federal Ministry of Labor to oversee union elections and settle conflicts across unions for representation (*encuadramiento*). Unions were organized into confederations at the national and provincial levels.[21] At both levels, the dominant central became the General Labor Confederation (CGT, *Confederación General del Trabajo*), although almost always there were rival factions, such as the CTA.[22] In addition to factions among unions, there were, from the beginning, elements of the labor movement that existed completely outside of the formal union structures, but these elements were consistently marginalized.

The historical alliance between the union movement and the Peronist PJ remained a central aspect of Argentina's labor movement. Perón's support for labor gained him the loyalty of many workers and union leaders, creating the foundations for the partisan alliance between Peronism and the labor movement.[23] Under Perón, union leaders who were politically loyal were approved by the state and given power, while those who were not had their unions declared illegal and were replaced.[24] The complex relationship between Perón and the unions evolved into a partisan alliance between the unions and the PJ.[25] The PJ's main base of support came from the labor movement, but, unlike working class parties in other countries, there were no formal rules to give union leaders power within the party. The structure of the PJ granted politicians flexibility to pursue policies that were not supported by organized labor.[26] In addition, in the 1990s, the PJ began to rely more on clientelism than on mobilizing labor unions, resulting in a diminished position for organized labor in the party. Given the nature of the Peronist movement, PJ politicians often differed in terms of ideology and orientation toward economic policy (notably, Menem undertook a radical market reform). Nevertheless, the

---

[21] There are confederations of unions across industry and within industry structures. Within each industry, there are two main forms of organization. One is a "union," such as the construction workers' union UOCRA, which is one organization. Another is a federation, such as the sugar workers' union FOTIA, which groups individual unions at a lower level. There are significant formal organizational differences between these two structures. For example, in "federations" the union budget is controlled at the local level, while in "unions" the budget is set in Buenos Aires.

[22] For example, in Córdoba there are two CGTs that are aligned around the metal workers' union and auto workers' union, which have been rivals since the 1950s. See: Brennan 1994

[23] Levitsky and Way 1998; Murillo 2001; Levitsky 2003

[24] See: Collier and Collier 1979; Buchanan 1985; Collier and Collier 2002

[25] This relationship between the PJ and the unions has been analyzed extensively. See: James 1988; McGuire 1997; Levitsky 2003

[26] Levitsky 2003

partisan alliance between the PJ and organized labor proved an important element of Argentine politics. Contestation over market reforms and labor law in the 1990s revealed that partisanship and ideology were important for explaining political support for labor.[27] Specifically, the alliance between the PJ and unions was key to blocking attempts to weaken labor regulations and to support the subsequent reversal of the deregulation that did occur. This pattern of labor politics was similar to that of other Latin American countries with histories of labor mobilization and labor-based parties.[28] At the same time, partisan loyalty restrained labor militancy and helped support cooperation between politicians and unions during market reforms.

In the period following the economic crisis of 2001, union strength was on the rise. The 1980s and 1990s had been a time of weakness, due initially to the oppression they suffered during the military regime, and, later, to structural changes in the economy.[29] During the end of the 1990s and early 2000s, a new unemployed workers' movement threatened to displace traditional unions.[30] But after the 2003 crisis, unions mobilized to make political and economic gains and to take center stage. The number of strikes increased substantially – ranging from between 200 and 300 a year during the late 1990s, to nearly 600 in 2005.[31] With the friendly Kirchner government in power, the increase in labor conflict focused around economic issues, such as wages and working conditions, instead of political issues. At the same time, collective bargaining was reactivated (the number of new agreements increased) and became more centralized with agreements at the industry-level outpacing those at the firm-level. These shifts have led observers to argue that unions gained "more autonomy than in the pre-neoliberal period from both the state and the increasingly fragmented party system."[32] One place where Argentine unions have not been particularly well developed is in representation on the shop floor, with active union delegates in only a small minority of firms covered by collective bargaining agreements.[33] Nevertheless, in comparative context, the Argentine union movement was very strong. Unionization rates were among the highest in the Americas, with approximately 38% of salaried workers being union members and 60% of workers covered by a collective bargaining agreement.[34]

The revival of the union movement did not, however, include all workers. At the beginning of this period, union affiliation rates were highest in manufacturing, utilities, construction, commercial, and transport sectors.[35] In addition, provinces with a PJ governor in power tended to have higher union affiliation rates (all things being equal).[36] Not surprisingly, registered workers in sectors with powerful unions fared better from the gains of union mobilization than did workers in the informal economy. A substantial number of workers operated in the informal economy and were employed by firms that were not

---

[27] Murillo 2001   [28] Murillo and Schrank 2005   [29] Palomino 2005   [30] Garay 2007
[31] Etchemendy and Collier 2007   [32] Etchemendy and Collier 2007 p. 365
[33] Schneider 2013   [34] Data for 2006. Source: Hayter and Stoevska 2011   [35] Marshall 2006
[36] Marshall 2006

Unions, businesses, and partisan politics

registered in any way. Thus, while many aspects of a neo-corporatist system came into place, the system was decidedly segmented.

The line between formal and informal was, however, blurred in many instances. Even in sectors for which unions won large wage increases, a substantial number of workers remained in the "grey" area between formality and informality. That is, workers who were employed by otherwise formal firms were not paid according to collective bargaining agreements; were registered for only parts of their time (i.e., were paid off the books for a portion of their work); and/or were denied legally mandated severance pay. In addition, some workers in sectors that were dominated by insiders, such as the metal sector, were not even formally registered.[37] Where compliance was weak, the impacts of the gains that the unions achieved in collective bargaining were muted.

A large number of unions developed capabilities to support workers who had individual problems with their employers. Within local union offices, specialized staff (often called *asuntos gremiales*) acted as a one-stop shop for workers with grievances. Generally, unions took matters directly to employers and then, if the issue could not be resolved, to labor inspectors.[38] By supporting workers who were subject to violations of labor law, unions could maintain membership and support. For example, a leader from the metal workers' union described how helping unregistered workers advances the union's interests: "We respond to workers because when they are not registered, they can't be affiliates of the union. Therefore, we have to respond to them so that they can formalize their employment and affiliate ... we say 'muchacho, we did our part, it is now your turn to affiliate with the union.'"[39] Unions also had financial interests in enforcement; only registered workers paid dues and contributed to union-run social funds (*obras sociales*) that were an important source of revenue and organizational strength.[40]

Not all unions, however, had capabilities or strategies that were oriented toward playing an active role in enforcement. Unions that were relatively weak, with few members or delegates, could not advocate effectively for workers. In addition, there were differences in strategies among unions that were potentially powerful. For example, the commercial workers' union accounted for 12% of inspection requests in the city of Córdoba compared with 0.1% in the Federal Capital, even though the union had made substantial gains in collective bargaining and the commercial sector had high degrees of violations in both jurisdictions (and are of similar sizes relative to the overall economy).[41]

---

[37] Interviews with dozens of union leaders and labor inspectors. Details on specific sectors and provinces will be discussed in Chapters 4 and 5.

[38] Interview: B47, Tannery Workers' Union, Avellaneda, Province of Buenos Aires, 2/18/2009

[39] Interview: C07, Metal Workers' Union (UOM), Córdoba, 3/18/2009   [40] McGuire 1997

[41] Data on inspection request from Auditoria General la Ciudad Buenos Aires 2006 and internal data from the Córdoba government. On commercial workers and collective bargaining, see Etchemendy and Collier 2007. On the relative size of the sectors, I draw on census data from 2000 that commercial workers make up 10% and 12% of the workforce in the Federal Capital and in Córdoba, respectively. Also draw on interview: B85, Commercial Workers' Union, Buenos Aires, 9/16/2008

Given the fact that supporting enforcement was not in the core organizational interests of unions and did not impact all members, it is not surprising that there would be variation in union efforts to support enforcement.[42] In some circumstances, unions were challenged by other organizations advocating on behalf of workers (two examples will be discussed in Chapter 5), but by and large, unions remained the dominant worker organizations in the post-crisis period.[43] Explaining variation in union organization and strategy is beyond the scope of this analysis,[44] but recognizing the heterogeneity in the union movement will be important for understanding patterns of enforcement.

For their part, business organizations resisted labor law regulations and supported efforts to deregulate, but they did not take a strong stance regarding enforcement. At the peak level, the Industrial Union of Argentina (UIA) lobbied hard against labor laws that it considered too strict and that amounted to "a hope rather than a reality."[45] Business associations in Argentina were, however, "among the weakest and most fragmented in the region."[46] In addition, there was no electorally relevant right-leaning party to which businesses could ally at the national level.[47] Under de la Rua, only one cabinet official was appointed from the business, and none during the Kirchner administration (compared with substantial numbers Chile, Colombia, Mexico, and Peru).[48] Not surprisingly, given the strength of unions, businesses were consistently unable to gain labor reforms that they sought.

While business organizations resisted policies that made labor laws more protective, business associations were not nearly as active in fighting enforcement. Representatives of the main peak association, the UIA, claimed that they were "not against strong administration" as long as laws were reasonable. Indeed, UIA did not publicly oppose enforcement campaigns or efforts to increase numbers of labor inspectors. Similarly, a representative from the construction association claimed that "The association has always been for compliance with the laws ... because if not, there is illegal competition ... [one] company is complying with all of the laws, and others are not, creating an inequality."[49] Broadly, associations were against strict regulations, but held public positions in favor of compliance with those laws on the books.

The firms that did comply with regulations, and could potentially be disadvantaged by competitors who cut costs by not complying, largely did not use business associations to support enforcement. For example, a representative from the leather industry association in Córdoba explained that taking action against "illegal competition" is "difficult and complicated because participation in the association is voluntary, and ... we need members."[50] With differential levels

---

[42] On union interests, see: Murillo 2001; Madrid 2003; Murillo and Schrank 2005; Cook 2007
[43] Etchemendy and Collier 2007   [44] See, for instance: Ahlquist and Levi 2013
[45] Interview: B58, Political and Social Department, Argentine Industrial Union, Buenos Aires, 4/9/2008
[46] Schneider 2004   [47] Fairfield 2010   [48] Schneider 2013 p. 146
[49] Interview: B01, Argentine Construction Association (CAC), Buenos Aires, 10/7/2008
[50] Interview: C12, Córdoba Leather Industry Association, Córdoba, 3/5/2009

Decentralized labor administration

of compliance across the membership, and with all members relying in some way or another on clients or providers that did not comply with labor laws, business interests were further fractured. Instead of coming out for or against enforcement in a strong way, associations tended to support efforts in the interests of all businesses. When associations did take an active role in regulatory compliance, it was more often through education campaigns directed at firms about legal requirements than through direct advocacy against regulators.[51]

The fact that business associations generally did not take a strong stance against (or in support of) enforcement did not mean, of course, that individual businesses did not have power and did not resist regulations.[52] Instead of working in a coordinated way, individual businesses fought enforcement on their own by hiring lawyers, threatening to use market power, and sometimes bribing officials. This placed the role of business in the politics of enforcement very much in the shadows of administrative procedures and negotiations over individual workers. This type of "quiet" or "low salience" politics, where individual businesses press for their interests out of the view of the broader public, was typical in many policy areas and countries in Latin America.[53]

In sum, within the context of Argentine labor politics, we can map the sets of interests that should be central to determining whether or not there was political support for enforcement. Given the importance of the partisan alliance between the PJ and unions in the politics of labor regulation (and the relatively marginal role of business associations), our expectation is that this alliance should play a central role creating political support for enforcement. Yet, to influence enforcement, these political forces needed to work through a state apparatus that was in many ways internally incoherent. Moreover, within these national tendencies, there was substantial variation across the provinces and industries where the politics of enforcement took place. The next section turns to labor administration and builds on the analysis here by undertaking a preliminary evaluation of competing explanations for enforcement.

DECENTRALIZED LABOR ADMINISTRATION

Argentina did not inherit a labor inspectorate that matched the strength of the regulations on the books. For example, assessments by the ILO of labor inspection in the 1980s and late 1990s were highly negative, finding a lack of training, inadequate resources, and pervasive conflicts of interests.[54] National-level assessments of Argentine inspection are, however, limited in their ability to measure labor law and enforcement because inspection was decentralized and highly uneven across provinces.

---

[51] Interview: S24, Industrial Federation of Santa Fe, Rosario, 5/13/2009; T16, Industrial Union of Tucumán, Tucumán, 4/15/2009; C13, Industrial Union of Córdoba, Córdoba, 6/19/2008

[52] Etchemenedy's analyses of which firms were compensated under liberalization demonstrates the power of individual firms and particular industries. See: Etchemendy 2011

[53] Culpepper 2011; Schneider 2013   [54] ILO 1989; ILO 2000

60	*Labor regulation in Argentina*

While the federal Ministry of Labor was the most important state bureaucracy involved in labor policy, unions, and collective bargaining, historically, it has played a marginal role in enforcement. Only for certain periods of time did the Ministry of Labor have jurisdiction over enforcement. For example, in 1943 Perón removed control of labor administration and inspection from the provinces and created seventeen geographic zones for labor administration that were under the federal government's control (this centralization was one aspect of Perón's rule that did not fundamentally reshape institutions and was only short lived).[55] Under Alfonsín in the 1980s, labor inspection was decentralized for the last time, and nearly all provinces passed laws that made the provincial government the sole authority for administering labor matters in the provincial territory.[56] Since that time, the federal government did not take many direct actions in oversight or funding of provincial agencies.[57] After the crisis of 2001, Néstor Kirchner appointed a union lawyer, Carlos Tomada, to be the Minister of Labor. Tomada tried, but failed, to recentralize inspection as part of the reform of 2004.[58] For the next ten years, provincial dominance over inspection remained firm, with federal agencies identifying parts of laws that they could enforce (such as social security) and leaving the bulk of labor law to provincial governments.[59] Provincial-level actors generally did not try to leverage national-level resources beyond using funds available for health and safety inspection.

Without a strong central body to coordinate administration, there was tremendous variation across inspectorates. The nature of the unevenness is as important, if not more so, than the overall averages due to the distributional

---

[55] Initially, some Argentine provinces established their own labor offices to enforce legislation – including Córdoba (1914) and Santa Fe (1923) – while the federal government maintained jurisdiction only over the Federal Capital (the city of Buenos Aries) and a few provinces. Poblete-Troncoso 1935

[56] Vasquez Vialard and Julio Navarro 1990

[57] Interview: B79, Superintendent of Workplace Risks , Buenos Aires, 4/3/2008

[58] *Clarín* "Policía del Trabajo, el centro de la discordia de la nueva ley laboral" 02/22/2004; *Página/12* "Apuradas y problemas para la reforma laboral" 02/23/2004; "El martes, Diputados tratará de aprobar la nueva reforma laboral" 02/26/2004

[59] Tomada created the National Plan for Regularization of Work (PNRT Plan Nacional de Regularización del Trabajo), which evolved into a massive effort to register workers. The PNRT involved deploying inspectors throughout the country to enforce social security registration. There was substantial investment in the administrative resources to make the PNRT possible. The federal Ministry of Labor and Social Security (MTESS) increased its staff dedicated to enforcement tenfold by hiring 400 new "labor inspectors." While Tomada and other senior officials publically portrayed the PNRT as full labor inspection, the program only covered a very small part of labor law. "Inspectors" from the MTESS could not enforce many aspects of labor law that were commonly violated, such as nonpayment of wages, illegal overtime, unsafe working conditions, and violations of the terms of collective bargaining agreements. For many skeptics in the labor movement and in provincial governments, the program was seen as "tax collection," and people involved in inspection emphatically stated that the officials were not truly labor inspectors. In May of 2014, Tomada proposed a law to expand the federal government's role, but as of this writing, that law has not been implemented.

Decentralized labor administration

TABLE 3.1 *Provincial Cross-Section*[60]

	Party in Power (2008)	Population (2010)	Average Income (USD 2010–11)	Union Density (2001)(%)	Size Public Sector (2008)
Federal Capital	PRO	2,890,151	8,475	44	NA
Corrientes	UCR	992,595	3,543	24	46,572
Córdoba	PJ	3,308,876	3,821	39	106,841
Santa Cruz	PJ	273,964	8,983	44	23,903
Santa Fe	PS	3,194,537	3,522	47	108,564
Tucumán	PJ	1,448,188	3,062	36	66,608

benefits of who gains protections through enforcement. If implementation was concentrated in some provinces and not in others, or in some sectors and not in others, the segmented nature of the labor market would be reinforced by enforcement. In addition, examining provincial variation provides an opportunity to examine competing explanations for variation in enforcement.

We begin our analysis with a cross-sectional examination that focuses on the relationship between the partisan affiliation of governor (as a proxy for ideology and partisan alignments) and the organization and resources of inspectorate (as a proxy for state capacity for enforcement). Thus, we focus on the explanatory variable, partisanship, that was key to accounting for regulatory reforms at the national level. Because no comprehensive, nationwide data exist on variation in enforcement, this analysis necessarily will be preliminary until I develop the case studies of specific provinces. For the broadest possible cross-section analysis, I use original survey data gathered from six provinces during 2008–2009. The survey included the four case study provinces that varied in terms of partisanship (Córdoba and Tucumán were led by Peronist governors, the Federal Capital by the right-leaning PRO, and Santa Fe by the center-left Socialist). In addition, I selected two additional provinces that provide variation on income, region, and partisanship. Corrientes is a northern province governed by a conservative branch of the Radical party (UCR), and Santa Cruz is a southern province ruled by Peronists.[61] Thus, we have an array of cases that differ across variables that might influence political support for labor regulations and, therefore, inspectorates.

Tables 3.2, 3.3, and 3.4 describe variation in levels of administrative resources and organizational features of the inspectorates that are central in the literature. Table 3.2 compares the number of inspectors across these

---

[60] Sources: Population, income (only for urban residents), and size of public sector from Ministry of Economy. Union density based on author's calculations using government SIEMPRO database. Based on methodology from Marshall 2006

[61] A written survey was distributed to inspectors in the provinces through senior officials. Inspectors were given the survey and envelope to seal and return the survey to officials, who then returned the surveys to the researchers. The response rate was 70%. The total N was 166.

62   *Labor regulation in Argentina*

TABLE 3.2 *Inspectors per Capita*

Province	Party	Number of Inspectors	Inspectors per 10,000 People	Inspectors as Percent of Public Employees
Santa Fe	Non-PJ	28	0.09	0.026%
Corrientes	Non-PJ	10	0.10	0.021%
Tucumán	PJ	18	0.12	0.027%
Córdoba	PJ	56	0.17	0.052%
Federal Capital	Non-PJ	95	0.33	NA
Santa Cruz	PJ	32	1.17	0.134%
All PJ	–	*102*	*0.13*	–
All non-PJ	–	*133*	*0.19*	–

TABLE 3.3 *Inspector Education Levels*[62]

Province	Party	Primary (%)	High School (%)	Incomplete University (%)	Technical (%)	University (%)	Post-graduate (%)
Federal Capital	Non-PJ	0	0	0	0	64	36
Corrientes	Non-PJ	10	20	30	30	10	0
Santa Fe	Non-PJ	10	24	5	24	5	33
Córdoba	PJ	3	24	34	18	11	8
Santa Cruz	PJ	19	57	14	5	5	0
Tucumán	PJ	28	33	17	17	0	6
All PJ provinces	–	10	26	22	19	6	14
All non-PJ	–	3	8	4	9	44	31
PJ starting year	–	16	35	19	17	8	3
Non-PJ starting year	–	1	9	12	6	40	32

provinces, normalized by population (a variant on the standard way of measuring inspectorates) and the size of the public sector. Tables 3.3 and 3.4[63] contain indicators of key organizational features, such as education levels, civil service protection, meritocracy, and training (in Chapters 4 and 5, organizational features of the inspectorates will be examined in much greater detail

---

[62] Self-reporting in inspector survey.   [63] Non-responses are not shown.

Decentralized labor administration

TABLE 3.4 *Inspector Contracts, Civil Service Exams, and Training*[64]

Province	Party	Civil Servant		Civil Service Exam		Training in Past Year	
		Yes (%)	No (%)	Yes (%)	No (%)	Yes (%)	No (%)
Federal Capital	Non-PJ	2	98	53	43	66	34
Corrientes	Non-PJ	60	40	10	90	70	20
Córdoba	PJ	82	16	57	38	86	10
Santa Cruz	PJ	38	57	34	66	89	11
Santa Fe	Non-PJ	48	52	0	95	57	43
Tucumán	PJ	94	0	22	72	33	67
All PJ	–	75	22	–	–	68	32
All non-PJ	–	19	81	–	–	71	27
PJ starting year	–	73	25	11	86	–	–
Non-PJ starting year	–	21	78	54	44	–	–

using a wider array of data sources). In addition to the provincial-level measures, the tables contain totals summed up across provinces by partisanship. The totals are computed in two ways, contrasting PJ provinces versus non-PJ provinces (at the time the survey was conducted), and contrasting inspectors who were hired under PJ governors with those who were hired under other governments (new governors do not mean a complete change in personnel, and this measure allows us to disaggregate the inspectorate that the party in power inherited from the inspectors that a party hired).

Overall, these data show that the size of the inspectorate and four core features of bureaucratic organization in the state capacity literature (civil service protection, meritocracy, education levels, and training) do not co-vary across the provinces. For example, Tucumán had a mid-range number of inspectors who had civil service protection, but they had the lowest levels of education, were not hired through a merit-based process, and were not provided training. By contrast, the Federal Capital had a large number of highly educated inspectors, but very few inspectors had civil service protection.[65] In addition, these data show that none of these six inspectorates included had features that remotely approach the Weberian ideal-type; the inspectorates with features suggesting meritocracy did not offer civil service protection to insulate inspectors from political interference, and vice versa.

To put these features of the inspectorates in comparative context, these data suggest that the Argentines are much closer to the norm than to countries

---

[64] Self-reporting in inspector survey.
[65] Interviews with officials in the Federal Capital indicate that there still was substantial patronage in hiring that will be discussed in Chapter 5.

64 *Labor regulation in Argentina*

that have been noted for having strong inspectorates. Most inspectorates in the world share the features of these Argentine provinces – they lack "professionalism, independence, and impartiality of inspectors."[66] Yet, some countries, such as the Dominican Republic (DR) and Brazil, boast civil service protection entrance exams as well as frequent training for all inspectors. In addition, all wage and hour inspectors are lawyers in the DR, and, in Brazil, all inspectors have college degrees and 34% have graduate degrees.[67] The Argentine cases are all substantially different from these exceptional examples of countries that have reformed their inspectorates, making them a useful context in which to study variation in enforcement under the conditions of weak state institutions.

The cross-sectional variation suggests that there are some systematic differences across provinces that correlate with partisanship, but the data do not yet match any clear theoretical expectations. The tendency in the PJ provinces was toward inspectors who were comparatively less educated and less likely to have taken a civil service exam, but who were more likely to hold a civil service contract (and thus have *de jure* protection from political influence). Examining the year that inspectors were hired only exacerbates differences in inspector education (although it does not change the differences in contracts). At the aggregate level, there was no substantial difference between inspector training related to partisanship. In some ways, this finding is not surprising given the number of factors that influence bureaucratic reform and the varied factions within the Peronist party.[68] Nevertheless, these initial results suggest that there is more going on in the provincial labor inspectorates than a simple explanation of strong inspectorates being created by organized labor's traditional allies.

To further examine the influence of politics, it is helpful to depart from standard measures of bureaucratic quality and size, and turn to the different ways in which the provincial bureaucracies were porous to political influence. By doing so, we can begin to assess the usefulness of the argument outlined in the previous chapter. The inspector survey contained a series of questions about inspector-union relationships (Table 3.5 contains a subset of these questions) that can be used to measure inspector-union linkages. For example, the inspectors were asked how often they rely on a union's car or use information from a union leader. These questions specifically measure the relative strength of inspector-union linkages that have the potential to both expand the capabilities of regulators and to give unions a political opportunity to influence the way enforcement occurs. (At this stage, we examine the average across all unions. In Chapters 4 and 5, we will go down to the level of particular unions and sectors).

These data suggest a strong relationship between partisanship and inspector-union linkages. For nearly all of the questions, inspectors in the PJ provinces

---

[66] ILO 2006c p. 4   [67] Pires 2009; Schrank 2009
[68] Although some of intra-PJ differences might be reduced by the fact that governors of all three PJ provinces were part of the *Frente Para la Victoria*.

Decentralized labor administration

TABLE 3.5 *During Inspections, How Often does a Union Representative...*[69]

		Never (%)	Sometimes (%)	Almost Always (%)
Accompany the inspection	PJ	8	49	43
	Non-PJ	22	56	22
Provide a car	PJ	19	52	29
	Non-PJ	37	51	12
Orient the inspector toward the most important problems	PJ	19	55	26
	Non-PJ	35	46	18
Help the inspector with knowledge about the collective bargaining agreement	PJ	17	47	36
	Non-PJ	35	45	20
Help the inspector collect information from the workers	PJ	23	47	31
	Non-PJ	60	33	6
Collaborate with follow-up after the inspection	PJ	19	43	38
	Non-PJ	47	35	19

indicated greater union participation than in the non-PJ provinces. For instance, only 23% of inspectors in the PJ provinces indicated that unions *never* help the inspector collect information from workers during inspections, whereas 60% of inspectors in non-PJ provinces chose this response. Responses to other questions about union leaders accompanying inspections, providing cars, orienting inspectors toward the most important problems during inspections, and collaborating with follow-up after the inspection all had similar results. Thus, this evidence suggests that there were substantial differences in linkages between inspectors and unions that derive from political alliances.

There could be, however, other factors besides politics that drive these differences in linkages. To control for these and other variables, I statistically examined the relationship between partisanship and inspector-union linkages using a series of regression analyses. To operationalize the indicators of inspector-union linkages, I scored all responses to questions about the frequency of union participation (never=-1, sometimes=0, and almost always=1). I then created a "union score" for each individual inspector based on his or her average responses to the union participation questions. The main explanatory variable of interest is the party of the governor in power (coded using a simple dummy variable).

---

[69] Non-responses are not shown. Columns do not add up to 100 because of rounding and non-responses. N=166.

66   *Labor regulation in Argentina*

The regression controls for a series of potential compounding factors. First, the number of inspectors per capita controls for whether or not the correlation between linkages and partisanship is merely a product of different levels of staffing. Second, the percent of workers who report they pay union dues in the province is an indicator of the power of unions, independent of partisanship, which could have an effect on linkages.[70] Third, field research indicated that health and safety inspectors, for a variety of reasons, tend to have a different relationship with unions than with wage and hour inspectors.[71] Therefore, the regression analyses include a dummy variable for inspectors who work primarily in health and safety. Fourth, inspector-union linkages may be influenced by the inspectors' attitudes toward enforcement, instead of by partisanship. To control for whether or not inspectors with more strict attitudes toward enforcement are more apt to work with unions, the regressions include a variable coded by inspector agreement with the statement: "Sometimes, it is more important that the workers have jobs than that the firm complies with all of the laws." Finally, linkages could be the result of bureaucratic practices, such as civil service protection, that could make inspectors more or less comfortable working with unions. Therefore, for each inspector, a variable is included that indicates whether the inspector has a short-term contract or civil service protection.[72]

Table 3.6 presents the results of regressions that analyze the average union score, as well as the particular union actions during inspections. The results of all the regressions indicate that governor-union partisan alliances are correlated with strong inspector-union linkages, even after including controls.[73] In the first regression (Model 1), which analyzes the union score, the estimated effect of the dummy variable for governor-union partisan alliance is positive and statistically significant. Of the controls, only two were significant.[74] The remaining regressions (Models 2–4) examine responses to questions about select types of union participation.[75] For each individual question, the coefficient on the governor-union alliance variable is positive and statistically significant.[76]

---

[70] All data from the survey of inspectors. Union strength data is calculated from the SIEMPRO National Survey in 2001. This method is imperfect, but it is one of the best available estimates of union strength. See: Marshall and Perelman 2004.

[71] The reason for health and safety inspectors having different relationships with unions appears to stem from union priorities – many union leaders are more concerned with, and knowledgeable about, wage and hour issues than health and safety issues.

[72] This captures whether or not unions are more likely to be linked with inspectors who are most exposed to political influence.

[73] Model 1 uses a simple linear regression, with standard errors clustered by province.

[74] Inspectors in provinces with more inspectors per capita and health and safety inspectors are less likely to work with unions.

[75] These regressions use an ordered logit model with standard errors clustered by province.

[76] With the exceptions of union strength in Models 3 and 4, the controls that have significant coefficients are all in the expected direction.

Provincial pathways to enforcement

TABLE 3.6 *Partisanship and Inspector-Union Linkage Regressions[77]*

	(1) Total Union Score	(2) Provide Car	(3) Gather Information	(4) Follow-up After
Governor-union partisan	0.31**	1.8**	1.9**	0.93*
alliance	(0.07)	(0.59)	(0.29)	(0.43)
Provincial insp./	−0.60**	−3.5**	−0.97**	−1.6**
population	(0.05)	(0.84)	(0.28)	(0.33)
Provincial union	−0.19	2.7	−8.8**	−6.8*
affiliation rate	(0.31)	(1.6)	(2.8)	(2.9)
Health and safety	−0.52**	−2.9**	−0.71	−1.7*
specialist	(0.09)	(0.74)	(0.76)	(0.78)
Flexibility on jobs vs.	0.07	0.066	0.14	0.41
compliance	(0.08)	(0.31)	(0.49)	(0.27)
Civil service protection	0.22	0.042	0.03	1.1*
	(0.11)	(0.61)	(0.43)	(0.5)
Number of observations	153	148	146	145

In addition, the number of inspectors per capita in the provinces was negatively correlated with inspector-union linkages. While these regression analyses have limitations in making causal inference (we do not know which way a causal relationship is going), they show that the partisan alliances between the PJ and unions are correlated with stronger inspector-union linkages and lower numbers of inspectors per capita.

PROVINCIAL PATHWAYS TO ENFORCEMENT[78]

The cross-sectional snapshot provides a starting point and suggests that we need to do more than examine the dominant features of state capacity highlighted by the literature. It does not get down to the level of enforcement, nor does it include all relevant interest groups, or address changes over time. The following sections preview, in short form, the analyses of the coming chapters. These cases tie the overall structures of Argentine labor politics to the specifics of enforcement at the provincial and industry level. Building on the discussion above and the theoretical expectations that we have from the literature, the case studies are organized in terms of partisanship – first discussing a pair of provinces that were governed by Peronists in the

---

[77] Clustered standard errors are in parenthesis. Model 1 is a linear regression with robust standard errors clustered by province. Models 2–4 are ordered probit models with standard errors clustered by province. *p<0.05; **p<0.01. Descriptive statistics are available upon request.

[78] The cases of Córdoba and the Federal Capital were analyzed in: Amengual 2014a; Amengual 2014b

68   Labor regulation in Argentina

TABLE 3.7 *Summary of Main Cases of Labor Regulation*

Industry (Province)	Societal Organization Support for Enforcement	Linkage Strength	Administrative Resources	Pattern of Enforcement	Level of Enforcement
Brick-Kilns (Córdoba)	Low	High	Low	Society-dependent	Low
Metal (Córdoba)	High	High	Low	Society-dependent	Medium
Construction (Córdoba)	High	High	Medium	Co-produced	High
Citrus (Tucumán)	Low → High	High	Low	Society-dependent	Low → Medium
Construction (Tucumán)	Medium	High	Low	Society-dependent	Low
Construction (Santa Fe)	Low	High → Low	Low → High	Society-dependent → State-driven	Low → Medium
Garment (Federal Capital)	High	High → Low	High	Co-produced → State-driven	High → Low

post-crisis period, and then a pair of provinces that had transitions and were
not governed by Peronists.

Córdoba and Tucumán: partisan alliances with neo-corporatist unions

The cases of Córdoba and Tucumán illustrate the role of partisan exchange
between Peronist governors and labor unions in shaping enforcement. In Córdoba, the first governor after the return to democracy in the 1980s was from
the Radical party. Just as President Alfonsín made concessions to mobilized
unions at the national level, the governor of Córdoba attempted to placate
unions by investing considerable resources in the inspectorate and by appointing a widely respected lawyer to lead the provincial labor ministry. This legacy
was partially broken during the right-wing governor who followed and down-
sized the inspectorate. When the Peronists took control of the province at the
end of the 1990s, they encountered an inspectorate with a very weak wage and
hour division and a modestly resourced health and safety division. Despite
many promises by politicians to augment the resources in the inspectorate
and to improve the quality of inspectors, such investments were never made.
There was a continued separation between the wage and hour division, which
had extreme resource shortages, and the health and safety division, which had

Provincial pathways to enforcement

marginally greater resources. Instead of reforming the bureaucracy, Peronist governors appointed union leaders to key positions inside the inspectorate. For example, of the three labor secretaries during this period, two were union lawyers and one was the secretary general of the public sector union. The result of this period was a bureaucracy that did not have Weberian features; had internal differences in administrative resources (with the wage and hour having low levels, and health and safety having higher levels); and was extremely porous to unions with privileged access to inspectors.

As a result of this structure, enforcement was concentrated in sectors where strong unions pursued strategies to support workers who were, or could potentially be, affiliates, but were subject to violations of labor laws. In the metal industry, for example, the union created a sophisticated apparatus to monitor compliance and to work with inspectors on enforcement. Enforcement in the metal industry reached medium levels in a society-dependent pattern, despite the fact that employers in the industry were well positioned to resist. In other sectors that did not have strong or active unions, such as the brick-kilns, the society-dependent pattern resulted in low levels of enforcement. Only in the construction industry, which was the primary responsibility of the health and safety inspectors, did the pattern of enforcement more closely resemble co-production and were the levels of enforcement high. In sum, the partisan exchange between the PJ and unions resulted in an inspectorate with limited administrative resources but strong linkages with unions, leading to variation in both levels and patterns of enforcement.

In Tucumán, the only pattern of enforcement in the post-crisis period was society-dependent. Governors from the Peronist party controlled the province for all but two brief periods (federal intervention in 1991, and one term of a right-wing governor in the second half of the 1990s). No governor in Tucumán invested in reforming or professionalizing the labor inspectorate. Labor inspectors were hired based on their connections with unions or party activists, which helps account for the extremely low levels of education among inspectors (discussed above). Instead of reforming the inspectorate, the Peronist governors responded to labor demands by making strategic appointments of union leaders to run labor administration. As a result, the inspectorate was highly porous to union leaders who pursued strategies to leverage enforcement. With extremely scarce resources and internal incoherence, Tucumán's inspectorate was completely dependent on unions for enforcement. In some industries, such as the citrus sector, inspectors gathered information about violations, took actions to enable and incentivize employers to comply, and were able to resist even strong employers. Thus, the pattern of enforcement in citrus was society-dependent at medium levels. By contrast, in the construction industry, the union did not have sufficient capabilities to make up for deficiencies in the state. Consequently, society-dependent enforcement was at very low levels.

The cases of Tucumán and Córdoba show the limitations of alternative explanations for enforcement. Contrary to state capacity theories, enforcement did occur in these provinces despite highly flawed inspectorates, and there was substantial variation that could not be explained with reference to the coherence of the bureaucracy. In addition, political control of the bureaucracy did not occur primarily through labor's partisan allies allocating resources and support for enforcement broadly. Instead, partisan exchange led to appointments in the bureaucracy that structured access to the porous state. Ultimately, the non-autonomous bureaucracies were not equally porous to all groups; variation in enforcement could not be accounted for by the actions of nonunion groups, including business associations. Instead, the privileged access of unions to the state pushed out other groups. Thus, to account for the presence of enforcement, and for variation across industries, we need to examine the relationship between partisanship, administrative resources, and the structures of linkages.

Santa Fe and the Federal Capital: transitions and non-partisan based enforcement

The partisan and union-dominated aspects of Argentine politics did not, however, result in only one outcome. The cases of Santa Fe and the Federal Capital depart from those discussed above. For the first twenty-five years after the return to democracy, Santa Fe was governed by Peronists, and its labor administration appeared extremely similar to those in Córdoba and Tucumán. The inspectorate was understaffed and under-resourced; those who were hired to work as inspectors were selected based on connections to unions or party activists rather than on merit. These officials had strong linkages with union leaders and drew on union resources for enforcement. As a result, across a variety of industries, enforcement very much resembled that of Córdoba and Tucumán, characterized by high levels of dependence on unions.

In 2007, however, the center-left Socialist candidate, Hermes Binner, was elected, breaking the lock of Peronist rule. Binner removed union-affiliated political appointees and replaced them with technocrats. These officials took steps to reform the inspectorate, including hiring health and safety inspectors through a competitive exam and increasing their access to resources. Simultaneously, officials reigned in union leaders' access to the inspectorate, thereby weakening linkages. The result was a redistribution of enforcement in the economy. The case of the construction industry illustrates the results of these changes. Under the Peronist governments, enforcement levels were society-dependent at a low level in construction due to a combined weakness in the inspectorate and in the union. The Socialists, however, hired professional health and safety inspectors who prioritized construction and undertook a far-reaching enforcement campaign. Changes in enforcement could not be explained by increases in union power or mobilization, or by a new weakness in business interests. Instead, bureaucrats with resources and autonomy took steps to implement regulations in a sector with high levels of violations. Thus, the construction industry was an instance of state-driven enforcement at a medium level.

Conclusion

The Federal Capital also underwent changes in the pattern of enforcement. Under center-left governments in the early 2000s, resources were allocated to hire a substantial number of highly educated inspectors. Steps were not taken, however, to create an autonomous regulatory agency; inspectors, for example, were never given civil service protection. Therefore, the inspectorate had a particular characteristic of having resources, but not coherence. The structure of linkages in the Federal Capital was also different from those of Peronist provinces. Unions did not dominate, and nonunion groups gained the opportunity to establish linkages with inspectors. This structure of linkages reflected the left-leaning coalition that governed the Federal Capital.

Analysis of enforcement at the industry level illustrates the results of high levels of administrative resources and the possibility of forming linkages with groups that are not unions. The most salient case of enforcement in the Federal Capital during this period arose in the garment industry, in which there were extreme violations of labor law. To combat these violations, inspectors in the Federal Capital formed strong linkages with a community organization called La Alameda that mobilized against exploitation in the garment industry. The combination of the resources of the inspectors and the support (political and operational) of La Alameda led high levels of enforcement that followed the co-produced pattern. Inspectors closed down thousands of workshops and leveraged supply-chain relationships systematically to deter violations. The enforcement campaign, however, lasted only two years and ended with the election of the right-wing PRO government in 2007. The right-leaning government did not reduce the resources available to the inspectorate, but instead cut off ties between inspectors and La Alameda. Thus, the garment industry case in the Federal Capital demonstrates the way that the formation, and destruction, of linkages influences enforcement.

CONCLUSION

The overall objective of this book is to develop an explanation for variation in enforcement in order to better understand the workings of uneven states in the face of institutional weaknesses at a general level. The politics of enforcement are, however, heavily shaped by the institutional context in which they are embedded. Therefore, general propositions about the nature of enforcement politics need to be grounded in the particulars of specific places and policies. To that end, this chapter has described the regulatory, interest group, and administrative aspects of Argentine labor politics.

First, the regulatory landscape of labor law in Argentina was characterized by protective laws based on a template established under Perón, but compliance was far from widespread from the 1990s onward. Thus, Argentine labor regulation exhibited a typical kind of institutional weakness – legal protections were restored after a modest deregulation, but noncompliance was allowed to grow substantially.[79] Second, the chapter identified the main interest groups and political players that were involved in labor politics. Specifically, there were strong unions with high levels of affiliations bolstered by an alliance with the PJ, and comparatively weak business organizations. The interests, power, and relationships among these groups kept strong labor laws in place, but did not create an enforcement bureaucracy with the classic features of state capacity. Both unions and business associations had more fractured interests when it came to enforcement when compared with regulatory reform. Enforcement primarily influenced a subset of union members, specifically workers who were subject to violations but who could potentially become affiliated with unions. In addition, unions in different sectors and provinces had varying capabilities with which to support enforcement. For their part, business associations did not take stands against legality and generally had to appeal to firms that were in and out of compliance. The locus of conflict was, in many cases, at the level of individual businesses that fought enforcement on a case-by-case basis.

Third, this chapter introduced the administrative structures of labor enforcement. Importantly, enforcement of labor law was decentralized to the provincial level from the 1980s onward. Therefore, the national-level bureaucracies mattered less than did the provincial level ones. Building on the analysis of labor-regulatory reform at the national level, we began to explore variation at the provincial level by examining the relationship between the partisan affiliation of governors and the bureaucratic organization of the inspectorates. This preliminary analysis showed that there was variation across parts of the Argentine state that did not map neatly on to the dimensions of the degree of Weberian bureaucracies. Instead, there were substantial differences in the ways inspectorates were porous to unions that were correlated with the partisan affiliation of the governor. The preview of the cases provided a broad overview of the relationship between those differences and enforcement at the industry level. Chapters 4 and 5 will expand on this analysis, identifying variation of enforcement at the industry level and contrasting the ability of competing explanations to account for these patterns.

---

[79] Levitsky and Murillo 2013

4

Enforcement with unions in the driver's seat

Enforcing labor regulations is particularly challenging in places where regulatory agencies are politicized and have highly limited resources. This chapter analyzes enforcement by labor inspectorates in Córdoba and Tucumán, where regulatory agencies have faced many bureaucratic shortfalls. Agencies in both places were staffed with patronage employees appointed not for their merit but for their political connections. Moreover, both agencies had limited numbers of inspectors who had no reliable access to transportation and, in some cases, not even to paper necessary for writing up inspection reports. In short, nearly all of the features associated with capable bureaucracies were missing, making enforcement in both provinces seem highly unlikely. Notwithstanding these serious constraints, in some industries, such as metal manufacturing in Córdoba and the citrus industry in Tucumán, inspectors were able to enforce labor regulations. Thus, these cases illustrate pathways to enforcement that do not involve the creation of an internally coherent bureaucracy.

Enforcement, however, was highly uneven in both provinces. In some industries, such as brick-making in Córdoba and construction in Tucumán, inspectors have largely failed to take meaningful actions. Differences in enforcement across industries did not reflect the programmatic priorities of bureaucrats, the degrees of organization of business interests, or the economic costs of regulations. Nor was enforcement universally targeted to parts of the labor market where institutions were weakest or workers in most need of state support. This chapter addresses the puzzles that arise from the uneven enforcement in Córdoba and Tucumán. How are inspectors able to enforce regulations at all with such substandard bureaucratic organization? What explains variation in enforcement across industries in this context?

Córdoba and Tucumán is a useful comparative set of cases because of their political similarities and contrasts in economic conditions. On the one hand, Córdoba had substantially higher levels of socioeconomic development than

73

did Tucumán (higher incomes, levels of education, health outcomes etc.,). Córdoba is part of the more economically developed central region of Argentina and has been highly industrialized for many years, while Tucumán is part of the Northwestern region that historically has been the poorest and most underdeveloped in the country. Overall, Córdoba's economy was more diversified (exporting both agricultural commodities and manufactured products) as compared with Tucumán's, which relied heavily on just two industries, citrus and sugar. On the other hand, in the post-crisis period, both Córdoba and Tucumán were dominated politically by the labor-based PJ party that controlled the legislatures and held the governor's seat.[1] As Chapter 3 showed, the PJ was key in supporting labor regulation and in the cross-section analysis; provinces governed by the PJ tended to have stronger inspector-union linkages and fewer inspectors per capita. Therefore, analyzing these two cases allows us to narrow in on the similar effect of partisanship in very different contexts. Together, these cases illustrate a partisan mechanism of forming linkages that structure state-society relations and, ultimately, patterns of enforcement. The remainder of this chapter is divided into two principal sections, one for each province. Each section describes the patterns of enforcement in particular industries and contrasts alternative explanations for within-case variation.

CÓRDOBA – ENFORCEMENT WITH UNION ALLIES

Córdoba's Labor Secretariat (*Secretaría de Trabajo*, STC) conducted more than 10,000 wage and hour inspections and 3,000 health and safety inspections per year in the post-crisis period.[2] Put in comparative context, there were 8.6 wage and hour inspections per thousand residents in Córdoba's capital – a figure that is equal to or greater than that of other countries (e.g., Chile 8.3, Dominican Republic 5.1, France 2.8, Mexico 0.3).[3] The STC found a substantial number of violations (approximately 25% of inspections resulted in infractions in 2008). These inspections triggered a process through which regulators negotiated a plan for the firm to come into compliance and, at times, pay a fine. In some cases, regulators forced firms to pay back wages, or they suspended operations in unsafe worksites.[4] An official at the STC illustrated this process with the example of an inspection at an auto mechanic shop:

---

[1] In Córdoba, governors from the PJ were in power from 1999 through 2011 and the PJ block in the provincial legislature controlled 57% of the seats from 2003 to 2007 and 53% from 2007 to 2011. In Tucumán, the governors were also from the PJ from 1999 through 2011 and the PJ held 65% of the seats in the *Camara de Diputados* from 2003 to 2007 and 55% from 2007 to 2011.

[2] Data compiled by author from STC records.

[3] Inspections per capita are used instead of per worker because of the large uncertainty in estimates of the number of workers in Argentine provinces. Federal Capital and Córdoba data are for 2007. Chile: Figuera Valenzuela 2005; Dominican Republic: Secretaría de Estado de Trabajo; France are for 2013: ILO; Mexico: Romero Gudiño 2008.

[4] Dozens of interviews with labor leaders, business leaders, and officials.

Córdoba – enforcement with union allies

One time we did an inspection at a workshop that maintained vehicles, trailers, trucks, buses … We went into the worksite, [where] we saw two or three people, but with many vehicles. There was no way that only these workers were maintaining all of these cars … There was also a big bus in the shop and the inspector asked the employers to open it. The people didn't want to do it, and the inspector forced it open to find eighteen workers inside; the managers had hidden the workers. The inspector took the names of the workers … In the end, we registered half the workers [and] … they had a happy ending.[5]

In this case, inspectors were not deterred by the reluctant employers, and a significant number of workers gained the legal protections associated with being registered, including health insurance, legally mandated vacation time, social security protection, and the right to collect severance pay. This same type of action was repeated hundreds of times by inspectors who gathered information about violations and crafted concrete responses. Using common indicators, it would appear that Córdoba's inspectorate was enforcing labor regulations at high levels. However, as will be shown next, these numbers provide only a partial view of enforcement, which was highly uneven in the economy.

Data from the survey of inspectors, Table 4.1, shows the industries in which wage and hour enforcement is concentrated, along with an indicator of which unions request the most inspections.[6] These data show that there was a very strong relationship between union demands and enforcement; the correlation between union requests and inspections is high (0.92). In addition, according to internal data from the STC, in 2007 and 2008, 73% of wage and hour inspections were at the request of unions, and 27% were either programmed or had resulted from individual complaints. Therefore, the inspectors themselves selected only a small percentage of the firms that were visited. In sum, the distribution of enforcement was not only skewed toward industries with active unions, but enforcement occurred largely in firms selected by union leaders.

The allocation of inspection described previously contrasts sharply with that of other countries that have professionalized inspectorates. For example, in the Dominican Republic, the percentage of programmed inspections in 2006 was more than 60%, and the great majority of the complaints were made by *individual* workers, not unions.[7] The high ratio of programmed inspections, which was the result of a political decision by top officials, enabled inspectors to protect workers who have difficulty lodging complaints, such as those in the sugar plantations.[8] The French labor inspection service also differs substantially from that of Córdoba in the allocation of enforcement. The French

---

[5] Interview: C45, Senior Official, Córdoba Labor Secretariat, Córdoba, 6/19/2008

[6] The survey results are consistent with available data from the STC of the number of union-led inspections over a five month period; nine out of ten of the top unions identified by inspectors in the survey were also in the top eleven unions requesting inspections in the archival data.

[7] Source: "Memoria 2006," Secretaría de Estado de Trabajo de la República Dominicana, Santo Domingo.

[8] Schrank 2009; Amengual 2010

76 *Enforcement with unions in the driver's seat*

TABLE 4.1 *Distribution of Wage and Hour Inspections and Union Requests in Córdoba*[9]

Sector	Which Sectors are Inspected the Most?(%)	Which Unions Request the Most Inspections?(%)	Difference Between Inspections and Requests(%)
Commercial	21	20	1
Construction	17	17	0
Restaurants	11	6	5
Metal	10	15	-5
Gas stations	7	7	0
Shoes	6	7	-1
Cleaning	4	2	2
Health clinic	4	5	-1
Hair cutting	3	2	0
Private security	3	2	1
Transportation	3	7	-5
...			

inspectors gather information from a variety of sources, including individual complaints, consultation with unions, and journalists. Once this information has been collected, regulators allocate inspections in the ways that they believe would have the strongest influence on working conditions, even if this allocation does not directly reflect the distribution of the demands that inspectors receive.[10] As a result, the industries that are inspected are not necessarily those with the most active unions. Therefore, the way the state unevenly responds to violations is qualitatively different in Córdoba than in these two cases.

Analysis of a cross-section of three industries that vary in a variety of dimensions – including levels of violations, strength of unions, organization of business, and what part of the inspectorate is responsible for the industry – provides further granularity in the distribution of enforcement in Córdoba and allows for further examination of alternative explanations of enforcement.

Brick-making industry in Córdoba: extreme violations and low levels of enforcement

The production of bricks in Córdoba is a highly marginalized activity. The basic technology and method of production are rudimentary – workers form mud into bricks and bake them in relatively small kilns. The brick-kilns are

---

[9] Analysis of the responses of 29 inspectors listing top 5 industries and top 5 unions.
[10] Piore and Schrank 2008b

concentrated around the periphery of the metropolitan area of the city of Córdoba. In total, there were approximately 700 worksites that employed workers from approximately 4,000 families.[11] These worksites ranged from just a handful of workers to larger operations of more than forty workers. The labor was unskilled, and more than 50% of workers were migrants, mainly from Bolivia and Peru. During the mid to late 2000s, the industry was growing rapidly and did not face external competition, creating little threat that production could be moved in response to enforcement. The industry did not export, nor did it compete with imports. Its primary market was local construction, which was booming after the economic crisis.

Labor violations in the brick-making industry were pervasive and severe by all measures in the post-crisis period. First, estimates of labor informality in the sector were extremely high. In 2006, a survey of workers in the sector found that 96% of them were informal, which means that nearly all workers were denied their legally mandated benefits, such as social security, and had little chance of collecting severance pay.[12] The rate of informality in brick-making was much higher than the provincial average of 39% in 2006.[13] In addition, many of the workers, 65% according to a survey conducted by the STC, were unregistered immigrants. There were also reports that human traffickers tricked workers and forced them to labor long hours to pay off debts incurred during migration.[14] The combination of labor informality and high numbers of unregistered migrants made these workers especially vulnerable to abuses by employers.

Second, wages in the industry were often not paid according to the collective bargaining agreement. In 2007, a labor inspector summed up wages in the industry, stating: "On the brick-making worksites, they treat the horses better than the workers ... The employers get 95% of the profits, they spend 3% or 4% on the animals, and 1% or 2% on the workers."[15] These practices were violations of labor law. For instance, on some worksites, laborers were paid $3 for each thousand bricks instead of the $20 mandated by the collective bargaining agreement (the bricks were then sold for approximately $100 per thousand on the local market).[16] There were also widespread reports of

---

[11] *La Voz del Interior* "Intensificarán controles en los cortaderos" 11/08/2008
[12] The STC even conducted a study of working conditions in the brick-making and horticultural worksites surrounding the city of Córdoba (Pizaro 2008). *La Voz del Interior* "Flojos de papeles" 12/24/2006
[13] Author's calculations based on the *Encuesta Permanente de Hogares*.
[14] *La Voz del Interior* "Investigación por bolivianos esclavizados" 10/20/2007, "¿Patrones o traficantes?" 09/09/2007
[15] *La Voz del Interior* "A los caballos los tratan major" 9/09/2007
[16] *La Voz del Interior* "El otro lado del 'boom' inmobiliario" 4/16/2006, "Intensificarán controles en los cortaderos" 11/08/2008. There were further increases in the salary negotiated in 2009, but there is no indication that those changes translated to increased pay. Ministerio De Trabajo, Empleo y Seguridad Social Secretaria De Trabajo Resolución No 894/2009 Registros No 800/2009, No 801/2009, No 802/2009, Buenos Aires 21/7/2009

workers being denied their wages, including one incident of a worker who demanded payment being chased off a worksite by an employer with a gun.[17]

Third, health and safety conditions on the worksites were well below standards. Workers were not given the basic safety equipment (gloves, boots, etc.,) required by the collective bargaining agreement. In addition, workers lived in encampments on the worksites in substandard conditions, often lacking potable water, sewage, and electricity.[18] Fourth, because entire families lived and worked in the industry, child labor was often a problem. An article in a local newspaper described a worksite found within the city of Córdoba in 2008:

The labor inspector from the STC could not believe what he saw: children who were two or three years old covered in dirt, hidden with their dogs in holes left behind by piles of recently baked bricks. No adults were nearby. Other children, less than three feet tall, ran after one another in a pool of water that is used to knead the mud in one of the first stages of the production process. It was that same green and smelly pool where, two weeks earlier at 5 PM, Gilda Valdivia Mendoza, who was only six years old, was found dead floating in the water.[19]

In sum, this industry was easily one of the most precarious in Córdoba. Rules and regulations (both laws and the collective bargaining agreements) failed to protect workers or structure employment relations. Clearly, if there was a rational planning process for enforcement that prioritized industries based on need or opportunities for improvement, the brick-kilns would be near the top of the list.

Notwithstanding the salient need, enforcement levels remained relatively low in the brick-making industry for the entire period after the economic crisis. Officials in the STC were aware of the problems in the brick-making sector for years.[20] In the post-crisis period, a number of incidents potentially could have triggered enforcement but did not result in sustained efforts in the industry. In 2006, the Cordobés newspaper, *La Voz del Interior*, ran a series of investigative articles about migrant Bolivian workers in the brick-making sector, bringing widespread awareness to the issue.[21] At the same time, the Center for Bolivian Residents of Córdoba (*Centro de Residentes Bolivianos en Córdoba*), which

---

[17] *La Voz del Interior* "Investigan nuevas denuncias por maltrato a bolivianos" 06/15/2006

[18] *La Voz del Interior* "Buscan normalizar situación de inmigrantes" 04/21/2006

[19] *La Voz del Interior* "Clausuran por primera vez un cortadero" 11/07/2008

[20] At least since 1998, when the problems were discussed in an annual report about labor regulation. Source: Annual communication from Governor Mestre to the legislature of Córdoba, *Archivo del Poder Legislativo*, Córdoba 1998.

[21] Pizaro 2008. This media coverage was spurred on by the fire in a Buenos Aires garment workshop that killed a family of workers (discussed in detail in Chapter 5). The tragedy in Buenos Aires focused national attention on the problems of migrant workers and spurred debate about similarly situated workers in Córdoba. As evidence that these newspaper reports generated attention, the reporter who wrote the articles, Edgardo Litvinoff ,was a finalist in 2007 for an award from the Inter American Press Association.

Córdoba – enforcement with union allies

organized the Bolivian community since the 1950s,[22] took the plight of the workers in the brick-kilns to a variety of government agencies seeking assistance.[23] A senior official from that time recalled how after a few high profile accidents involving migrants, "... they put the issue of 'those poor migrant Bolivian workers' in fashion, but this wasn't even the case because the Bolivians weren't unique; the brick-kilns were exploiting children ... Paraguayans, and Argentines, whoever was working."[24]

In response to these problems, the provincial government created a formal structure, the Permanent Roundtable of Dialogue for the Rights of Immigrants, to coordinate the efforts of related agencies and civil society organizations. The Permanent Roundtable was convened by the *Defensor del Pueblo* (a type of ombudsman) and included the STC, the federal Ministry of Labor, the Ministry of Security, the National Department of Immigration, the Department of Human Rights, the Bolivian Consulate, the Center for Bolivian Residents of Córdoba, and the Pro-Bolivia Foundation.[25] The first step of the Permanent Roundtable was to diagnose the problem by gathering information through inspections and a survey of workers that verified the extremely high levels of violations among both migrants and Argentine nationals. In addition, the Center for Bolivian Residents gave the STC a list of firms violating labor laws. Using this information, the STC conducted a series of inspections to put pressure on a handful of employers and to try to regularize the workers.

Officials from the STC, however, never formed long lasting ties with the leaders from the Center for Bolivian Residents, and the enforcement campaign did not reach beyond a few worksites. The head of the STC at the time concluded that despite these changes "more needed to be done" to have an impact on the brick-making industry.[26] By 2007, the ironically-named "Permanent" Roundtable was dissolved. The attempt to formally institutionalize ties between inspectors and civil society organizations had failed. There were few additional inspections in the sector, and enforcement essentially ground to a halt.

In 2008, there was another series of changes that could have, once again, increased enforcement in the sector. The first shift was the appointment of a new Secretary of Labor, Omar Sereno, who made child labor a priority.[27] With support from Governor Schiaretti, he created a child labor committee called COPRETI,[28] which effectively replaced the Permanent Roundtable as a forum

---

[22] Ortiz 2002   [23] Defensor del Pueblo de la Provincia de Cordoba, "Informe Anual 2006"

[24] Interview: C04, Former Senior Official, Córdoba Labor Secretariat, Córdoba, 3/11/2009

[25] Defensor del Pueblo de la Provincia de Cordoba, "Informe Anual 2006"

[26] Interview: C04, Former Senior Official, Córdoba Labor Secretariat, Córdoba, 3/11/2009

[27] Interview: C45, Senior Official, Córdoba Labor Secretariat, Córdoba, 6/19/2008. *La Voz del Interior* "Comisión provincial para eliminar el trabajo infantil" 04/10/2008; "Hallan a niños que trabajan en cortaderos" 06/12/2008

[28] *Comisión Provincial de Prevención y Erradicación del Trabajo Infantil*

connecting the STC to other government agencies and civil society organizations. In 2009, the STC formally presented a plan to combat child labor that highlighted the problems in the brick-making industry.

At the same time, a second change occurred within UORLA, the union that represents brick-markers.[29] UORLA's leadership did not push for enforcement until 2008, when its provincial leadership was dismissed by the central union office (in Buenos Aires) and a new head was appointed. The new union leadership was more active and helped officials from the STC, but UORLA still lacked resources to provide the inspectors.[30] For example, in 2009, UORLA could count only 200 workers as affiliates, giving the union a relatively small network from which to gather information.[31] UORLA's operational capacity was also weak since, with fewer than 10% of workers registered, the union could collect very limited dues. In sum, starting in 2008 there were two factors working toward enforcement – new union leadership and officials who made the brick-kilns a formal priority.[32]

The combined top-down decisions and the more active union resulted in only a modest increase in enforcement efforts for a short time. When in 2008 two more children died by drowning in the worksite of brick-kilns,[33] the STC began once again to send inspectors to conduct operations on the sites.[34] It was during this campaign that an inspection resulted in the first closing of a worksite.[35] Enforcement was not sustained, however, as the brick-kilns were quickly superseded by other industries with stronger unions. The inspectors never closed more than a handful of brick-making sites, and inspection operations quickly came to an end. In the second half of 2008, there was an average of 1.8 inspections a month in the brick-making industry, which constituted only 0.2% of all inspections conducted by the STC. In the survey of inspectors conducted in 2009, not one inspector listed brick-kilns as being part of the top five most inspected sectors.[36] According to officials at the STC, the lack of union resources in the brick-making industry limited what the STC could do, even after a policy decision was made to focus on child labor.[37] Ultimately, the appointment of an official who prioritized child labor and a change in union leadership resulted in only a small increase in enforcement for a short time.

---

[29] *Unión Obrera Ladrillera de la República Argentina*
[30] Interview: C42, Senior Official, Córdoba Labor Secretariat, Córdoba, 3/9/2009
[31] *La Voz del Interior* "Cortaderos de ladrillos, tumba para 5 niños" 12/09/2009
[32] Interviews: C42, Senior Official, Córdoba Labor Secretariat, Córdoba, 3/9/2009; C44, Senior Official, Córdoba Labor Secretariat, Córdoba, 6/26/2008
[33] *La Voz del Interior* "Ladrilleros reclaman por muerte de dos nenas" 11/11/2008
[34] *La Voz del Interior* "Intensificarán controles en los cortaderos" 11/08/2008
[35] *La Voz del Interior* "Clausuran por primera vez un cortadero" 11/7/2008   [36] See Table 4.1
[37] Interviews: C22, Senior Official, Córdoba Labor Secretariat, Córdoba, 06/23/2008, 03/05/2009, and 03/07/2009; and C42, Senior Official, Córdoba Labor Secretariat, Córdoba, 3/9/2009

Córdoba – enforcement with union allies

The failures in the brick-making industry are particularly striking because of the combination of extreme violations and high saliency both in the press and among leaders of the STC. In this case, awareness and decisions by top officials to focus on the industry did not translate into enforcement. Both the Center for Bolivian Residents and UORLA failed to spur on enforcement. The Center for Bolivian Residents was unable to maintain ties with inspectors, and UORLA, which had ties to inspectors, did not have resources. Ultimately, there was a lack of routine information gathering about specific worksites through inspections or through civil society organizations that regulators could use to monitor the industry, and regulators crafted only sporadic responses to the violations that they found. In sum, enforcement in this case can be coded as *low* (see Chapter 2 for definitions of the different levels of enforcement).

Without controls, working conditions did not improve in the industry. Levels of informality remained extremely high, and children kept dying on brick-making sites throughout 2009. A leader from the union UORLA said at the end of 2009 that "without a state policy, without an open space for discussion that brings together all of the actors in the sector, without control and without penalties against the people who violated the law, this [problem] is not going to be solved."[38] The former head of the inspectorate concluded that "more needed to be done" for enforcement.[39]

Metal in Córdoba: medium-levels of union-induced enforcement

The metal industry in Córdoba contrasts sharply with brick-making in many ways, most notably in its relatively lower levels of violations and higher levels of enforcement. In 2004, the metal sector consisted of 1,800 firms, small and large, that manufacture parts for farm machinery and other industries.[40] There were violations of labor laws in the metal industry, but they were significantly less extreme and less prevalent than those in the brick-making sector. Approximately 30% of workers were informal (unregistered) in the metal industry, lower than the provincial average and much lower than that of the brick-making sector.[41] Two of the main problems in the industry were violations of the collective bargaining agreement and the use of subcontracting to avoid contract obligations.[42] After the reactivation of the economy, with high growth in the sector, the metal union (*Union Obrera Metalurgica de la*

---

[38] *La Voz del Interior* "Cortaderos de ladrillos, tumba para 5 niños" 12/09/2009
[39] Interview: C04, Former Senior Official, STC, Córdoba, 3/11/2009
[40] According to the Economic Census of 2004 there were 1,877 localities.
[41] Using the household survey EPH to construct an estimate of informality rates reveals rates of around 30% in 2008–2009 (N=194 households in which people reported working in the sector). Even if this is an underestimate by ten percentage points, the informality rate would be much lower than in brick-making.
[42] Interview: C46, Metal Workers' Union (UOM), Córdoba, 3/18/2009

Republica Argentina, or UOM) made large gains in collective bargaining.[43] Part of the challenge of enforcement was making sure employers respected the agreements. However, due to comparatively better working conditions, a bureaucratic planning process that prioritized industries based on violations would find the metal workers clearly to be in *less* need of enforcement than those in brick-making industry.

Even though the metal industry was not the place of the most egregious (or the highest rates of) violations, it was one of the sectors in which the STC concentrated enforcement. The STC gathered ample information about violations through a high rate of inspections. For instance, in 2008, on average there were 28 inspections per month in the metal industry (in contrast with the 1.8 inspections per month in the brick-making industry).[44] Though employing fewer than 2% of the workers in the province, the metal industry accounted for nearly 10% of the inspections.[45] Moreover, inspectors collected detailed information about the firms to target inspections from UOM, which had a group of nine leaders who regularly checked compliance in the metal workshops. UOM also conducted its own operations; in 2004, for example, the union completed a series of checks for informality that involved more than 1,400 workers. UOM leaders also identified inspection targets using their network of approximately 200 delegates, 16,000 affiliates, anonymous complaints to their toll-free number, and conversations with workers who came to UOM's health clinic and pharmacy. In addition, inspectors counted on UOM to provide transportation to inspection sites, intelligence during inspections, and post-inspection follow-up to check on firm compliance.[46] In short, inspectors had relatively large amounts of information about violations in the metal industry in contrast with other industries in Córdoba.

Once inspectors found violations, they used a variety of tools to respond to firms that failed to comply. In most cases, the inspectors used a combination of "coercion" through fines, "persuasion," and negotiation.[47] Often they gave firms a period of time, approximately a month, to come into compliance. Firms were

---

[43] These national level agreements (which were at the same level of other powerful unions) increased salary in the order of 16% in 2007, 28% in 2008, and 18% in 2009 (after a tough fight with industry). Sources: *Página/12* "La UOM cerró por el 16,5" 05/04/2007; *La Nación* "Metalúrgicos y mecánicos lograron aumentos salariales de casi un 30%" 05/27/2008; *Página/12* "Se firmó el último gran acuerdo salarial" 08/06/2009. Interview: B41, Lawyer, Metal Industry Association of Argentina (ADMIRA), Buenos Aires, 2/18/2009

[44] Author's analysis of data from the STC.

[45] Percentage of workers based on the 2001 Argentine census. "Cuadro 9.24 Total País. Población ocupada de 14 años o más por provincia según rama de actividad económica."

[46] Interviews: C07, Metal Workers' Union (UOM), Córdoba, 3/18/2009; C46, Metal Workers' Union (UOM), Córdoba, 3/18/2009. In addition, *La Voz del Interior* "La reactivación también sumó nuevas afiliaciones a los gremios" 10/16/2006

[47] Interviews: C38, Inspector, Córdoba Labor Secretariat, Córdoba, 7/18/2008; C43, Inspector, Córdoba Labor Secretariat, Córdoba, 6/25/2008; C07, Metal Workers' Union (UOM), Córdoba, 3/18/2009

Córdoba – enforcement with union allies

induced to register workers who were informal so that they could gain full employment protections and back pay. Enforcement also ensured that employers respected the collective bargaining agreement. Negotiations over the terms by which the firm would come into compliance almost always involved union leaders, and, at times, even the powerful head of UOM, who was also a member of the provincial legislature. This political support helped inspectors overcome opposition from firms. In addition, in order to protect workers who gave them information about violations, inspectors investigated problems in firms on a broad basis instead of singling out the worker who alerted the inspectors to a problem. For instance, if a worker brought an inspector's attention to a problem, the inspector checked a cluster of firms (including the problematic one) to make it impossible for the employer to seek retribution.

In sum, enforcement was at a *medium* level in the metal industry in Córdoba – clearly a much higher level than that of the brick-making industry, but still a lower level than those in other industries in other provinces. Union leaders certainly would have preferred more state action in their industry, and they were quick to complain about the poor condition of the STC. But by comparison with other industries in Córdoba, metal was doing relatively well. There was also evidence that, aided by enforcement, levels of informality dropped in the industry from the peak reached during the crisis. For example, according to surveys conducted by union leaders, 52% of workers were unregistered at the beginning of 2004, but by the end of the year this number had dropped to 40%. Although there are many factors that influence compliance, in this case, the union leadership attributed the reduction in violations to the joint inspections of UOM with the STC.[48]

In some ways, greater enforcement in the metal industry than in the brick-making industry is surprising. First, there was clearly less of a need for state intervention on behalf of the workers in the metal industry, in which infractions were comparatively minor. Second, unlike in the brick-making industry, firms in the metal industry compete in a market that extends beyond Córdoba, and, in the 2000s were under particular stress because they had been losing ground to their chief competitors in Brazil.[49] As regulations can increase costs, the industry can be expected to push back on enforcement. In addition, firms had a strong organization[50] with enough political weight to gain key cabinet appointments in the provincial government. In contrast, the brick-kiln association was not influential and scored no major appointments. All of these factors point to the likelihood that the costs of enforcement for the STC should be much greater in the metal manufacturing industry than in the brick-making industry. Yet, these differences clearly *did not* determine the enforcement levels.

---

[48] *La Voz del Interior* "Acción de la UOM por trabajo en negro" 12/17/2004. These estimates align with survey data from the *Encuesta Permanente de Hogares*.

[49] Interview: C37, Córdoba Metal Components Industry Association, Córdoba, 7/15/2008

[50] *Cámara de Industriales Metalúrgicos y Componentes de Córdoba*

84   *Enforcement with unions in the driver's seat*

Construction – high levels of broad enforcement

During the commodity boom that followed the economic crisis in 2001, the number of construction workers in Córdoba increased rapidly – from 1,600 registered workers in 2004 to 20,000 in 2005, and up to nearly 30,000 by 2008.[51] The rebound in the residential and commercial construction industry was driven by new investors who had profited from soaring agricultural exports. These investors challenged the traditional, integrated construction firms by creating new firms that relied heavily on subcontracting and that were dissolved when projects were completed.[52] The combination of rapid expansion of the industry and new, unstable firms brought a sharp increase in the risk of accidents that challenged regulators.[53] Ensuring that this increased risk did not translate into more workplace accidents was primarily the responsibility of the health and safety division, called CYMAT (*Condiciones y Medio Ambiente de Trabajo*), which operated somewhat independently from the wage and hour division. Thus, we introduce yet another dimension of variation – the part of the labor inspectorate tasked with enforcement.

By all measures, CYMAT met the increase of workplace risks in the sector with substantially more enforcement than did the industries discussed previously. CYMAT inspectors were able to gain a substantially large and constant flow of information about working conditions in the construction industry. One source of intelligence for inspectors was the construction union (UOCRA), which transmitted tips about unsafe worksites. UOCRA had a technically trained health and safety expert leading a team of five union employees who patroled the construction sites and gathered information from workers. UOCRA also had an extensive network of delegates and a union office that received workers with a variety of individual problems and then communicated information about conditions into the STC.[54] In its extensive infrastructure to support enforcement, UOCRA was similar to UOM. However, unlike the wage and hour inspectors who work with UOM, CYMAT does not rely entirely on union requests. A senior official in the inspectorate explained that, in the construction industry, he does not wait for the union because "if I had to wait for UOCRA to accompany the inspections, we would only do 1,000

---

[51] Data provided by the *Instituto de Estadística y Registro de la Industria de la Construcción* (IERIC). The numbers only include workers registered in the *obra social* of UOCRA. Given the high levels of informality in this sector, there were likely twice the number of workers.

[52] By the account of industry leaders, new firms that were created lacked the experience and commitment to address health and safety issues. They would mitigate the risks of accidents by insulating investors through layers of subcontracting, instead of through investment in prevention. Interview: C15, Argentine Construction Association (CAC), Córdoba, 3/3/2009

[53] Interview: C32, Health and Safety Specialist, Construction Workers' Union of Argentina (UOCRA), Córdoba, 06/20/2008 and 03/09/2009

[54] Interview: C47, Construction Workers' Union of Argentina (UOCRA), Córdoba, 6/26/2008

inspections [a year]."[55] Instead, CYMAT took the initiative and conducted more than 2,000 inspections a year in the industry (190 a month, nearly 7 times the number conducted in the metal sector).

Nearly all of CYMAT's inspections were programmed internally, which is evidence of an enforcement stance that goes beyond responses to union complaints.[56] When a new construction project was planned above a minimum size, CYMAT regulators routinely conducted an initial inspection of the worksite to ensure that construction plans included health and safety considerations. These programmatic inspections were supported by the union. A leader from UOCRA explained "the inspectors have a list of construction sites that comes from above. We know that they have to progress in making it through this list of sites, so we don't call them except when we know that there is a problem."[57] Inspectors also conducted joint campaigns with the municipal government, which is in charge of safety external to construction sites (e.g., people in the nearby street and surrounding buildings).[58] Moreover, CYMAT received tips from the national Superintendent of Workplace Risks (*Superintendica de Reisgos de Trabajo*) about worksites that have had accidents.[59]

Using this confluence of information sources, regulators put together programmed inspection campaigns that both responded to immediate risks and were preventative. Inspections also went beyond union demands, reaching a broad swath of construction sites, even if the union had not made a direct request. These practices contrasted sharply with those that the inspectors took in response to the brick-kilns and the metal industry. In addition, when compared with enforcement in the construction industries of other provinces, there was a substantially higher level of information gathering in Córdoba. For example, in the city Rosario of the neighboring province of Santa Fe, approximately the same size as Córdoba and with a similar construction boom, in 2006, health and safety inspectors reached only 30 worksites a month (the Córdoba inspectors averaged 190 a month).[60]

A second indicator of high enforcement levels is the existence of credible penalties. In the construction industry, suspensions of unsafe workshops are the most important penalties because they impose immediate and high costs (unlike fines, which can be appealed and often do not reach large sums). A business

---

[55] Interview: C22, Senior Official, Córdoba Labor Secretariat, Córdoba, 06/23/2008, 03/05/2009, and 03/07/2009
[56] Interview: C22, Senior Official, Córdoba Labor Secretariat, Córdoba, 06/23/2008, 03/05/2009, and 03/07/2009
[57] Interview: C32, Health and Safety Specialist, Construction Workers' Union of Argentina (UOCRA), Córdoba, 06/20/2008 and 03/09/2009
[58] *La Voz del Interior* "Para prevenir accidentes habrá control de obras" 04/02/2009
[59] Interview: C36, Córdoba Labor Secretariat, Córdoba, 7/14/2008
[60] Interviews: S41, Construction Workers' Union of Argentina (UOCRA), Rosario, 5/13/2009. *La Capital* "En un año, 6 albañiles muertos y 10 heridos" 03/13/2006; "Cuestionan a empresas que no cuidan a obreros de la construcción" 11/01/2006

leader observed that "when the inspectors shut down a worksite, it causes a lot of pain" for the construction firm in terms of lost time and money.[61] CYMAT inspectors have the ability to unilaterally shut down, or suspend, operations, and the inspectors do exercise this power. In 2004, for example, accidents began to increase, and the construction union, UOCRA, publicly criticized CYMAT for not being tough enough on violators.[62] The inspectors responded by drastically increasing suspensions of activity on construction sites that violated norms in a way that posed an immediate danger to workers. Prior to the criticism by UOCRA, inspections resulted in suspensions 1.6% of the time; the following month, this number shot up to 19%.[63] After this incident, inspectors adjusted to combining penalties with other approaches. Between February 2007 and 2009, inspections resulted in partial closures of construction sites 10% of the time, and full suspensions 4% of the time.[64] To put these rates in comparative context with those of other provinces, in 2008 in the Federal Capital, inspections resulted in a closure only 1% of the time.[65]

Penalties are rarely enough to improve compliance on their own, especially for health and safety standards. A third indicator of enforcement levels is the degree to which regulators enable firms to comply. When CYMAT inspectors found problems that did not pose an immediate risk, they offered advice to construction managers and workers on how to comply. For example, on one construction site, health and safety inspectors instructed managers on methods for identifying conditions that led to workers falling from high floors of unfinished buildings and showed them simple ways to reduce accidents (e.g., putting plywood barriers around open elevator shafts to prevent workers from falling). These steps helped managers and workers anticipate impending changes in the worksite that could create new risks.[66]

Beyond providing instruction during inspections, CYMAT has also systematically taken preventative steps to reduce accidents that go beyond inspection. These actions grew out of a Four-Part Construction Commission that includes the business association (*Cámara Argentina de la Construcción,* or CAC), UOCRA, the STC, the City of Córdoba, and various professional associations. Established in the late 1980s, the Commission served as a way to coordinate

---

[61] The firms are required to continue paying workers in these cases, and by all indications they often do. Interview: C15, Argentine Construction Association (CAC), Córdoba, 03/03/2009

[62] *La Voz del Interior* "La seguridad laboral se relajó" 03/09/2004

[63] Author's analysis of internal inspection data provided by the STC. The average was taken for the year before the public criticism.

[64] Source: Database of inspections from the STC.

[65] Interview: B07, Federal Capital Labor Subsecretariat, Buenos Aires, 10/01/2008

[66] Interviews: C35, Health and Safety Inspector, Córdoba Labor Secretariat, Córdoba, 06/24/2008 and C36, Córdoba Labor Secretariat, Córdoba, 07/14/2008. In addition, I observed health and safety inspections of construction sites during which inspectors interacted with managers from firms.

activities across major actors. A senior official in the STC described one of the initiatives that came out of the Commission:

We have designed training days in the worksites. That's to say ... we ask for permission from the firm—either UOCRA asks or I ask. Then representatives of the STC and UOCRA go, and on the day of the training, the firm changes the work schedule so that we can meet with all of the workers and managers. Two of my inspectors talk specifically about what workers are doing (on the site) and what health and safety measures they should take in a practical way.[67]

For close observers, including union leaders, these *in situ* trainings were a *valuable* way of reducing accidents in the long run and of addressing the root causes of violations.[68] In addition, the Commission worked with local universities that train architects in order to improve education about safety in construction. This effort, advocated by inspectors and UOCRA, showed architects how to incorporate worker well-being into the planning of projects from the very beginning.

In sum, there is ample evidence that CYMAT was actively implementing labor regulations in the construction industry. The flexibly applied mixture of actions in Córdoba – penalties with real teeth along with instruction – is a textbook example of best practices in regulation.[69] CYMAT also appears to have had an effect on safety in the industry (even though there are clearly multiple factors that ultimately determine compliance levels). Most notably, there has not been an increase in the number of accidents even as the number of workers has increased substantially, which union leaders and officials view as an indicator of successful enforcement.[70] While most certainly there were limitations to enforcement in this industry – union leaders have not yet reached their goal of eliminating accidental deaths, and inspectors would prefer to have more resources with which to conduct even more inspections – the *relative* level enforcement was *high* when compared with that of other cases. In addition, the *distribution* of enforcement in Córdoba's construction industry was distinct from that in the other industries; regulators clearly took actions that went beyond reacting to the union's daily demands.[71]

---

[67] Interview: C22, Senior Official, Córdoba Labor Secretariat, Córdoba, 06/23/2008, 03/05/2009, and 03/07/2009

[68] Interview: C32, Health and Safety Specialist, Construction Workers' Union of Argentina (UOCRA), Córdoba, 06/20/2008 and 03/09/2009

[69] See for example: Ayres and Braithwaite 1992; Pires 2008

[70] Interview: C32, Health and Safety Specialist, Construction Workers' Union of Argentina (UOCRA), Córdoba, 06/20/2008 and 03/09/2009. Data on accidents are notoriously bad. The best estimate comes from combining employment data from the *Obra Social del Personal de la Construcción* and deaths in the industry from the STC and SRT. Using these numbers, it appears that deaths have fallen per-thousand workers (in 2002, there were 3.6 deaths per 1,000 workers, while in 2007 there were only 0.3).

[71] In addition, looking beyond the construction industry, CYMAT inspectors carve out resources to address industries with weak unions. For example, CYMAT has inspectors who are dedicated

88   *Enforcement with unions in the driver's seat*

Explaining uneven enforcement

An explanation of enforcement in Córdoba needs to account for its dominant features. By all measures there was enforcement, but it was very uneven across sectors of the economy. The unevenness was not random, but instead was skewed toward industries with large numbers of union demands. How can this pattern of enforcement be explained?

First, enforcement cannot be easily accounted for using standard bureaucratic assessments of state capacity. Quite simply, the STC lacked most of the features of bureaucratic autonomy. Although most inspectors had civil service protection, they were largely patronage hires chosen not based on merit but for their political connections.[72] In addition to their official duties, most inspectors held jobs outside of the state bureaucracy, a practice that was tolerated by senior officials who recognized their staff's need to (unofficially) supplement low salaries.[73] The bureaucracy was governed more by "uses and customs" than by "written down rules" that would indicate a rational, Weberian bureaucracy.[74] These informal norms left significant opportunity for organized interests to influence the inspectorate directly. Indeed, senior officials worried that in some cases union influence was so strong that their own control over the agency completely broke down.[75] Direct influence of unions created, in the words of a senior official, a "deformation" that "impedes" the STC from "creating a plan that is based on a map of informal work, fraudulent firms, and child labor" to target enforcement.[76] In short, enforcement was not made possible by bureaucratic autonomy.

Second, standard political approaches could not explain enforcement. If the principals of the STC were simply pro-labor, the STC should have been given ample resources. Inspectors should have been able to respond to the problems in the brick-kilns because: there was political support in the leadership of the STC who articulated a policy of helping the brick workers; there was no strong employer association that could push back; and stories about the brick-kilns in the media embarrassed the administration. Enforcement in the metal industry, by contrast, could have been more problematic as the metal industry association had enough political weight in the provincial government to gain key cabinet appointments. Consequently, the costs of enforcement for STC's

---

     to other industries and they actively seek out unions in high-risk industries that do not come looking for inspections, such as mining.

[72] Multiple interviews with labor inspectors. For example, when the Bank of Córdoba was privatized, politically connected civil servants who previously worked in the bank were transferred as health and safety inspectors to avoid laying them off. *La Voz del Interior* "25 ex bancarios ya dependen de la Secretaría de Trabajo" 09/15/2004

[73] Interview: C31, Senior Official, STC, Córdoba, 7/17/2008

[74] Interview: C42, Senior Official, STC, Córdoba, 3/9/2009

[75] Interview: C31, Senior Official, STC, Córdoba, 7/17/2008

[76] Interview: C45, Senior Official, STC, Córdoba, 6/19/2008

Córdoba – enforcement with union allies

principals could have been greater in the metal manufacturing than in the brick-kiln industry. Yet, these differences clearly did not determine the enforcement level; the metal industry association largely did not use its collective voice to push back against individual enforcement actions, leaving individual businesses to negotiate directly with inspectors.[77]

By contrast, to understand enforcement in Córdoba, we need to examine the way the structures of linkages interacted with levels of administrative resources in the bureaucracy. Inspectors in Córdoba had strong linkages with labor unions (and only with labor unions). Union leaders had unfettered access to the inspectors and could contact them directly.[78] For example, at the beginning of each day, inspectors routinely waited for labor union leaders to arrive at the STC headquarters before deciding where to conduct inspections. There were no barriers between inspectors and union leaders that prevented regulators from mobilizing union resources.

Linkages help explain the ability of inspectors to undertake the key tasks of enforcement. Regulators gained information from unions throughout the entire process: before inspections, when union leaders request action; during the act of inspection, when union leaders act as "auxiliaries"[79] by interviewing workers and directing inspectors toward violations; as well as after inspections, when union leaders follow up to see if firms corrected the problems.[80] Unions also furnished transportation and even gave direct benefits for inspectors who worked overtime, allowing regulators to visit firms that would otherwise be out of their reach. For example, a union leader explained "In order for me to conduct an operation related to informality, I could talk with the Secretary of Labor ... and say, 'Look, I need so many inspectors. I need a week for me.' ... But we need money, not to pay the inspectors, but to pay for their food, and for the cars to bring them to the inspection sites."[81] An official described the relationship with the unions, "We complement one another. When the unions have a problem, we advise them ... and they ... come with the cars ... which they put at our service so we can complete our objectives and conduct inspections."[82]

Inspector-union linkages also provided a way for inspectors to draw on the political support of unions during enforcement – indeed, they compelled inspectors who might be otherwise uninterested in enforcement to be

---

[77] A representative from the metal association said that the main concern of the association were mass layoffs and subsidies that impacted the whole industry, rather than compliance issues that only impact some members. Interview: C37, Córdoba Metal Components Industry Association, Córdoba, 7/15/2008

[78] Multiple interviews, including: C38, Inspector, STC, Córdoba, 7/18/2008; C43, Inspector, STC, Córdoba, 6/25/2008

[79] Interview: C43, Inspector, STC, Córdoba, 6/25/2008

[80] Interview: C33, Garment Workers' Union (SOIVA), Córdoba, 6/25/2008

[81] Interview: C03, Union of Pastry, Pizza, and Alfajor Workers, Córdoba, 7/16/2008

[82] Interview: C44, Senior Official, Córdoba Labor Secretariat, Córdoba, 6/26/2008

responsive to union demands. As described previously, in the metal industry union leaders directly observed the inspection processes and oversaw how each inspector exercised discretion. Once violations were uncovered, inspectors coordinated with unions so that union leaders could be present when the firm and the inspector negotiated how to resolve violations. Consequently, the union was able to put its weight behind a push for strong enforcement, even when a powerful firm resisted or the inspector might have been uninterested. Where unions failed to provide this political support, enforcement simply did not occur.

The porous nature of the state had a particular structure to it; not all groups had equal access to the inspectorate. There were approximately 12,000 civil society organizations in Córdoba, more than two-thirds of which worked on social assistance, on issues related to workers, or with vulnerable groups.[83] Yet, labor inspectors did not draw on these organizations for resources because of a lack of structures crossing the state-society divide to facilitate collaboration. Thus, focusing on linkages instead of on the unfiltered demands of civil society also helps reveal why enforcement is tied to unions rather than to pressure from all sources.

The importance of linkages that allow union resources to ensure the operation of the STC becomes most clear when we take into account levels of administrative resources that constrained the inspectors – beginning with the wage and hour inspectors and then turning to health and safety. With approximately fifty inspectors, the wage and hour division was in range of the ILO recommendations for inspectors per worker, and at a medium level compared with other Argentine provinces. The number of inspectors, however, is only one component of administrative resources.[84] A major limitation of the STC has been inspector salaries. In 2008, for example, inspectors were paid between $477 and $636 per month.[85] Some inspector pay has even been off the books, prompting inspectors to complain: "How are we supposed to give a fine to a firm that pays workers off the books when we also are paid off the books?"[86] In a sympathetic comment, a union leader noted that "it is very difficult for the inspectors ... what they are paid is not sufficient ... it is somewhat ironic."[87] The low pay created a need for inspectors to work secondary jobs in the afternoons.[88] As a result, while there was a medium number of inspectors on staff, the number of actual hours that they were paid by the province to work was limited, thereby reducing capacity for enforcement. In addition, the quality

---

[83] Luna and Cecconi 2004

[84] There are approximately 35,000 economically active workers per inspector in the province (including health and safety).

[85] Interview: C31, Senior Official, Córdoba Labor Secretariat, Córdoba, 7/17/2008

[86] *La Voz del Interior* "Sueldos en negro, en la cartera que debe evitarlos" 06/18/2005

[87] Interview: C07, Metal Workers' Union (UOM), Córdoba, 3/18/2009

[88] Interview: C31, Senior Official, Córdoba Labor Secretariat, Córdoba, 7/17/2008

Córdoba – enforcement with union allies

of inspector training was relatively low, and there was no minimum educational requirement to be an inspector; only 10% of inspectors completed university, and 4% of inspectors went only to elementary school.[89] These levels of educational attainment fail to meet the MERCOSUR standards requiring all inspectors to have university degrees by 2010, and are extremely low in international comparative context.[90]

Limited material resources and the organizational capacity to plan inspections also limited the STC in undertaking enforcement campaigns on its own. In the wage and hour division, inspectors had extremely insufficient means of transportation – in 2008 there were only two cars for approximately 50 inspectors – which limited their ability to take action without union cars.[91] Furthermore, the STC was "technologically very bad," having no information management system that would allow it to assess which firms had been inspected and what the inspection results were.[92] A senior official explained that essential resources were missing for the STC. "To design and undertake a concentrated inspection operation, we need three very basic tools: people, cars, and a computer. Nothing more than that."[93] Yet in their absence, he admitted that key sectors of the economy were left out. "We haven't done many inspections in agriculture because we didn't have cars, and the union did not come."[94] Despite some efforts, the STC's wage and hour division has been unable to institute long- or medium-term planning processes to prioritize enforcement and has undertaken few programmatic inspection campaigns.[95] Ultimately, the combination of limited transportation resources and no information management system effectively prevented active enforcement campaigns. These constraints cemented the importance of the unions' resources, making inspectors highly dependent on unions for the most basic tasks.

---

[89] To put the education levels into context, MERCOSUR countries agreed in 2006 that all labor inspectors should have completed university.

[90] MERCOSUR 2006

[91] Interview: C22, Senior Official, STC, Córdoba, 06/23/2008, 03/05/2009, and 03/07/2009

[92] Information management, until very recently, entailed inspectors writing the number of inspections they conducted in the month on the wall. In the middle of 2009, steps were taken to modernize the system, but there were still no concrete changes.

[93] Interview: C22, Senior Official, Córdoba Labor Secretariat, Córdoba, 06/23/2008, 03/05/2009, and 03/07/2009

[94] Interview: C22, Senior Official, Córdoba Labor Secretariat, Córdoba, 06/23/2008, 03/05/2009, and 03/07/2009

[95] Interviews: C22 and C45, Senior Official, Córdoba Labor Secretariat, Córdoba, 6/19/2008. The inspection campaigns that do exist are generally short bursts that occur in reaction to a crisis or a lull in union demands. For example, during January vacations union demand for inspections decreases and there is a spike of short-term employment in the tourism sector of the province. Taking advantage of the opportunity created by fewer union requests, the wage and hour division conducted a campaign in the tourism industry in 2009 for one month. They found high levels of violations of worker registration laws – as expected – but they were unable to follow-up systematically with inspections after the campaign to bring firms into compliance.

Greater enforcement in the construction industry was made possible by the pocket of administrative resources in CYMAT. Health and safety inspectors had priority access to material resources (e.g., cars), which enabled inspectors to take action even when there were no immediate resources available from the unions. There were still shortages of cars and the inspectors used unions for transport, but they were not nearly as constrained as the wage and hour inspectors. Also, in contrast to the wage and hour division, CYMAT had a computer system that gave it the basic ability to plan inspections and keep systematic records of its actions. This capability, although quite elementary, was fundamental for the inspectorate to identify firms to inspect, monitor rates of violations in industries, and keep track of the actions of inspectors.[96] Note that these differences did not make CYMAT more Weberian; many of the inspectors gained their positions through patronage, not merit.[97] Nevertheless, with comparatively greater resources dedicated to enforcement, CYMAT inspectors were able to go beyond immediate demands.

Revisiting the strategies and capabilities of the unions in the three industries described in light of the structures of linkages and distribution of administrative resources, clarifies the different patterns of enforcement in Córdoba described previously. In the brick-kilns, the union had very few capabilities to help inspectors with the operational tasks of enforcement. With few punctual demands and no administrative resources, enforcement did not occur. The outcome was society-dependent enforcement at a low level. In the metal industry, there were greater political and operational resources that both pushed and enabled inspectors to focus on this sector. But since the metal workers mainly engaged the wage and hour inspectors, there were few administrative resources within the state to allow inspectors to enforce if they were not being subsidized by the union. Here, the outcome was society-dependent enforcement at a medium level. Finally, in construction, the union was powerful and had considerable resources to help inspectors, including a trained health and safety expert. In addition, the state was able to respond to political pressure by going beyond the punctual demands of UOCRA and to undertake more programmatic inspections in the sector due to the pocket of administrative resources in CYMAT. These programmatic efforts were supported by UOCRA, which undertook an explicit strategy to give inspectors space to go beyond union demands. In this industry, the outcome was co-produced enforcement at a high

---

[96] Interview: C36, Córdoba Labor Secretariat, Córdoba, 7/14/2008

[97] For example, when the Bank of Córdoba was privatized, politically connected civil servants who previously worked in the bank were transferred as health and safety inspectors to avoid laying them off. In addition, many inspectors had side consulting businesses that clearly conflicted with their official duties. Multiple interviews with labor inspectors. *La Voz del Interior* "25 ex bancarios ya dependen de la Secretaría de Trabajo" 09/15/2004

Córdoba – enforcement with union allies

level. Thus, the combinations of administrative resources and the capabilities and strategies of linked-organizations help explain the distinct enforcement outcomes across these industries.

In sum, enforcement in Córdoba cannot be explained by the traditional components of state capacity, the balance of political power of societal interest groups contesting over enforcement in a particular industry, or hierarchical control by which formal political principals in the state hierarchy determine where enforcement takes place. Instead, to understand how and where enforcement occurred, we need to look at the way linkages allowed certain groups to access the inspectorate and provide both political and operational support, as well as how these groups combined with administrative resources inside the state. By doing so, we can reveal the particular ways in which the state is uneven in its responses to regulatory violations.

Political origins of linkages without administrative resources

Tracing the history of labor administration in the province further clarifies the politics of enforcement by identifying the origins of the particular combination of linkages and administrative resources. By doing so, we are also able to distinguish more clearly the politics of regulatory reform (discussed in Chapter 3) from the politics of enforcement. Córdoba did not always have an inspectorate wherein internal components of state capacity were weak and linkages were strong. The first governor elected in Córdoba after Argentina's return to democracy was Eduardo Angeloz from the Radical Party (UCR). The UCR's main opposition was the PJ, which was allied with organized labor (the two factions of the provincial General Labor Confederations, or CGTs).[98] Under Angeloz, Córdoba formed a Ministry of Labor (MTC, *Ministerio de Trabajo de Córdoba*) in 1985. Creating a cabinet level ministry, as opposed to an agency lower on the hierarchy of the executive branch, resulted in greater budgetary resources being allocated to labor administration. To head the MTC, Angeloz selected a labor lawyer, Jorge Sappia, who was respected by both labor and business.[99] Córdoba soon became the only province in Argentina to use meritocratic criteria (a competitive civil service exam) to hire its first inspectors. By 1988, the MTC had 57 labor inspectors (0.21 per 10,000 residents). Sappia also created CYMAT and the Four-Part Commission in the construction industry, laying the groundwork for greater resources in that area years later. During this time, inspectors were required to take training courses of seventy hours per year and were given relatively high wages within the

---

[98] The Radicals also controlled both changes of the provincial legislature, dominating the province.
[99] Interviews: C13, Industrial Union of Córdoba, Córdoba, 6/19/2008; C03, Union of Pastry, Pizza, and Alfajor Workers, Córdoba, 7/16/2008; C46, Metal Workers' Union (UOM), Córdoba, 3/18/2009

94   *Enforcement with unions in the driver's seat*

provincial government's civil service system.[100] In addition, these inspectors had access to cars and other basic material resources.

The use of linkages with unions to enhance state enforcement was, by contrast, comparatively modest. Labor union leaders could come to the inspectorate and request enforcement on particular firms, but they were limited to prevent the loss of hierarchical control within the bureaucracy. For example, unions could not subsidize the inspectors' salaries by paying for food or overtime. In addition, inspectors would mostly use their own cars, but when they needed to, could use union transportation. Overall, there is consensus among those involved in labor politics in Córdoba – from unions, industry, and within the state – that this initial period was the high point of labor inspection in the province, due largely to the investments in the bureaucracy.[101]

After Governor Angeloz left office in 1995, the new right-leaning governor, Ramón Mestre (also from the UCR), shifted the programmatic emphasis away from building capacity in labor inspection.[102] The MTC was downgraded three levels to become a Sub-Secretariat of Labor, leaving it diminished in terms of political strength and budgetary resources. The number of inspectors was reduced drastically between 1995 and 1996 from 56 to 36.[103] These decreases in the internal components of capacity were not supplemented with stronger ties to unions. Appointed officials made it even harder for inspectors to work with unions by putting in place a system that curtailed union collaboration to specific days of the week. Consequently, the capacity of the state to enforce labor regulations declined.

The decline in capacity under a governor who was ideologically opposed to labor regulation is not surprising. What is surprising, however, was the trajectory of the inspectorate after the allies of labor unions gained power in 1998. For the first time since the return to democracy, a PJ candidate, José Manuel De la Sota, was elected governor. In 2003, De la Sota was reelected, and in 2007 was followed by his ally from the PJ, Juan Schiaretti.

---

[100] Interview: C01, Former Senior Official, Córdoba Labor Secretariat, Córdoba, 06/18/2008 and 03/10/2009
[101] The consensus was apparent based on dozens of interviews in Córdoba. Indicators of enforcement outputs indicate that there were substantial actions taken by inspectors in the 1980s. For example, in the Capital region, the MTC conducted 13,590 inspections in 1987 and 20,881 in 1990. These numbers were substantially greater than the 10,078 inspections conducted in 2007 (when the economy was substantially larger). While inspection numbers are not a definitive measurement of enforcement, they support the view held by all local actors that state capacity was particularly high in the 1980s. Source: Archival data from the provincial government.
[102] During Mestre's administration, the province had a debt crisis, unemployment spiked, and the provincial government worked with the World Bank to institute a series of structural reforms.
[103] This rate was much greater than the overall reduction in Córdoba's public sector. The number of public sector employees per 1,000 inhabitants in Córdoba dropped only from 28 to 26. Source: Ministerio de Economía y Finanzas Públicas, Direccion Nacional de Coordinacion Fiscal con las Provincias.

Córdoba – enforcement with union allies

At the beginning of the twelve-year period that the unions' traditional partisan allies were in power, De la Sota rewarded unions for their support by elevating labor administration from a Sub-Secretariat to a full Secretariat, the *Secretaría de Trabajo* (STC). However, going against union requests, he stopped short of restoring labor administration to the level of a ministry and of providing resources to augment the internal capacity of the agency. Just before the elections in 2007, union leaders had argued that the STC should become a full ministry because it was suffering due to "budgetary limitations."[104] After Schiaretti had won the election, a group of unions from both CGT factions argued once again: "We want it to stop being a secretariat, and to be changed to the level of a ministry."[105] As an official in the STC (and union leader) explained: "Everyone wants there to be a Ministry of Labor. The structure, a ministry ... more than anything is about the budget ... If they convert us into a ministry, we will be able to act in a different way. It would be ideal, for the population, for the people inside, for the unions, for everyone."[106] In short, the unions fought, repeatedly and unsuccessfully, for a ministry of labor.[107]

In response to union demands, the Peronist governors made promises to double the number of labor inspectors, increase the number of cars, build new regional offices, and upgrade the information management system.[108] These investments in administrative resources, however, were never made. The number of inspectors did not double as promised – instead it initially decreased from 58 in 1998 to 45 in 2006, and then leveled off at 56 in 2008. The ratio of inspectors per population (a commonly used measure) was lower in 2008 than it had been in 1988 due to growth in the province (0.17 inspectors per 10,000 inhabitants in 2008 compared with 0.21 in 1998). The one pocket of greater capabilities within the state, CYMAT, was directly subsidized by the SRT at the national level and thus did not require allocation of scarce resources.

While the Peronist governors did not invest budgetary resources in labor inspection, they did promote linkages between inspectors and unions. Nearly all senior officials appointed during this period had previously worked for unions, mainly as lawyers. They came into office with a substantial network and an ideological affinity to the labor movement. For example, when the head of one union was appointed Secretary of Labor, he explained that "the general secretaries of the unions all had my cell phone number, no one in the waiting room, no one asking for an official hearing. They had totally free access to my

---

[104] *La Voz del Interior* "Cautela de gremios por gestión de Trabajo" 02/12/2007
[105] *La Voz del Interior* "Gremios por un Ministerio de Trabajo" 11/20/2007
[106] Interview: C31, Senior Official, Córdoba Labor Secretariat, Córdoba, 7/17/2008
[107] Unions waited until November 2011 for a governor to restore the Ministry of Labor, after the period of time of this case study.
[108] *La Voz del Interior* "Schiaretti duplica la cantidad de inspectores laborales" 04/29/2008

office."[109] These appointment patterns and practices continued throughout the period in which the PJ was in power.[110] As a result of this political support from the governors, routinized processes were established that facilitated tight coordination and collaboration between inspectors and unions.

While nonunion organizations could put pressure on the STC and attempt to hold it accountable, they could not enable the STC to act; demands from society do not automatically translate into action. The failure of enforcement in the brick-kiln industry is a striking illustration of the lack of linkages between inspectors and civil society organizations that are not unions. The Center for Bolivian Residents, which was not a union, attempted to hold the STC accountable, but collaboration between the Center and inspectors never developed in a way that could enable enforcement. The inspectors only maintained linkages with the union. There was a disagreement between the Center and the union over which group truly represented the interests of workers, and the Center was unable to displace the union and establish linkages.[111]

In sum, the trajectory of the state in Córdoba went from: investment in the internal components of state capacity; to a period of dismantling; and then to an emphasis on linkages with unions that enabled the state to implement policies. This shift could not be accounted for by the nature of political competition among parties. Investment in internal state capacity was greatest when politics was the least competitive – the Radical party beat the PJ in 1983 by seventeen points, the widest margin in the democratic history of the province. By contrast, in 2007 the PJ beat the Radicals by only one point. Thus, the more competitive period coincided with the least investment in internal components of state capacity. Nor could this trajectory be reduced to a simple extension of the politics of labor law. Whereas theories of labor politics would predict that unions should be best positioned when their partisan allies are in power and face political uncertainty,[112] unions did not gain investment in internal forms of state capacity during Schiaretti's administration, which met both of these conditions. However, enforcement was increasingly supported by linkages with unions throughout the Peronist period, even when elections were not close (such as in 2003, when the PJ won by fifteen points). Thus, while in some ways labor politics functioned similar for legislation as for enforcement – outcomes favored organized interests – in other ways the dynamic was distinct due to the lack of sensitivity to political uncertainty.

By contrast, investment in the internal components of state capacity in the early years of the inspectorate can be explained by the combination of the governor's programmatic goals and the opposition of the unions. The Radical governor felt real pressure from the unions to develop state capacity

---

[109] Interview: Co4, Former Senior Official, Córdoba Labor Secretariat, Córdoba, 3/11/2009
[110] Interview: C45, Senior Official, Córdoba Labor Secretariat, Córdoba, 6/19/2008
[111] *LV* "Cruce entre un abogado y el gremio" 11/08/2008   [112] Murillo 2005

Tucumán – society-dependent enforcement

to regulate labor relations.[113] A union leader contrasted the politics under Radical and Peronist governors:

When Angeloz was the governor and Sappia the Minister, they were from the other party—because unionism is Peronism—we demanded a ton and they were afraid ... and because of that, they complied with our demands. When we were from the same party as the governor, they would say "Not so fast, wait." It is because there is an alliance. We won much more in the years of the Radicals than in the years of the Peronists.[114]

The Radicals did not want to hand over control to the unions but needed to respond to their demands; so they invested scarce resources in the internal components of state capacity and used ties to the unions in limited ways.

The dynamics changed in the later period when the unions' allies were in power. Labor did not win all of the investments that the movement wanted – unions would have preferred a full ministry with its own internal resources. A leader from one of the major Córdoba unions explained:

We have lost ... The unions created the possibility that their people could be a part of the STC. [This way] the STC would give them more weight ... Therefore, if the governor gave unions positions in the STC, ... it didn't matter [to them] that it was Secretariat, when in reality it should be a Ministry.[115]

As this leader suggests, the governors were able to respond to labor demands through appointments that created ties between unions and regulators, thus satisfying the unions that were advocating for strong enforcement without having to allocate scarce resources to the budget of the inspectorate. However, unlike pure patronage (e.g., appointments given to political allies with no special interest or ability to further labor regulation) this political exchange did further enforcement in specific industries.

TUCUMÁN – SOCIETY-DEPENDENT ENFORCEMENT

Tucumán's Labor Secretariat (TST) conducted nearly as many inspections as did Córdoba's, comparing favorable international standards in terms of enforcement outputs (approximately 7.6 per 1,000 residents compared with Córdoba's 8.6).[116] During these inspections, workers gained protections that they would have otherwise been unable to secure. For instance, inspectors collaborated with the metal workers union to induce employers to register workers and ensure that salaries were paid in full.[117] Just as in Córdoba,

---

[113] Córdoba's labor unions had mobilized substantial protests in the past Brennan 1994, and a series of general strikes had pushed the Radical party at the national level to take a conciliatory tone with unions McGuire 1997 pp. 202–203.

[114] Interview: C17, Construction Workers' Union of Argentina (UOCRA), Córdoba, 7/15/2008

[115] Interview: C46, Metal Workers' Union (UOM), Córdoba, 3/18/2009

[116] Interview: T56, Head of Inspection, Secretaría de Trabajo de Tucaman, Tucumán, 11/6/2008

[117] Interview: T57, Metal Worker's Union (UOM), Tucumán, 4/21/2009

98　　　　　　　　　　　　　　　*Enforcement with unions in the driver's seat*

TABLE 4.2 *Sector Distribution of Inspections and Union Requests in Tucumán*[118]

Sector	Which Sectors are Inspected the Most?(%)	Which Unions Request the Most Inspections?(%)	Difference Between Inspections and Requests(%)
Commercial	22	22	0
Construction	16	17	−1
Metal	12	9	+3
Transport/ trucking	10	11	−1
Citrus/ agriculture	9	12	−3
Restaurants / hotels	7	9	−2
Domestic workers	4	0	+4
Sugar	4	4	0
Bakery	3	2	−1

enforcement was highly skewed to union demands; more than 80% of inspections were conducted at the requests of unions. Using the survey data, Table 4.2 shows the distribution of sectors that were most inspected along with those unions that requested the most inspections. Just as in Córdoba, there was a strong correlation between union requests and inspection. The following two sections examine the citrus and construction sectors in detail.

Citrus industry – responsive enforcement[119]

One of the most important industries in Tucumán's economy, by employment and revenue, is the citrus industry. Tucumán is home to lemon growers, "packing" facilities that process fresh lemons for export, and industrial plants that transform lemons into a number of commodities (e.g., essential oils and frozen pulp) for export. The industry took off in the 1990s, driven mainly by the growth in demand from European markets. Between 1992 and 2007, employment in the industry quadrupled, reaching approximately 30,000 workers.[120] By 2007, citrus accounted for more than half of the province's

---

[118] N=90. Analysis of the responses of 18 inspectors listing top 5 industries and top 5 unions.
[119] I am grateful to Sutti Ortiz for her insightful comments on labor issues in the citrus sector of Tucumán.
[120] Between 1992 and 2007, employment in the citrus industry increased four fold. Gobierno de Tucumán, *Censo Citrícola Provincial 2006*.

Tucumán – society-dependent enforcement

exports.[121] Workers in this industry are divided among field laborers, workers in fresh fruit packing facilities, and industrial workers in citrus processing facilities. Although conditions differ among these subsectors, toward the end of the 1990s labor law violations were rampant throughout the industry. There were extremely high levels of informality – the majority of workers were denied benefits – and conditions were extremely poor as evidenced by the fact that workers were transported to the fields in trucks *like cattle*.[122] The citrus workers union, UATRE, was largely subdued and did not fight strongly for labor law enforcement or wage increases.[123] Enforcement levels from the TST were also extremely low. Quite simply, during the 1990s, regulators did little to reduce widespread violations.

Low levels of enforcement appear to be especially likely in this case for two reasons. First, the industry is labor intensive and exports cost-sensitive commodities. These market conditions should give firms strong incentives to avoid compliance when doing so will reduce costs. Second, the industry was well organized in the Tucumán Citrus Association (ATC) that includes all of the citrus growers, fresh fruit packing plants and citrus processing plants. The ATC has been a strong advocate for the industry. For example, the ATC convinced the government to lobby countries to open up their markets to fresh lemons from Argentina.[124] With a cost-sensitive, labor intensive, and highly organized industry, dominant theories would expect that political pressure against enforcement that could increase labor costs should have been strong. Yet, like other associations, the ATC's largest members were the ones that were most likely to comply (they were under pressure from the union and expected to be operating legally by their clients), creating a competitive advantage for smaller firms that could dodge regulatory requirements. Therefore, the large firms would gain from enforcement, while the small firms would lose out. With these conflicting interests, the ATC's position was that the STC should "regulate everyone so that everyone complies with their obligations," but at the same time the ATC would not act against some of its own members.[125] Ultimately, the ATC did not take a strong stand either for institutional strengthening or less state regulation, leaving firms to advocate for themselves.

---

[121] In 2007 and 2008, citrus sectors accounted for 51% and 53% (respectively) of the value of all exports. Source: Tucumán Ministry of Production.

[122] Interviews: T51, Union of Agricultural and Rural Workers (UATRE), Tucumán, 4/15/2009; T12, Senior Official, Tucumán Labor Secretariat, Tucumán, 10/27/2008 and 11/12/2008

[123] Multiple interviews. See also: Aparicio, Ortiz, and Tadeo 2008

[124] Interview: T09, Tucumán Citrus Association, Tucumán, 10/28/2008. Additional evidence of their strength comes from their independence. The ATC was part of the FET (*Federación Economica de Tucumán*), but separated from it after the industry became large enough to focus more on its own interests without needing the support of the FET. Instead, the ATC is associated with the substantially weaker UIT (*Union Industria de Tucumán*), the regional organization of the powerful national industry confederation UIA.

[125] Interview: T09, Tucumán Citrus Association, Tucumán, 10/28/2008

When the economy began to reactivate, there were a number of changes in the industry. The union began to fight hard in collective bargaining for wage increases and for the inclusion of citrus workers in the government sponsored "inter-harvest" program that provides payments to workers between harvests. The inter-harvest program gave UATRE and workers extra incentives for registration – only registered workers could benefit from the payment. UATRE had incentives to support enforcement and, in turn, increase union members and contributions. At first, the number of inter-harvest beneficiaries was small, but it increased substantially over time. In 2006, the Secretary of Labor Roberto Jiménez noted that in the citrus sector "there are not as many problems [with enforcement] because the workers are aware of the need to be registered."[126] Second, as UATRE became more active, it developed resources that labor inspectors could use; transportation and staff with money gained through the union social fund. UATRE also organized political action by putting forward candidates in local elections. Its secretary general became the head of the union confederation, the CGT-Tucumán (beating out the powerful secretary general of the transport union, UTA, who became Secretary of Labor in 2004).[127] In sum, there was greater activity as well as significant organizational and political resources in UATRE.

During this time, enforcement increased dramatically in the citrus sector. First, the TST dedicated a number of inspectors just to the citrus sector, sending them out regularly to conduct inspections. Although exact figures are unavailable, the survey of inspectors indicates that the citrus industry accounted for approximately one tenth of all inspections (see Table 4.2). The TST also gathered information through UATRE's network of sixty delegates in packing firms, as well as from union representatives who work in UATRE's social fund and who control compliance with union dues. Also, UATRE had a constant stream of workers seeking a variety of union-offered services, thereby generating another flow of intelligence. Combined, these sources created an influx of information about working conditions, and the citrus sector became one of the top industries wherein inspections were concentrated.[128] Second, inspectors issued fines and pushed firms to formalize their workers. To avoid problems of corruption and any pushback from industry, the union leaders kept photocopies of all records to ensure that the inspections resulted in compliance (and not in a bribe to the inspector).[129] Enforcement in this industry was not able to escape corruption completely, but close observers all agree that union oversight has resulted in lower levels of corruption than in other industries. In short, in the period after the crisis, the TST was able to gain information

---

[126] *LGT* "En Tucumán, 112.000 empleados están en negro" 04/02/2006
[127] *LGT* "El PE exige cambios en la conducción de la CGT" 04/07/2007
[128] Interview: T55, Inspector, Tucumán Labor Secretariat, Tucumán, 11/11/2008
[129] Interview: T51, Union of Agricultural and Rural Workers (UATRE), Tucumán, 4/15/2009

Tucumán – society-dependent enforcement

about violations and respond in a way that was consistent with recognized enforcement practices and robust against political interference.

In sum, even with many factors working against enforcement in the citrus industry, in the period after the economic crisis, enforcement changed in level from *low* to *medium*. Compared with levels in Córdoba's brick-making industry, levels of enforcement in Tucumán's citrus industry were clearly greater. There is also evidence that enforcement has contributed to improving working conditions in this sector. Precise data are not collected at the industry level, but, by all accounts, levels of informality have dropped precipitously in the packing plants. Union leaders estimate that in 2001 the citrus sector had very few registered workers receiving the inter-harvest benefit, but numbers increased dramatically from 1,000 in 2002, to 3,000 by 2003, and 18,000 in 2008. By 2009, approximately 27,000 workers were registered and receiving benefits of the union's social fund. And in 2009, nearly all workers in the packing plants were registered, which is a feat for any sector in Argentina, let alone an agro-industrial sector.[130] From the view of those most closely involved with inspection, this change was created in part by enforcement. Even if the estimates are inflated and market pressures from European buyers contributed to improving levels of compliance,[131] the numbers are congruent with the conclusion that labor regulations have been enforced in a context with an extremely weak and politicized bureaucracy.

Failed enforcement in construction

The construction industry in Tucumán offers a sharp contrast to the citrus industry. After the economic crisis of 2001, the construction industry in Tucumán exploded; in May 2005 there were 6,600 registered workers, and by May 2008 this number reached 15,800.[132] Tucumán was no exception to the high levels of violations of labor laws in this industry. As the industry grew, accidents increased – two reported deaths in 2004, five in 2005, and six in 2007.[133] These numbers, which only include registered workers, likely understate the

---

[130] Interview: T51, Union of Agricultural and Rural Workers (UATRE), Tucumán, 4/15/2009

[131] In order to export fresh lemons, the most lucrative segment of the citrus sector, Tucumán's firms had to meet European phytosanitary standards. They also had some incentives from European buyers to comply with local legislation. Ultimately, in order to compete in the fresh fruit market, firms had to undertake a number of work organization changes and upgrade production methods to increase quality. These changes had positive effects on labor compliance, which complemented the increasingly stringent state enforcement. Ortiz and Aparicio 2006a; Ortiz and Aparicio 2006b; Ortiz and Aparicio 2007; Aparicio, Ortiz, and Tadeo 2008

[132] These numbers greatly underestimate the total employment in the sector because the majority of workers were unregistered. Data Source: IERIC "Cantidad de Trabajadores Registrados en la Construcción por Provincia. Argentina. Serie Mensual. Julio 2002/2003/2004 – Enero 2005 – Mayo 2008"

[133] Data Source: *Superintendencia de Reisgos de Trabajo*

102 *Enforcement with unions in the driver's seat*

magnitude of the problem. In short, the construction sector was widely understood to be one of the most problematic health and safety industries in the province.

Notwithstanding the concentration of violations in the construction industry, enforcement levels remained very low.[134] With only three health and safety inspectors, the TST could not, on its own, keep up with the rapid turnover in hundreds of construction projects. As a result, the great majority of worksites went uninspected. Unlike UATRE in the citrus industry, the construction union (UOCRA) did not have its own union-"inspectors" actively controlling sites and thereby supplementing the TST. UOCRA's network was relatively small; with sixty delegates, the union did not have even one delegate per large worksite, and the union had no delegates in many smaller construction sites.[135] Even though UOCRA – being one of the main leaders of the provincial CGT – had the political strength necessary to access inspectors, the union was operationally unable to generate high quality information. UOCRA gave inspectors long lists of worksites that *might* have had issues, as a health and safety inspector explained:

UOCRA, to date, is asking me on average 500 inspections a month. I have three inspectors who aren't completely dedicated to UOCRA ... For the operational capacity that I have, it is impossible to comply with this demand ... Therefore, if you want to evaluate impact in the construction sector ... it is very limited. Yes, it is certain that each time an inspector goes to a worksite they gain some benefits for the worker, a pair of boots, gloves, a helmet ... and we can get the firm to incorporate a system [of health and safety]. But I have 500 requests a month from UOCRA and the result is that I only have the operating capacity to do ... 16 inspections a month.[136]

The only reason that inspectors were able to get out at all was because "UOCRA gives us the cars for the work of the inspector,"[137] and if the inspectors need to work late, UOCRA "pays them, gives them a car, gives them lunch, and dinner."[138] There remained, however, serious barriers because UOCRA simply did not have enough resources to make up for the TST's deficits. In sum, the TST's inability to collect intelligence about violations in the construction industry is evidence of relatively low levels of enforcement.

Second, the TST struggled to react to violations in ways that could improve compliance. Unlike other provinces that have tripartite commissions through which inspectors work along with the industry association and UOCRA to find solutions to recurring problems in the industry, in Tucumán there was no such

---

[134] Data on Table 4.2 indicate that the construction industry is inspected at a relatively high rate compared with other industries, but these inspections are mainly around wage and hour violations, not health and safety.

[135] Interview: T06, Construction Workers' Union of Argentina (UOCRA), Tucumán, 4/14/2009

[136] Interview: T39, Senior Official, Tucumán Labor Secretariat, Tucumán, 4/17/2009

[137] Interview: T39, Senior Official, Tucumán Labor Secretariat, Tucumán, 4/17/2009

[138] Interview: T06, Construction Workers' Union of Argentina (UOCRA), Tucumán, 4/14/2009

Tucumán – society-dependent enforcement

coordination. Even on a case-by-case basis, regulators often lacked the ability to conduct follow-up inspections when they found violations. For instance, one inspector explained that "after having done an inspection and suspending a part of a worksite, I am unable to go back and check [on their progress] because I am too busy [with new inspections]."[139] In addition, corruption was a constant problem in the industry. Inspectors often did not resist employers' bribes. For example, in one incident an inspector went to a worksite asking for a bribe in exchange for canceling an inspection planned for the following day.[140] One of TST's main strategies for avoiding corruption was to have union leaders accompany inspectors.[141] In the construction industry, however, UOCRA lacked the staff to follow inspectors (in contrast with the citrus workers' union's ample staff).[142]

The problems of enforcement in the construction industry were brought into sharp focus when a serious accident killed three workers on a construction site in March 2007. The accident stirred up social unrest as relatives of the victims threw stones at the police, bringing the issue of construction safety immediately to the media's attention.[143] UOCRA had requested an inspection of the site a week before, but the TST still had not visited it.[144] The Secretary of Labor explained to the local newspaper that "there are many construction sites and there aren't enough personnel to conduct the inspections."[145] The fact that the owner of the construction company was a cousin of the governor José Alperovich gave the feeble opposition an opportunity to attack the administration.[146] Notwithstanding this public accident and the ensuing scandal of a magnitude that in other cases triggered serious regulatory responses, there were few changes to enforcement in Tucumán's construction industry.[147]

In sum, based on the available data and the assessment of those involved most directly with the construction industry – UOCRA, the industry associations, and the TST – enforcement was at a *low level*.[148] There was also no evidence that violations were reduced in the period after the economic crisis. For these reasons, enforcement in construction contrasts sharply with that in

---

[139] Interview: T45, Inspector, Tucumán Labor Secretariat, Tucumán, 10/31/2008
[140] Interview: T06, Construction Workers' Union of Argentina (UOCRA), Tucumán, 4/14/2009
[141] Interview: T12, Senior Official, Tucumán Labor Secretariat, Tucumán, 10/27/2008 and 11/12/2008
[142] Interview: T06, Construction Workers' Union of Argentina (UOCRA), Tucumán, 4/14/2009
[143] *LGT* "Un muro se derrumbó y causó una tragedia" 03/22/2007
[144] *LGT* "Dos de las tres víctimas trabajaban en negro" 03/24/2007
[145] *LGT* "Ediles le quitan responsabilidad al municipio" 03/23/2007
[146] *LGT* "Aseguran que el Estado debe controlar las obras" 03/24/2007
[147] In 2009, TST attempted to hire more health and safety inspectors, but the process was continually delayed.
[148] Interviews: T48, Argentine Construction Association (CAC), Tucumán, 10/29/2008; T53, Tucumán Construction Association, Tucumán, 11/4/2008; T06, Construction Workers' Union of Argentina (UOCRA), Tucumán, 4/14/2009; T39, Senior Official, Tucumán Labor Secretariat, Tucumán, 4/17/2009

104   *Enforcement with unions in the driver's seat*

the citrus industry. This outcome is somewhat surprising considering that the construction industry is not very mobile (firms cannot shift production just because of enforcement). Furthermore, the industry is not very well organized; two industry associations, actively competing against one another, divided employers' voice.[149] One industry association, the Tucumán Construction Associations (*Cámara de Construcción de Tucumán*, CCT), is tied to the local Economic Federation of Tucumán (*Federación Economica de Tucumán* FET), while the other is a local branch of the national Argentine Construction Association (*Cámara Argentaina de la Construcción*, CAC). Still, even with a comparably less organized industry that cannot easily relocate, enforcement levels remained low.

Explaining enforcement in Tucumán

Enforcement in Tucumán clearly cannot be explained by virtue of the province having a coherent bureaucracy. In fact, the TST has all of the characteristics that the literature suggests should lead to universal failure. Inspectors were selected not due to their education or merit but mainly by their political connections to Peronist activists or to unions.[150] Although formally they were given civil service protection, in practice there were multiple instances in which retaliatory action was taken against inspectors.[151] Corruption was a serious problem that was openly acknowledged by officials.[152] Multiple times between 2002 and 2009, inspectors were publically exposed for taking graft.[153] Inspectors were accused of various schemes, including accepting bribes from businesses for tipping them off about pending inspections, charging workers for free paperwork, and conducting inspections after hours so as to collect the fine without reporting it to the central office. Moreover, there were tense conflicts within the TST over efforts to crack down on corruption that sometimes escalated into violence. Clearly, enforcement in Tucumán was not made possible by bureaucratic coherence or autonomy.

Nor can enforcement be explained simply in terms of political support. As will be described in more detail next, Governor Alperovich clearly took steps to support implementing labor regulations, but these actions did not reliably translate into action. Some unions, like UATRE, were able to induce enforcement, but others, like UOCRA, were not. This difference cannot be accounted for by lack of political power on the part of UOCRA, which

---

[149] Interview: T48, Argentine Construction Association (CAC), Tucumán, 10/29/2008
[150] Multiple interviews with inspectors and officials in 2008 and 2009
[151] They were moved to undesirable positions in other parts of the provincial administration.
[152] *LGT* "En Trabajo hay inspectores que son 'ciegos y sordos'" 07/27/2009
[153] *LGT* "Funcionario detenido por presunto soborno" 05/22/2002; "Filmaron y grabaron el presunto soborno" 05/23/2002; "El ex funcionario Ibarra fue condenado por pedir coimas" 05/03/2003; "Neme y Cabral asumen" 09/20/2002; "Pocas Palabras" 10/26/2002

occupied key positions in the political hierarchy of organized labor. Therefore, enforcement is not simply a reproduction of the distribution of political power.

Part of the explanation for the inability of the TST to respond directly to political inputs lies in the extreme lack of administrative resources. The bureaucracy operated without basic technology – there were no computers, and inspectors had to compete for access to manual typewriters to write reports.[154] Inspectors also lacked access to transportation (there was only one car, and it was often not available to inspectors) as well as to basic supplies, such as paper and pens. For a period of time, the TST regional division in the city of Concepción even lost its office space and had to operate out of borrowed space in the sugar workers' union regional headquarters.[155] The TST had no system for monitoring which firms had been inspected in the past or for planning enforcement campaigns in the medium term. Even short-term planning was hampered by organizational failures. For example, inspectors, though given a list of firms to be checked within a given week, were unable to execute the tasks, and the practice of weekly planning quickly stopped.[156]

In terms of human resources, the TST had deficiencies in the quantity and quality of inspectors. As of 2009, the TST had only eighteen inspectors, considerably fewer in per capita terms than in other provinces, and below internationally recognized standards.[157] There was no health and safety division as in Córdoba that augmented the number of inspectors dedicated to certain industries. More important than number, the quality of the inspectors was extremely low. Only one inspector had completed university studies, and nearly a third of the inspectors had only primary education. Finally, as in Córdoba, inspectors had low salaries (approximately $530 dollars per month), and most had additional jobs outside of the state to supplement their income.[158] Consequently, the TST was limited to paying inspectors for their time for a half-day's work.

Combined, deficiencies in material resources, human capital, planning capability, as well as pervasive organizational conflict and corruption, created tremendous constraints. Consequently, the TST could not generate its own information about violations, craft its own responses, or withstand the actions of interest groups intent on blocking enforcement by bribing inspectors. These failings help explain why, just as in Córdoba, enforcement did not occur in industries like the ones where unions lacked resources to supplement the state.

---

[154] Multiple interviews with inspectors in 2008 and 2009.

[155] *LGT* "Se inicia la mudanza de Trabajo" 08/02/2002

[156] Interview: T56, Inspector, Tucumán Labor Secretariat, Tucumán, 11/6/2008

[157] There are approximately 80,000 people in the province for each inspector, which translates to about one inspector per 40,000 economically active workers. The ILO's recommendation is that there should be 1/20,000 workers in "transition economies" but fewer than 1/40,000 workers in "developing countries": ILO 2006c

[158] One even runs a business of training and certifying soccer referees from his desk in the TST.

Conversely, strong linkages between many unions and inspectors enabled and encouraged officials in the TST to leverage societal resources and overcome constraints for enforcement in select industries. There were routinized processes in which a series of unions came to request inspections.[159] For example, when the metal workers' union (UOM) discovered a violation that could not be remedied by union action, the leader would call the TST and could get an inspector that very day.[160] These interactions kept a stream of information coming into the inspectorate. Linkages also facilitated the flow of resources, such as cars, from the unions to the TST, allowing inspectors to respond to violations.

Finally, union participation in inspections was key in overcoming resistance from firms to enforcement or instances in which inspectors would see it in their individual interest not to enforce. Even though there was occasional collusion between corrupt inspectors and union leaders, senior officials in the TST (as well as union leaders) found that the presence of a union leader during inspections was a way to reduce the inspectors' opportunities for soliciting bribes from employers.[161] One union leader noted that, "The quality of the inspection depends on the union leader. If you leave the inspector alone, he will do all kinds of things." As a result, to combat corruption, officials in the TST created a policy that inspectors be accompanied by unions leaders whenever possible.

In sum, the TST was a porous bureaucracy; its porosity, however, was structured in a way that gave unions preferential access. There were more than 2,000 civil society organizations in the province, many of which were involved in labor or social issues and could offer resources to inspectors.[162] But the TST worked with approximately only two dozen unions that had the operational capabilities and pursued strategies congruent with enforcement. This structure was crucial in shaping how the politicized state leveraged resources for action. In addition, the dependence of the inspectors on unions for operational support explains why enforcement did not follow solely from the political power of the union. UOCRA, for example, could exercise influence in the PJ coalition, but the union did not have enough staff to make up for the TST's deficiencies. Thus, linkages to a well-resourced organization was a necessary (and sufficient) condition for enforcement in Tucumán.

Political origins of society-dependent enforcement in Tucumán

How did linkages form between inspectors and unions? Why was enforcement in Tucumán so heavily dependent on unions? The origin of underinvestment in

---

[159] Interview: T58, Inspector, Tucumán Labor Secretariat, Tucumán, 11/11/2008; T32, Inspector, Tucumán Labor Secretariat, Tucumán, 4/16/2009
[160] Interview: T57, Metal Worker's Union (UOM), Tucumán, 4/21/2009
[161] Interview: T57, Metal Worker's Union (UOM), Tucumán, 4/21/2009
[162] Luna and Cecconi 2004

Tucumán – society-dependent enforcement

administrative resources combined with the creation of strong union linkages can be found in a partisan dynamic similar to that of Córdoba's. Peronists ruled the province of Tucumán with only two interludes: a period of federal intervention in 1991, and the one-term rule of the right-wing Antonio Domingo Bussi (*Fuerza Republicana* 1995–1999). Allied with the unions, Peronist governors appointed union leaders to positions in the TST. A longtime veteran of the TST describes the influence of the union leaders running the inspectorate: "Of all of the Secretaries of Labor, only two were lawyers. The rest were union leaders, which means that there was a strong mark of union participation in all of the decisions and in the management of the TST."[163] The first governor after the return to democracy, a Peronist named Fernando Rivera (1983–1987), appointed union leaders from his coalition to managerial positions and hired Peronist party activists as labor inspectors.[164] The governors who followed took a similar approach. The result of these appointments was support for inspector-union linkage formation from TST's senior officials.

Ties with unions were not, however, supplemented with investment in administrative resources. When the TST was formed, staff members were given no systematic training, and by 1991 the TST had only eleven inspectors for the entire province of more than a million people and almost no administrative resources.[165] Unions wanted greater investment in administrative resources, but just as in Córdoba, these investments did not come.[166] When conflict over the lack of enforcement heated up, governors responded with appointments of union leaders. The same strategy persisted through a series of Peronist governors: linkages with unions were used as a substitute for the internal components of state capacity.

On two occasions, governors attempted to depart from this strategy but failed. Governor Ramón Ortega (PJ, 1991–1995) appointed Rogelio Mercado, a labor lawyer who was a technocrat and not a union ally, as Secretary of Labor. Mercado attempted both to remove inspectors accused of corruption and to improve training. But these reforms never materialized; Mercado lacked political support from the unions and was forced out after a year in office to be replaced by union leaders.[167] Ten years later, José Alperovich (PJ) attempted similar reforms. In response to extremely high levels of unregistered work in the wake of the financial crisis, Alperovich faced pressure from the federal

---

[163] Interview: T12, Secretaría de Trabajo de Tucumán, Director Provincial, Tucumán, 10/27/2008 and 11/12/2008

[164] Interview: T12, Secretaría de Trabajo de Tucumán, Director Provincial, Tucumán, 10/27/2008 and 11/12/2008

[165] ILO 1989

[166] *LGT* "Habría 8.000 obreros azucareros en negro" 06/28/2004; "Jiménez asumió y pidió un mayor presupuesto" 08/20/2004

[167] Interview: T37, Former Secretario de Trabajo, Secretaría de Trabajo de Tucaman, Tucumán, 4/14/2009

108 *Enforcement with unions in the driver's seat*

government to take action.[168] He tightened provincial regulations and used tax inspectors to supplement labor enforcement.[169] In addition to these measures, he started an initiative to reform the TST.

As part of this effort, Alperovich broke with the tradition of appointing union leaders to the top Secretary of Labor slot and once again selected Rogelio Mercado.[170] Mercado, along with other top officials at the TST, traveled around Argentina to learn from other provinces about best practices in labor inspection that could be emulated. The officials concluded that Tucumán should: introduce merit based hiring to bring in *professionals,* improve training, and prohibit inspectors from having employment outside the state – many of the same steps that Sappia took in Córdoba in the 1980s.[171] Senior officials also decided that they needed to replace the existing inspectors so as to reduce corruption. To complete the reform, senior officials concluded that they needed to initiate a number of steps that would reinforce bureaucratic coherence and autonomy, as well as increase administrative resources.[172] Part of this plan was to use subsidies from the SRT to augment the health and safety division, just as in Córdoba.

This attempt at reform, however, was costly to Alperovich. In the face of losing control of the inspectorate, powerful union leaders criticized the governor for not investing in inspectors and called for Mercado's resignation.[173] Union leaders did not believe that new inspectors would be any better than the old ones, and they did not want to lose linkages that enabled them to support enforcement.[174] Moreover, with the support of the public sector unions, labor inspectors who saw their jobs threatened went on strike and blocked roads.

---

[168] Interview: T12, Senior Official, Tucumán Labor Secretariat, Tucumán, 10/27/2008 and 11/12/2008

[169] The law also called for firm closures between three and ten days and a prohibition on these firms receiving public contracts. It was of questionable legality due to the federal structures that set rates for fines in the entire country. *LGT* "Alperovich anunció sanciones contra el trabajo no registrado" 05/12/2007; "Se intensifica la lucha contra el trabajo en negro" 06/12/2007; "Aplicarán duras penas a quienes tengan personal sin registrar" 01/17/2008; "Rentas va por el blanqueo de 14.000 empleadas doméstica" 11/03/2007; "Rentas apunta a 89 negocios que pueden ser clausurados" 11/23/2007; "Por el empleo no registrado, controlan hoteles y helader ías" 12/01/2007; "El control de empleo en negro derivó en la clausura de un local" 02/14/2008; "Controlarán día y noche que no haya empleo en negro" 01/30/2000; "La construcción es el sector con la mayor cantidad de empleados en negro" 02/04/2008; "El Gobierno detectó hasta ahora 88 empleados en negro" 02/07/2008

[170] Alperovich did select a union leaders' Sub-Secretary of Labor (Ramón Aguirre) and Director (Jorge Blasco), thus maintaining the ties between the TST and the unions.

[171] Interview: T37, Former Senior Official, Tucumán Labor Secretariat, Tucumán, 4/14/2009

[172] *LGT* "'Blanquean' a obreros por la presión official" 12/17/2003; also there is some pushback against enforcement in the agricultural sector: "Alivia a los productores el repunte en el precio de la papa" 11/13/2004

[173] *LGT* "Los gremios marcharán mañana y el jueves por un básico de $ 350" 05/27/2004; "Habría 8.000 obreros azucareros en negro" 06/28/2004

[174] Interviews: T57, Metal Worker's Union (UOM), Tucumán, 4/21/2009

Tucumán – society-dependent enforcement

The conflict escalated; fist-fights broke out in the TST and eventually some inspectors were arrested.[175] Alperovich tried to resist the pressure, proclaiming that he would "support [Mercado] to the death."[176] He also proposed legislation that the TST could keep the money from fines to supplement its budget – a policy that would increase administrative resources. [177] But as the conflict intensified and further threatened the governor's alliance with key unions, Mercado was forced out and the reform halted.

To keep his coalition together, Governor Alperovich reinstated the exchange with unions and appointed as Secretary of Labor the leader of the "62" Peronist Organizations (the political wing of the unions aligned with the governor) Roberto Jiménez, who also continued to serve as head of UTA, the powerful transport workers' union.[178] The exchange was successful in subduing conflict; as a union leader observed: "The governor chose Roberto Jiménez so that he could control us, the unions, so we don't go out on the street and mobilize ... Jiménez is a sort of bridge, a nexus, between the unions and the governor."[179] Jiménez continued, without success, to demand greater resources, but whatever additional resources had been slotted for the TST by the governor were channeled elsewhere.[180]

The case of Tucumán brings into relief the politics of linkage formation and underinvestment in the internal components of state capacity. First, linkages key for enforcement were developed through the partisan alliance between unions and Peronist governors. The unions supported the governors, and, in exchange, gained appointments in the TST that supported linkage formation. Unlike a pure patronage strategy that could have appointed supporters uninterested or uninformed in labor policy, this type of partisan exchange led to linkages with groups broadly aligned with the goal of enforcement. Second, most Peronist governors in Tucumán responded to demands for enforcement by substituting linkages for administrative resources. Governors who departed from this strategy and tried to undertake reforms that would exercise more hierarchical control over the inspectorate found the changes politically unfeasible. In both cases, they returned to the exchange of political support for linkages.

---

[175] *LGT* "Jornada de paro en la Secretaría de Trabajo" 06/05/2004

[176] *LGT* "Alperovich avaló con un abrazo a dos funcionarios de su gabinete" 05/27/2004; "Se autofinanciaría la Secretaría de Trabajo" 06/14/2004; "Trompadas en la Secretaría de Trabajo" 06/06/2004; "Empleados de la Secretaría de Trabajo cortan el tránsito" 07/14/2004

[177] *LGT* "Se autofinanciaría la Secretaría de Trabajo" 06/14/2004; "Trompadas en la Secretaría de Trabajo" 06/06/2004; "Empleados de la Secretaría de Trabajo cortan el tránsito" 07/14/2004

[178] *LGT* "Alperovich suma a un sindicalista al PE" 08/17/2004; "Repercusiones sobre la modificación en Trabajo" 08/17/2004; "Jiménez asumió y pidió un mayor presupuesto" 08/20/2004

[179] Interview: To6, Construction Workers' Union of Argentina (UOCRA), Tucumán, 4/14/2009

[180] The governor hired additional tax inspectors to respond to the problem of unregistered work.

CONCLUSION

The cases of Córdoba and Tucumán demonstrate how enforcement, although limited, is possible even where regulatory bureaucracies are far from the ideal. In both provinces, there were widespread violations of basic labor regulations, including payments of wages, registration to receive benefits, and safety practices. These violations were evidence of weak labor institutions that often did not structure employment relations. At times, the state, in both provinces, did respond to these weaknesses and activate institutions. These responses required both political support and the administrative capabilities to undertake the tasks of enforcement, but the specific pathways that were taken to enforcement in these cases differed substantially from standard models of bureaucratic reform. Unlike countries where professionalization was key to enforcement, such as the Dominican Republic and Brazil, these two provinces continued to lack many of the bureaucratic features that are often described as prerequisites for effective states. Notwithstanding these flaws, inspectors still managed to enforce labor regulations under certain conditions. Thus, these cases show that a particular type of enforcement can become possible without autonomy.

Enforcement was, however, limited and highly uneven with puzzling differences across industries that could not be explained by standard explanations. It was clear that enforcement targets were not chosen by coherent and autonomous bureaucracies that planned actions based on programmatic instructions or policy goals. At the same time, variation could not be accounted for by economic and political conditions that could increase the costs of enforcement. Industries in which firms were exposed to international competition and were highly organized were subject to higher levels of enforcement than other industries that lacked the features often attributed to business power. While this finding may appear surprising, considering theories of regulation that fall out of economic interests, it is consistent with cross-national statistical evidence. A study of firm-level survey data from seventy-two middle-income and developing countries found that firms that export are more likely to be inspected than those that do not.[181] Also, according to this study, firms that are members of business associations that might exercise political power on their behalf are more likely to be inspected than not members. These results are inconsistent with the theoretical expectations based on potential economic costs and firm organization leading to increased political efforts to block enforcement, but they are largely congruent with the findings in Córdoba and Tucumán.

Instead of bureaucratic planning or capture by those who stood the most to gain from blocking enforcement, a close look revealed specific patterns of enforcement built upon close ties between inspectors and unions. Where administrative resources were lacking, enforcement was made possible through linkages with unions that had capabilities and interests in reducing noncompliance

---

[181] Almeida and Ronconi 2012

Conclusion

among specific workers. Where the state had greater resources and unions were active, as in construction safety in Córdoba, enforcement was at higher levels and targeted firms both with and without union delegates. In sum, to understand uneven state action – specifically who benefits from enforcement and how it occurs – it was necessary to identify the way that the state was porous to specific groups.

Finally, the patterns of enforcement in these cases arose out of specific political conditions. A key similarity between Córdoba and Tucumán was the dominance of Peronist governors who shared a historic partisan alliance with labor unions. Partisanship served as the basis for the creation of strong linkages between unions and inspectors. It did not, however, lead to investment in the internal components of state capacity. As a result, partisanship and ideology, which are often pointed to as drivers of pro-labor policies, led to a particular type of enforcement that privileged unions but did not lead to the building up of broad capabilities in the state for more programmatic enforcement actions. This type of state unevenness had its roots in the political coalitions formed around the labor regulatory enforcement at the provincial level. Unions were able to be politically accommodated with linkages, removing a potentially powerful advocate for administrative resources. Ultimately, the pattern of enforcement reinforced the segmented neo-corporatist nature of the Argentine labor relations system by responding to sectors with strong unions. Chapter 5 moves to provinces that were not continually governed by the union allies in the post-crisis period, furthering the analysis of the politics of enforcing labor regulations.

5

State-driven and co-produced enforcement in labor regulation

This chapter examines enforcement in Santa Fe and the Federal Capital, two provinces that departed from the patterns of strong union influence described in Chapter 4.[1] For nearly twenty-five years after the return to democracy, Santa Fe's labor inspectorate was highly dependent on unions for enforcement. In 2007, however, the province reformed part of its inspectorate and undertook an enforcement campaign in the construction industry without drawing on union resources. Similarly, labor inspectors in the Federal Capital responded to violations in the garment industry with an intense enforcement campaign, even though the garment workers' union did little to support those efforts. Inspectors in the Federal Capital took substantial actions on their own and leveraged resources from a neighborhood organization to further their reach. In both cases, the ways in which the state was porous to different interests and how it mobilized resources for enforcement differed substantially from those of society-dependent enforcement, which is tightly coupled with union interests. While state responses to weak regulatory institutions certainly remained uneven in Santa Fe and the Federal Capital, the state did offer protection to workers who did not have strong unions.

What explains these distinct patterns of enforcement? The answer cannot be found in standard political analyses of labor-regulatory reform; dominant theories of labor politics suggest that governments with partisan alliances to unions produce pro-labor outcomes, especially when leaders face electoral threats.[2] Chapter 4 has shown how partisan alliances led to the creation of inspector-union linkages but did not result in substantial investments in

---

[1] Although the Federal Capital is not technically a province, for the purposes of labor enforcement it functions like a province.

[2] For example: Murillo 2005

Santa Fe 113

administrative resources. By contrast, in the cases that I analyze in this chapter, opponents of the unions' partisan allies in the PJ won elections. For center-left elected leaders with a programmatic interest in enforcement, linkages with unions could not further solidify their base of support. As a result, they responded to demands for enforcement with investments in administrative resources.

In Santa Fe, allocation of resources to the inspectorate was coupled with a reform that insulated a part of the bureaucracy from political pressure. Thus, the province took the well-known pathway to enforcement. In the Federal Capital, however, features of autonomy remained absent even though a substantial number of inspectors were hired. Notwithstanding the lack of many organizational features of bureaucratic coherence considered necessary for enforcement, inspectors in the Federal Capital, for a period of time, were able to find political support for enforcement through linkages with a nonunion civil society organization called La Alameda. In sum, these two cases shared one fundamental feature – when linkages alone could not placate demands for enforcement, political leaders with an interest in enforcement allocated administrative resources to the bureaucracy, thereby making the departures from the society-dependent pattern possible.

The remainder of this chapter is organized into two main sections, one for each province, followed by a conclusion. For each province, I describe the trajectory of administrative resources and linkages, thus contrasting the ability of alternative explanations to account for the combinations and changes. I also describe changes in enforcement in key industries – construction in Santa Fe and garment in the Federal Capital – that were triggered by the political changes. These two industries became the focus of attention for regulators and thus reveal the process of prioritization (e.g., responses to societal demands versus strategic planning) and the ways inspectors mobilized resources for enforcement; to understand the pattern of enforcement in either place, it is essential to account for these high-profile industries. In the conclusion, I place these cases in comparative context with those of Chapter 4.

SANTA FE

The trajectory of Santa Fe's labor inspectorate was, in many ways, the reverse of Córdoba's (described in Chapter 4). For the first eight years after the return to democracy, Santa Fe was led by Peronist governors closely allied with organized labor. The first governor, José María Vernet (PJ), had been an accountant for the metal workers' union, and the second governor, Víctor Reviglio (PJ), drew on unions for significant support.[3] In 1985, the province

---

[3] Zapata 1994; Levitsky 2003 pp. 93, 123

114   *State-driven and co-produced enforcement in labor regulation*

formed the *Secretaría de Estado de Trabajo de Santa Fe* (STSF).[4] The governors put labor administration at the second highest level of the hierarchy of the executive (a cabinet-level secretariat), not giving labor administration the status of a full ministry as had been done in Córdoba in the early period.

The Peronist governors of the 1980s and 1990s did not invest in administrative resources. The STSF essentially had only a minimum budget to cover the salaries of the officials; to fund all nonsalary operating costs, the STSF was expected to rely on money collected through fines, not enough revenue to procure basic goods (e.g., transportation).[5] Nor did the governors insist on meritocratic recruiting of the best candidates. Instead, as in Tucumán and Córdoba (during the later period), the staffing of the STSF was heavily marked by rewards to PJ's union allies:

When they were forming the agency, unions sent lists of people who could work for the inspectorate, and the governor chose from those lists. Labor inspectors were not selected based on their education, experience, or an exam ... [Instead], a scheme of politically designated people was put together.[6]

There was also no effort to train these inspectors to become professionals.[7] In short, there was minimal investment in administrative resources under the first wave of Peronist governors.

Under the following four Peronist governors, administrative resources continued to lag. Staffing was inconsistent and the material resources for enforcement were further reduced.[8] Between 1995 and 1997, the number of labor inspectors fluctuated rapidly – dropping from 41 to 10, and then increasing to 22, where it stayed until 2000.[9] Even during the peaks, the number of inspectors in Santa Fe were lower than those of Córdoba, despite the provinces' similar levels of economic prosperity, economic structures, populations, and sizes (Santa Fe had 0.13 inspectors per 10,000 residents at its peak in 1995, compared with the 0.21 in Córdoba in 1988). The cuts made in personnel in

---

[4] The legislature passed the law to authorize the STSF in 1985 under Vernet, but the province did not hire staff and fully take over the task of labor administration until 1988 when Reviglio was in office; as a consequence, both governors played a key role in the early days of the STSF. Interview: S12, Senior Official, Santa Fe Ministry of Labor and Social Security, Santa Fe, 12/12/2008; S27, Labor Lawyer and advisor to CGT, Rosario, 5/13/2009

[5] This arrangement greatly influenced the behavior of the inspectors; one of their central goals was *tax collection* to keep the organization going. To evaluate their actions, inspectors were asked *how much did we collect this month?*, not *what was the result of inspection?* Interview: S12, Senior Official, Santa Fe Ministry of Labor and Social Security, Santa Fe, 12/12/2008

[6] Interview: S12, Senior Official, Santa Fe Ministry of Labor and Social Security, Santa Fe, 12/12/2008

[7] Interview: S15, Inspector, Santa Fe Ministry of Labor and Social Security, Santa Fe, 12/11/2008; S02, Senior Official, Santa Fe Ministry of Labor and Social Security, Rosario, 5/5/2009

[8] Interview: S19, Senior Official, Inspection Department, Santa Fe Ministry of Labor and Social Security, Rosario, 5/7/2009

[9] Data from various sources, including data compiled by Lucas Ronconi. See: Ronconi 2010

Santa Fe   115

Santa Fe happened during a period when the number of public employees in the province had actually increased, indicating that the reductions in staffing for labor inspection were not merely part of a broader policy of state downsizing.[10] For the inspectors who remained through these changes, there were even fewer material resources to use for enforcement. Regulators had to share one vehicle to cover the entire province, which is more than 400 miles long. No efforts were made to train inspectors or to hire staff with higher levels of education. Moreover, with the series of economic crises that occurred during this period, self-financing through fines became extremely difficult.[11] And as salaries stagnated, corruption festered.[12]

As did their counterparts in Córdoba and Tucumán, organized labor advocated for increasing the resources allocated to the STSF. Union complaints about the lack of inspectors were reported frequently in the press; the head of a local branch of the commercial sector union was quoted in the newspaper saying: "To control the cascade of abuses that we know are occurring, [our union] would need ten inspectors every day ... but today there are no more than seven inspectors for all of the unions."[13] According to union leaders, the STSF simply "did not have the resources" it needed for enforcement.[14] In response, officials said that there had been "a political decision by Governor Jorge Obeid to reinforce [labor inspection]" and that the STSF made it "a top priority to hire more agents and to train them."[15] But new inspectors were never hired; a senior official explained: "We didn't get to hire new staff, and we lost some to retirement. The Governor was very strict ... with funding."[16] The resources were simply not forthcoming. In one delegation of the STSF, the head of the local office complained that: "From 2005 to today (2007) we have put three formal requests to the STSF asking for more people and a car, but nothing changed."[17] In reply to requests to open a new delegation in a growing industrial city, the STSF opened the office but gave it no resources; a union leader complained "the delegation doesn't have personnel, a telephone ... or even a car for the officials. Like this, they can't regulate ... and businesses are never going to respect them."[18]

---

[10] The provincial public sector increased from 28 public employees per 1,000 residents in 1990 to 34 per 1,000 in 2000. Source: Ministry of Economy and Public Finance data.

[11] Interviews: S32, Former Senior Official, Santa Fe Labor Secretariat, Santa Fe, 12/15/2008

[12] Interviews: S35, CGT Rosario, Rosario, 5/4/2009; S38, Labor Lawyer and advisor to CGT, Rosario, 5/5/2009

[13] *La Capital* "Por gremio: cuántos son y cuánto ganan" 11/30/2003

[14] Interview: S35, CGT Rosario, Rosario, 5/4/2009

[15] *La Capital* "En Rosario se detectó un 30% de empleo informal" 04/28/2005.

[16] Interview: S11, Former Senior Official, Santa Fe Labor Secretariat, Reconquista, Santa Fe, 12/16/2008

[17] *La Capital* "Limitaciones para combatir trabajo en negro" 07/19/2007

[18] *La Capital* "Firmat-Piden una delegación de la Secretaría de Trabajo" 08/25/2004; "Nuevo local de la Secretaría de Trabajo en San Lorenzo" 04/07/2005; "Murió un joven al caer del techo de

As in Córdoba and Tucumán under the Peronists, the governors of Santa Fe did pave the way to the formation of linkages between inspectors and unions by appointing a series of senior officials from the main labor confederations. A bureaucrat recalled: "When the STSF formed, the Secretary of Labor was from a union, below him the Director was from a union, and the Sub-director was from a union."[19] With labor leaders placed throughout the agency, inspectors could easily rely on unions to make up for their lack of capacity. Regulators drew on union leaders for much of their material resources; one inspector from this period recounted, "when you have few cars, and you have to do a number of inspections that aren't local, the union leaders say 'Come in our car' and you go."[20]

With the help of the unions, the STSF conducted more than 7,000 inspections in 2005 (2.3 inspections per 1,000 residents), and officials estimated they registered 13,000 workers who had been informal.[21] However, for a number of years the STSF conducted inspections only with the support of unions, leading to strong bias toward industries with active unions. In the metal industry of Rosario, for instance, the union (Union Obrera Metalurgica de la Republica Argentina, UOM) drew on a twelve-person commission that was able to go to the STSF and automatically get access to an inspector. With 145 delegates in firms throughout the region, the union gathered ample information about noncompliance and worked with inspectors to *pressure* firms that were violating labor laws.[22] Enforcement in the metal industry is not surprising, considering that one of the second ranking officials in the STSF was a member of the UOM. Similarly, in the commercial laundry industry, union leaders facilitated a steady stream of inspections targeted at noncompliant firms.[23] Thus, linkages with unions served as an operational substitute, albeit a highly imperfect one, for administrative resources.

In sum, throughout twenty-five years of Peronist rule in Santa Fe, the labor inspectorate was marked by low levels of investment in administrative resources, but policy implementation was possible in some industries due to linkages with unions. This pattern was extremely similar to those in Córdoba

---

un silo en Timbúes" 03/16/2006. Interview: S19, Senior Official, Inspection Department, Santa Fe Ministry of Labor and Social Security, Rosario, 5/7/2009

[19] Interview: S15, Inspector, Santa Fe Ministry of Labor and Social Security, Santa Fe, 12/11/2008. These officials included union leaders from the water utility union and the food workers' union. Interview: S02, Senior Official, Santa Fe Ministry of Labor and Social Security, Rosario, 5/5/2009

[20] Interview: S12, Senior Official, Santa Fe Ministry of Labor and Social Security, Santa Fe, 12/12/2008

[21] *La Capital* "Alto índice de empleados en negro el año pasado en Santa Fe" 01/17/2006. In the first half of 2006, the STSF conducted 2,600 inspections that officials estimated resulted in 8,500 informal workers being registered. *La Capital* "Empleo Negro" 07/13/2006.

[22] Interview: S37, Metal Workers' Union (UOM), Rosario, 6/1/2009

[23] Interview: S44, Laundry Workers' Union (UOETSYLRA), Rosario, 5/8/2009

Santa Fe 117

and Tucumán described in Chapter 4. Repeated attempts by unions to push governors to invest budgetary resources in labor inspection were met with responses that supported linkages. This reaction functioned as a politically expedient operational substitute for the allocation of resources to enforcement. The pattern persisted despite an increasingly competitive political climate, in which the PJ was challenged by the rising Socialist party. In 2003, governor Obeid (PJ) won the election but did not even have a plurality (the PJ's total vote share was only 43%).[24] There was clearly a viable alternative party, the Socialists, that could displace the PJ. According to theories of the effect of competition on state formation, such a dynamic should have led to the formation of a more autonomous bureaucracy.[25]

The literature also suggests that union-party alliances under pressure (due to tight elections or competition among unions) are key for triggering labor-friendly legal reforms. By these criteria, the period after the crisis was ripe for increases in capacity because there were competitive elections and tensions in the governing coalition.[26] Within the diverse currents of organized labor, a faction of unions (that had broken off from the main Peronist centrals) gave its support to an opposition deputy who had proposed a reform that would increase the STSF budget nearly 60% and authorize the hiring of more inspectors.[27] Even so, substantial resources were not allocated to the STSF under the Peronists.

The Socialist party and reform

The 2007 elections pitted the Peronist candidate, Rafael Bielsa, against the center-left Socialist candidate, Hermes Binner, who had been the mayor of Rosario. Just before the election, the head of the political organization of the CGT-Rosario stated, "the union leaders clearly understand that the enemy is not Peronism, but . . . Hermes Binner."[28] Despite the opposition of organized labor, for the first time, the unions' ally did not prevail; Binner won with 54% of the votes, beating out Bielsa, who received only 43% of the votes.

Upon his election, Binner made three important decisions to signal that he was serious about building capacity in the provincial government to enforce labor laws. First, he passed a law upgrading labor administration from a cabinet-level secretariat to a full ministry, transforming the STSF to the Santa

---

[24] In 2003, Santa Fe had a double simultaneous voting system, which gave Obeid victory because the total votes for the PJ (43%) were greater than those for the rival PS (38%). Obeid's ticket, however actually won a smaller portion of votes (21%) than the main Socialist candidate, Hermes Binner (36%).

[25] Geddes 1994; Grzymala-Busse 2007   [26] Murillo 2001; Murillo 2005

[27] *La Capital* "Gremios del cordón impulsan una reforma laboral" 07/13/2006

[28] *La Capital* "Las 62 dieron libertad para elegir candidato" 03/14/2007

Fe Ministry of Labor and Social Security (MTSF).[29] This move allocated greater funds and more political power to labor administration within the executive branch (and gave labor administration in Santa Fe a rank higher than 80% of Argentine provinces); Binner's actions won recognition even from opposition politicians, one of whom observed: "When you create a ministry, you are signaling that labor is a priority, and you are going to incur costs."[30] Second, Binner signed a memorandum of understanding with the International Labor Organization's (ILO) Argentine office to create a provincial program for "decent work."[31] The agreement constituted a mechanism by which the MTSF could draw on technical assistance from international experts and gave legitimacy to the reform.[32]

Third, Binner appointed a technocrat with an impeccable resume, Carlos Anibal Rodríguez, to be the new Minister of Labor. Rodríguez had led the national occupational health and safety agency (SRT) under President Néstor Kirchner, worked with the ILO in Turin (Italy) as a representative of labor, and held various faculty positions in universities in Argentina and Europe. His background contrasted with that of previous heads of labor administration in Santa Fe, who were either labor union leaders or well-connected Peronists with little experience in labor issues. Although the unions opposed Binner, they could not criticize the new Minister.[33] Union leaders attested that, although they opposed the Socialists, "the designation of Carlos Rodríguez as Minister of Labor has been well received. He is an excellent person, familiar with the ILO, [and] a friend of Carlos Tomada [the federal Minister of Labor under President Kirchner]."[34] For key appointments, Rodríguez chose a mixture of officials that included technocrats (e.g., former labor inspectors from the federal Ministry of Labor and the Federal Capital) and a Socialist Party (PS) activist with experience working on labor issues (including a stint with the ILO). Only one member of the appointed staff was from organized labor.

With respect to both administrative resources and the quality of the organization, Rodríguez came into office with plans for reforms that were textbook investments in the internal components of state capacity.[35] While his rhetoric was not substantially different from that of the PJ, the actions that followed were. Rodríguez focused his attention on the health and safety division, where

---

[29] Law 12.817, adopted 12/06/2007
[30] Interview: S39, Deputy, Santa Fe Chamber of Deputies, Rosario, 5/6/2009
[31] Provincia de Santa Fe. "*Agenda Provincial de Trabajo Decente en Santa Fe*" April 2009
[32] Santa Fe was the first Argentine province, and the second subnational government in all of South America, to work directly with the ILO. Later, in 2009, Rodríguez was invited to present the changes in the MTSF to an ILO meeting in Germany, giving him positive press. *El Litoral* "Santa Fe expone en la OIT su inspección de trabajo decente" 09/28/2009
[33] Interview: S37, Metal Workers' Union (UOM), Rosario, 6/1/2009. See also: *La Capital* "Futuro, dirigencia gremial y Ministerio" 11/25/2007
[34] *La Capital* "Seguridad: el gran desafío" 10/16/2007
[35] *La Capital* "Rodríguez: 'Haremos cumplir los derechos del trabajador'" 12/21/2007

Santa Fe

the existing inspectors had short-term contracts and could easily be removed (unlike the wage and hour inspectors, who had civil service protection).[36] He fired the existing inspectors and began a meritocratic process for recruiting new inspectors, using a civil service exam and imposing a set of educational requirements (70% of the new health and safety inspectors had post-graduate degrees). This was the first time since the 1980s in Córdoba that an exam was used to hire inspectors in Argentina.[37]

New inspectors were awarded probationary contracts to be converted into full civil service contracts after one year. New hires were required to sign a "code of ethics" that placed strict limits on actions that were not considered professional.[38] Unlike those in other provinces (and in Santa Fe in previous years), the new inspectors were not allowed to have secondary jobs and were paid a salary that was competitive with private sector employment. An official explained: "No one makes less than (US) $1,450 ... We already had to fire someone because ... he was consulting outside. There is zero tolerance."[39] When inspectors were hired, they were given two months of full-time training, in contrast to the almost nonexistent training that had been given in the past.[40] Finally, the inspectors had access to transportation, and each two-person team of inspectors was issued a laptop, enabling them to complete reports while still in the field. Overall, there was tremendous investment in administrative resources under the Socialists. The transformation, however, was not complete due in part to the civil service protection of wage and hour inspectors that prevented Rodríguez from firing them and left part of the Ministry weak. Nevertheless, the resources committed to enhancing state capacity were substantially greater than during any other period.

Binner used investments in the administrative resources available to the bureaucracy to deflect criticism from the opposition and the unions. When unions complained to the press about the lack of progress in enforcement, Rodríguez responded with credible statements about improvements.[41] In private, union leaders even admitted that the PS did more than the PJ had ever done; a former official in the STSF, who was a Peronist political appointee,

---

[36] Health and safety inspectors were not actually paid by the province, but by the federal government's SRT.

[37] Interview: So6, Senior Official, Santa Fe Ministry of Labor and Social Security, Santa Fe, 12/10/2008

[38] "Codigo de Etica de la inspección de Trabajo" Resolution 001/2008, Minsterio de Trabajo y Seguridad Social, Santa Fe

[39] Interview: S26, Health and Safety Inspector, Santa Fe Ministry of Labor and Social Security, Rosario, 5/13/2009. This is similar to the insider-outsider dynamic that Schrank found in the Dominican Republic. Schrank 2009

[40] Interview: So9, Health and Safety Inspector, Santa Fe Ministry of Labor and Social Security, Rosario, 5/12/2009

[41] For example, see: *La Capital* "La provincia sacará 20 inspectores a la calle" 01/06/2009; "Seguridad: mayores exigencias para la exhibición de cartelaríam en obras" 07/22/2008

described the changes under Binner as "excellent" because when the PJ was in power "occupational health and safety ... had been totally abandoned."[42]

In addition to the reform of the bureaucracy, there were changes in the nature of the relationships between labor inspectors and unions under the PS. While under the PJ administrations union leaders would go directly to their fellow unionists inside the government, under Binner there were no more unmediated ties – the heads of the unions had to go to Rodríguez or to a number of newly created commissions when they wanted access to the upper levels of the MTSF.[43] The operating procedures that Rodríguez put into place specified that "no union leader [could] come here and just take an inspector." Moreover, union leaders were not allowed to work with inspectors "without the coordinator knowing."[44] Unions that collected information about working conditions (such as the commercial laundry workers' union) continued to give health and safety inspectors lists of firms with violations, but did so under modified conditions.[45] An inspector described the new system: "If a union wants to make a complaint ... we go and conduct the inspection ... [but] we always manage the inspection ourselves."[46] This structure allowed inspectors to access union information, but limited their use of material resources so that, in the words of the inspectors, "we do not become the arm of any union."[47] In total, these efforts reduced the practice of inspectors drawing on unions for resources and reinforced hierarchical control within the bureaucracy.

The investments, especially their emphasis on administrative resources, cannot easily be accounted for by dominant approaches to labor politics or to state capacity. Explanations rooted in labor politics suggest that workers should win when the party in power has an alliance with unions, but this clearly was not the case. Explanations of bureaucratic reform focus on the collective action benefits of reform, but the reform in Santa Fe was undertaken to deflect criticism by a specific interest group, not to create collective benefit of good government.[48] Instead, the way political alliances prevented linkages from being used as a politically viable substitute for the internal components of capacity was a key development leading to the reform.

---

[42] Interview: S32, Former Senior Official, Santa Fe Labor Secretariat, Santa Fe, 12/15/2008
[43] Interview: S35, CGT Rosario, Rosario, 5/4/2009
[44] Interview: S26, Health and Safety Inspector, Santa Fe Ministry of Labor and Social Security, Rosario, 5/13/2009
[45] Interview: S44, Laundry Workers' Union (UOETSYLRA), Rosario, 5/8/2009
[46] Interview: S20, Health and Safety Inspector, Santa Fe Ministry of Labor and Social Security, Rosario, 5/12/2009
[47] Interview: S26, Health and Safety Inspector, Santa Fe Ministry of Labor and Social Security, Rosario, 5/13/2009
[48] Similar reforms were not undertaken in other regulatory bureaucracies of Santa Fe. For example, the Environment Ministry was downgraded in the hierarchy and new hires were not given civil service protection. Interview: S01, Senior Official Santa Fe Environmental Secretariat, Rosario, 4/30/2009; S13, Inspector, Santa Fe Environmental Secretariat, Rosario, 4/30/2009

Santa Fe 121

Changes in enforcement in the construction industry (2003–2009)

Without looking at the actions of the MTSF, it is difficult to assess what concrete differences in enforcement resulted from these investments in administrative resources and alterations in linkages. The case of enforcement in construction in the city of Rosario – an industry that was highly salient due to the high rates of fatal accidents – provides a way to examine the consequences these changes had for enforcement. This section recounts the shift from *society-dependent enforcement* at *low* levels under the PJ, to *state-driven enforcement* that reached *medium* levels under the PS.

There was a tremendous increase in construction activity in Rosario in the post-2003 boom.[49] With rapid expansion there were dramatic workplace accidents that made unsafe conditions in the industry highly salient.[50] The principal local newspaper, *La Capital*, began to keep count of the deaths, which regulators estimated reached one hundred workers every year in the province.[51] In addition to the deaths and serious injuries, investigations found atrocious practices, including "1,500 migrant construction workers living on the construction sites" in dangerous conditions.[52] The construction industry was clearly in crisis; nearly every month there was a newspaper article focusing on the horrific consequences of labor law violations (calling significantly more attention to the industry than to any other).

By their own assessment, officials in the Obeid administration stated that responding to these challenges in construction was *one of our failures*.[53] After the death of two workers on a construction site in 2005, the Secretary of Labor, Gianneschi, was quoted in *La Capital* as saying: "In Rosario, where we have nearly 200 construction sites of tall buildings and 8,000 small sites at the same time, we have only three employees for inspection."[54] After yet another accident, officials stated that there "exists a marked impotence of the state" in tackling the

---

[49] The increases in registered construction workers in the province illustrate this explosive growth. In July, 2004, there were 1,208 registered workers. This number shot up to 27,915 by July 2005, and reached 35,925 by July 2007. Source: *Instituto de Estadística y Registro de la Industria de la Construcción* (IERIC)

[50] *La Capital* "Un obrero murió al caer al vacío desde un 14° piso" 06/07/2005; "Murió un obrero en San Lorenzo al caer desde 20 metros de altura" 12/22/2005; "En un año, 6 albañiles muertos y 10 heridos" 03/13/2006; "Un paredón de una escuela cayó sobre dos obreros" 10/27/2006; "Otro albañil sufrió lesions" 11/01/2006; "Cuestionan a empresas que no cuidan a obreros de la construcción" 11/01/2006

[51] *La Capital* "En un año, 6 albañiles muertos y 10 heridos" 03/13/2006; "Descartan que paraguayos vivan dentro de una obra" 03/06/2007; "Cuestionan a empresas que no cuidan a obreros de la construcción" 11/01/2006

[52] *La Capital* "Más de 1.500 albañiles migrantes viven en obras en construcción" 09/10/2006; "Los inmigrantes ven la cara oscura del 'futuro mejor' que buscan en el país" 08/13/2006.

[53] Interview: S11, Former Senior Official, Santa Fe Labor Secretariat, Reconquista, Santa Fe, 12/16/2008

[54] *La Capital* "Pocos inspectores para evitar los accidentes laborales" 01/13/2005

problem.[55] In 2006, the STSF attempted to step up enforcement in the industry using what resources it had along with some borrowed from the SRT. Inspectors conducted what they called a "mega operation" over eleven days and issued 200 fines for violations, but they did not suspend any worksites. In addition, this campaign quickly ended after the initial burst of action.[56] Enforcement efforts during this period were limited mostly to suspending worksites after accidents, not to preventative efforts.[57] In short, levels of enforcement remained *low* throughout the Obied administration.

Why such an inadequate reaction from the government to the challenges in the construction industry? Part of the answer is the lack of administrative resources. As described previously, under the PJ, the STSF simply did not have the inspectors or resources sufficient for enforcement. In a similar fashion to enforcement in the cases analyzed in Chapter 4, enforcement in Santa Fe under the PJ was highly dependent on unions, and in Rosario the construction union did not have its own health and safety specialist to check the worksites.[58] In addition, UOCRA's Rosario office had serious problems with internal corruption; union leaders had a reputation for soliciting bribes from employers who wanted to avoid inspections. The limiting factor was not the inspectors' access to UOCRA (linkages were strong), but problems within the union itself. With their allies in power, UOCRA-Rosario did not publicly criticize the government for its failures; in fact, in most of the press coverage, UOCRA was less critical about the lack of enforcement than were government officials.

There was one additional civil society organization (formed in 2005) that advocated for worker safety in the construction industry, *Manos a la Obra*. The group, which functioned as a loose cooperative of workers, directly challenged UOCRA by going to sites after accidents, protesting, denouncing union leaders, and trying to organize workers in an alternative movement. Officials at the STSF could have allied with this group to gain a vocal partner in civil society, but inspectors stayed with the union, even though UOCRA was not helping with enforcement. Leaders from *Manos a la Obra* approached the STSF with little success: "Everyone sent us ... to the STSF. They sent us to the viper pit. We went ... [and] they threatened me and told me to keep my mouth shut."[59] In short, the low levels of enforcement were due to the general *society-dependent* pattern in which the linked groups on which the state relied were not effective.

---

[55] *La Capital* "Un obrero murió al caer al vacío desde un 14° piso" 06/07/2005

[56] *La Capital* "La seguridad laboral" 03/14/2006; "Inician plan de inspección en obras de construcción en Santa Fe" 03/21/2006; "Detectan fallas de seguridad en la construcción" 03/21/2006

[57] *La Capital* "La Secretaría de Trabajo clausuró la obra donde se mató un albañil" 06/08/2005; "Suspendieron las obras del edificio del que cayó un tirante a un jardín" 09/01/2007

[58] Interview: S41, Construction Workers' Union of Argentina (UOCRA), Rosario, 5/13/2009

[59] Interview: S23, Manos a la Obra, Rosario, 5/7/2009

Santa Fe

The pattern of enforcement drastically changed after the election of the Socialists. Even before Rodríguez was able to hire new inspectors, he undertook an intensive campaign in the industry.

We came into office on December 11 ... on the 18th we put together an inspection operation using people from the office in the city of Santa Fe, because the inspectors in Rosario were very questionable. It was a huge shock to the industry. After a week, we visited 33 construction sites, and we suspended operations in 32 ... This was all without notifying anyone in advance. Afterwards, we had a press conference. It was a way of marking the field to say: "Here we are and we aren't going to permit these violations."[60]

The message was received by the industry as intended. Representatives of the local industry association described the operation "as a shock," noting that "some firms complained ... because some of the violations were small and did not merit closures."[61] A few days later, the MTSF met with firm owners to initiate dialogue about how to reduce construction accidents.[62] Shutting down 32 out of 200 major construction sites operating in Rosario was very significant, but inspections did not stop after this initial operation. Whereas under the Obied administration, the STSF fined (on average) one firm a week and suspended operations after major accidents, during the first year of the Binner administration, inspectors were averaging 8.3 suspensions a week.[63] These actions indicate a tremendous increase in penalties for firms that violated health and safety laws.

Once the process of hiring and training new inspectors was complete, enforcement increased even more in construction. The MTSF mapped out different zones of Rosario where there were worksites, and the regulators systematically inspected each one.[64] By 2009, in the Rosario metropolitan area there were 2,800 health and safety inspections, the majority of which were in the construction industry.[65] In comparison with its actions during the previous period, the MTSF collected more information about violations, had a stronger response to these violations, and did not succumb to resistance and kept shutting down worksites.

The change in enforcement cannot be traced back to any new ability of pro-enforcement civil society organizations to work with the state. Mired in its

---

[60] Interview: S06, Senior Official, Santa Fe Ministry of Labor and Social Security, Santa Fe, 12/10/2008. Also reported in: *La Capital* "Rodríguez-Haremos cumplir los derechos del trabajador" 12/21/2007; "Suspenden 31 obras en construcción por 'faltas graves' en seguridad" 12/21/2007

[61] Interview: S08, Argentine Construction Association (CAC), Rosario, 4/29/2009

[62] *La Capital* "Obras en las que detectaron fallas vuelven a trabajar" 12/28/2007

[63] Source: Internal data from the MTSF

[64] Interview: S26, Health and Safety Inspector, Santa Fe Ministry of Labor and Social Security, Rosario, 5/13/2009

[65] *La Capital* "Trabajo provincial realizó 2.800 operativos en 2006" 02/20/2007; "Trabajo tiene sólo 13 inspectores para controlar siete departamentos" 01/14/2010.

own conflicts, UOCRA remained with very little operational capacity and never was able to hire its own health and safety officer to work with the state.[66] Notwithstanding the reining in of inspector-union linkages in Santa Fe by Rodríguez, leaders in UOCRA did not have problems accessing the new inspectors – one leader explained that officials in the MTSF "never impeded the union, and never rejected requests for information."[67] But the MTSF found that the information provided by UOCRA to the MTSF was not very accurate or useful; an inspector explained that in the one month during 2009, 62% "of the UOCRA's requests were inconclusive, meaning that the address did not exist or the construction project had ended."[68]

The MTSF restructured linkages with other civil society organizations through the creation of the Tripartite Construction Commission that helped inspectors with enforcement. The Commission, overseen directly by Rodríguez, met monthly and included UOCRA, the construction industry association (CAC), and various other professional associations. One of the first problems that the CAC brought to the table was the prevalence of subcontracting in the industry with fly-by-night construction firms that undercut the established firms and increased safety problems.[69] This was an issue that UOCRA had already brought up during the Obeid administration, citing the trouble in fighting "ghost" firms that are "insolvent" and that stay in business solely for "constructing one building."[70] In response, Binner issued a decree mandating that all construction sites have a large sign indicating all of the involved investors, managers, architects, and insurance companies.[71] This new rule helped the inspectors identify those responsible for putting workers at risk. The initiative was praised by the business community and worker advocates because it "separated the wheat from the chaff" when it came to construction firms.[72]

The MTSF's relationship with organizations outside of the state was not, however, always cooperative. Industry associations and unions pushed back on

---

[66] In 2008, there was an election for secretary general that was actually a contested election (the first contested election since the 1980s). To make sure there was no violence, there were 160 police officers present to ensure that the elections occurred without violence. The incumbent secretary general won with only 791 of the 9,000 affiliates voting. After the election, in 2010, a group of union leaders attempted to displace the secretary general of the union because of his lack of effort in protecting the workers and alleged corruption. *La Capital* "Sin violencia ganó el oficialismo en la Uocra" 12/12/2008. *Rosario/12* "Secretario cuestionado" 07/28/2010. Interview: S43, Construction Workers' Union of Argentina (UOCRA), Rosario, 5/13/2009
[67] Interview: S41, Construction Workers' Union of Argentina (UOCRA), Rosario, 5/13/2009
[68] Interview: S26, Health and Safety Inspector, Santa Fe Ministry of Labor and Social Security, Rosario, 5/13/2009
[69] Interview: S08, Argentine Construction Association (CAC), Rosario, 4/29/2009
[70] *La Capital* "La Uocra develó la cara oculta de la construcción" 07/18/2007
[71] *La Capital* "Seguridad: mayores exigencias para la exhibición de cartelacríam en obras" 07/22/2008
[72] *La Capital* "La provincia sacará 20 inspectores a la calle" 01/06/2009

Santa Fe 125

plans to create new health and safety committees in the workplace.[73] And although leaders of UOCRA privately praised the efforts of the MTSF, they publicly criticized the provincial government for not doing enough to reduce accidents.[74] During the Obeid administration, UOCRA and the other CGT unions had never protested about health and safety problems in the worksites or petitioned the Secretary of Labor in the media. Not even four months after Binner took power, UOCRA organized a protest of one hundred workers who marched to the MTSF to demand "implementation of safety measures and the provision of inspectors because without these actions the accidents, many of them fatal, will not stop."[75] As the accidents continued, demands from the unions increased, protests persisted, and the CGT-Rosario insisted on more inspections.[76] The local newspaper quoted the head of the CGT as stating "from November until today (May 2008), every time an inspector is requested they aren't there. It took people dying once again to get the inspectors out into the street."[77] These statements, which contrast sharply with the private accounts of a number of unions praising Rodríguez (including UOCRA), illustrate the more aggressive political stance that unions took against a governor with whom they had no partisan alliance.

In summary, the case of the construction industry demonstrates how shifts in the MTSF translated into changes in patterns of enforcement. Under the PJ, administrative resources in health and safety inspection were few, the state was dependent on unions for enforcement, and UOCRA did not have the resources to make up for the state's deficiencies. The union had unfettered access to the few inspectors who were on staff, and neither UOCRA nor CGT protested or made public statements demanding more resources for health and safety inspection in construction. As a result, despite the saliency of the crisis in the industry, there was failed *society-dependent* enforcement at *low* levels.

Everything changed when the PS came into power. With investments in administrative resources, enforcement was made possible even without inspectors drawing on material resources from society. Enforcement increased sharply due to decisions made by Rodríguez, without any major change in the capabilities or actions on the part of UOCRA (thus, union power remained constant). In addition, with their opponents in power, UOCRA and the CGT went on the offensive and publically demanded more state action and investment, keeping the pressure on Binner. The MTSF did not cut off all linkages with society, but the inspectors did not draw on resources of outside groups as

---

[73] Interview: S24, Industrial Federation of Santa Fe, Rosario, 5/13/2009

[74] Interviews: S43, Construction Workers' Union of Argentina (UOCRA), Rosario, 5/13/2009; S41, Construction Workers' Union of Argentina (UOCRA), Rosario, 5/13/2009

[75] *La Capital* "Trabajadores de la construcción marchan en reclamo de más seguridad" 03/07/2008; "Obreros de la construcción marcharon para exigir seguridad" 03/08/2008

[76] *La Capital* "La Uocra y otros 35 gremios irán con reclamos a Trabajo" 05/19/2008

[77] *La Capital* "Ahora la CGT pide controles más frecuentes en las obras" 05/22/2008

126 *State-driven and co-produced enforcement in labor regulation*

extensively as they had in the earlier period or as in the cases analyzed in Chapter 4. Instead, regulators mainly were on their own, and the increases in enforcement were a result of bureaucratic decision processes within the MTSF.[78] Ultimately, enforcement in the construction industry became *state-driven* at *medium* levels.

FEDERAL CAPITAL

While most provinces in Argentina gained jurisdiction over labor law in the 1980s, the Federal Capital (also called the Autonomous City of Buenos Aires) did not become independent from the federal government until the late 1990s. As a result, the Sub-Secretariat of Labor (STBA) in the Federal Capital was created in 1999, many years later than were the other inspectorates included in this study. Power was transferred slowly to the Federal Capital, leaving the STBA barely functional during its first three years of official existence. After the financial crisis, however, administrative resources quickly increased; the STBA's staff grew from only 11 inspectors in 2002 to 54 in 2003. In 2006, there was yet another expansion, and the number of inspectors reached more than one hundred (0.35 per 10,000 people). The inspectors were, by comparison with those in the other provinces, highly educated professionals (e.g., lawyers and accountants). Also, divisions were created for health and safety, construction, general wage and hour employment, and, eventually, for home-based work. The STBA was given a budget sufficient for an information management system that enabled the inspectorate to identify industries as well as geographic areas where violations concentrated. These data allowed, for instance, the Auditor General of the government to conduct a detailed analysis of all enforcement action in 2006.[79] Such advanced information systems stand in stark contrast to those in other provinces, where data analysis was often just a totaling up of daily handwritten counts by inspectors. In sum, in just three years the STBA gained a large number of highly trained inspectors who had relatively more resources than any other inspectorate in the country.

Notwithstanding the substantial administrative resources allocated to the STBA, the inspectorate did not have the features commonly associated with a coherent or autonomous bureaucracy. While inspectors were required to have a minimum level of education, political interference and patronage in the hiring process prevented true meritocracy.[80] Civil service protection, for instance,

[78] And although enforcement clearly increased, the number of fatal accidents did not decline in 2009 and 2010. It is uncertain what exactly was driving the high levels of accidents. *Rosario/12* "El récord más triste del año" 01/21/2011
[79] Auditoria General la Ciudad Buenos Aires. Informe Final: Dirección General de Protección del Trabajo. 2006
[80] Interview: B39, Former Senior Official, Federal Capital Labor Subsecretariat, Buenos Aires, 2/6/2009

Federal Capital 127

is crucial for inspector independence, but nearly all of inspectors in the STBA had precarious contracts that could be terminated at any time.[81] Some in the STBA were even falsely contracted as "interns" though they were acting as full employees.[82] One inspector described the limitations that his short-term contract posed: "In this position, if you don't have civil service protection, you are prone to all kinds of pressure ... You feel somewhat constrained in front of powerful corporations."[83] In addition, many inspectors held jobs outside of the STBA to supplement their income (a practice that was tolerated by senior officials). As one inspector explained, "the majority of the inspectors have clients in their independent consulting or legal practices," which are mainly outside of the jurisdiction of the Federal Capital.[84] These characteristics put the STBA at a distinct disadvantage compared with other inspectorates (such as Brazil, the Dominican Republic, and Santa Fe after the reform) that had many more Weberian organizational features.[85]

As in other cases of investment in administrative resources, linkages with unions were relatively constrained. While inspectors could collaborate with unions, structures were put into place to prevent unions from exercising large degrees of control over where enforcement took place. Unlike in Peronist provinces (where union leaders had free access to inspectors), in the STBA appeals for inspection came through a centralized office that monitored and filtered requests before forwarding them to the inspectors.[86] In addition to limitations on access, unions also had a more circumscribed role during inspections than they did in other provinces. For instance, one inspector recounted that "the only thing union leaders can do is be present. They cannot intervene."[87] Inspectors did not draw on unions for transportation or follow-up after inspections, but instead relied on their own resources. In sum, although inspector-union linkages were not completely blocked, compared to the cases discussed in Chapter 4, and to Santa Fe under the PJ, these linkages were substantially weaker (this finding is also supported by the survey data analyzed in Chapter 3).

What explains this combination of high levels of administrative resources (but not bureaucratic coherence) and weak inspector-union linkages? Although the Federal Capital has higher levels of socioeconomic development than do the other provinces included in this study, income does not simply translate into the ability to hire more officials across the cases. (For example, the significantly poorer province Tucumán had a greater number of public employees per capita

---

[81] *Página/12* "La paradoja de los inspectores" 09/18/2008
[82] *Página/12* "En casa del herrero ..." 04/10/2007
[83] Interview: B16, Inspector, STBA, Buenos Aires, 10/14/2008
[84] Interview: B36, Inspector, Federal Capital Labor Subsecretariat, Buenos Aires, 10/21/2008
[85] Schrank 2009; Pires 2011
[86] Interview: B22, Federal Capital Labor Subsecretariat, Buenos Aires, 9/15/2008
[87] Interview: B16, Inspector, STBA, Buenos Aires, 10/14/2008

128 *State-driven and co-produced enforcement in labor regulation*

than did the Federal Capital).[88] Nor, as is often suggested in the literature on administrative reform, could the political underpinnings of investment in the internal components of capacity be found in strategies to provide a collective benefit. The official who put together the political support for the expansion described the process as assembling a "critical mass ... with a little support from the unions" and the support of "legislators [who] wanted ... the prospect of creating new government positions so that they can influence the hiring."[89] Thus, there was an investment in administrative resources but no depoliticization of the bureaucracy.

Instead, the political dynamic in the Federal Capital involved a center-left head of government with a programmatic interest in enforcement but with no union alliance. These political conditions in the Federal Capital were extremely similar to those in Córdoba (under the UCR) and in Santa Fe (under the PS) that led to greater investment in administrative resources than in ties with unions. The head of government of the Federal Capital from 2000 to 2005, Aníbal Ibarra, was from the center-left *Alianza Fuerza Porteña*. Although he was supported by some Peronists, Ibarra had a much broader leftist coalition and did not rely on the traditional partisan alliance that the PJ had with the labor movement. Labor union leaders, therefore, did not have to be rewarded with positions in labor administration, leaving space for a leadership with a different set of political commitments. For Sub-secretary of Labor, Ibarra selected Alejandro Pereyra, a labor lawyer who had links to Alianza political activists (not CGT unions).[90] Below Pereyra, the position of Director of Labor Protection was given to a lawyer, Florencio Varela (from the PJ), who could serve as a bridge to the major unions.[91] In total, there was only one appointment with strong ties to unions in the entire leadership.

Ibarra was followed by Jorge Telerman (2005–2007), also from the *Alianza Fuerza Porteña*. Telerman initially kept the same appointed team, but in the height of the controversy over migrant garment workers, Varela and Pereyra were forced to resign. The political circumstances of their removal were not clear – some, including Pereyra himself, interpreted it as a reprisal for his aggressive enforcement on the garment industry, but the continued enforcement after Pereyra is strong evidence that this was not the case.[92] Telerman selected Ariel Lieutier to be his new Sub-secretary of Labor. Lieutier was an economist

---

[88] In 2006, the Federal Capital had 43 public officials per 1,000 residents, while Tucumán had 47. Source: MENCON
[89] Interview: B39, Former Senior Official, Federal Capital Labor Subsecretariat, Buenos Aires, 2/6/2009
[90] Interview: Alejandro Pereyra, Former Subsecretario, Federal Capital Labor Subsecretariat, Buenos Aires, Buenos Aires, 2/6/2009
[91] Interview: B19, Union Obrera Metalurgica de la Republica Argentina (UOM), Asesor Gremial, Seccion Capital Federal, Buenos Aires, 2/12/2009
[92] *Página/12* "Despido y polémica" 09/09/2006. *La Nación* "Una renuncia sorpresiva" 09/10/2006. Interviews: Alejandro Pereyra, Former Subsecretario, Subsecretaría de Trabajo, Ciudad

Federal Capital

with connections to the alternative worker organizations, including the alternative union central, the CTA (*Central de Trabajadores de la Argentina*). Unlike the Secretaries of Labor in the PJ provinces, Lieutier did not come into office with politically predetermined allies with whom he had work to maintain the coalition.[93] As did Pereyra, Lieutier kept one team member with connections to both the CTA and the CGT who could serve as a bridge. Still, officials drawn directly from unions in no way dominated management positions in the STBA. Lieutier's career, like that of Pereyra, was not dependent on his connections with unions either. There was, ultimately, sufficient flexibility to form alliances with nonunion civil society organizations.

What was the result of the combination of substantial administrative resources (without bureaucratic organization necessary for autonomy) and comparatively weak inspector-union linkages? Examining outputs, it is clear that there was enforcement. Regulators conducted 30,000 inspections in 2007, resulting in a per thousand residents inspection rate of 9.7 (compared with 8.6 in Córdoba),[94] and found infractions 32% (2006)[95] of the time.[96] The percentage of inspections triggered by complaints, however, was substantially lower in the Federal Capital than it was in other provinces (~47% in 2006 and 2007).[97] Moreover, in stark contrast with places where unions dominated complaints, only a minority of inspection requests in the Federal Capital (40% in 2005) came from unions, while the majority came from individuals or other government agencies. Furthermore, there was no direct relationship between the industries where enforcement was concentrated and union demands. In 2005, 66% of all requests came from the construction union, but the construction industry had only 36% of all inspections. On the other end of the spectrum, only 0.1% of requests were from the commercial workers' union, but 7% of inspections were in the commercial sector.

In sum, these overall indicators show that there was enforcement (by most common measures), and the pattern was not society-dependent. A full account of the politics of enforcement, however, requires a close examination into the events that surrounded the garment industry. Not only was this industry the locus of a tremendous enforcement effort, but the saliency of the problems

---

Autonama de Buenos Aires, Buenos Aires, 2/6/2009; Gustavo Vera, Fundación La Alameda, Buenos Aires, 2/23/2009

[93] Interview: B66, Former Subsecretario, Subsecretaría de Trabajo, Ciudad Autonama de Buenos Aires, Buenos Aires, 2/24/2009

[94] The inspection rate was particularly high in 2007, but in other years it was lower than that of Córdoba.

[95] Auditoria General la Ciudad Buenos Aires. *Informe Final: Dirección General de Protección del Trabajo*. 2006. p. 23

[96] These numbers are not terribly different than the 8.6 inspections per capita and 26% infraction rate in Córdoba (2008).

[97] Source: Internal report from the STBA

State-driven and co-produced enforcement in labor regulation

in the garment industry played a key role in linkage formation and investments in administrative resources.

Garment industry[98]

Garment manufacturing in the Federal Capital accelerated rapidly during the period of economic growth after the financial crisis of 2001. Between 2002 and 2006 there was a 70% increase in activity in the sector nationally, much of it concentrated in the Federal Capital.[99] Although the industry did not have substantial exports, domestic producers did compete with imports, which account for 25% of consumption. An integral part of the industry was a vast network of small home-based workshops that operated through a system of outsourcing and piecework for local and foreign apparel brands; 74% of producers had fewer than five employees, and 23% had between six and forty employees.[100] It is impossible to know the precise number of workers and workshops, but officials estimated that in 2009 there were between 3,000 and 3,500 workshops in the Federal Capital.[101]

Work in this sector was regulated by the general law of labor contracts and by a special law of home-based work that regulates putting out piecework.[102] A commission of unions, industry associations, and the federal Ministry of Labor (MTESS) set the piece rates for wages in the industry. This bargaining structure gave the sector a degree of flexibility that goes beyond the general Argentine system of collective bargaining, but problems of compliance rendered the details of formal rules (and any flexibility built into them) moot.

By all measures, the garment industry in the Federal Capital had extremely high levels of labor violations. The factors that contribute to poor working conditions in all garment industries – relatively low-skilled workers, highly fluctuating demand, and low levels of investment[103] – were amplified in the Federal Capital by the large number of undocumented migrant workers. The migrants, who were mostly from Bolivia, for the most part did not have legal status in Argentina. Many were brought to Buenos Aries in human trafficking networks and had to repay their debt.[104] Their illegal status made them

---

[98] A version of this case study was published in *Creative Labour Regulation: Indeterminacy and Protection in an Uncertain World*, edited by Deirdre McCann et al., International Labor Organization, Geneva, 2013, and in Spanish as: "Cambios en la capacidad del Estado para enfrentar las violaciones de las normas laborales: los talleres de confección de prendas de vestir en Buenos Aires," *Desarrollo Económico* (Argentina) Vol. 51, N° 202–203, 2011

[99] Centro de Estudios para la Producción. "Las marcas como motor del crecimiento de las exportaciones en el sector indumentaria" 2007

[100] Fundación el Otro 2007

[101] *Clarín* "Imágenes de los talleres clandestinos, una forma de esclavitud moderna" 4/12/2009

[102] Law 12.713   [103] Abernathy, Dunlop, Hammond, and Weil 1999; Piore 2004

[104] *La Nación* "Una ruta clandestina: de Bolivia a Retiro" 04/01/2006; *Página/12* "Una cámara oculta para comprobar cómo opera la trata de personas" 05/05/2007

Federal Capital   131

especially vulnerable because workers believed (erroneously) that they would be deported if they complained to government authorities about labor conditions – a belief cultivated by workshop owners, themselves often Bolivian migrants.[105] Descriptions of working conditions in the industry were staggering. In 2008, industry leaders estimated that nearly 80% of workers were informal (unregistered).[106] An inspection operation in 2006 found that 1,600 of 13,000 workers checked were in conditions that approximated "slavery," and worker advocates estimated that in total 25,000 Bolivian migrants were "reduced to slavery in clandestine workshops."[107]

An investigation from the *Defensor del Pueblo*[108] described conditions in two workshops in the Parque Avellaneda neighborhood.[109] The workshops produced various garment products for domestic brand name apparel companies; one had twenty-one machines and twenty-five employees; the other had fifteen machines and twelve employees. The workers – undocumented migrants – lived in crowded, illegally operated workshops in buildings that were not approved (or safe) for factories. The workshops violated nearly every labor law: they did not meet basic health and safety standards; there was no legal payroll; working days began at seven in the morning and lasted until past midnight with only short breaks for meals; salaries were only 100 dollars per month; and workers were denied all legally mandated benefits. When the workers' children returned from school, they were locked in small, unsafe rooms with exposed wires. The workshop owners bribed local police for protection and threatened workers with arrest and deportation if they complained to officials. Workshop owners also kept the workers' passports under their control to prevent escape. Workers who were fired were denied their last payment and tossed out in the street. The bosses would then travel to Bolivia to look for new workers and then traffic them to Buenos Aires.

Unfortunately, the workshops described previously were hardly unique; thousands of small factories that were spread out in wide swaths of the city had similar conditions.[110] Responding to these extreme violations of labor (and

---

[105] Interview: B11, Senior Official, Federal Capital Labor Subsecretariat, Buenos Aires, 02/12/2009 and 02/17/2009
[106] *La Nación* "Talleres clandestinos: el negocio de la explotación" 05/11/2008
[107] *La Nación* "Aún quedan 25.000 bolivianos que trabajan como esclavos" 10/16/2006
[108] The *Defensor del Pueblo* is a mix between an ombudsman and a public prosecutor.
[109] Court filings from the *Defensor del Pueblo* against Juan Carlos Salazar Nina in case N° 158, 03/05/2005
[110] Interviews: B46, La Alameda Foundation, Buenos Aires, 2/23/2009; B11, Senior Official, Federal Capital Labor Subsecretariat, Buenos Aires, 02/12/2009 and 02/17/2009; B20, Lawyer, Argentine Human Rights League, Buenos Aires, 3/25/2009; B13, Defensor del Pueblo, Buenos Aires, 2/26/2009. See also: Lieuxref> and var/xref> and various media reports, including: *La Nación* "Descubren que hay 'esclavos' bolivianos en dos talleres" 10/28/2005; "Denuncian que hay casos de esclavitud" 11/18/2005; "El drama de vivir como esclavos" 04/01/2006; "Clausuraron otros once talleres textiles" 04/05/2006; "Nueva denuncia por trabajo esclavo en talleres textiles" 04/27/2006; "Aun quedan 25,000 bolivianos que trabajan como esclavos"

other) laws posed a formidable challenge to regulators. Workshops were hidden in residential buildings and changed location constantly. In addition, workers were reluctant to come forward with complaints. Once regulators discovered violations, they had the complicated task of ensuring that displaced workers did not wind up in more dire circumstances on the streets. This meant finding housing and employment for workers as well as helping them with immigration issues. Enforcement also entailed confronting a powerful industry that was reliant on low-wage workers in factories located near the largest retail centers of the country.

Before 2006, notwithstanding extensive and extreme violations of labor laws, there were low levels of enforcement in the garment industry. One barrier to action was the incomplete power transfer from the federal MTESS to the STBA. Even after the STBA was created, the MTESS continued to regulate the "putting-out" agreements that were the norm in the garment workshops. As a result, the STBA was not in a position to respond fully to the violations.[111] This barrier was resolved in 2006 after a garment workshop fire killed two adults and four children, all Bolivian migrants, and set off a flurry of criticism targeting both the STBA and the MTESS.[112] The STBA, which had been blamed even though it lacked jurisdiction to enforce the home-based work law, began taking ownership of the problem. At first the STBA defied the formal jurisdictional barrier, and later a new agreement was reached to transfer power formally.[113] In the eleven days that followed the fire, a series of operations by inspectors from STBA closed 122 workshops. In 40% of these workshops, the workers (and often their families) lived and worked in the same place. The closures immediately resulted in the displacement of 110 Bolivian migrants who had been employed in the shut-down workshops or who had been thrown out by their employers in anticipation of inspections.[114] By September of 2006, the STBA had conducted 1,700 inspections in the sector and closed 500 clandestine workshops. The crisis quickly grew in scale – officials from the Bolivian embassy became involved, and displaced workers had to be housed in government shelters.

The initial reaction of the STBA to the fire was somewhat expected, but enforcement did not end after saliency of the issue waned. Instead, the STBA

10/16/2006; *Página/12* "Centro clandestino, esta vez de confección" 03/31/2007; *Clarín* "Imágenes de los talleres clandestinos, una forma de esclavitud moderna" 04/12/2009

[111] For a discussion of the period before 2006, see: Amengual 2011a

[112] *Página/12* "El infierno del trabajo esclavo" 3/31/2006. *La Nación* "Mueren seis personas en un incendio" 3/31/2006

[113] Interview: B39, Former Senior Official, Federal Capital Labor Subsecretariat, Buenos Aires, 2/6/2009. On June 22, 2006, the government of Federal Capital formally signed an agreement (Convenio N° 14-GCBA/06) with the MTESS to take primary jurisdiction over home-based work. This agreement did not go into legal effect until the end of 2007, but its existence made it possible for the STBA to increase its involvement in regulating the garment sector.

[114] *Página/12* "Tras los controles, las textiles ilegales ya se mudan al conurbano" 4/11/2006; *La Nación* "Tras el incendio, combaten el empleo ilegal" 04/01/2006; "Bolivia en Buenos Aires: la vida después de las clausuras" 04/26/2006

Federal Capital

began a multipronged effort to reduce the worst forms of abuse in the garment industry. The STBA undertook an extensive campaign to gather information about the industry. Working with La Alameda, the STBA targeted workshops that produced for well-known local brands. In one case, the government of the Federal Capital found production for Kosiuko in a violating workshop. As part of its response, inspectors forced the brand to provide addresses of its other suppliers. Inspectors then worked with La Alameda to send Bolivian undocumented migrants to look for work in these factories. At least one *spy* was given a job and found a workshop that violated a series of laws, including a lack of fire extinguishers, no emergency exits, and salaries that did not conform to wage and hour regulations. La Alameda then passed this information back to the STBA, which followed up with inspections.[115] The information that La Alameda generated through its network in the community of Bolivian migrants was extremely valuable – inspectors found violations in 97% of the workshops identified by La Alameda.[116] To put this number into context, wage and hour regulators in the United States' garment industry found violations in 49% of their investigations between 1996 and 2000.[117]

With the information gathered, the STBA took far-reaching steps to raise the costs of noncompliance for workshops that continued illegal practices; to prosecute the firms at the top of the supply chain that sourced from clandestine factories; and to create employment in cooperatives that did not exploit workers. Inspection campaigns and extensive closures continued over a full year after the fire. In the first eight months of 2007 alone, the STBA closed down 713 workshops.[118] To complement this strategy, inspectors, with their allies in the public prosecutor's office and La Alameda, started mapping out the entire supply chain of the garment industry and began a campaign against lead firms. The first brand that the STBA publicly denounced was a local apparel firm called Cheeky. Inspectors linked Cheeky to a number of clandestine workshops, a move that resulted in a series of articles detailing exploitation and child labor among Cheeky's suppliers.[119] After a number of investigations, the STBA put together information on five more local brand name apparel firms that produced in clandestine workshops and then held a press conference to publicize the information.[120] This put direct pressure on the firms, embarrassing them and sparking public protests in front of their stores.

The campaign in the media was complemented with new judicial actions against firms that sourced from clandestine workshops. The STBA made an

---

[115] *Clarín* "Trabajo esclavo: usaron a espías para investigar talleres" 09/06/2006; "Se infiltró en un taller ilegal para denunciar a una marca de ropa" 09/07/2006.

[116] Auditoria General la Ciudad Buenos Aires 2006   [117] Weil 2005 p. 242

[118] *Clarín* "Trabajo esclavo: la Comuna denunció a seis marcas textiles" 07/31/2007

[119] *Página/12* "Ropa infantil con manchas legales" 01/16/2007; "Nos pagaban centavos por prendas que en vidriera estaban a 30 pesos" 01/17/2007

[120] *Página/12* "Denuncian a cinco marcas deportivas por explotar a los indocumentados" 07/30/2007. Interview: B66, Former Senior Official, Federal Capital Labor Subsecretariat, Buenos Aires, 2/24/2009

134   *State-driven and co-produced enforcement in labor regulation*

effort to use laws that make firms responsible for the actions of their subcontractors as a way of pressuring firms further up on the supply chain. In justifying this tactic, a former Sub-secretary of Labor explained that the "function" of the STBA "was not to inspect, but to change the working conditions."[121] Collaborating, once again, with La Alameda and the public prosecutors, the STBA identified an intermediary supplier that produced for a number of brands (including Puma) and that had a network of smaller clandestine subcontractors. Inspectors were able to locate these workshops, which were in extreme violation of labor laws, and not only shut them down, but also prosecuted the intermediary factory.[122] These actions imposed a cost on the workshop owners, had a far-reaching effect up the supply chain, and consequently served as a greater deterrent.[123]

Not all cases were successful in court. One case in which prosecution failed involved a local apparel brand called SOHO.[124] Inspectors learned about the brand's direct use of clandestine workshops from employees of a firm that supplied SOHO with materials. Upon investigating, the STBA discovered four workshops in the Federal Capital that produced for SOHO. A series of inspections revealed serious labor law violations in these workshops, including illegal overtime, wage violations, and health and safety violations. The STBA worked with prosecutors to take both the brand and the workshop owners, who were themselves Bolivian nationals, to court on charges of exploitation and violation of immigration statutes. A judge, however, ruled in favor of the workshop owners on the grounds that their actions were legitimate "cultural" practices of Bolivians. The ruling was widely criticized as ridiculous, prompting condemnation from the Bolivian embassy and the Argentine association of anthropologists, with both parties claiming that exploitation of workers was hardly an accepted cultural practice.[125] Notwithstanding these setbacks, multiple prosecutions against firms at various levels of the supply chain put significant pressure on workshops that violated labor laws.

In addition to penalizing violators, the STBA worked with the National Institute of Industrial Technology (*Instituto Nacional de Tecnología Industrial,* INTI) to create two programs which would support garment production that did not exploit workers. One program, modeled on international private-

---

[121] Interview: B66, Former Senior Official, Federal Capital Labor Subsecretariat, Buenos Aires, 2/24/2009

[122] See: Lieutier 2010 p. 169

[123] This practice is somewhat similar to the highly effective use of the "hot goods provision" by the U.S. Department of Labor to increase costs for firms that source from illegal workshops. See: Weil 2005

[124] *Página/12* "Otra marca de ropa en el banquillo por una denuncia de trabajo esclavo" 03/28/2007; "Allanan un taller clandestino en Parque Avellaneda" 11/20/2007; "Con la marca del trabajo esclavo" 12/13/2007

[125] *Página/12* "Explotación, esa 'costumbre ancestral'" 05/15/2008; "Rechazo del cónsul de Bolivia" 05/15/2008; "La explotación no es herencia cultural" 06/27/2008

Federal Capital 135

voluntary regulation, was designed to reduce labor abuses by using the power of consumers and brand name firms.[126] Brands could participate in the program and have their supply chain certified by INTI as being free of the worst forms of labor abuses. INTI would offer training on management systems to help brands upgrade their supply chain. This program ultimately failed because brands did not sign up. A second program, to create employment for displaced workers, was successful in building a cooperative.[127] A coordinator for INTI explained that "due to the labor inspections, which have closed many workshops and left hundreds of workers out in the street and without employment ... we are working to develop a garment cluster that will provide job opportunities for these people." The cooperative became a part of La Alameda and employed 200 people who had worked in the clandestine factories. The cooperative sold the clothing under the brand "No Chains" in the fashionable Palermo neighborhood of Buenos Aires, and it was also given a contract to make uniforms for the police and Ministry of Defense. Eventually, the cooperative developed international ties with a similar organization in Bangkok, teaming up with international designers and even being featured on the international news broadcast of international news channel CNN.[128]

Finally, the STBA was able to resist pressure against enforcement from those firms that had immediately benefited from labor law violations. The garment industry supported enforcement in 2004 on the presumption that most illegal workshops were producing knock-offs that undercut the brands.[129] When regulators began to investigate, they found many workshops that produced for the larger local brands (e.g., Cheeky). After these investigations, there were no statements from the industry association calling for enforcement. Instead, the industry lobbied against enforcement, putting pressure on the STBA. Inspectors came to see the industry associations as an enemy, not an ally.[130] The large brands, however, made little progress altering the behavior of the agency, and so industry changed tactics. Instead of preventing enforcement, industry attempted to rewrite the law to reduce lead firms' responsibility for compliance in their supply chains.[131] This legislative strategy also failed. Finally, resistance from businesses failed was ineffective at the street-level; even though workshop owners were able to bribe police for protection, there is no evidence that they were able to bribe labor inspectors.

---

[126] "Programa de Certificación INTI Compromiso Social Compartido Empresas de Indumentaria" Instituto Nacional de Tecnología Industrial, 2006
[127] Interview: B46, La Alameda Foundation, Buenos Aires, 2/23/2009. See also: Lieutier 2010
[128] La Alameda was featured in CNN's project on modern-day slavery in April of 2011.
[129] Clarín "El 50% de la ropa se vende en negro" 01/11/2004; "Preocupa más a empresas la economía en negro" 12/17/2004
[130] Interview: B11, Senior Official, Federal Capital Labor Subsecretariat, Buenos Aires, 02/12/2009 and 02/17/2009
[131] Clarín "Ya se generó polemica por la ley contra 'el trabajo esclavo'" 8/21/2008. This proposed law was eventually defeated.

In sum, over a two-year period (2006–2008) enforcement levels were sustained at *high levels,* and the actions undertaken by the STBA approximated best practices of labor inspection.[132] While there were limitations – notably in the prosecution of SOHO and the failure of the INTI program to engage lead firms as collaborators – enforcement was substantial when compared with the cases discussed in Chapter 4. For instance, after the children of workers died in the brick-making sites in Córdoba, only a handful of worksites were closed down, and inspection operations quickly ended. Whether or not the inspections had an impact on working conditions in the garment industry is a difficult question to answer (the workshops, after all, are clandestine and no reliable data exist on working conditions). Illegal workshops still remained in the Federal Capital after the campaign, but there was also a noticeable change.[133] Between 2005 and 2008 nearly 1,000 workshops were closed down, thereby creating a real deterrent for garment producers who selected the low road of exploitative workshops.[134] A lawyer with the *Defensor del Pueblo,* who was closely involved in defending the rights of migrant workers, described the changes this way: "My view is that this effort already created a change ... From the total impunity at the beginning, to not having total impunity."[135] In short, the institutions that were meant to structure the labor market became somewhat stronger.

What made this dramatic enforcement campaign possible? The fire in the workshop clearly set the change into motion, but the event itself was by no means decisive.[136] There were other cases of tragedies in Argentine workplaces of equal (or greater) magnitude that did not result in intense enforcement, including the episodes of children dying on brick-kiln worksites in Córdoba discussed in Chapter 4.[137] In 2006, more than 600 registered workers were killed on the job in Argentina, yet there were few (if any) enforcement campaigns of this intensity.[138] How did the inspectors in the STBA undertake a broad, sustained, enforcement campaign that went well beyond merely responding to complaints?

First, the structure of linkages was key. If the STBA could have worked only with unions, as did the inspectors in other cases analyzed in Chapter 4, enforcement levels would likely have been much lower. The garment workers' union, SOIVA, simply did not request many inspections of the STBA.[139] For instance,

---

[132] Many of the steps taken by the STBA fit in the model of "strategic inspection." See: Weil 2008
[133] Some workshops have also moved out of the Federal Capital, where enforcement has been less concentrated.
[134] *La Nación* "El lado oscuro del negocio textil" 5/11/2008
[135] Interview: B13, Defensor del Pueblo, Buenos Aires, 2/26/2009
[136] Tragedies of this nature are often cited as the prime causal force behind reforms, but they are usually not decisive. Many tragedies fail to trigger change, and for those that do, a variety of factors influence what kind of policy change occurs. See: Carpenter and Sin 2007
[137] See: Amengual 2011b   [138] Superintendencia de Riesgos del Trabajo 2007
[139] Auditoria General la Ciudad Buenos Aires. "Informe Final: Dirección General De Protección Del Trabajo" 2006

Federal Capital 137

an official in the division of the STBA responsible for the garment workshops recounted, "To me, the unions don't come."[140] Senior officials at the STBA invited SOIVA to participate in the operations and the press conferences when clandestine firms were discovered and closed, but the union did not.[141] In fact, there were widespread accusations that SOIVA (a *yellow* union) was captured by management that discriminated against Bolivian migrants.[142]

While the union did not take steps to assist regulators, La Alameda offered ample resources for enforcement. A lawyer closely involved with the industry explained that La Alameda's great advantage was that *it worked directly with the people* in the workshops. These ties with workers in the industry began around the time of the economic crisis of 2001, when La Alameda started a soup kitchen to address social needs of its neighborhood:

They began to build rapport with the Bolivian workers because the bosses from the clandestine workshops sent their workers to the soup kitchen to eat, so they didn't have to pay. After workers started to go and eat, leaders of La Alameda began to understand what was going on ... workers started to tell stories ... and La Alameda began to help people escape from the workshops and to make formal complaints.[143]

Thus, La Alameda had resources that could help enforcement. According to officials from the STBA, La Alameda became a key partner in providing "logistics, and [information] before, during, and after" inspection operations.[144] An inspector explained that the people from La Alameda are crucial because they "provide training and teach the garment workers. They tell them what their rights are, what to do when a labor inspector comes, how they can collaborate with the inspectors." The inspector went on to explain that these actions are important "because the bosses scare workers by saying that if they go out in the street or see the police, they will be deported to Bolivia ... It is all a lie. They won't be sent to Bolivia. We don't deport anyone. We help them get their documentation."[145] The intermediary role of La Alameda was essential to making worker collaboration with regulators possible.

---

[140] Interview: B11, Senior Official, Federal Capital Labor Subsecretariat, Buenos Aires, 02/12/2009 and 02/17/2009

[141] Interview: B66, Former Senior Official, Federal Capital Labor Subsecretariat, Buenos Aires, 2/24/2009

[142] Interviews: B13, Defensor del Pueblo, Buenos Aires, 2/26/2009; B29, Federal Capital Labor Subsecretariat, Buenos Aires, 6/30/2008. To put pressure on the union, workers involved with La Alameda began running in shop elections contesting SOIVA's delegates. They also created their own union, the *Unión de Trabajadores Costureros de Buenos Aires* (UTCBA) to challenge SOIVA to represent the workers. This action created competition for SOIVA, but still little changed.

[143] Interview: B13, Defensor del Pueblo, Buenos Aires, 2/26/2009

[144] Interview: B39, Former Senior Official, Federal Capital Labor Subsecretariat, Buenos Aires, 2/6/2009

[145] Interview: B11, Senior Official, Federal Capital Labor Subsecretariat, Buenos Aires, 02/12/2009 and 02/17/2009

138   *State-driven and co-produced enforcement in labor regulation*

The simple fact that La Alameda had resources did not mean that they could automatically be used for enforcement by inspectors. How did La Alameda form linkages with inspectors? Part of the answer lies in the partisan conditions described previously; La Alameda had the opportunity to build linkages because there was no union dominance created by partisan exchange. An additional crucial step was the ability of La Alameda to generate political strength by taking to the streets. The leader of La Alameda describes how he secured access to the STBA in 2006:

> *After the fire, the STBA went and did a ton of inspections in small workshops that worked for small brands. They said that they didn't find large brands, so we brought together all of the media outlets and went to knock on the doors of the clandestine workshops of the large brands. All the while we were making the government look ridiculous in the view of the public ... During that time, La Alameda was really well known and had a strong relationship with the journalists in the press. For this reason, politicians were afraid ... In this way, La Alameda had a lot of weight ... and that is the way we got access. Not for any other reason.*[146]

At first, there was a lot of *distrust* between the two sides, which had not known each other beforehand. But with political expediency and congruent objectives, linkages began to develop. Senior officials saw value in collaborating because La Alameda came with "ideas and suggestions" to go beyond an "indiscriminate policy of inspection from workshop to workshop" in order to have a greater impact.[147] As evidence for the strength of the relationship, the central senior official (Secretary of Labor Pereyra) provided council to La Alameda after he left the STBA.[148]

Linkages to La Alameda were initially shaken by the transition to a new set of individuals leading the STBA with the appointment of Ariel Lieutier as Sub-secretary of Labor in 2006. Lieutier did not have a prior relationship with La Alameda, but he was selected by the head of the government, in part, because he had experience working with unemployed workers' movements. When he came into office, Lieutier "went looking for allies" so he could address the problems in the garment industry, and La Alameda was the biggest player. No matter what Lieutier did, La Alameda was going to be in the press,

---

[146] Interview: B46, La Alameda Foundation, Buenos Aires, 2/23/2009. On the protests and attention that La Alameda was able to generate, see: *La Nación* "Marcha de trabajadores bolivianos" 04/05/2006; "Protesta contra el trabajo esclavo" 09/15/2006

[147] Interview: B39, Former Senior Official, Federal Capital Labor Subsecretariat, Buenos Aires, 2/6/2009

[148] The motivations for firing of Pereyra are not obvious, but it is clear that his replacement was not discouraged from enforcing labor law in the garment sector. There was speculation in the press and observers that Pereyra was fired because of pressure coming from the garment industry, but this explanation does not appear to be true because, if anything, Lieutier *increased* pressure on the garment industry. *Pagina/12* "Despido y polémica" 09/09/2006; *La Nación* "Una renuncia sorpresiva" 09/10/2006

collaborating with the *Defensor del Pueblo* to prosecute the brands and the workshops. At first, Lieutier and La Alameda had trouble coming to an agreement; it took some time before they could work together, but once again the power of La Alameda coupled with the objectives they shared with the regulators allowed the two to build strong linkages. By the end of 2006, the STBA, under Lieutier, had gained significant intelligence from La Alameda, which laid the groundwork for the 2007 enforcement campaign described previously.

The linkages with La Alameda were extremely important, but they alone cannot explain why enforcement had such a broad reach. If the STBA relied on La Alameda for every one of its inspections (as did regulators in Córdoba, Tucumán, and Santa Fe under the PJ), there simply could not have been such a large enforcement campaign. To understand how the STBA was able to conduct thousands of inspections, we need to revisit the administrative resources of the STBA. As described previously, by 2006 STBA had well over one hundred inspectors who were trained professionals equipped with information technology needed to keep track of their enforcement efforts.

In addition, in 2007 the STBA created a specialized division within the labor inspectorate to enforce regulations only in home-based work. The creation of a new division dedicated a number of inspectors, more than 15% of the total, to the problem of the clandestine workshops. This change ensured that inspection capacity would be apportioned to the garment industry, even if other industries demanded many inspections. This tactic contrasts strongly with that of the inspectorates analyzed in Chapter 4. In Córdoba, Tucumán, and Santa Fe (before the reform), the demands of powerful unions occupied most of the time of the inspectors, and there was little effort to reduce these pressures on a segment of inspectors. The creation of the dedicated group also allowed inspectors to specialize and receive training in human rights, child welfare, and migration issues that prepared them to deal with the complex, and often extremely difficult, problems they encountered in the clandestine workshops.[149] While the STBA still lacked many of the features considered necessary for an autonomous inspectorate – such as civil service protection – the resources allotted to the inspectors proved crucial in making the enforcement campaign in the garment industry so intensive.

In sum, the STBA was able to undertake such a far-reaching enforcement campaign in the garment industry due to a combination of linkages with La Alameda and a high level of administrative resources. Without linkages with La Alameda, it would have been nearly impossible for inspectors to identify so many hidden garment workshops. And without some administrative resources, inspectors would not have been able to go beyond the immediate demands of La Alameda and to conduct such broad operations.

---

[149] Interview: B11, Senior Official, Federal Capital Labor Subsecretariat, Buenos Aires, 02/12/2009 and 02/17/2009

Changes under Macri

The election of the right-leaning Mauricio Macri (PRO), in December 2007, to the head of government marked a shift in labor politics in the Federal Capital. Clearly on the ideological right, Macri was not the favorite candidate of many unions or workers' advocates (he had support of only two, relatively small, private sector unions).[150] This section recounts the changes to the STBA in 2008, as well as the shifts in enforcement in a variety of industries, including garments.

Senior officials appointed by Macri took steps to limit inspector linkages with societal organizations but did not drastically reduce administrative resources. With a small number of unions, the Sub-secretary of Labor, Jorge Luis Ginzo, drew up formal agreements that gave the unions a limited number of inspectors per week in return for the unions providing free access for disabled workers to their training centers. The intention of these agreements, from the point of view of appointed officials in the STBA, was to bring union-inspector interactions "into the light ... to give a structure so that the inspector does not feel uncomfortable if the union leaders participate in the inspection ... to make everything on top of the table."[151] Most worker organizations and unions were completely left out of the agreements, and thus they lost access to the inspectors. For example, the auto workers' union (Sindicato de Mecanicos y Afines del Transporte Automotor de la Republica Argentina, SMATA) was able to work with inspectors before Macri came to office, but afterward they had delays of five to six months, which for them was "a huge cost not to have inspection."[152] Other unions experienced similar problems, and many were effectively locked out of inspection.[153] The percentage of complaint-driven inspections dropped to just 33% in 2008.[154] Although linkages were changed, the traditional components of enforcement capacity remained relatively untouched. There was no restructuring of the STBA that could further erode bureaucratic autonomy. For instance, the inspectors did not have civil service protection before, and they were not given any under Macri.

---

[150] *Clarín* "Los gremios también juegan sus porotos por los candidatos" 05/24/2007
[151] Interview: B08, Subsecretaría de Trabajo, Ciudad Autonama de Buenos Aires, Buenos Aires, 9/23/2008
[152] Interview: B80, Sindicato de Mecanicos y Afines del Transporte Automotor de la Republica Argentina (SMATA), in the office of the Secretaria Gremial (Federal Captial Section), Buenos Aires, 2/16/2009
[153] Interviews: B49, Union Leader, Unión Obreros y Empleados Tintoreros, Sombreros y Lavaderos UOETSYLRA, Buenos Aires, 6/30/2008 and 10/20/2008
[154] Internal data provided by the STBA. The difference between Buenos Aires and Córdoba is understated by the way these numbers are calculated. The 32% in Buenos Aires includes all complaint-driven inspections – individual and union – while the 80% estimate for Córdoba only includes union complaints.

Federal Capital

Moreover, administrative resources stayed comparatively high.[155] The STBA, for example, still had access to computer systems and employed a sizable number of inspectors (85 in 2009).

In the garment industry, the political changes under Macri resulted in a clear decline in enforcement. A close observer of the industry noted that the new Sub-secretary of Labor "has not stopped working on this issue, but he does not do it as well as the others."[156] Inspections continued in the industry, but there were no more efforts to take a strategic approach to getting at the root causes of violations by enforcing up and down the supply chain. La Alameda and its allies were highly critical of the new administration, writing in an open letter to the STBA:

> *During the period 2006–2007, the Defensor del Pueblo and the STBA closed hundreds of clandestine workshops, denounced dozens of brands, and brought workshop owners to Federal justice for servitude, human trafficking, and slavery and significantly reduced the quantity of workshops with a policy of inspection, penalties, and publicity ... After [Macri] took office, there was a significant reduction in the fight against slave labor ... His policy consisted of bean counting inspections without penalties for factories that exploited undocumented workers nor collecting fines that were placed on closed workshops that have once again mysteriously began functioning recently.[157]*

Congruent with this account, clandestine workshops were discovered in 2010 and 2011 by neighbors who alerted the police, yet the STBA did not undertake enforcement campaigns.[158] In sum, the enforcement in the garment industry was reduced substantially.

Enforcement in the garment industry declined despite the fact that inspectors in the STBA continued to recognize the industry as being problematic. Even without reducing administrative resources, inspectors lost the ability to respond to violations in the industry. The new administration replaced a number of the senior officials at the STBA, removing many of those who had developed ties with La Alameda.[159] When the newly appointed officials then took steps to curb linkages, they cut off a key political and operational resource for inspectors. A leader of La Alameda recounted:

---

[155] There were some decreases in the number of inspectors, but the STBA continued to have the highest administrative resources of any provincial-level inspectorate in Argentina. Interview: B11, Senior Official, Federal Capital Labor Subsecretariat, Buenos Aires, 02/12/2009 and 02/17/2009

[156] Interview: B13, Defensor del Pueblo, Buenos Aires, 2/26/2009

[157] An open letter from La Alameda and the *Asociación Civil Que no se Repita* to Mauricio Macri 9/27/2010. See also: *Página/12* "Una carta abierta sobre la corrupción" 9/27/2010

[158] *Clarín* "Hubo incidentes tras allanamientos en ocho talleres textiles ilegales" 06/04/2010; "Villa Lugano: rescatan a 50 personas que vivían en dos talleres textiles clandestinos" 04/14/2011

[159] In a similar fashion to previous changes in leadership, a few of these officials continued to work with La Alameda as advisors after they left office. This is further evidence of the strength of ties between these officials and La Alameda.

> *With Macri, we have tried to collaborate. We have sent more than 200 addresses of workshops that have not been denounced [by the STBA]. ... Nor have they denounced any of the brands that work with those workshops. We have waited a year, patiently, for them to act – the time has already passed by.*[160]

The weakening of linkages with La Alameda meant that the overall political support and operational resources that could be mobilized for enforcement were substantially reduced. Even though inspectors had the same levels of discretion on the street, there was little that they could do to override the will of the political appointees when it came to large campaigns in collaboration with La Alameda. And because the political change also weakened inspectors' linkages, inspectors could no longer use their alliance with La Alameda to muster the backing for strong actions against violators. La Alameda still had the same (if not more) capacity to generate information about violations and to bring attention that could translate into political support, but these resources were now much more difficult for inspectors to mobilize.

Changes in linkages under Macri translated into shifts in enforcement in other industries as well. For example, inspectors had worked with union leaders in the metal industry before Macri came into office. From 2003 to 2005, the STBA responded to leaders from the union (UOM), but also conducted more inspections in the metal sector than there were requests from the union.[161] Even though inspectors sometimes regulated metal firms on their own, they also drew upon the union as a resource for information. The STBA was able to extend its capacity by working with UOM, for which inspection was a *great tool* to be used when employers were recalcitrant.[162] After the election of Macri, STBA inspectors stopped responding to UOM's requests and stopped working with the union. A leader from UOM charged with handling worker problems explains what happened:

> *Now they don't give us any more inspections. Today we have problems because ... it is going to be a year since we put in five requests for inspections and we still haven't gotten any response ... I believe that it was because of the political change, and the change in the management [of the STBA], the two things together ... They closed the door on us.*[163]

UOM was unable to get around political hierarchy to continue with inspections. Enforcement in the industry declined, with inspectors spending their resources on other industries.[164]

---

[160] Interview: B46, La Alameda Foundation, Buenos Aires, 2/23/2009
[161] Auditoria General la Ciudad Buenos Aires 2006
[162] Interview B19, Union Obrera Metalurgica de la Republica Argentina (UOM), Asesor Gremial, Seccion Capital Federal, Buenos Aires, 2/12/2009
[163] Interview B19, Union Obrera Metalurgica de la Republica Argentina (UOM), Asesor Gremial, Seccion Capital Federal, Buenos Aires, 2/12/2009
[164] In the survey of inspectors in 2008, the metal industry did not come close to one of those identified by inspectors as being a focus of enforcement.

Conclusion 143

While it is not surprising that the right-leaning government sought to limit enforcement, the way the limitations developed does not meet the expectation of standard theories. The change was not in the resources allocated, which declined only slightly, leaving the STBA better-equipped than in places where union-allies were in power. Nor was it related to changes in the power of pro-enforcement groups – if anything, La Alameda grew in relevance as its leader, Gustavo Vera, won a place in the legislature of the Federal Capital. Rather, the key change was in the relationship between the state and pro-enforcement groups. The lack of porosity of the bureaucracy to these particular groups limited the ability of unions and other organizations to provide political and material support to inspectors. As a result, the political influence of these groups and the operational capacity of the inspectorate declined simultaneously. Thus, politics of enforcement worked through linkages.

CONCLUSION

Chapters 4 and 5 have analyzed enforcement of labor regulations in four distinct provinces. From the numerous industry-level cases in these provinces, it is clear that enforcement is possible even with flawed bureaucracies. Moreover, differences in the degree or distribution of enforcement cannot be explained with reference only to approximation of the regulatory bureaucracy to the ideal-type. While there was some variation in the traditional features of state capacity – Santa Fe under the PS compared with all other inspectorates that were missing most, if not all, elements of bureaucratic autonomy – detailed examination of the patterns of enforcement in each province reveals variation that cannot be accounted for using dominant theories. Nor was enforcement a simple reflection of the interests of the formal political principals of regulatory bureaucracies. Political support of elected principals was important for enforcement, but not through directing agents who then worked on their own. Instead, political support indirectly influenced enforcement through shaping the porosity of the state to different groups.

To summarize, in Córdoba (when it was under the PJ), Tucumán, and Santa Fe (when it was under the PJ) enforcement was closely tied to union action. Regulators did take steps for enforcement, but this occurred primarily when there was a union with operational and political capacity to make such actions possible. By contrast, regulators in both Santa Fe (under the PS) and the Federal Capital (under the *Alianza*) responded to violations without relying on unions at all. In Santa Fe, enforcement in the construction industry was state-driven, immediately made possible by a reform of the inspectorate that improved administrative resources and introduced some organizational features that could lead to autonomy. In the Federal Capital, the far-reaching campaign in the garment industry is better described as co-produced – regulators worked closely with La Alameda but used their own internal capabilities to go beyond the group's immediate demands. Inspectors in the Federal Capital never enjoyed civil service protection or insulation, but that did not completely block enforcement when there was political support for linkages. These cases of enforcement without traditional bureaucratic reform are theoretically important because they reveal different pathways to enforcement that have been overlooked by the literature.

To identify dimensions of variance of bureaucratic organization and interest group politics obscured by dominant approaches, these chapters have highlighted the key differences in state-society linkages, as well as the administrative resources that were allocated to the inspectorates. Therefore, key to explaining the puzzling differences across cases is accounting for the way politics influences linkage formation and investments in administrative resources. Evidence from all four provinces demonstrates the important role that partisanship played in inspector-union linkages. Both cross-sectional comparisons of provinces and changes within provinces over time reveal that there is a robust relationship between the party in power and the way inspectors work with unions. Moreover, process tracing in each case shows how political appointments enabled linkage formation in all provinces with a union-governor alliance.

The finding that partisanship is central to enforcement is consistent with the broader literature on labor politics in Latin America.[165] By extending this analysis to enforcement, it becomes clear that in many cases linkages with unions were used as a substitute for reform and for investment in administrative resources. Even without investing in administrative resources, political leaders were able to, in some circumstances, use linkages to allow enforcement to be allocated in ways that please specific interest groups. This strategy was unavailable to center-left politicians not aligned with unions. Under these conditions, substantial resources were allocated to inspectorates. To better understand the processes that lead to distinct patterns of enforcement beyond the confines of the particular interest organization of labor politics, the following section of this book turns to environmental regulation.

---

[165] Murillo 2001; Murillo 2005

PART II

ENVIRONMENTAL REGULATION

6

Chaotic environmental regulation in Argentina

The second part of this book shifts from labor to environmental regulation. Over a thirty-year period, Argentina gradually built up a set of institutions to regulate pollution, beginning with the establishment of an environmental secretariat by Perón in 1973; the inclusion of the right to a clean environment in the constitution of 1994; and the General Environmental Law of 2002. These formal institutions, however, had substantial challenges in structuring social and economic activity to foster more sustainable development. Environmental regulatory institutions in Argentina were born weak and did not have the support of electorally relevant organized interests. In some industries, nearly all firms violated environmental laws without any real threat of action. Yet, in other cases, state responses to violations resulted in regulators taking far-reaching steps to give force to regulations. This variation across industry, geography, and time, presents another puzzle of uneven state responses to breakdowns in formal institutions.

This chapter introduces the politics and administrative structures of environmental regulation in Argentina with three main objectives. First, it situates the provincial cases that follow in the national context of policies, environmental organizations, and administrative structures. By doing so, this chapter identifies the sources of institutional weaknesses and maps general arguments about enforcement onto the specifics of environmental politics in Argentina. Within the range of salient environmental policy issues – such as conflicts over mining, forestry, and pesticide use – the focus of the analysis is on regulations that control pollution from industry. These policies are important in their own right, as achieving inclusive and sustainable development requires institutions that can provide the incentives and abilities for firms to improve environmental performance. At the same time, these policies are theoretically useful because they present an opportunity to examine competing explanations for enforcement; there are bureaucracies charged with enforcing regulations that have

147

varying levels of capacity and are operating in the contexts of intense contestation by interest groups. Second, this chapter explicitly places environmental and labor politics in a comparative light in order to highlight this important dimension of variation. While some aspects of environmental regulation are the same as with labor – notably, the very same provincial governments, businesses, and economies are involved – there are many substantial differences. Most important for our analysis, the structure of societal organizations, the lack of partisanship, and the role of the courts and federalism are each distinctive in environmental regulations. These differences provide a way to probe the politics of enforcement beyond what would have been possible if the focus was solely on any one policy area. Third, the chapter sets up the detailed analysis of enforcement politics by previewing the provincial cases that are analyzed in Chapters 7 and 8.

CREATION OF ENVIRONMENTAL REGULATIONS WITHOUT SOCIAL MOBILIZATION

Environmental regulation in Argentina is a case of institutional creation through top-down processes without the support of strong organized interests. For most of the twentieth century, legislation related to environmental issues focused on establishing national parks and managing specific types of natural resources (mining, water, land, etc.), instead of on addressing the environment in an integrated fashion.[1] Argentina began to take the first steps toward creating comprehensive environmental policies in the early 1970s, when international attention turned to environmental issues. Perón launched the first environmental agency, the Secretariat of Natural Resources and the Human Environment (*Secretaría de Recursos Naturales y Ambiente Humano*), in 1973, under the Ministry of Economy. Argentina also became a signatory to many international environmental agreements and established additional laws governing specific environmental issues.[2] Perón's actions to create environmental institutions did not come from domestic social actors pressuring the government or an attempt to gain favor with particular groups. Instead, this development has been attributed to Perón's conforming to broad international trends of creating environmental ministries and policies.[3]

After this initial period, environmental policies were created in a nonlinear process with many stops and starts. There were substantial setbacks during the military dictatorships, and the agency created by Perón was removed in 1976.[4] During the first years after the transition to democracy, there were several proposals for environmental policy reform at the national level, but in

---

[1] For example: Law 13273 "Ley de defensa de la riqueza forestal," 1948. See: Hopkins 1995; Devia, Coria, Flores, Lamas, Nonna, and Villanueva 2008
[2] Hopkins 1995; Acuña 1999 [3] Gutiérrez and Isuani 2014 [4] Hochstetler 2002

Creation of environmental regulations

the context of macroeconomic and political crises, the proposals were not carried through.[5] Beginning in the 1990s, there was an *explosion* of new legislation regulating environmental issues.[6] The hazardous waste law (passed in 1992) was the first national environmental law that went beyond management of natural resources.[7] Also, in 1991, President Carlos Saúl Menem recreated the national environmental agency, the Secretariat of Natural Resources and Environment (*Secretaría de Recursos Naturales y Ambiente*).[8] Although not a full ministry, the Secretariat of Natural Resources and Environment reported directly to the president, placing it near the top of the hierarchy of government agencies. In addition, the Federal Environmental Council (COFEMA, *Consejo Federal de Medio Ambiente*) was established to serve as a space for dialogue and exchange among provincial and federal environmental agencies; the Council was the country's first real attempt to coordinate across levels of government.

Another critically important development that occurred during the 1990s was the inclusion of an environmental clause (Article 41) in the 1994 constitution.[9] Beyond the symbolic significance of enshrining the right to a healthy environment in the constitution, the clause created the conditions for future legislation that could address the barriers of federalism by enabling the federal government to establish minimum environmental standards for all provinces.[10] Although Article 41 gave policy-making power to the federal government, a separate provision, Article 124, gave provincial governments original dominion over natural resources. In effect, the constitution created the ability of the federal government to pass laws, but left the provincial governments responsible for implementing them. The constitution also empowered individuals (and groups) to bring lawsuits on behalf of collective damages created by environmental degradation (Article 43).

The most important legislative barriers to environmental regulation in Argentina were finally overcome when, using the power given to the federal government by the 1994 constitution, Congress passed laws in 2002 mandating

---

[5] Gutiérrez and Isuani 2014   [6] Coria, Devia, Lamas, Nonna, and Villanueva 1998 p. 118

[7] Di Paola 2002a

[8] Hopkins (1995 p. 68) argues that Menem acted primarily in response to an oil spill in Chubut that had very high levels of saliency.

[9] Article 41 of the 1994 constitution states: *All inhabitants are entitled to the right to a healthy and balanced environment fit for human development in order that productive activities shall meet present needs without endangering those of future generations; and shall have the duty to preserve it. As a first priority, environmental damage shall bring about the obligation to repair it according to law. The authorities shall provide for the protection of this right, the rational use of natural resources, the preservation of the natural and cultural heritage and of the biological diversity, and shall also provide for environmental information and education. The Nation shall regulate the minimum protection standards, and the provinces those necessary to reinforce them, without altering their local jurisdictions. The entry into the national territory of present or potential dangerous wastes, and of radioactive ones, is forbidden.*

[10] Sabsay and Di Paola 2002

minimum environmental standards (*presupuestos mínimos*). Though debates over federalism did not end, the minimum standards marked a turning point in environmental policy by formally establishing a floor of regulations that was applicable in the entire country.[11] These laws included the first General Environmental Law of Argentina, as well as a series of laws addressing specific issues, such as managing industrial waste, PCBs, water, public information, and household waste.[12] These laws established the basic institutional framework to regulate pollution at the national level.

As with the creation of the initial environmental agency by Perón, the constitutional clause and subsequent regulatory policies did not have their origins in broad social mobilization. Instead, the constitutional clause was rooted in "efforts of the government ... to adapt to the new normative frameworks and international ideologies" that had formed around environmental protection.[13] Congruently, the passage of environmental regulations was supported by international organizations, such as the Inter-American Development Bank that loaned Argentina 30 million dollars between 1993 and 2000 to build environmental institutions. In some cases, international loans for specific projects, like large infrastructure, were contingent on the creation of environmental regulations that conformed to international standards.[14]

While environmental groups supported the creation of stronger environmental protections, the key group of domestic political actors involved in the passage of the laws in the early 2000s was a small set of political leaders. By all accounts, business, for its part, did not energetically oppose many of the new policies. As long as noncompliance stayed the norm, regulations did not create an immediate cost for business. The main problem created by unenforced laws was "judicial uncertainty;" by operating outside the law, businesses were exposed to the possibility of enforcement. Nevertheless, instead of fighting in the legislature, businesses found it much easier to engage in "quiet politics" and to "neutralize the law during application."[15]

Many of the provincial environmental policies followed similar trajectories as those at the federal level. When provinces were reforming their constitutions after the return to democracy, many (at least eleven) conformed to new international standards and included environmental clauses.[16] Provinces also created their own legislation, often copying federal or international standards. For instance, Córdoba created a Sub-Secretariat of Environmental

---

[11] Schiffrin 2005

[12] Devia, Coria, Flores, Lamas, Nonna, and Villanueva 2008. After this initial burst, additional minimum standards laws were gradually adopted, including a law to protect native forests and a controversial law passed in 2010 to protect glacial areas.

[13] Gutiérrez and Isuani 2014 p. 307

[14] Gutiérrez and Isuani 2014. On "quiet politics," see: Culpepper 2011

[15] Interview: B02, Environment and Natural Resources Foundation, Buenos Aires, 4/7/2009. See Culpepper 2011

[16] Díaz 2009

Creation of environmental regulations 151

Management and, in 1985, passed a General Environmental Law, regulating a broad range of activities.[17] Later on, they "cut and pasted" laws from Spain.[18] Similarly, in Santa Fe, the former head of the provincial regulatory agency noted, "What has happened in Argentina ... is that it is really easy to pass a law. ... Today the Internet even gives us the ability to see and copy whatever are the best laws from the United States Environmental Protection Agency or the European Union. ... This is a defect in our regulatory framework. ... In some cases Argentina has stricter rules than the EU and USA."[19] In a similar statement, an official in an environmental agency from Corrientes stated that the law of environmental impact assessments (EIA) "was practically copied from what was one of the first environmental impact laws in Spain."[20] Provinces were able to conform to international and federal norms with little cost, as long as they controlled enforcement. The lack of expectations of true implementation meant that the legislation would often go unopposed and not fully debated.[21]

Put in comparative context, some of the attributes of the formation of environmental institutions in Argentina are typical of middle-income and developing countries. One of the central mechanisms in the creation of environmental institutions around the world was the diffusion of institutional blueprints promoted by the international community; many countries formed environmental agencies in the 1970s that were influenced by the example of the Environmental Protection Agency (EPA) in the United States.[22] For example, Brazil created the Special Secretariat for the Environment in 1973 that was modeled, in part, on the US EPA.[23] It was often the case, however, that top-down processes were substantially supported and modified by domestic activists and grassroots organizations that were decisive in determining how the global blueprints were translated to domestic institutions. This was the case in Brazil, where policy agendas were shaped by domestic environmentalists, who, often working within the government, were engaged in "guerilla activity" to advance their agendas.[24] Similar processes played out in Bolivia, Chile, and Peru, although the timing was different across these countries.[25] In many cases, there were social networks that bridged state bureaucracies and environmental organizations, giving individuals substantial opportunities for shaping policy.

---

[17] Interview: C23, Former Official, Córdoba Environmental Protection Agency, Córdoba, 6/3/2009
[18] Interview: C21, Center for Human Rights and the Environmental (CEDAH), Córdoba, 3/20/2009
[19] Interview: B12, Senior Official, Santa Fe Environmental Secretariat, Buenos Aires, 5/26/2009
[20] Interview: CR8, Corrientes Water and Environmental Agency, Corrientes, 9/12/2008. These laws were adopted as "window dressing" to comply with the requirements of international finance organizations Levitsky and Murillo 2009.
[21] Interview: T10, Cleaner Production Center, Tucumán, 11/11/2008
[22] Frank, Hironaka, and Schofer 2000   [23] McAllister 2008
[24] Hochstetler and Keck 2007 p. 29   [25] Steinberg 2001; Orihuela 2014

In Argentina, by contrast, environmental activists and their organizations tended to be detached from state structures during the creation of key institutions. While the first environmental agency was established in Brazil in 1973, an environmental activist was put at the helm. In Argentina, it took 33 years for the first (and only) person affiliated with the environmental movement, Romina Picolotti, to be selected to lead the environmental agency (and she was not a central figure in many of the most important domestic environmental organizations). In addition, it was not until the mobilizations of the mid-2000s, for policies like the Native Forest Law and the Law to Protect Glaciers, that environmental organizations had a substantial impact on state policy.[26]

These features of a relatively top-down process of policy formation not only contrasted with the histories of similarly situated countries, but also were markedly different from labor politics in Argentina. As described in Chapter 3, labor laws were created with the explicit intention of building a coalition with masses of workers who were entering the political arena. The more recent labor reforms that took place after the return to democracy involved political contestation that pitted powerful unions against political incumbents. The debates in the 1990s and early 2000s were highly salient, and laws were kept in place, or strengthened, largely due to union power. Also, unlike the supportive role of international organizations in strengthening environmental institutions, international organizations recommended the dismantling of labor laws.

In sum, these politics of environmental policy-making have direct implications for the ways in which political institutions became weak, and inform our analysis of competing theories of enforcement. Environmental regulatory institutions were born weak, largely because they were created through institutional borrowing and did not reflect the *de facto* distribution of power at the time of creation. The pronounced form of the top-down institutional development meant that environmental regulations were created without any mass of support that could hold politicians accountable for implementation. Therefore, expectations from standard bureaucratic control theories suggest that enforcement of environmental regulation should be less likely than enforcement of labor regulation. Moreover, compared with other countries in the region, Argentina did not have the thick networks between parts of the state responsible for environmental regulation and societal organizations that were forged during policy-making. Therefore, the opportunities for technical (apolitical) ties between the state and environmental groups were diminished, creating further challenges for enforcement. To gain a better understanding of the role of environmental groups in the politics of enforcement, the next section turns to the environmental movement.

---

[26] Brailovsky and Foguelman 1991, see: Chapter 6; Gutiérrez and Isuani 2014

The environmental movement

THE ENVIRONMENTAL MOVEMENT

The environmental movement took shape in Argentina primarily after the return to democracy in the 1980s and 1990s. Before this period, there had been some organizations dedicated to wildlife protection, nature, and conservation, but they were not templates for most of the organizations that would follow (and eventually become the primary protagonists).[27] According to one of the early leaders of the movement, only "after the fall of the military government and the beginning of democracy" was there a "boom" and a "spectacular emergence of NGOs."[28] There are no good estimates of the exact number of environmental organizations that became active in Argentina, but there was clearly a "boom" with hundreds, if not thousands, of organizations being founded across the country.[29] By the mid-2000s, approximately 1.7% of the public reported being active members in environmental organizations, and 55% of the public reported that they had confidence in the environmental protection movement, placing Argentina in the middle of countries ranked in terms of participation and perception of organized environmentalism.[30] Unlike in other countries in the region, such as Brazil and Bolivia, environmental issues in Argentina did not draw much international attention; as a result, there is little question that the protagonists of the movement were primarily domestic.[31] The patchwork of environmental organizations grew to be extremely heterogeneous in its bases of support, modes of action, and organizational structures.[32]

---

[27] Some early organizations were: Asociación Ornitológica del Plata founded in 1916 and Asociación de Amigos de los Parques Nacionales founded in the 1940s. In the 1960s, there was the *Fundación Bariloche* that gained international prominence through the creation of the Latin American Model that recast the influential Limits to Growth model. One of the first environmental NGO to focus on both conservation and social issues, *Fundación Vida Silvestre Argentina* formed in 1977, was the only major organization founded during the military dictatorship. Aguilar 2002 See also: *La Nación* "25 años en favor del medio ambiente" 12/22/2002. See also Gutiérrez and Isuani 2014

[28] Interview: C24, Environmental Defense Foundation, Córdoba, 3/5/2009

[29] Data from a survey of civil society associations conducted in 2004 indicated that 5% of the approximately 100,000 civil society organizations reported working on environmental issues. See: Luna and Cecconi 2004

[30] Source: Author analysis of World Values Survey data from 2005 to 2009. For participation, although Argentina is near the middle of the ranking, the worldwide average for active membership is substantially higher, 8% of population. For perception of environmentalists, 6.5% report having a "great deal" and 48.5% "quite a lot" of confidence in the environmental movement. While 32.9% report having "not very much at all" and 10.4% "none at all." Compared to the world average, Argentines approximate the averages, but are somewhat more skeptical of the environmental movement.

[31] While recent accounts of environmental movements in Latin America have gone to length to correct dominant accounts that focused only on international actors, there are no such debates about the Argentine movement. See: Steinberg 2001; Hochstetler and Keck 2007

[32] This is typical of Latin America. See: Christen, Herculano, Hochstetler, Prell, Price, and Robberts 1998

154   *Chaotic environmental regulation in Argentina*

For analytical purposes, it is helpful to identify two ideal types of environmental organizations around which many groups cluster.[33] Each type has different capabilities and repertoires of political action. One type is the professional organization, which tends to have staff (or members) who are highly educated elites. Professional environmental organizations have the capability to take cases to court and to conduct scientific analyses of environmental problems. One example is the Environmental and Natural Resources Foundation (*Fundación Ambiente y Recursos Naturales*, FARN), founded in 1985, which has played an important role in the development of Argentine environmental policy and jurisprudence. Based in the Federal Capital, FARN has a paid staff of professionals, a board of directors, and a number of volunteers (who are often college or law students from the United States).[34] To support its activities, FARN raises money from members, international organizations, and foundations, such as the Ford Foundation and the William and Flora Hewlett Foundation. Two of FARN's key roles have been to lobby Congress for stronger environmental legislation at the national level and to conduct legal research to inform policy. In addition, FARN has continually run courses in environmental law, training students, judges, and government officials. Starting in 1994, FARN published an environmental law supplement to the periodical *La Ley*, which in its first year reached over 10,000 lawyers throughout the country. Finally, through its legal clinic, FARN gives legal aid to groups that take environmental issues to court. Combined, this set of capabilities has made FARN one of the more formidable players in Argentine environmental politics at the national level.

A second ideal type of organization is the small, neighborhood group that becomes involved in environmental issues at the local level. Such groups did not surge to prominence until after 2003, when a series of high-level conflicts brought them into contact with the state.[35] Neighborhood organizations are often primarily not concerned with environmental issues; rather they respond to pressing environmental matters in their community. These groups lack the human and financial capital of the professional organizations and must depend on government actors, such as *Defensores del Pueblo*, or professional environmental organizations to take cases to court. Some groups also lack formal organizational structures and fashion themselves as "self-convening" (*autoconvocados*), implying that they have no institutional interests (e.g., they do not need to raise money to perpetuate themselves and will disband when the problem is solved). Despite their organizational weaknesses, neighborhood

---

[33] For a similar classification, see: Gutiérrez and Isuani 2014
[34] Its staff included high influential figures in the Argentine legal community. For example, in a poll conducted of lawyers to determine candidates to the Supreme Court in 2003, FARN's former director, Daniel Alberto Sabsay, was the favorite. *La Nación* "Sabsay y Kemelmajer, preferidos" 07/06/2003
[35] Gutiérrez and Isuani 2014

The environmental movement

groups often have greater capacity than professional environmental organizations to mobilize protests, and, in the eyes of politicians and courts, tend to have more legitimacy. As a result, while neighborhood groups are not at the forefront of policy research or lobbying Congress, they have played a key role in demanding implementation of environmental regulations in the courts and the streets.

The La Boca Neighborhood Association (*Asociación Vecinos La Boca*), also in the Federal Capital, is an example of a small, neighborhood environmental organization. When it was founded in 1997, the La Boca Neighborhood Association did not organize around environmental issues.[36] Instead, the primary concerns of its founders were typical issues of a working-class urban neighborhood: crime, education, and public health. These issues, as a leader from the association explained, led them to taking on problems of environmental contamination in the Riachuelo River:

The area by the Riachuelo River was a beachhead for criminals because, just as the river was degraded, the properties by the river were degraded and criminals occupied and lived in them. The hospital was collapsing due to its proximity to the river ... The schools are in the same neighborhood, and with their closeness to the river they were run down. Everything was happening in the riverfront, making it the center [of the problems]. We said: "Enough. We are going to get ourselves involved in this [problem]. Enough with working on individual issues." It was this way that we started working on environmental issues.[37]

The La Boca Neighborhood Association had an extremely limited budget, supported by dues of approximately twenty members who paid three dollars per month. Yet, the group was surprisingly effective in promoting implementation of environmental laws in the Riachuelo. After years of campaigning with little success, in 2005 the Association came in contact with the *Defensores del Pueblo* of the Federal Capital and Nation, as well as with a number of professional environmental organizations (including FARN). With their help, a case from the community made it all the way to the Supreme Court.[38] In the effort to enforce regulations that followed, the La Boca Neighborhood Association was a key societal actor. Although not many organizations make it to the Supreme Court, the La Boca Neighborhood Association is typical in terms of its small size, limited resources, local focus, and its ability to gain allies with technical expertise.

The different modes of political action and capabilities of professional and small neighborhood organizations provide a source of variation that can distinguish among political processes that shape enforcement. If enforcement

---

[36] The Association was founded in 1997, but it was not until 2000 that it registered to get *personaría juridical*, which enables organizations to take cases to court.

[37] Interview: B24, "La Boca" Neighborhood Association, Buenos Aires, 10/4/2008

[38] *Página/12* "Un fallo para salvar el Riachuelo" 06/21/2006

156   *Chaotic environmental regulation in Argentina*

politics occurs mainly through formal participatory structures that favor expertise over capabilities to mobilize protests, differences in enforcement should be better explained by the actions and density of professional organizations than by those of neighborhood organizations. Similarly, if networks formed around professional communities with more technical than political content, the actions of professional organizations should dominate. By contrast, if the informal and highly political ties to the state are required for enforcement, then the actions of small neighborhood organizations with the capacities to protest should influence more than those of professional organizations. The only strategies that the two types of organizations occasionally share are the use of the courts and alliances with Defensores del Pueblo; thus, we cannot use differences between these types of groups to gain analytical traction on the importance of these two institutional means of influencing enforcement.

Notwithstanding heterogeneity in the environmental movement, it has several general features that contrast with those of the labor movement in Argentina. These differences provide additional opportunities to probe competing explanations for enforcement as well as the scope conditions of the argument. First, environmental groups are highly pluralistic, not corporatist; in any given locality, or around any given issue, multiple environmental groups can be active simultaneously, and there is no state regulatory agency that determines which organization can represent a particular issue (as the Ministry of Labor does for unions). The only type of government oversight of environmental organizations is not mandatory or onerous – many groups apply for legal incorporation (*personaría jurídica*) to have standing in court.

Second, environmental groups do not have a formal hierarchical confederation as do labor unions in the CGT. When environmental organizations collaborate, they are most often structured by relatively horizontal partnerships, federations, or networks. At the national level, there are a number of networks of organizations. For instance, in 1984 groups formed the National Network for Ecological Action (*Red Nacional de Acción Ecologista*) that, over the years, waxed and waned in importance.[39] At the provincial level, there are additional federations, such as the Federation of Environmental Non-governmental Organizations of Tucumán, (*Federación de Organizaciones Ambientales No Gubernamentales de Tucumán*), formed in 1987, which brings together professional associations and environmental groups. However, because these environmental federations lack the hierarchy of national or provincial labor confederations, there are fewer possibilities of collective action at a large scale and also less of a possibility that one group could prevent others from taking action. This pluralist structure might have weakened the environmental movement in some ways by not providing the inducements for

---

[39] Interview: C24, Environmental Defense Foundation, Córdoba, 3/5/2009

creating and sustaining large organizations, but it also prevented the state from easily taking control of environmental organizations.

Third, the environmental organizations that formed in Argentina did so without any attachment to a particular political party; instead, most went out of their way to avoid partisan alliances. When the movement began to take shape in the 1980s, environmental issues were not a central cleavage point in electoral politics. None of the major political parties in Argentina had (or has) a reputation for being more pro-environmental than the others. There is Green Party, founded in 2006 by the former Minister of Environment of the Federal Capital, but it is extremely small and includes only a handful of active politicians.[40] Unlike labor unions, most environmental organizations tend to cautiously guard their independence and avoid entanglement with any political party.[41] When they have directly engaged in electoral politics (as groups did in Santa Fe and Córdoba) it has been to invite candidates of all parties either to clearly state their positions or to sign a statement documenting their commitment to environmental issues. The distance between environmental organizations and party politics precluded the types of partisan exchanges behind the formation of linkages between the state and unions that are found in many of the labor cases. Therefore, environmental regulation provides the possibility to examine distinct mechanisms of linkage formation (such as the one observed in the Federal Capital garment case).

In sum, the environmental movement was highly pluralistic and heterogeneous. Organizations did not, for the most part, align with any one party nor did they play a major role in electoral politics. Nevertheless, environmental groups used a variety of tactics to promote environmental protection – some groups took to the courts and the streets, while others conducted studies, lobbied the government, and provided legal support. Each of these strategies has the potential to promote enforcement under different sets of political conditions. If state bureaucrats are responsive to technically trained groups that lobby for programmatic policy shifts (either through formal channels or technical networks), professional organizations should be able to influence enforcement. If state bureaucrats are responsive to social mobilization using informal channels of pressure and grassroots monitoring of pollution, community organizations should have a greater influence on enforcement.

ENVIRONMENTAL ADMINISTRATION – WEAK AND DECENTRALIZED

The provincial governments that had the primary responsibility for enforcement operated in the context of federal and municipal governments that could

---

[40] Interview: B44, Green Party, Buenos Aires, 10/9/2008
[41] Based on interviews with scores of leaders from environmental organizations in 2008 and 2009

indirectly influence implementation. While the constitution of 1994 made it clear that the role of the federal government was to create a policy floor (*presupestos mínimos*) and that the provinces had enforcement jurisdiction, the constitution and the following laws left many jurisdictional issues unclear and did not fully specify the roles of different levels of government.[42] At the local level, municipal governments in many provinces had the responsibility to control land use and sanitation, potentially giving them the opportunity to intervene in environmental controversies. Municipal governments, however, often lacked the authority and ability to implement pollution control regulations.[43] As a result, for pollution control from industries, the most relevant agencies sat in the provincial governments that were formally tasked with enforcing the minimum standards set by national law (and any provincial laws that went above those standards). Political leaders from municipalities could leverage their positions to pressure provinces, but these actions happened outside of standard administrative channels.

At the federal level, the environmental agency had a series of organizational shortcomings that, on top of jurisdictional restrictions, limited its action. For example, when a federal hazardous waste law was adopted, the Secretariat of Natural Resources and the Environment did not have any staff trained to enforce the law and, even more crucially, there was no facility in Argentina that could receive and process the waste in a way that met the legal standards.[44] Moreover, under the Menem presidency, the federal agency was plagued by corruption at the highest levels of the agency.[45] In 1999, the Secretariat of Natural Resources and Environment was demoted and moved under the Ministry of Social Development.[46] Staff were scattered in the new Ministry and many well-trained officials left the state, further compromising the federal government's ability to implement policies.[47] Under Kirchner, the agency stabilized, but it always remained understaffed, with an extremely limited budget, and open to political influence. These problems are typical of environmental agencies in middle-income and developing countries, which

---

[42] World Bank 1995; Bertonatti and Corcuera 2000; Di Paola 2002a; Nonna 2002

[43] Municipal governments were much more important in sanitation and household waste issues. See: Gutiérrez 2012

[44] World Bank 1995 p. 68; Coria, Devia, Lamas, Nonna, and Villanueva 1998 p. 275

[45] In 1998, the Inter-American Development Bank (IDB) gave a 250 million dollar loan to Argentina to clean up the Riachuelo. Investigations of the Secretary of Environment Alsogaray revealed that much of this money was effectively embezzled through fraudulent contracts. As a result, Argentina was fined 6 million dollars by the IDB. *Página/12* "La Plata es lo de Menos" 01/03/2000; "Amenazan con denunciar al Estado por la contaminación del Riachuelo" 12/05/2003; "Riachuelos de lágrimas" 08/16/2003. She was convicted for corruption involving privatization of the telephone company Entel and for various actions as Secretary of Environment. On her arrest and conviction: *Página/12* "Coleccionista de juicios" 08/08/2003; "María Julia está a punto de mudarse" 08/08/2003 "Una prueba de que el dinero no hace la felicidad" 05/22/2004.

[46] Hochstetler 2003   [47] Espach 2009 p. 67

Environmental administration – weak and decentralized

often have bureaucrats who are poorly paid, suffer from corruption, and lack training or equipment.[48]

Notwithstanding jurisdictional limitations due to federalism and organizational weaknesses, the national government had three channels through which it could play a role in enforcement. First, federal courts and prosecutors could directly intervene in implementation. When Argentina created a constitutional right to a clean environment and created federal laws of minimum standards, individuals and organizations gained standing to appeal to federal courts. As a result, there was a substantial increase in judicial involvement and a series of cases in federal courts in which individuals, organizations, and governments took action against individual polluters or governments that were responsible for implementation. In some cases, courts have used this jurisdiction to order firms and governments to alter their practices.[49] In this sense, the courts could circumvent authority of provincial governments to implement federal and local laws. There were, however, many instances in which court orders were ignored or implementation was problematic. As one environmental lawyer explained, "the sentence can solve part of the problem; afterwards the issue remains under the discretion of politics."[50] Thus, courts created a channel by which actors could exert pressure on firms and regulators, but judicial decisions were often not sufficient to make enforcement occur.

One landmark case, mentioned previously, was the Supreme Court ruling that the government of the province of Buenos Aires and the Federal Capital had failed to implement environmental policies in the Matanza-Riachuelo watershed. The court's ruling required that the responsible governments take a wide range of projects to clean up pollution, improve infrastructure, and relocate slums along waterways. The court also ordered the implementation of regulations controlling pollution in the hundreds of firms that operate in the watershed. To respond, the federal and provincial agencies created an interjurisdictional initiative called the Matanza-Riachuelo Watershed Authority (ACUMAR, *Autoridad de Cuenca Matanza Riachuelo*).[51] While this entity was overseen, in part, by the courts, the judicial system could not guarantee timely implementation. The real power to act on a day-to-day basis and implement regulations was located in the governments of the Federal Capital, the province of Buenos Aires, and the federal Environmental Secretariat. After years of building up capabilities and hundreds of millions of dollars of

---

[48] Dwivedi and Vajpeyi 1995; Hettige, Huq, Pargal, and Wheeler 1996; McAllister 2008; Henry 2010

[49] Di Paola 2006

[50] Interview: C21, Center for Human Rights and the Environmental (CEDAH), Córdoba, 3/20/2009

[51] Inspections by the Environmental Secretariat increased from an average of approximately 100 per year from 2003 to 2005, to 464 in 2007, and 598 in 2008. Source: Response of Environmental Secretariat to information request from researcher

support from international organizations, compliance with the order of the Supreme Court was partial. While the court's decisions triggered a wide range of important moves, such as the development of capacities to assist firms in upgrading their production systems, enforcement remained highly dependent on political support and capabilities of regulatory agencies.[52] In sum, the courts were a potential point of power by actors looking to circumvent the administrative process and demand action by governments, but the courts were not a substitute for regulatory agencies; in many cases, the tasks of implementation still needed to be taken by administrative agents who were out of the direct control of the courts and often lacked the capabilities to follow through on court orders.

Second, there were some pockets of capabilities in the federal environmental agency that developed at the end of the 1990s and could provide support for provincial governments. One of the few initiatives touted by officials as successful was the Cleaner Production Program (PPL, *Plan de Producción Más Limpia*). In September 1999, officials from the Department of Technology, Processes and Environmental Services (*Dirección de Tecnología, Procesos y Servicios Ambientales*) joined the Industrial Union of Argentina (*Union Industrial Argentina,* UIA) and the Argentine Council for International Relations to organize a seminar in green-upgrading in industry.[53] The meeting brought together international experts, governmental officials, firms and environmental groups to lay the groundwork for a series of projects, supported by the federal government, to help firms adopt cleaner production practices. The first pilot began in the province of Salta in 2000, and the first large program was launched in Tucumán in 2002.[54] These projects created spaces for collaboration between industry and regulators to identify technological processes and managerial programs that would improve environmental and economic performance. Similar programs were started in countries around the world and were heavily promoted by the United Nations Environment Programme. Although PPL did not bolster the punitive side of enforcement, it became one of the primary ways by which the federal government could foster improvement in industries through collaborative efforts. The primary role of the federal government was to support and advise provincial governments, as well as to provide credit for firms to improve their processes – federal officials could not force provincial authorities to take specific actions.

---

[52] FARN, "El Plan de Saneamiento del Riachuelo a Sies Años del Histórico Fallo de la Corte," July 8, 2014. See also: Gutiérrez and Isuani 2014

[53] Dirección de Tecnología, Procesos y Servicios Ambientales, de la Secretaría de Recursos Naturales y Desarrollo Sustentable, Secretaría de Ambiente y Desarollo Sustentable. "*Seminario Internacional Sobre Producción Limpia.*" Buenos Aires, 1999

[54] Interview: B28, Federal Secretariat of Environment and Sustainable Development, Buenos Aires, 9/22/2008

Environmental administration – weak and decentralized 161

Third, while jurisdictional constraints precluded the national-level environmental agencies from becoming directly involved in many issues surrounding enforcement, there were some national-level controversies that influenced provincial-level debates over pollution, even if there was no formal political power by which the federal government could intervene. One of the most important conflicts in the 2000s was triggered by the construction of a paper mill in Uruguay, dubbed "Botnia." The mill was built across the River Paraná and the Argentine city of Gualeguaychú in Entre Rios province, with international capital and financial support from the World Bank's International Finance Corporation. In response to the threat of water contamination, a series of community groups formed that eventually led to the Gualeguaychú Environmental Assembly (*Asamblea Ambiental de Gualeguaychú*). This organization mobilized massive protests that took the Argentine environmental movement to new levels.[55] In April of 2005, an estimated 40,000 people marched on the international bridge connecting Argentina and Uruguay to protest the construction of a paper mill.[56] The bridge – one of the most important land routes between Argentina and Uruguay – was blockaded for long periods of time, sometimes lasting more than forty days. The protesters generated so much attention that in May 2006 President Néstor Kirchner held a rally in Gualeguaychú to support the Gualeguaychú Environmental Assembly, which was attended by nineteen governors, all of Kirchner's cabinet, and 35,000 people.[57] And in December 2007, the first major protests about environmental contamination took place in the symbolically important Plaza de Mayo in Buenos Aires.

For a period of time, Botnia moved environmental issues from the margins to the center of the political agenda. Many players involved in environmental politics understood that if the movement turned inward toward Argentine firms, such as the paper mills located on the very same river and just as polluting as Botnia, Néstor Kirchner's government would be facing a major problem. To stave off this possibility, Kirchner replaced the Secretary of Environment, Atilio Savino,[58] with Romina Picolotti, a lawyer who was representing the assembly of residents of Gualeguaychú in international tribunals in The Hague.[59]

---

[55] For a journalistic account, see: Toller, Verónica. *Daños Colaterales: Papeleras, Contaminación y Resistencia en el Río Uruguay*, Editorial Marea, Buenos Aires, 2009.

[56] *Página/12* "Una marcha rioplatense" 05/02/2005

[57] *Página/12* "Es una cuestión ambiental que atañe a todo el país" 05/06/2006. Days later, during a photo session of heads of state attending the European Union-Latin American summit in Vienna, the queen of the carnival in Gualeguaychú surprised the delegation in her carnival costume with a sign protesting Botnia. *Página/12* "Mueva, mueva, mueva, no a las papeleras" 05/12/2006

[58] Atilio Savino was not supported by environmental organizations when he was appointed and had an extremely quiet three-year tenure in which he barely had a presence in policy debates. *Página/12* "Medio Ambiente" 09/12/2003; "La Deuda Ambiental" 07/06/2006

[59] *Página/12* "Vos hacé lo que tengas que hacer" 06/28/2006; "Desde una ONG a La Haya" 06/28/2006. *La Nación* "Kirchner nombró a una nueva secretaria de Medio Ambiente" 07/17/2006. *La Nación* "Llega al Gobierno una enemiga de las papeleras" 07/28/2006

Picolotti was the president of the Center for Human Rights and Environment (CEDAH, *Centro de Derechos Humanos y Ambiente*), which she co-founded in 1999 after working in Washington, D.C. as a human rights lawyer. Although Picolotti had become a key figure in the Botnia conflict, she was somewhat unknown in the broader Argentine environmental movement and in national politics. If Kirchner wanted to co-opt the environmental movement through Picolotti, he was mistaken; though Picolotti maintained support of the principal groups involved in the Botnia conflict, most major environmental organizations saw her as an outsider and never endorsed her.[60]

Picolotti's two-year tenure as Secretary of Environment was marked by controversy.[61] The international conflict over Botnia continued, mostly outside of the primary competency of Picolotti. Ultimately, Picolotti was forced out at the end of 2008 amidst accusations of corruption and mismanagement.[62] Nevertheless, during her tenure, Picolotti was a visible official in the Kirchner administration, advocating for a variety of environmental policies, including stronger enforcement both generally and specifically in the Matanza-Riachuelo watershed – a much different role from that of other Secretaries of Environment, who generally kept lower profiles. Thus, the controversy of Botnia indirectly (and temporarily) amplified efforts of the national environmental agency to put political pressure on various other government actors to improve implementation.

The analysis of the regulatory institutions reveals three features of enforcement politics. First, the federal and municipal parts of the state apparatus do not have direct control over enforcement of industrial pollution in most circumstances – this power was squarely held by the provinces. Second, federal agencies meant to implement environmental policy under certain jurisdictions were chronically under-resourced, were internally incoherent, and lacked political autonomy. These attributes of the federal regulatory apparatus are typical of many countries and contrast with the exceptional countries, like Brazil, that formed pockets of strong central bureaucracies capable of leveraging their autonomy for enforcement.[63] Third, despite the many constraints, federal actors could intervene in provincial enforcement politics indirectly. The federal

---

[60] Interviews with multiple environmental organizations. See also: *La Nación* "Algunos asambleístas respaldaron a Picolotti y otros celebraron su salida" 12/03/2008

[61] *La Nación* "De defensora de los asambleístas, a cuestionada por su gestión" 12/02/2008; *Página/12* "No le quedó ni un cuarto de ambiente" 12/03/2008; "La secretaria antiBotnia" 12/03/2008; "Ambiente caldeado" 12/03/2008; *Clarín* "Al final, la Presidenta echó a la secretaria de Ambiente" 12/03/2008.

[62] Picolotti was replaced by Homero Bilboni, who had a much lower profile. Bilboni was fired in 2010, presumably for failing to manage the clean-up in the Riachuelo. He was replaced by Juan José Mussi in 2010, who was known primarily for his loyalty to President Cristina Fernandez de Kirchner, not his credentials in environmental issues. *La Nación* "La Presidenta sumó a Mussi al Gabinete" 12/29/2010

[63] McAllister 2008

Provincial pathways to enforcement

government could provide resources (such as supporting PPL), exercise some power through court rulings, and place informal pressure on provincial governments. That said, the levers of the federal government were far from sufficient for enforcement and required political action through provincial governments.

PROVINCIAL PATHWAYS TO ENFORCEMENT[64]

To understand enforcement and the uneven state in environmental regulation, we need to turn our attention to variation at the provincial level. Not surprisingly, given the lack of strong coordinating institutions, there was tremendous variation across provinces in environmental administration. Even the basic structures of administration differed tremendously; for example, some provinces created a Ministry of Environment (e.g., Misiones), while others created sub-departments under a water authority (e.g., Santiago del Estero) or the Ministry of Development and Production (e.g., Tucumán). In addition, there was substantial variation in political factors, such as the structure and strength of environmental groups. For example, Córdoba had approximately 575 civil society organizations that addressed environmental concerns, compared with 190 in Santa Fe and 106 in Tucumán.[65] Moreover, there were substantial differences in the attributes of the economy that might make compliance costly (or enhance the power of business in resisting regulation); some provinces depended on polluting and heavily concentrated industries, while others had more diversified economies. Variation across provinces in key explanatory factors is methodologically important because it can be used to contrast alternative explanations of enforcement, all within the same context of weak institutions.

No comprehensive data on the necessary variables exist at a national (or even regional) level, making it impossible to analyze all provinces. Instead, we will need to focus our attention on the case-study provinces – Santa Fe, Córdoba, and Tucumán – where it is possible to construct detailed accounts. In this section, I briefly describe the empirical findings that will be developed more completely in Chapters 7 and 8.[66]

The provinces of Santa Fe and Córdoba are cases of society-dependent enforcement. In both provinces, inspectors had some of the formal organizational trappings of a Weberian bureaucracy – civil service protection, professional training – but the agencies were understaffed, with only a handful of inspectors to cover thousands of industrial firms. With few resources,

---

[64] The cases of Santa Fe and Tucumán were also analyzed in: Amengual 2013

[65] Luna and Cecconi 2004. Normalized by population (organizations per 10,000 residents), Córdoba had 1.73, Santa Fe 0.59, and Tucumán 0.73.

[66] The Federal Capital is not included because of the complications due to overlapping jurisdiction in the Riachuelo watershed.

TABLE 6.1 *Summary of Provincial Cases*

Province	Córdoba	Santa Fe	Tucumán
Administrative resources	Low	Low	Low → High
Civil service protection in regulatory bureaucracy	Strong	Strong	Strong → Weak
Density of professional environmental organizations	High	Medium	Low
Linkage structure	Ties to select neighborhood groups	Ties to select neighborhood groups	Ties to select neighborhood groups and industry
Enforcement pattern	Society-dependent	Society-dependent	State-driven → Co-produced
Level of enforcement in specific industry	Medium for single firms (e.g., tannery), low for industry more broadly	Medium for single firms (e.g., agro-industry), low for industry more broadly	Low → High in sugar and citrus industries

regulators were able to gather compliance information only on an extremely small set of firms; when regulators identified violations, in most cases they were unable to make penalties stick due to resistance by power businesses that could evade them. The lack of systematic enforcement across a broad set of industries is not surprising considering the constraints and the general weakness of state institutions.

Yet, even under these conditions, enforcement did occur in both provinces. For example, in Santa Fe, regulators made a substantial effort to enforce pollution rules violated by an agro-industrial plant. Inspectors collected consistent information about air and water pollution, and the plant eventually made substantial investments in pollution-control technologies. Enforcement in this case was made possible by a mobilized community group that put pressure on the plant and developed linkages with regulators. Through these linkages, the neighborhood group was able to extend operationally the surveillance capability of the regulators and to put political pressure directly on street-level agents charged with enforcement. This particular agro-industrial plant was not the only instance of such mobilization and enforcement – in both provinces, there was a broader pattern of society-dependent enforcement that occurred across a number of industries and localities.

Provincial pathways to enforcement

These cases hold a number of key findings. First, they show, once again, how enforcement is possible without traditional features of a strong state. The most salient feature of state responses to violations was its unevenness, not its absence. Second, it demonstrates society-dependent enforcement beyond the dynamic of partisan politics identified in the labor cases. Linkages clearly mattered, as not all groups were able to influence enforcement. Those that could, employed strategies that created ties with regulators and, through these ties, shared information with officials and politically influenced the regulatory process. Notably, professional environmental organizations in both provinces were unable to form linkages with regulators in the way that neighborhood organizations could. Third, when put in comparative context with the analysis of labor politics, the similarities between these two cases suggest that enforcement politics are not reducible to the overall political dynamics of the provinces. Notably, the reforms in Santa Fe's Ministry of Labor that led away from society-dependent enforcement did not occur in environmental regulation.

While the patterns of enforcement in Santa Fe and Córdoba held steady in the post-crisis period, in Tucumán the pattern of enforcement shifted dramatically, illustrating a case of transition to co-produced enforcement. This outcome is particularly puzzling because, compared with Santa Fe and Córdoba, Tucumán has relatively lower levels of socioeconomic development, a smaller number of professional environmental organizations, and the two most important industries in the province have characteristics that make environmental regulation potentially costly (highly polluting commodities, and in the case of citrus, competition in international markets). Moreover, as illustrated in Chapter 4, the labor regulatory bureaucracy in Tucumán was mired with corruption and political influence. There was no provincial-level push toward good government indicating that a reform in environmental administration would be possible. All of these factors lead to the expectation, according to conventional analyses, that enforcing environmental regulations would be more unlikely in Tucumán than in Santa Fe or Córdoba.

In fact, for many years, all sugar mills and citrus processing plants polluted with near impunity. Regulators could gather information about violations, but they could do little about it. Inevitably, they would be blocked at some stage by firms with political and economic strength to prevent regulators from issuing fines or shutting down operations. There were environmental groups that could potentially have been allies to regulators and support enforcement, but they lacked linkages to the state. A series of shocks beginning in 2001 – which included the activation of courts, pressure from the neighboring province of Santiago del Estero, and protests against pollution – changed the relationship between regulators, environmental groups, and businesses. Bureaucrats slowly were able to establish linkages with environmental groups that earlier would have been politically untenable. In addition to developing linkages, the regulatory agency gained administrative resources through the creation of plans for cleaner production. The bureaucracy did not, however, become autonomous. If anything, as time went on, bureaucrats were more exposed to outside pressures because newly hired staff had short-term contracts and no civil service protection.

Conventional theories would expect little change in enforcement because without establishing some form of autonomy, or at least a strong enough organization to respond to hierarchical control, there would be no way these bureaucrats could resist the influence of powerful firms that sought to avoid enforcement. Contrary to these expectations, enforcement increased to high levels in these two industries. For the first time, regulators were able temporarily to shut down firms that were intransigent, and regulators used combinations of advice, sanctions, and joint problem-solving to find ways to reduce pollution. The resulting pattern was co-produced enforcement, made possible by tight interactions between regulators and a variety of organizations and administrative resources within the state.

The case of environmental regulation in Tucumán reveals an alternative pathway to enforcement. Once again, enforcement became possible without standard reforms to increase state capacity. In this case, the pattern of enforcement shifted as regulators gained resources and established ties with various groups in society that could further the operational capabilities of the state while exercising political influence. This finding suggests that the patterns of enforcement identified in Argentina are not self-reinforcing equilibria, but are instead susceptible to change when there are shifts in informal ties between state and society. While the process of linkage formation (mobilization by neighborhood organizations) was similar in Tucumán as in other cases, the increases in administrative resources were not. In Tucumán, two decisive factors – activation of the courts and the provision of resources by the federal government – contributed to the increased administrative resources necessary for co-production. Although this process was substantially different from those observed in the cases of labor regulation, it shared one key similarity; namely, linkage formation was not a viable political substitution for the allocation of administrative resources to address mobilization.

CONCLUSION

Environmental politics provides another opportunity to explore the central question of this book: what explains variation in enforcement in the context of uneven states and weak institutions? To answer this question, we must examine the politics that are embedded in particular contexts. To that end, this chapter has described the adoption of regulatory institutions, the societal organizations that advocate for enforcement, and the administrative structures involved in environmental regulation. In the process, the discussion revealed a series of opportunities for further refining the theory advanced in the book while contrasting it with alternative explanations.

Conclusion 167

First, environmental regulatory institutions in Argentina were largely created through top-down processes against the grain of de facto power structures. Although this process of creating weak institutions is typical, it differs from that of labor regulation – namely, the formal institutions never reflected the distribution of power in society.[67] There is no equivalent of the strong legacy of Argentine organized labor in the environmental movement. Therefore, analyzing environmental regulation provides an opportunity to examine how the state responds to a different type of institutional weakness, one that occurs broadly around the world in countries that adopt policies more to conform to international standards than to respond to domestic interest groups.

Second, the organization of interests in environmental politics had features that help distinguish political pathways to enforcement. Professional environmental organizations wielded power related to technical expertise, while neighborhood organizations could mobilize protest. These two different capacities create a way of analyzing the types of groups regulators respond to and through which institutional processes they do so. Moreover, both types of groups differ from labor unions in a number of key areas. Crucially, the environmental movement was pluralist, non-partisan, and lacked the substantial economic power of unions, thereby creating the opportunity to examine whether the dynamics identified in Chapter 5 can be extended beyond strong, centralized, electorally relevant groups.

Finally, the administrative structures in environmental regulation make regulators responsive to provincial political conditions, therefore creating variation across key outcomes and explanatory factors. While the municipalities, judiciary, and the federal government can potentially play roles, these channels for political influence work through the provincial bureaucracies. Therefore, these channels create opportunities for environmental groups (and businesses) that are distinct from the largely partisan politics of labor regulation, allowing for further tests of the theory advanced in this book.

---

[67] Levitsky and Murillo 2013. There was always a strong constituency for labor regulations, but non-enforcement was used as a strategy for de facto changes in policy without facing the strong veto of labor unions in the legislative arena.

7

Putting out fires in Santa Fe and Córdoba

This chapter turns to provincial-level analysis of the environmental regulations and their enforcement. The discussion begins with the province of Santa Fe where, under most circumstances, regulators undertook a routine process of enforcement that was highly limited. The size of the industrial sector in the province, combined with the relatively infrequent actions of regulators, left most industries in scarce contact with regulators. In the majority of cases, those firms that were inspected by regulators could avoid penalties or corrective actions by employing delaying tactics. Although the province had a relatively well-developed set of environmental organizations (compared with Tucumán, which will be analyzed in Chapter 8) and, as discussed in Chapter 5, had undertaken at least a partial reform of its Ministry of Labor, in most cases enforcement was at very low levels. In many ways, this is the outcome expected by theories of political will and state capacity – few officials championed environmental regulation, and there was a generalized inability of the state to withstand political pressure by businesses.

However, in certain cases, state officials were able to enforce regulations with substantial results. They pressured firms to change practices, worked with managers to resolve problems in implementing technologies, and mediated between industries and angry public. Although these actions were limited in scope, they gave regulatory institutions force in specific places and times. Regulators helped communities protect themselves from illegal pollution and, simultaneously, brought order to contentious conflicts threatening to shut down those plants accused of releasing toxics. In other words, the state was highly uneven in a particular pattern.

What explains this pattern of enforcement? While attributes of the regulatory agency or the environmental organizations in the province are important, they alone cannot account for the actions of regulators. Instead, it is necessary to examine which civil society organizations became linked with regulators and

168

Santa Fe 169

to trace how the capabilities of these groups combined with those of the state. In other words, we must investigate how and where the state became porous to groups that have interests and capabilities aligned with enforcement. In the case of Santa Fe, regulators lacked administrative resources and could not work with professional environmental organizations that had the potential to support enforcement aimed at an industry or region. Instead, regulators formed linkages only with small community groups that could generate the conflict necessary to become politically viable partners. Under certain circumstances, these groups enabled the state to enforce regulations only in a highly concentrated way on specific firms. Thus, the uneven nature of the state becomes intelligible, and it is possible to explain why enforcement occurs in some cases and not others.

Analysis of Santa Fe suggests that linkages are crucial for explaining environmental enforcement. To further test this proposition, the second section of the chapter briefly analyzes a shadow case of Córdoba, which by most measures (e.g., funding, expertise, and international connections) has even stronger professional environmental organizations than does Santa Fe. Notwithstanding the robust professional environmental organizations in Córdoba, the pattern of enforcement is extremely similar to that in Santa Fe. Groups that otherwise would seem to be able to wield political power are not able to establish linkages or make enforcement possible. This additional case provides stronger evidence that analyzing both linkages and administrative resources is necessary for explaining the dynamics of environmental enforcement.

These two provinces exhibited stability in patterns of enforcement during the post-crisis period. Close investigation of the dynamics of contention reveal that conflicts around particular plants did not trigger investments in regulatory agencies needed to go beyond a firefighting type of enforcement. This finding suggests that, just as in labor regulation, the political possibility of building linkages can undermine support for broader reforms. Chapter 8 will further explore this possibility by examining changes in the pattern of enforcement in Tucumán.

SANTA FE

The Santa Fe *Secretaría de Medio Ambiente* (SFSMA) is the primary government agency responsible for implementing environmental regulations on industry in the province.[1] As introduced previously, examining the actions of regulators reveals two main logics of enforcement. One logic involves routine inspections to gather and analyze pollution samples, followed by attempts to penalize firms in violation. Officials estimated that in 2008 they conducted

---

[1] The agency was created when the provincial water authority (DIPOS) was privatized in the 1990s. It was initially formed as a *secretaría del estado* but was downgraded in rank under the Binner administration (in 2007) to a normal *secretaría*.

260 such inspections, which were a mixture of programmed actions and responses to complaints.[2] The inspections differed by media (e.g., air, water, and solid waste), but they generally involved surprise visits in which the regulators would "take a sample, talk with the manager, review the plant, the processes, and systems of waste treatment." Regulators used a strategy that is at once pedagogical and punitive:

> We have a double function. On the one hand, we monitor the firms and the way they are being managed. On the other hand, we have to convince firms to manage the environment well and minimize their impacts so the firm can really grow. [This way,] they are going to have fewer difficulties, no problems with their neighbors or with the courts ... In this aspect we guide firms, telling them what technology exists ... and which consultants they can hire who do good work.[3]

In sum, there are routine processes in the SFSMA for collecting information about compliance and fashioning responses; these actions aim to incent, convince, and enable firms to come into compliance. If the analysis of enforcement focused entirely on style, it would appear that the SFSMA is approximating best practices in regulation.

After looking more closely, however, it becomes clear that these routine actions have resulted only in low levels of enforcement across broad swaths of industry. First, when placed in context of the vast number of polluting firms concentrated in the province, the number of inspections was very low. In the economic census of 2004, there were nearly 10,000 industrial facilities operating in the province that were potential contaminators.[4] This number undoubtedly grew substantially in the post-crisis boom, indicating that inspectors visited *fewer than 3% of facilities*. Therefore, regulators were just scratching the surface in terms of information gathering. Officials from the SFSMA estimated that there were some 5,000 firms that were "not totally identified" and operating completely outside of the regulatory system.[5] This is no small deficiency. A study released by researchers in the National University of Rosario's medical school in 2011, in collaboration with the United Nations, found that Santa Fe's industry posed the highest risk of contamination in the country.[6] Yet, regulators were not consistently monitoring the majority of firms.

---

[2] There are no precise figures available for the number of inspections that fluctuates year to year. Nor are there any exact figures available for the portion of these inspections that were programmed or in response to complaints; in air pollution, officials estimated that half of the inspections were triggered by complaints, while in water pollution, the number is closer to 20%. Interviews: S49, Inspector, Santa Fe Environmental Secretariat, Santa Fe, 12/10/2008 and S50, Inspector, Santa Fe Environmental Secretariat, Santa Fe, 12/10/2008
[3] Interview: S49, Inspector, Santa Fe Environmental Secretariat, Santa Fe, 12/10/2008
[4] Source: Economic Census of 2004, INDEC
[5] Interview: S01, Senior Official Santa Fe Environmental Secretariat, Rosario, 4/30/2009
[6] *La Capital* "Rosario es una de las zonas con mayor contaminación del país" 05/08/2011

Santa Fe 171

Second, after issuing violations, inspectors had difficulty taking steps that could alter firm behavior. For one, the process of using fines was often blocked; out of the inspected firms in 2008, upward of 50% were issued notices that they were out of compliance, but only 5% were issued penalties.[7] This was not due to a strategic use of flexibility, but instead stemmed from interrelated formal and informal failures in the regulatory system. Formally, Santa Fe's environmental laws made it difficult, although not impossible, to penalize firms that violate air pollution provisions in some industries. Air regulations in Santa Fe limited the amount of ambient pollution in any particular area, but did not specify exact fines for emissions.[8] As a consequence, the normal administrative processes of fines could not be used in these cases. There were, however, ways around this problem.[9] For example, the SFSMA could void the firm's license to operate by finding that the firm was not following the management plan described in its EIA, or by working with the municipality to shut the firm down. Also, in specific industries, like grain silos, there were supplemental pieces of legislation that could be used to issue fines.[10] Furthermore, a number of national and international statutes could be applied by provincial regulators (the *presupuestos minimos* described in Chapter 6). Therefore, provincial legislative weaknesses were not completely constraining.

Perhaps even more important than the formal limitations in regulatory rules was an additional set of weak points in enforcement across media (i.e., air, water, and solid waste). The formal penalties that did exist were easily evaded by firms that put up resistance either by exploiting organizational failings in the SFSMA or by taking advantage of the limited appetite for punitive measures among senior officials.[11] As a result, even in areas like water pollution, in which regulations specified clear penalties, the SFSMA rarely executed fines.[12] When combined with the low rate of information gathering, the weakness in the SFSMA's ability to overcome resistance and to make penalties stick resulted in very low levels of enforcement across all industries.[13]

---

[7] Interview: S01, Senior Official Santa Fe Environmental Secretariat, Rosario, 4/30/2009

[8] Interview: S13, Inspector, Santa Fe Environmental Secretariat, Rosario, 4/30/2009

[9] Interview: S18, Taller Ecologista, Rosario, 5/14/2009

[10] Interview: S48, Inspector, Santa Fe Environmental Secretariat, Santa Fe, 12/10/2008

[11] Interview: S13, Inspector, Santa Fe Environmental Secretariat, Rosario, 4/30/2009

[12] Interviews: S01, Senior Official Santa Fe Environmental Secretariat, Rosario, 4/30/2009; and S04, Taller Ecologista, Rosario, 6/3/2009

[13] The inability for the SFSMA to overcome resistance is somewhat surprising considering the fact that, compared with most of other bureaucracies analyzed thus far in this dissertation, the SFSMA has some features that tend toward bureaucratic autonomy. Even though they were not hired through a meritocratic process, all officials in the small team that enforce environmental regulations had civil service protection and university degrees. These organizational features, however, were insufficient in the face of pressure from firms.

172 *Putting out fires in Santa Fe and Córdoba*

The SFSMA was not, however, always a crippled agency, and there was an entirely different logic of enforcement that coexisted with the routine practices described previously. When there was social pressure over pollution in a specific community or firm, regulators could surmount the formal and informal limitations in their monitoring abilities and power to penalize firms. One inspector described the difference when there was conflict:

We can demand more because the firms feel very pressured because there can be a protest and blockade of the plant so that no one can go to work. Everything functions like that here. When there is popular pressure, everything gets really interesting. We have had cases in which popular pressure was the only way to get a firm that was out of compliance to change.[14]

Firms have to worry about the direct effects of social protests (e.g., blockades) as well as civil suits filed in court that strengthen the hand of regulators.[15] In short, the political pressure generated by social conflict can, under some conditions, create opportunities for inspectors to overcome barriers when they want to enforce, and place pressure on inspectors who might not want to enforce.

In circumstances of conflict, inspectors can also leverage connections with the local actors to continually monitor firms. For example, one inspector in northern Santa Fe recalled:

The most successful case that I have seen was in Rafaela. There were three firms that the population systematically denounced ... one dairy plant and two meat packing plants. An NGO, the municipality, and city councilors all started moving [against the firms]. They put together a commission with the SFSMA to keep checking on the firms. This was due to social pressure ... We went to inspect them ... [and] social pressure made the three firms create first-rate wastewater treatment plants, which are functioning really well.[16]

In this case, regulators were not only getting political backing from civil society organizations and the municipality, but they were also extending their capacity to collect information (particularly important in this case because the firms were located some distance from the nearest office of the SFSMA). Regulators did not draw on civil society just for political support; they relied on civil society to make up for operational weaknesses in information gathering. In sum, examining all cases of enforcement in Santa Fe during this period reveals that they only occurred when there was mobilization.

Santa Clara and the dynamics of conflict

The case of the Santa Clara Plant, which processes soy and sunflower seeds to produce vegetable oil in the city of Rosario, is illustrative of how social conflict

[14] Interview: S13, Inspector, Santa Fe Environmental Secretariat, Rosario, 4/30/2009
[15] Interview: S29, Inspector, Santa Fe Environmental Secretariat, Santa Fe, 12/10/2008
[16] Interview: S28, Inspector, Santa Fe Environmental Secretariat, Santa Fe, 12/10/2008

Santa Fe 173

translates into successful enforcement. This case is methodologically useful because it concerns an economically powerful firm that became the center of one of the most substantial conflicts that regulators faced in the industrial heart of the province. The Santa Clara plant is owned by Molinos Río de la Plata, an Argentine agro-industrial firm that produces primary products (soy beans, sunflower, and rice), vegetable oils, biodiesel, and a variety of processed food products. Molinos Río de la Plata is a large firm that grew extremely rapidly during the commodity boom to reach 1.7 billion dollars in sales, 1.3 billion dollars in exports, and 5,000 employees in 2007.[17] In the 2000s, many of the firm's principal operations were in the province of Santa Fe, which was one of the leaders in the agro-industry sector.[18] In total, Molinos controlled significant economic resources in the province, making it no easy target for regulators.

Santa Clara, one of five plants owned by Molinos, had the capacity to process a massive amount of soy and sunflower seeds (4,500 tons per day). This industrial process results in a variety of pollutants that need to be treated (in the air: particulates, hexane, nitrogen oxides, ammonium, and residual pesticides; in the water: oils, fats, and sulfates).[19] When Santa Clara began its operations, the area around the plant was essentially farmland. As the city of Rosario expanded, housing was built nearby, and the plant became engulfed on three sides by working-class residential neighborhoods. By the 2000s, the plant was operating without complying with a variety of environmental laws, thereby exposing its neighbors to contaminants.

Inspectors from the SFSMA were well aware of the environmental problems caused by Santa Clara, which were common in the industry. But regulators were largely unable to take steps that would lead to compliance. According to inspectors, Santa Clara's air "emissions were very bad because they were burning sunflower seed shells to fire the boiler, which created high levels of particulates and noise. We confirmed all of this ourselves. As always, we required changes, but there were no penalties. We required the changes again, and there were no penalties again. It was a closed loop."[20] In short, the firm was intransigent, and inspectors could do little to surmount its resistance. In addition to air pollution, regulators later discovered that Santa Clara was violating water pollution laws by releasing fats, oils, and sediments through an illegal connection to a storm water drain.[21] The former Secretary of Environment, who was leading the agency at this time, recounted: "The state ... was not

---

[17] Source: Annual Report, Molinos Río de la Plata, 2007
[18] In 2004, it proposed an 80 million dollar investment in the province.
[19] Torres de Quinteros, Zulema et al. "Condicones ambeintales y salud en el área influencia de la Aceitera Santa Clara (Distrito Sudoeste de Rosario-Argentina)" *Investigación en Salud* vol. 8, número especial, 2007
[20] Interview: S13, Inspector, Santa Fe Environmental Secretariat, Rosario, 4/30/2009
[21] *La Capital* "Una inspección detectó un desagüe clandestino en la aceitera Santa Clara" 06/15/2004; "Intiman a la aceitera Santa Clara por el desagüe pluvial clandestine" 06/16/2004

174   *Putting out fires in Santa Fe and Córdoba*

complying with its own rules to apply penalties and implement legislation."[22] There were routine inspections of the plant during which violations were found, but the SFSMA was unable to force investment in technologies that would lead to compliance. In short, Santa Clara, like many of the cereal processing facilities in Santa Fe, was violating laws and causing serious environmental damage, but responses from regulators did little to mitigate the pollution.[23]

The trigger for change in this case was a series of fires and explosions that occurred at the plant in April 2004.[24] The fires were caused by improper ventilation in silos that held sunflower seeds, leading to gas build-ups that eventually ignited.[25] These incidents frightened nearby residents and brought the problems at the plant to the attention of officials in the municipal government. People living in the surrounding neighborhoods had a longstanding conflict with the plant, but, until this point, they had little success finding allies to help them press their demands.[26] After the fire, there was a local protest, and a city councilor met with residents to demand greater pollution control.[27]

One of the most vocal neighborhood groups was an informal collection of residents called the *Vecinal Santa Teresita*, which came to represent the community in a number of local forums. The leaders of the *Vecinal* had on their side several factors that allowed them to mobilize a serious campaign against Santa Clara.[28] First, when attention was focused on the plant, the provincial government was under the control of the *Partido Justicialista* (PJ), while the municipal government was controlled by the opposition Socialist Party (PS). This condition was important because various actors in the municipal government aligned with the neighbors to demand action by the provincial government, which had jurisdiction over enforcing environmental regulations through the SFSMA. In short, exploiting the conflict between political parties operating at different levels of government enabled the *Vecinal* to gain powerful allies outside the main regulatory system.

Soon after the fire, health officials from a local clinic revealed to the press that there had been disproportionately high rates of asthma in the Santa Teresita neighborhood.[29] The city health department then conducted a

---

[22] Interview: B12, Senior Official, Santa Fe Environmental Secretariat, Buenos Aires, 5/26/2009
[23] For example, see an editorial from the environmental group *Taller Ecologista: La Capital* "Más cerealeras, más deuda ecológica" 02/20/2004
[24] *La Capital* "Explotó un silo y provocó gran incendio en una aceitera" 04/06/2004; "Un incendio destruyó un silo en una aceitera" 04/07/2004; "Un incendio en la aceitera Santa Clara arrasó un silo" 05/09/2004; "Otro incendio en un silo de la aceitera Santa Clara" 05/11/2004
[25] Interview: S36, Manager, Cereal Industry Firm, Rosario, 5/13/2009
[26] Interview: S25, Vecinal Santa Teresita, Rosario, 5/8/2009
[27] *La Capital* "Piden controlar los silos de la planta aceitera Santa Clara" 05/11/2004
[28] In addition to the ones listed below, the *Vecinal Santa Teresita* connected with students in the National University of Rosario's communications program to produce a documentary on the problems of pollution and draw attention to the problem.
[29] *La Capital* "Advierten que aumentaron los casos de asma cerca de una planta aceitera" 05/25/2004

Santa Fe 175

household survey of the conditions in the neighborhoods surrounding the Santa Clara plant.[30] The results, published in 2007, found that there were high levels of illnesses commonly associated with air pollution. The study went beyond health issues and surveyed residents about their opinions regarding Santa Clara. Its findings revealed broad support for the claims of those in the neighborhood in favor of more enforcement, indicating that more than 90% of residents felt that there were serious environmental problems in the community, and 60% felt that the plant should be relocated.[31] Second, neighborhood leaders connected with a law firm that began to file civil suits on behalf of the individuals against the owner of the plant. As one neighborhood leader described: After the fire, "we were all under the smoke and ash, with people evacuated from their houses. The first issue was health, and afterwards, the lawyers. . . . We made it so all of the people in the neighborhood started individual lawsuits. They received a lot of support from . . . the public health officials who had been studying the neighborhood."[32] The threat of civil legal action was, according to the neighbors, key in getting managers in the plant to pay attention to the community.[33]

As the conflict escalated, the managers began to feel threatened, fearing the community would demand the closing or relocation of the plant.[34] According to regulators, "the pressure of the neighbors was so strong that the firm had to solve the problems, or the plant could not keep working."[35] Regulatory institutions were completely failing; not only were pollution standards being ignored, but conflicts were in the courts and the streets instead of being structured by regulations. In response, provincial and municipal governments took steps to address the problem and resolve their conflicts by conducting joint inspections.[36] These inspections uncovered further violations in the plant, including the illegal wastewater discharges. These actions marked the beginning of an enforcement campaign on the part of the SFSMA, which grew into an intensive monitoring effort and led to the imposition of requirements that could not be ignored by the firm.

One key element of the change in enforcement came when neighborhood activists and city councilors started a *Monitoring Committee* to bring together

---

[30] Torres de Quinteros, Zulema et al. "Condicones ambeintales y salud en el área influencia de la Aceitera Santa Clara (Distrito Sudoeste de Rosario-Argentina)" *Investigación en Salud* vol. 8, número especial, 2007

[31] The methodology of the study was questionable, but nevertheless it gave a scientific endorsement to the claims of the neighbors who were against the plant.

[32] Interview: S25, Vecinal Santa Teresita, Rosario, 5/8/2009

[33] At the time of the research, some cases were still in court and their outcomes were uncertain.

[34] Interview: S36, Manager, Cereal Industry Firm, Rosario, 5/13/2009

[35] Interview: S13, Inspector, Santa Fe Environmental Secretariat, Rosario, 4/30/2009

[36] *La Capital* "Por la aceitera Santa Clara se reúnen provincia y municipio" 05/27/2004; "Controlarán las emanaciones que produce la aceitera Santa Clara" 06/01/2004

176   *Putting out fires in Santa Fe and Córdoba*

all the actors involved in the conflict.[37] The Monitoring Committee, which met at a local office of the SFSMA, included representatives from the neighborhood, the SFSMA, health professionals, and city council members.[38] Plant managers did not participate at first because they feared neighbors would make unreasonable demands, such as requiring the firm to buy houses for residents wanting to move or forcing the plant to relocate.[39] The "Vecinal Santa Teresita invited the managers from the plant. They did not come, but they sent union leaders, who almost wanted to kill us."[40] Through the union leaders, Santa Clara sent a message that enforcement threatened jobs. Despite this initial resistance, when the pressure did not abate, managers eventually came to the table and began an open dialogue with the neighbors and the SFSMA about how they could come into compliance.

The series of events greatly increased the capabilities of environmental inspectors to enforce regulations. The SFSMA became "a mediator, demanding actions from the plant and ... monitoring the plant to make sure the changes were adequate."[41] Now, according to the inspectors, the *closed loop* of violations repeating endlessly without a real response had been broken. In August 2004, managers from Santa Clara presented a plan of action outlining how they would reduce pollution and come into compliance within a two-year period. The plan included the installation of electrostatic filters in Santa Clara's chimneys to reduce air pollution and a change in grain-handling practices to further reduce air pollution. The plant management also promised to install a series of controls in the silos to reduce the risk of additional fires as well as an alarm system that would notify neighbors of any accidents. Finally, Santa Clara committed to undertaking a number of projects in the community, including planting a barrier of trees between the neighbors and the plant.[42]

These promises were important first steps because they pushed Santa Clara to begin seriously managing environmental issues; once the plant had a plan, it became clear that compliance was feasible and Santa Clara "was not just going to be shut down."[43] Still, inspectors from the SFSMA had to make sure that Santa Clara actually undertook the investments outlined in the plan. To do so, regulators from the SFSMA worked directly with the *Vecinal Santa Teresita* to conduct a series of inspections. According to neighbors, "When environmental officials come to inspect the plant, we go to the plant as well."[44] Residents called this a system of *neighborhood monitors*.[45] Managers at

---

[37] Interview: S25, Vecinal Santa Teresita, Rosario, 5/8/2009
[38] *La Capital* "Reunión de vecinos, funcionarios, empresarios y concejales" 06/15/2004
[39] Interview: S36, Manager, Cereal Industry Firm, Rosario, 5/13/2009
[40] Interview: S25, Vecinal Santa Teresita, Rosario, 5/8/2009
[41] Interview: S13, Inspector, Santa Fe Environmental Secretariat, Rosario, 4/30/2009
[42] *La Capital* "Santa Clara busca bajar la polución ambiental con un plan forestal" 08/23/2004
[43] Interview: S13, Inspector, Santa Fe Environmental Secretariat, Rosario, 4/30/2009
[44] Interview: S47, Vecinal Santa Teresita, Rosario, 5/8/2009
[45] In Spanish: *vecinos controladores*. Interview: S25, Vecinal Santa Teresita, Rosario, 5/8/2009

Santa Clara accepted this practice, which was not legally mandated; a manager explained, "I didn't have anything to hide, so I opened the doors to the neighbors and the government and let them in."[46] The SFSMA kept monitoring the plant, pushing it along and evaluating the technical aspects of the investments; all the while the community organization served as local observers and, in combination with the municipal government, kept political pressure on both regulators and the firm.

The process was anything but smooth, but this form of enforcing regulations with tight interactions between the SFSMA, the *Vecinal*, municipal government and Santa Clara persisted for more than two years. Along the way, there were challenges in keeping the firm on track with the investments. For instance, Santa Clara delayed in purchasing the air pollution filter. When the plant fell short on its commitments, new negotiations were triggered. Eventually, Santa Clara spent additional money to expedite the installation of the filter. By 2006, the firm made more than two million dollars in investments and completed the projects that it had proposed.[47] From the point of view of the regulators, enforcement was a success: "After two long years, a lot of tolerance from the neighbors, an effort from the firm, and an effort from us acting in between those two groups, Santa Clara managed to fix the emissions and made many improvements."[48] Representatives from the *Vecinal Santa Teresita* recognized noticeable improvements in the environment as well as to their health: "After they put in the chimney ... [my friend] did not have any more asthma crises. The children haven't had them either."[49]

For managers at Santa Clara, the transformed relationship with the community had long-term benefits. First, they stopped worrying about the plant being shut down because of popular pressure. Second, when they made new changes in the plant, they were able to talk them through with regulators and the community to gain their support. No longer did managers have to operate outside formal rules. For example, in 2009, Santa Clara needed approval from the city government for some alterations to the plant layout. Managers talked it over with the community leaders, who asked for some public works projects in the neighborhood and then agreed to support the plant in securing the permits. Plant managers called this the "cherry on the cake" of building a good relationship with the community.[50]

In sum, the Santa Clara case was an example of how, in the context of social conflict, regulators from the SFSMA could take steps that approximated high levels of enforcement in specific cases. These actions reinforced environmental

---

[46] Interview: S36, Manager, Cereal Industry Firm, Rosario, 5/13/2009
[47] *La Capital* "Avanzan las mejoras ambientales en la zona de la aceitera Molinos Río de la Plata" 08/09/2006. Interview: S36, Manager, Cereal Industry Firm, Rosario, 5/13/2009
[48] Interview: S13, Inspector, Santa Fe Environmental Secretariat, Rosario, 4/30/2009
[49] Interview: S25, Vecinal Santa Teresita, Rosario, 5/8/2009
[50] Interview: S36, Manager, Cereal Industry Firm, Rosario, 5/13/2009

178   *Putting out fires in Santa Fe and Córdoba*

regulatory institutions. Leaders from a professional environmental organization located in Rosario, who were not directly part of the Monitoring Commission but observed the process closely, also saw the efforts as a success: "It is a positive case because they made many environmental improvements."[51] There was complete consensus that, with a lot of help, environmental regulations had been enforced by the SFSMA.

The Santa Clara case was not unique, but rather indicative of a series of similar cases that occurred throughout the province. There was a similar case in the northern city of Rafaela, which also involved a commission of municipal government officials and neighborhood groups that monitored firms. Also, there were at least two other similar cases involving industry in the greater Rosario area.[52] All of these cases began with some sort of community mobilization and conflict, followed by actions of the SFSMA to take steps to enforce environmental regulations.

Not all of the cases, however, ended up with investment and compliance. The blocked installation of a car battery recycling facility in a small town in southern Santa Fe illustrates a somewhat different result of environmental conflict. In 2007, Ramsafé, an Argentine firm with investors from Buenos Aires, received permission for the plant from the SFSMA. The recycling facility promised to produce 120 jobs and was supported by the municipal government over the objections of some environmental groups. In response to their concerns, the mayor stated: "The municipal government and the SFSMA will conduct periodic inspections to ensure that the facility complies with all of the requirements contained in the over 400 pages of documentation that have been approved by the SFSMA."[53]

There were claims, however, that the EIA was highly flawed and had essentially overlooked a community that was located near the facility.[54] Just as the construction of the facility began, a group of residents, along with a small community organization, *Centro Ecologista Renacer*, and a few politicians, began to protest the facility. They argued that "if the project continues, within a few months all of our [agricultural] products will be contaminated."[55] The protests continued and, only three months later, the SFSMA reversed

---

[51] Interviews: S04 and S18, Taller Ecologista, Rosario, 5/14/2009 and 6/03/2009

[52] On Rafaela: Interview: S28, Inspector, Santa Fe Environmental Secretariat, Santa Fe, 12/10/2008. On Capitan Bermudez: S04, Taller Ecologista, Rosario, 6/3/2009 and *La Capital* "La Justicia ordenó la clausura de Petroquímica Bermúdez" 11/11/2006; "Celulosa y una medida a favor de los vecinos" 03/13/2008; "Hallan cianuro en lo que fue una laguna estabilizadora de Bermúdez" 06/05/2008. On Laser House: Interview: S13, Inspector, Santa Fe Environmental Secretariat, Rosario, 4/30/2009 and *La Capital* "Clausuran una fábrica que emanaba olores en zona norte" 03/22/2007; "Nueva denuncia contra una empresa por peligrosas emanaciones" 06/12/2007

[53] *La Capital* "Instalan una fábrica de baterías para automóviles en Fighiera" 05/11/2007

[54] Source: A presentation at a meeting of *Agenda Socioambiental Santafesino*

[55] *La Capital* "Pavón y Fighiera cortaron la ruta en rechazo a fábrica contaminante" 05/06/2007

Santa Fe 179

its decision, revoked the permission for the facility based on the faulty EIA, and effectively shut Ramsafé down.[56] In some ways, the outcome was not as positive as that of the Santa Clara case; instead of finding a solution that would allow development and environmental protection, the SFMSA stopped development altogether. Nevertheless, the SFSMA was able to take steps to enforce rules around the EIA process. Again, mobilization by the community made action by the regulators possible.

In sum, enforcement of environmental regulations in Santa Fe by the SFSMA in the period after the economic crisis was highly uneven, but not uniformly weak. On the one hand, when there was no social conflict, there were low levels of enforcement. Routine inspections were few, and, while regulators attempted to craft responses that involved penalties and pedagogy, the SFSMA was unable to withstand resistance from intransigent firms. The result was often a "closed loop," as one inspector described it, in which the regulators continually required firms to change their behavior while firms continually ignored those demands. On the other hand, when there was social conflict, the dynamics of enforcement shifted radically. In these cases, regulators focused their attention on one plant (or at most a handful), intensively monitored pollution levels, supplemented their data with accounts from small civil society organizations, and drew upon the political resources generated through social conflict to force firms to change their behavior.

This pattern of enforcement approximates the society-dependent ideal-type; social conflict appeared to be a necessary condition within the province. Enforcement remained piecemeal and local, as efforts to leverage conflicts and scale up enforcement to an entire industry in Santa Fe were fleeting.[57] In the late 1990s there was a conflict between the metal plating industry and the private wastewater treatment company that ran the city of Rosario's water system. Small metal plating firms had always discharged chemicals directly into the municipal system, but the effluents made it impossible for the private waste treatment company to comply. In 2000, the water company disconnected the firms. This action provoked a crisis in the industry, threatening all firms. Together, they worked with the SFSMA, city government, and the firm association on a Clean Production program to reduce pollution at the source. This program was successful in helping some firms improve their systems, but it quickly ended when the threat went away.[58] Under the Binner administration,

---

[56] *La Capital* "Marcha en Pavón contra un proyecto industrial" 08/05/2007; "Desautorizan la instalación de una fábrica en Fighiera" 08/22/2007. Interview: S01, Senior Official Santa Fe Environmental Secretariat, Rosario, 4/30/2009

[57] Interviews: S17, Senior Official, Santa Fe Environmental Secretariat, Santa Fe, 12/10/2008; S07, Metal Plating Association of Rosario, Firm Owner, Rosario, 5/14/2009

[58] The development of this program, even fleeting, is largely consistent with the argument advanced in this book, which holds that improvements in the capabilities of regulators should come when reactive enforcement (built upon linkages) fails to meet the needs of a substantial number of organized firms.

180   *Putting out fires in Santa Fe and Córdoba*

there were new attempts to create industry-level enforcement programs similar to Clean Production in the agro-industrial sector, but plans were never realized. Compared with the regulatory programs in Tucumán (analyzed in Chapter 8), Santa Fe's Clean Production efforts were underdeveloped, and the SFSMA never made substantial progress on systemic enforcement.

Instead, enforcement remained "a reactive plan" and regulators did not take action beyond the cases in which there was conflict.[59] This is not the pattern of enforcement that officials in the SFSMA preferred. As an inspector explained:

What we would like to do ... is to plan inspections with the most frequency for the most risky firms, and with less frequency for the less risky firms ... [To be] beyond the complaints that are always going to exist. But today we are still behind on this, and we are acting more as firefighters ... with complaints, and with judicial requests that have to be answered immediately.[60]

This sentiment, that rationalizing the enforcement process is an important goal, was expressed by nearly all of the officials in the SFSMA. It remained, however, out of reach.

Accounting for enforcement patterns in Santa Fe

What explains this pattern of enforcement in Santa Fe? Any account of enforcement would be incomplete without considering the extremely low levels of administrative resources in the SFSMA, which greatly constrained the action of regulators. First, the SFSMA had limited human resources for enforcement during the period after the economic crisis. In its Rosario office, the SFSMA had only one environmental inspector dedicated full time to control.[61] There was one official responsible for literally thousands of industrial facilities, large and small, in the industrial corridor that surrounds Rosario. In the north, which has fewer polluting industrial sites, there were five inspectors, bringing the total to between six and ten inspectors in the entire province (depending on how they are counted). This is an extremely small number of staff considering the number of sites that officials need to control and the sheer size of Santa Fe. From the point of view of the officials in the SFMA, resources were a huge constraint, leaving them with "little margin" for action.[62] Officials, by their own accounts, argued that the lack of human resources is at the root of their reactive approach: "with so few people, we react according to necessity."[63]

[59] Interview: B12, Senior Official, Santa Fe Environmental Secretariat, Buenos Aires, 5/26/2009
[60] Interview: S13, Inspector, Santa Fe Environmental Secretariat, Rosario, 4/30/2009
[61] This lasted from the early 2000s until late 2007 when some temporary officials, four or five, were hired to supplement the permanent inspector. It is unclear whether these temporary officials remained for long.
[62] Interview: B12, Senior Official, Santa Fe Environmental Secretariat, Buenos Aires, 5/26/2009
[63] Interview: S01, Senior Official Santa Fe Environmental Secretariat, Rosario, 4/30/2009

Santa Fe 181

In addition, the inspectors lacked the basic materials they needed to organize and execute the tasks of enforcement. They had access to one or two cars (depending on the office) and "more than one time we [inspectors] have had to pay for the gasoline ourselves to be able to get to the inspection site."[64] In addition, there was only one laboratory in the province, located in the north, creating delays in evaluating samples taken by the southern office (where most of the population and industry is located). The SFSMA also lacked basic computing technology: "There is no information system" to keep track of the firms, and officials "believe that getting IT technology is fundamental" to enforcing regulations systematically.[65] Even as other regulatory agencies in Santa Fe expanded in the post-crisis period, environment remained underfunded. For example, the Santa Fe Labor Secretariat was given money to purchase more than one hundred computers under Governor Obeid, and was upgraded to a full Ministry under Governor Binner and funded to hire new inspectors. There was no such investment in the SFSMA, and Binner actually lowered the rank of the agency.[66] In sum, low levels of administrative resources help account for why the inspectors cover such little ground in gathering information about compliance for the vast number of firms they are supposed to control.

Although the low level of administrative resources helps explain some of the limitations of the SFSMA, it is hardly a determinant on its own. Societal organizations clearly appear to be important. What about professional environmental groups? Can their interests or distribution explain the pattern of enforcement? In the north of the province, there are two major organizations. One is the Foundation Protect (*Fundación Proteger,* founded in 1991), which is run by a local professor and focuses on water and fish conservation in the Paraná river basin. Another is the Santa Fe Center for the Protection of Nature (*Centro Santafesino de Protección a la Naturaleza,* CEPRONAT founded in 1977), which publishes a monthly journal "The Environmentalist" (*El Ambientalista*) covering local and global environmental issues. In Rosario, the Ecological Workshop (*Taller Ecologista,* founded in 1984) and Center for Biodiversity and Environmental Research (*Centro de Investigaciones en Biodiversidad y Ambiente* ECOSur, founded in 1993) are professional organizations with members who include journalists, university professors, and lawyers. These organizations regularly conduct studies about environmental issues and are referents for the press in environmental matters. By most measures, these groups are comparatively well developed – they boast expertise, funding, and some even have international connections.

---

[64] Interview: S29, Inspector, Santa Fe Environmental Secretariat, Santa Fe, 12/10/2008
[65] Interview: S01, Senior Official Santa Fe Environmental Secretariat, Rosario, 4/30/2009
[66] Environment was reduced from a *secretaría del estado* to normal secretariat within a larger ministry.

Combining forces to influence local politics, thirty-two organizations joined together, creating the Socio-Environmental Agenda (*Agenda Socioambiental*) in 2007.[67] The group's initial purpose was to "acquaint those who aspire to govern the province ... about the key issues that should be addressed by provincial policies."[68] The group wrote public letters to the governor regarding policies and held meetings with members of government, professors, and environmentalists to debate environmental issues. Environmental groups, however, have been unable to leverage any partisan divide – none of the major political parties (Peronists, Socialists and PRO) has partisan alliances with environmentalists. Nor does one of the major parties have a particularly strong environmental agenda.

In spite of this limitation, environmental organizations could, at times, be influential. For example, in 2003 Governor Obeid appointed Oscar Quintero, a manager in a local chemical and industrial firm, to be head of the SFSMA. Quintero was heavily criticized by environmental groups arguing that his firm had a bad track record and that he would be easily captured by industry.[69] In front of the "pressure executed" by the unified opposition of environmental groups, Quintero's appointment was blocked.[70] In his place, Governor Obeid appointed Marcelo Terenzio, a lawyer who was not the favorite of any environmental groups but who had a more neutral profile and experience working on environmental issues in projects of the Inter-American Development Bank.[71] This episode suggests that, in some ways, the professional environmental organizations in Santa Fe have wielded power in provincial politics.

The political influence of these groups did not, however, directly translate into actions by the SFSMA. The geographic distribution, or interests, of professional environmental organizations cannot account for the cases of enforcement identified above. For example, one leading organization, *Taller Ecologista*, has campaigned since the late 1990s to push for greater enforcement in the Rosario area.[72] In 2005, *Taller Ecologista* started a specific project to address industrial pollution. The goal of the initiative was to create an enforcement plan "for the entire industrial corridor."[73] The change that *Taller Ecologista* was advocating was to move away from "firefighting" and toward systematic application of environmental laws – the exact goal expressed by officials in the SFSMA.

---

[67] Interview: S18, Taller Ecologista, Rosario, 5/14/2009
[68] *Agenda Socioambiental* "Una Agenda Socioambiental para Santa Fe Construyendo propuestas para sociedades sustentables" 2007
[69] *La Capital* "Confirmado" 12/19/2003; "La Secretaría de Medio Ambiente se usa para pagar favores políticos" 12/19/2003.
[70] *La Capital* "Rechazó el cargo el secretario de Medio Ambiente designado por Obeid" 12/20/2003
[71] Interview: B12, Senior Official, Santa Fe Environmental Secretariat, Buenos Aires, 5/26/2009
[72] Interview: S04, Taller Ecologista, Rosario, 6/3/2009
[73] Interview: S18, Taller Ecologista, Rosario, 5/14/2009

Santa Fe 183

Despite the congruence of their goals, *Taller Ecologista* has not played a large role in helping environmental inspectors with enforcement, which, as described previously, remained very much reactive. In addition, many of the episodes of enforcement that have been successful, even ones in Rosario where *Taller Ecologista* is based (such as the Santa Clara plant), did not directly involve professional environmental organizations, but instead were driven primarily by smaller, neighborhood-level associations, such as the *Vecinal Santa Teresita*. While professional groups might have been influential in policy-making, their actions cannot explain enforcement in the province.

To understand why professional environmental organizations, like *Taller Ecologista*, have had only modest and indirect influence enforcement patterns, it is necessary to examine the structure of linkages between the SFSMA and civil society organizations. Formal avenues of consultation, such as the Provincial Environmental Council – that is supposed to have a tripartite structure that includes the state, the private sector, and environmental NGOs – did not function. Quite simply, "the NGOs have never participated" in these formal meetings.[74] There were also few channels for informal connections to form.

Furthermore, civil servants at the SFSMA had norms against going out on their own to build relationships when they need support to do their jobs. As one inspector recalled, it would be easy to "talk with the radio, television, or someone [from an NGO] ... but it is going to create a mess ... No, we do not do it ...We aren't an environmental advocacy organization. We are the state. We regulate. The NGOs have the role of advocacy. We cannot go out and play politics from our position in the SFSMA. We are civil servants who work for the state."[75] Among politically appointed officials, there was little, if any, dialogue with professional environmental organizations. Under the Obeid administration, the secretary of environment summed up his view of professional environmental NGOs, stating "Some NGOs are only interested in being NGOs. Once they form, they choose an issue and focus on their own interests with an objective of just fundraising."[76] Among professional environmental organizations the feeling was mutual; one leader explains:

They were almost all bad relationships. Very cold. As an NGO we criticized them a lot ... they seemed less like Secretaries of Environment [working] to preserve the environment and the quality of life of the people, and more like the defenders of the firms.[77]

With these frosty relationships, professional environmental groups lacked linkages with the SFSMA.[78] This failure of linkage formation helps account for

---

[74] Interview: S46, Inspector, Santa Fe Environmental Secretariat, Rosario, 4/30/2009
[75] Interview: S29, Inspector, Santa Fe Environmental Secretariat, Santa Fe, 12/10/2008
[76] Interview: B12, Senior Official, Santa Fe Environmental Secretariat, Buenos Aires, 5/26/2009
[77] Interview: S04, Taller Ecologista, Rosario, 6/3/2009
[78] There were some nascent changes in the Binner administration, but they were too preliminary to assess whether they would be effective.

184   *Putting out fires in Santa Fe and Córdoba*

why, even when they have congruent goals, regulators have not drawn upon the resources of these groups for enforcement.

By contrast, relationships between regulators and small, neighborhood-level organizations took on a different dynamic. Neighborhood groups were able to become viable partners for regulators, making enforcement possible in many of the positive cases. For instance, in the Santa Clara case, the neighbors served as "monitors," joined regulators during inspections, and had direct interactions with staff at the SFMSA. In other cases, relationships with small neighborhood organizations even helped the SFMSA overcome their transportation shortages by getting a municipal government to send a car to pick up the inspectors.[79] The result was that the seemingly weaker neighborhood organizations – which lack expertise, budgets, and paid staff – were actually more likely to become sources of support for regulators in the SFSMA than were professional environmental organizations.

Why were these small groups able to create the conditions for enforcement? The key difference lies in the dynamics of linkage formation. Small neighborhood groups took a number of steps to generate social conflict in a way that professional environmental organizations did not. The professional environmental organizations, for the most part, did not bring cases to court and could not mobilize mass protests. The small neighborhood groups took both these courses of action. In addition, as in the Santa Clara case, some neighborhood groups formed alliances with municipal governments. For appointed officials, working with neighborhood groups has advantages: "When there was a high-conflict issue, it was necessary to give a response because of two interests. First, to defend the government so it isn't criticized. Second, so they don't fire me."[80] Once these conflicts got going, neighborhood groups became viable partners for regulators. The politics of linkage formation helps explain why civil servants were able to develop ties with neighborhood groups but not with professional environmental groups, which, in turn, accounts for the localized nature of enforcement.

In sum, environmental regulation in Santa Fe is distinctively society-dependent; social conflict that results from community mobilization was a necessary condition for enforcement in the province. Ultimately, the structure of linkages privileged small community groups over professional environmental organizations, and the low levels of administrative resources in the SFSMA need to be taken into account when explaining enforcement. The full implications of this particular combination of linkages and low levels of administrative resources will become clear in Chapter 8 with the comparative case of Tucumán. For the moment, however, it is important to note that firms did not advocate for or against the SFSMA. A senior official in the federation of

---

[79] Interview: S28, Inspector, Santa Fe Environmental Secretariat, Santa Fe, 12/10/2008
[80] Interview: B12, Senior Official, Santa Fe Environmental Secretariat, Buenos Aires, 5/26/2009

Córdoba as a shadow case

industry associations explained that in the 1990s, the federation "made a proposal, which we presented in the legislature, for the creation of an Environmental Secretariat" that eventually passed.[81] Industry wanted an "agency that was serious," one that could handle conflicts and offer *judicial security*. But when the economy suffered after the 2001 crisis, industry could no longer *prioritize* investment in environmental institutions. The example of Santa Clara helps clarify why industry was ambivalent about providing more resources to the SFSMA. Industry wanted legal certainty from regulators. Even with extremely limited staff, the SFSMA was able to provide some margin of certainty by putting out fires like the one around Santa Clara. This suggests that successful firefighting can actually undermine industry support for institutional strengthening. Without a conflict that requires a systematic response from the state, industry will not prioritize investment in the regulatory agency.

CÓRDOBA AS A SHADOW CASE

Is this pattern of enforcement unique to Santa Fe? Is it really the case that the politics of linkage formation are key? Are the professional environmental groups in Santa Fe, which appear to have many strengths, in fact weak? Juxtaposition with Córdoba, as a shadow case, is useful to put the Santa Fe case into comparative context. Córdoba is a helpful comparison because it is very similar in terms of the structure of the economy, level of socioeconomic development, and industrial composition.[82] However, there is one important difference: Córdoba had even stronger professional environmental organizations than did Santa Fe. For this reason, Córdoba provides a more difficult test of whether linkages are key intermediaries between regulators and society. If there is a direct relationship between enforcement and civil society organizations unmediated by linkages, then it should be apparent in a province like Córdoba.

There were two professional environmental organizations in Córdoba that have propelled their founders into the international stage. One organization, the Environmental Defense Foundation (FUNAM, *Fundación para la Defensa del Ambiente*) was established by Raúl Montenegro in 1982. Montenegro, a biology professor, was the Sub-secretary of Environment in Córdoba in the 1980s. During his tenure, he orchestrated the adoption of a set of environmental laws that made the province an early leader in Argentina.[83] He went on to undertake a series of national and international environmental campaigns against uranium mines, receiving recognition from the United Nations. In addition, he has been involved in campaigns in Córdoba against pesticides, mines, and municipal sewage. Furthermore, FUNAM often gave technical

[81] Interview: S24, Industrial Federation of Santa Fe, Rosario, 5/13/2009
[82] Mazorra and Beccaria 2007
[83] Interview: C24, Environmental Defense Foundation, Córdoba, 3/5/2009

186   *Putting out fires in Santa Fe and Córdoba*

assistance to neighborhood organizations concerned about contamination in their communities, and when the conflict over Botnia began, FUNAM conducted studies to support the claims of the residents of Gualeguaychú. Montenegro has developed strong global connections, attends international environmental conferences, and has collaborated with Greenpeace and other international organizations.

The other professional environmental organization, the Center for Human Rights and Environment (CEDAH, *Centro de Derechos Humanos y Ambiente*), was co-founded by Romina Picolotti and Jorge Daniel Taillant in 1999.[84] Prior to 1999, Picolotti and Taillant were working with international organizations and NGOs in Washington D.C. including the International Human Rights Law Group and the World Bank. With financing from the Hewlett Foundation and other international funders, Picolotti and Taillant returned to Córdoba and formed CEDAH with the explicit goal of linking human rights issues to environmental issues. They started working internationally and locally, trying to identify high-profile legal cases that could set precedents, and they opened a legal clinic that supports individuals and groups who want to take legal action in environmental cases.[85] CEDAH was thrust into the national spotlight in 2006 when Picolotti represented the Gualeguaychú Environmental Assembly in international courts, a role that led to her appointment as National Secretary of the Environment under Presidents Néstor Kirchner and Cristina Fernandez de Kirchner (see Chapter 6). When Picolotti was forced to resign, she returned to the helm of CEDAH. With substantial funding, international connections, and a high-profile leader, CEDAH was a formidable professional environmental organization.

In addition to FUNAM and CEDAH, the Córdoba Environmental Forum (*Foro Ambiental Córdoba*) is a third professional environmental organization comprised mainly of university professors.[86] The *Foro* became directly involved in local politics when, in 2007, it invited candidates for local office to sign a commitment to sustainability, sent a number of requests for information from

---

[84] Interview: C27, Center for Human Rights and the Environmental (CEDAH), Córdoba, 3/16/ 2009
[85] Interview: C21, Center for Human Rights and the Environmental (CEDAH), Córdoba, 3/20/ 2009
[86] The *Foro* grew out of an older conservation organization (*Comité Córdoba de Conservación de la Naturaleza*) involving a group of biologists who, in 1985, undertook a campaign to plant 800 trees in the province and, after one year, found that they all had been cut down. In 1986, members of the group decided what was most needed was general education in the province about environmental issues. They began visiting schools and giving short lessons on the environment, and then in 1987 they began educating teachers about environmental issues. These programs scaled up, reaching more than 100 schools. The Foro eventually grew into a small-scale organization made up of primarily of academics who undertook low-profile actions to influence local environmental policies in the province. Interview: C20, Córdoba Environmental Forum, Córdoba, 3/2/2009

Córdoba as a shadow case

the local government, and participated in local debates.[87] Combined, these three professional environmental organizations commanded significant resources, and, unlike many environmental organizations in Argentina, they had the ability to serve as brokers between domestic and international spheres. These are precisely the types of organizations that have been behind successful environmental campaigns in other countries in Latin America.[88]

Notwithstanding the presence of these groups, enforcement in Córdoba followed the same pattern as it did in Santa Fe. When there was no crisis, the Córdoba Environmental Secretariat (CSMA) conducted few inspections.[89] In fact, delays in inspections were a problem for the firms that needed certificates of environment compliance, and some firms actually paid for the transportation of the regulators to conduct inspections.[90] When the CSMA found violations, it was very vulnerable to the evasive tactics of firms, and it often took years before violations turned into penalties and fines.[91] Professional organizations were not able to trigger much in the way of enforcement either. But, as in Santa Fe, when local community groups mobilize, everything changes.

For example, in 2004, residents of the small town of Freyre mobilized against a leather tannery located in the town just fifty meters from the central square. The storyline is very similar to the cases in Santa Fe. Before the protests, regulators had done little to address violations from a known polluter. The community rallied against the firm, gained allies in the municipal government, and demanded that something be done about the tannery.[92] The municipality, on behalf of the mobilized community members, requested an inspection from the CSMA. Regulators found that the firm did have a waste treatment plant, but it was not functioning adequately.[93] In a manner similar to the Santa Clara case, the department of health (this time provincial) became involved and conducted a series of epidemiological studies, which found that residents had elevated levels of chromium in their blood.[94] Two hundred and fifty people marched in Freyre, and the CSMA finally conducted inspections that uncovered

---

[87] Foro Ambiental "Memoria de Las Actividades Del Foro 2006–2009," 2009. See also: *La Voz del Interior* "Compromiso por una Córdoba sustentable" 12/20/2007

[88] Steinberg 2001

[89] Multiple interviews, including: C29, Enforcement Department, Córdoba Environmental Secretariat, Córdoba, 3/19/2009; C21, Center for Human Rights and the Environmental (CEDAH), Córdoba, 3/20/2009

[90] Interview: C26, Inspectors, Córdoba Environmental Secretariat, Córdoba, 3/17/2009

[91] Interview: C29, Enforcement Department, Córdoba Environmental Secretariat, Córdoba, 3/19/2009

[92] *La Voz del Interior* "Fuerte debate en Freyre por una curtiembre en el centro de la ciudad" 11/15/2004; "Qué dice la empresa" 11/15/2004; "Actuará la Provincia" 05/18/2005

[93] Interview: C29, Enforcement Department, Córdoba Environmental Secretariat, Córdoba, 3/19/2009

[94] *La Voz del Interior* "Freyre: vecinos de una curtiembre muestran análisis de tóxicos en sangre" 05/18/2005; "Muestran análisis de tóxicos en sangre" 05/18/2005; "Curtiembre cuestionada por vecinos estudia trasladarse a San Francisco" 05/20/2005

188   *Putting out fires in Santa Fe and Córdoba*

serious violations.[95] The monitoring and protests continued for six months, until the CSMA shut down the tannery and gave it a 35,000 dollar loan to relocate to another city.[96] The Freyre case was not unique; other episodes of community protest triggered reactions from the CSMA and that resulted in enforcement.[97]

The reactive regulation of the CSMA can be traced back to the same structures of linkages and the relatively low levels of capacity that were apparent in Santa Fe. Although the strong professional environmental organizations were successful in advocating for regulation in many arenas, the administrative resources of the CSMA actually declined during the economic growth period starting in 2003, limiting regulators' ability to take actions on their own. Regulators in the CSMA had no routine interactions with professional environmental organizations from which they could have drawn significant resources. (One official went as far as saying he "believes" that regulators "should stay disconnected" from environmental groups.[98]) Instead, the CSMA was largely dependent on the mobilization of community organizations protesting specific instances of contamination. At times, community organizations were supported by the professional organizations, but only community organizations could generate local political resources on which the regulators could draw.

In short, the case of Córdoba suggests that even professional environmental organizations that appear to be very well endowed with resources cannot always help regulators. Crucially, linkages need to be formed through protests, which the professional environmental groups could not readily organize. Consequently, regulators relied mainly on community organizations. In the end, the *society-dependent* pattern of enforcement mirrored local mobilizations, not a bureaucratic plan or the demands of professional environmental groups.

CONCLUSION

The cases of Santa Fe and Córdoba have two main implications for the broader analysis of enforcement in the context of bureaucratic weaknesses. First, once again these cases show that enforcement does occur without the creation of traditionally strong bureaucracies. In Santa Fe, the state played a role in influencing the behavior of firms even if it was highly porous to political influence. In addition, unevenness in the state did not mean randomness – there was an informal political logic to when the state took steps to implement policies. Second, the pattern of enforcement in the cases analyzed here is comparable

---

[95] *La Voz del Interior* "Curtiembre: 250 personas marcharon en Freyre" 05/23/2005
[96] *La Voz del Interior* "Mañana cierra la curtiembre de Freyre" 11/28/2005
[97] For example: *La Voz del Interior* "Finalmente, Ambiente clausuró Tecnocuer en Villa del Rosario" 03/22/2007
[98] Interview: C29, Enforcement Department, Córdoba Environmental Secretariat, Córdoba, 3/19/2009

Conclusion 189

to the cases of labor regulation in Chapter 4. The labor inspectorates in Córdoba and in Tucumán enforced regulations when labor inspectors could draw upon linked-unions for resources. While there were some differences – the level of access that unions have to regulators was well beyond that of environmental groups – the cases of environmental regulation were in many ways highly similar. Mobilization by a specific category of civil society organizations is practically a necessary condition for state action. This similarity suggests that society-dependent enforcement is not only a product of corporatist labor institutions or the particular history of Peronist unions. Moreover, by contrasting environmental and labor cases it becomes clear that society-dependent enforcement is not just a relabeling of capture by organized labor. Even using an extremely broad definition, it would be impossible to interpret cases, like that of Santa Clara, as capture.[99]

Third, in the cases analyzed in this chapter, not all civil society organizations were viable sources of support for regulators. Just as in labor regulation, linkages were important. Different from labor regulation, however, the less formal civil society organizations were privileged over professional environmental groups, which were largely left on the outside of the day-to-day enforcement actions of regulators. The process of linkage formation in these cases was similar to the case of the labor regulation in the garment industry in the Federal Capital (Chapter 4), and not at all like that of partisan exchange described in the cases of Peronist unions. When small neighborhood groups generated conflict and gained allies outside of the regulatory system, their power within the system grew. This pathway to linkage formation was not immediately available to professional environmental organizations in these two provinces, neither of which directly collaborated with state regulators.

These conclusions raise a series of additional questions. Is society-dependent enforcement the only option for environmental enforcement in Argentina? If not, how can regulators develop administrative resources so that civil society organizations complement, rather than substitute, the state? How can patterns of environmental enforcement change? Chapter 8 explores these questions by examining environment regulation in the province of Tucumán.

---

[99] If anything, these cases are examples of so-called "not in my backyard" (NIMBY) behavior.

8

Pollution in the "Garden of the Republic"

The cases of society-dependent enforcement analyzed in Chapter 7 revealed how states take highly uneven actions to implement environmental regulations. The dynamics of political contestation over environmental regulation enabled the state to activate regulatory institutions in some instances, but did not result in the type of state action that might move toward compliance on a broader scale. While the state was not completely absent, enforcement was clearly limited. This chapter turns from cases of stasis to Tucumán, a case of shifting patterns of enforcement. By doing so, we can better understand the potential for moving out of society-dependent enforcement and toward a situation in which regulators more fully mediate between societal demands, formal policy, and the practices in the economy. In addition, this change creates another opportunity to contrast sets of competing theories – state capacity and political will – with the argument advanced in this book.

This chapter focuses on regulation in sugar mills and citrus processing plants that, within the range of industries in Tucumán, occupy a central position in the province's economy. These industries are particularly helpful for analyzing environmental politics because of the economic power concentrated in firms and their pollution profiles, which, combined, bring into relief two of the major challenges of enforcement. First, standard political accounts expect that enforcement should be unlikely in these industries because they concentrate economic power. The sugar industry historically has been the backbone of Tucumán's economy. In 2009, it accounted for 10% of the province's GDP and employed approximately 50,000 workers (during the harvest) in a province of 1.5 million people.[1] In the sugar supply chain, economic power was

---

[1] Source: "Indicadores de Evolución de la Provincia del Tucumán Informe 2 – Agosto 2009," Fundación del Tucumán, 2009

190

Pollution in the "Garden of the Republic"

concentrated in the approximately fifteen mills that operate at a key point in between the dispersed growers and the market. The sugar industry association, CART (*Centro Azucarero Regional de Tucumán*), had a monopoly on representation for the industry in collective bargaining agreements.[2] As further evidence for the industry's political weight, at various times (including the late 2000s) the head of CART was also the head of the main business association in the provinces, the FET (*Federación Económica de Tucumán*).[3] If sugar was the old guard, the newly ascendant industry in Tucumán was citrus. Argentina is the largest producer of processed lemons in the world, accounting for half of all lemons grown for processing worldwide, with nearly all of Argentina's lemon production in Tucumán.[4] The citrus industry accounted for 42% of the value of the province's exports in 2010.[5] Economic power in citrus industry was also highly concentrated; approximately 70% of the total lemon production in Tucumán was processed by only seven firms.[6] These firms were organized in the ATC (*Asociación Tucumana del Citrus*) and were successful in getting the government to lobby export markets to allow access to citrus inputs. If any industries in Tucumán should be able to use their economic might to block enforcement, they should be sugar and citrus.

Second, these industries became the focus of environmental politics because they are highly polluting.[7] Sugar mills and citrus plants produce copious amounts of water pollution.[8] One stream of pollution from sugar production is *cachaza* (wet organic solids) that contains high levels of organic pollutants. Moreover, when sugarcane is distilled into ethanol, it creates high quantities of a viscous substance called vinasse, also a potent organic pollutant. Similarly, processing lemons creates large amounts of organic wastes that, when dumped

---

[2] Interview: T60, Tucumán Regional Sugar Industry Association (CART), Tucumán, 11/14/2008

[3] There are 41 firm associations that are members of the FET, which include the commercial associations and sugar mills, that carry heavy economic weight in the province and have the ear of politicians. FET is one of the few associations that has competition for the leadership in closely watched and heavily contested elections.

[4] During 2008–2009, Argentina produced 1,035 metric tons of lemons for processing. The next largest producers were the United States with 340 metric tons and Mexico with 307. Source: United States Department of Agriculture. "Citrus: World Markets and Trade, July 2009 Citrus Update to the February Forecast," 2009

[5] Source: Ministerio de Economía y Finanzas Públicas

[6] Of the remaining 30%, 25% of the lemons are exported fresh, and 5% are for the internal market.

[7] Although there are certainly many additional environmental problems in Tucumán – including burning of sugarcane fields – in order to even begin to give environmental laws force and reduce contamination, pollution from industry has to be controlled. Environmental regulation historically proceeds from controlling "point sources" of pollution that are stable and easy to identify, to controlling "non-point sources" that are spread out and technically more difficult to control.

[8] There are also a variety of environmental problems associated with growing the cane, especially burning it in the field, but I am focusing this analysis on the mills. Goldemberg, Coelho, and Guardabassi 2008

straight into streams, cause rivers literally to run yellow. Combined, these pollution flows completely overwhelmed the river system in Tucumán. Beyond water pollution, sugar mills release particulate matter (soot) and a variety of other chemicals from burning excess cane called bagasse. Since the mills are located in densely populated communities, the mills blanketed residential areas with soot (it is literally called "black rain" by residents) and cause extremely high levels of particulate matter throughout the province.[9] Mitigating all of these pollution streams requires, at a minimum, technology that is costly to acquire and maintain, and, in some cases, more substantial shifts in production practices.

These conditions – economically powerful industries and extensive pollution that is costly to reduce – make Tucumán an even less likely place for successful enforcement of environmental regulations than are the provinces analyzed in the previous chapter. Indeed, for many years, environmental regulation was ineffective. Regulators were unable to overcome the political power of industry; there were no real consequences for firms that violated regulations, nor was there technical assistance to help managers find ways to improve environmental performance. Institutions failed and pollution steadily increased, yet the state did little to strengthen institutions through enforcement.

However, levels of enforcement shifted dramatically in the mid-2000s, beginning with a two-year program of voluntary agreements with firms to promote pollution reduction in industry. Enforcement then increased once again; regulators monitored firms, provided them with technical assistance, and, for the first time ever, penalized firms that were intransigent. This increase in enforcement is particularly puzzling because reforms of the regulatory agency introduced the very types of organizational shortcomings that are generally associated with capture and corruption. How was Tucumán able to increase enforcement without reforming its bureaucracy? What political processes led to this change?

To answer these questions, this chapter analyzes the increases in administrative resources in the state that expanded the staff and capabilities of regulators (even without making them more insulated from politics). Increased internal components of capacity were also combined with ties to environmental groups that both pressured and provided information to regulators. Ultimately, the increase in enforcement involved a transition to co-produced enforcement at a high level. The political origins of these changes can be traced to a set of demands from neighboring provinces, mobilized community groups, and a federal prosecutor who threatened the ability of all firms to operate. These threats triggered the allocation of resources by the federal government to expand the regulatory apparatus of the province, and industry supported this

---

[9] To make matters worse, the mills run at concentrated times during the harvest when many farmers burn the sugarcane in the fields, adding to the extremely high levels of air pollution.

Bureaucrats without backing (1990s –2001)

expansion because it could help business adapt to broad conflicts over pollution. Unlike the provinces discussed in the previous chapter, the political crisis in Tucumán prevented linkages from being used as a substitute for investments in the state, thereby creating conditions for systematic enforcement. This finding illuminates the possibilities for changes in patterns of action in the context of highly uneven states as well as the ways by which weak institutions can be activated by combinations of state and societal actors.

BUREAUCRATS WITHOUT BACKING (1990s–2001)

The main government agency tasked with controlling this pollution in the province was the Ministry of Health (*Sistema Provincial de Salud*, SIPROSA). Although the agency's staffing fluctuated over time, the environmental inspectors were able regularly to take samples from the pollution streams of the largest firms and to identify the levels of pollution.[10] SIPROSA, however, did not respond to violations in any meaningful way and was unable to withstand political pressure against enforcement. When inspectors found violations, they were unable to penalize those responsible or to enable firms to comply through instruction. An official explained the difficulties, "What happens is that the system of fines hasn't been applied as it should ... There would be a delay of at least five years before the fine was completely [processed]."[11] The regulatory system was full of weak points that could be exploited by firms with capable lawyers and political connections.[12] Quite simply, as one manager explained, "We have a lawyer who takes care of all of the legal issues. I can tell you that we never have paid a fine."[13] This pattern of action, of violations being discovered but no action being taken, is very similar to the "closed loop" described by the inspector in Santa Fe.

Apart from the attempted penalties, inspectors did little to take pedagogical actions that could help firms upgrade or promote gradual improvements. During their normal operations, regulators had few direct interactions with

---

[10] If there had been one hundred or so highly polluting firms across all industries, there were approximately ten firms for each SIPROSA inspector to regulate, which is a reasonable level of staff. The combined number of the most polluting sugar mills and citrus plants only total to around 30. Interview: T18, Environmental Inspector, Tucumán Ministry of Health (SIPROSA), Tucumán, 11/4/2008

[11] Interview: T18, Environmental Inspector, Tucumán Ministry of Health (SIPROSA), Tucumán, 11/4/2008

[12] Officials openly stated in 2003 to the press that the regulatory institutions were full of weaknesses: *La Gaceta de Tucumán (LGT)* "El PE reconoce que no cuida el medio ambiente" 08/02/2003

[13] Interview: T24, Environmental Specialist, Sugar Mill, Tucumán, 11/12/2008. Also: Interview T02, Environmental Specialist, Citrus Firm, Cevil Pozo, Tucumán, 4/17/2009; *LGT* "Inspección ambiental a la citrícola Citrusvil" 04/30/2002; "Citrusvil no detiene su avance hacia la calidad total" 08/23/2002

194   *Pollution in the "Garden of the Republic"*

firms. Instead, they mostly took samples and issued violations without engaging in discussions of the underlying causes of pollution.[14] Moreover, SIPROSA did not have any legal tools for inducing incremental improvements in performance. An inspector explained some of the legal barriers.

The sugar mills, with the vinasse, are at 60,000 BOD. They can, with treatment, lagoons, and liquid sewage, reduce to 300, 400, or 500, but they cannot get to 50 BOD.[15] It is 50 that is required by law, and one assumes that is the amount of oxygen that the life needs to be sustained. Well, to reduce BOD [from 60,000 to 500] is already a positive step, considering everything.[16]

Yet, SIPROSA had no ways of incentivizing firms to make these reductions. Compared to industry practices, environmental laws were considered so strict that they became almost irrelevant.

Why did SIPROSA fail to respond in a meaningful way to the violations it found? As did Santa Fe's SFSMA, SIPROSA had many of the characteristics often lauded by analysts of bureaucratic coherence. Its staff had technical training (nearly all held university degrees), civil service protection to give them employment stability, and even career ladders in government. The head of the enforcement department, for example, started her career in SIPROSA as a chemist in 1984, and, by 1995, became head of the laboratory that tests samples and then head of the department in 2005. Although these organizational features are often pointed to in the literature to explain why enforcement occurs,[17] in Tucumán they clearly did not create the conditions for enforcement. The bureaucracy was still subject to political pressures against implementing environmental regulations. One official in SIPROSA explained how it was politically impossible to close down polluting firms in the sugar industry:

Once the mill is going, it is very hard to close it because it is the economic base of Tucumán. Therefore, you have to be very careful because if you aren't, the society is going to come on top of you. For environmental issues, it isn't just complying with laws. It is achieving an equilibrium between the laws and what firms are able to do.[18]

That *equilibrium* meant, for many years, allowing sugar mills and citrus plants to violate laws with impunity. The regulatory bureaucracy was porous to

---

[14] Interviews: T18, Head of Environmental Inspection, Ministerio de Salud, Tucumán, Tucumán 11/4/2008. This is also supported from evidence from interviews: T07, T03, and others.

[15] BOD is a measure of the amount of oxygen consumed in the biological processes that break down organic matter in water. The greater the BOD, the greater the degree of pollution. The limit for industrial effluent according to national law is 50 BOD.

[16] Interview: T14, Environmental Inspector, Tucumán Ministry of Health (SIPROSA), Tucumán, 11/6/2008

[17] See, for example: McAllister 2008

[18] Interview: T18, Environmental Inspector, Tucumán Ministry of Health (SIPROSA), Tucumán, 11/4/2008

Mobilization against pollution

political demands of business, but not to those of environmental organizations that did not have any connections to the regulators.

In sum, even after more than ten years of regulation and the passage of various national and provincial laws, violations continued and there were very low levels of enforcement. Overall, pollution increased dramatically in the province at the end of the 1990s and beginning of the 2000s. The citrus industry grew nearly fourfold; sugar mills responded to increases in natural gas prices by switching to polluting biofuels without installing air filters; and incentives for ethanol production pushed more sugar mills to add large distilleries that increased water pollution. It was clear from scores of interviews with business leaders, regulators, and environmental groups that not a single firm complied with regulations during this period, and SIPROSA did very little to change this outcome.

In many ways, the outcome during this time conforms to dominant theories of the politics of enforcement. From the perspective of political will, the economic power of business in the economy and its organization suggest that it would be unlikely to see enforcement of regulations that impose a cost on business. From the perspective of state capacity, although SIPROSA had some formal elements of a Weberian bureaucracy, regulators were clearly susceptible to political influence. Informal features of the organization reduced their ability to implement policies. Going beyond standard approaches, we can also observe that regulators lacked linkages to societal organizations that possibly could have helped them surmount these challenges. Thus, the result was a pattern of state-driven enforcement that was failing.

MOBILIZATION AGAINST POLLUTION

As in the provinces discussed in the previous chapter, in Tucumán there were mobilizations against pollution by small neighborhood-level organizations, as well as demands for stronger enforcement made by more professional environmental groups. One neighborhood-level group, UniVec (*Union de Vecinos del Sur*), was formed in the beginning of 2003 in the town of La Trinidad. The town is home to sugar mill, by the same name, that blanketed La Trinidad with soot. Two neighbors, both school teachers, started lodging complaints about the increase in pollution with a wide range of government agencies and politicians.[19] Eventually, they took their complaints to the street:

We gathered all of the ash from the house of my neighbor ... We put it all in a container, put it in a wheelbarrow, and made a poster that said There Is No Right To Pollute. We went – my neighbor and our wives and kids ... this wasn't a big mobilization – through the central streets of the town, calling to everyone that we were taking the ash and

---

[19] *LGT* "La Trinidad padece por la contaminación" 08/02/2004. Interview: T21, Environmental Activist, Concepcion, Tucumán, 11/15/2008 and 04/16/2009

Pollution in the "Garden of the Republic"

returning it to the mill. From that moment, it was public, and that allowed neighbors in other places where mills are located to connect with us.[20]

The incident generated news stories in the local press and made the two neighbors focal points in the conflict against the pollution from the local mill.[21]

Another mobilization occurred in 2006 against odors from the wastewater treatment plant of a citrus plant. The firm Citromax, located in the city Tafí Viejo, installed a series of anaerobic lagoons to reduce wastewater pollution that previously had been discharged into canals only partially treated. This system was crucial to Citromax's compliance with pollution regulations, as an environmental engineer from the firm described:

We choose this system because, with the amount of land we have, this technology had possibilities ... And the effect of treating the water was really positive because the pollutants were removed and there was a reduction in [dissolved oxygen] ... From a pollution reduction point of view, it went well, but the collateral effect was the production of odors.[22]

The "collateral effect" in the densely populated city of Tafí Viejo turned out to be more than the community could stand. In July of 2006, two hundred people protested against Citromax because, "The odors that are produced are unbearable. During the night, there is a fog that covers all of the neighborhoods."[23] The situation became tense, and Pro-Eco, the local environmental NGO, mobilized as an opponent of the project, and as the moderator among the firm, state, and angry neighbors. The conflict escalated to the point where the firm sent workers into the neighborhood to break up assemblies; people started carrying machetes; and Peronist party activists (*punteros*) tried to find opportunities in the social unrest.[24] Eventually, Citromax was forced to stop using the treatment lagoons, lose its investment, *increase* its pollution, and continue to violate environmental regulations. This incident demonstrated the vagaries of local mobilization on environmental conflicts – neighbors pushed *against* enforcement of regulations in this case.

The mobilizations described here were similar to those in Santa Fe and Córdoba, but pressure to clean up Tucumán's environmental act went further than it did in the other provinces. A major force beyond neighborhood-level mobilization came through the judiciary.[25] The Federation of Environmental Non-Governmental Organizations (FA) in Tucumán filed a lawsuit against all

---

[20] Interview: T21, Environmental Activist, Concepcion, Tucumán, 11/15/2008 and 04/16/2009
[21] *LGT* "La Trinidad padece por la contaminación" 08/02/2004; "Piden que se ponga en vigencia una ley contra la polución" 07/21/2005
[22] Interview T05, Departamento de Medio Ambiente, Citromax, Tafí Viejo, Tucumán, 4/17/2009
[23] *La Gaceta de Tucumán* "Protesta vecinal contra una citrícola en Tafí Viejo" 07/27/2006
[24] Interview: T29, Presidente, Pro-Eco, Tafí Viejo, Tucumán, 11/1/2008
[25] *LGT* "La Justicia mejoró sus puntos de vista con respecto a los temas ambientales" 05/25/2003

Mobilization against pollution

of the sugar mills for noncompliance with air pollution regulations.[26] The FA decided to bypass SIPROSA, which they believed would only protect firms, and to take on the firms directly through a civil action.[27] The fact that the court agreed to hear the case and forced the mills to defend themselves was a victory in and of itself. Three of the mills settled with the FA and agreed to install filters by 2009. For the rest of the mills, there was an extended legal battle that the FA eventually won in 2008. This was a serious victory for the FA: "We undertook a conquest for the common good. It was David versus Goliath because an organization without a budget or resources confronted the sugar industry."[28]

In addition to the suits from environmental groups, firms had to deal with a new federal district attorney, Antonio Gustavo Gómez, who was transferred to Tucumán from Chubut, a Patagonian province where he had prosecuted a number of environmental cases. Gómez was personally invested in environmental issues and had developed legal theories that took extremely tough stances on pollution.[29] In 2002, Gómez began investigating relatively small instances of environmental crimes, strategically bringing cases against corrupt politicians who were dumping medical wastes in landfills. By doing so, he gained attention from environmental groups that began to seek his collaboration. Gómez quickly scaled up his cases to take more powerful groups to court (including the copper mine "Alumbrera" in the neighboring Catamarca province). By 2006 he had already investigated sixty cases of pollution, after which he began with the citrus and sugar industries.[30] Court filings in 2007, for instance, alleged that the La Trinidad sugar mill, which had been the target of protest of UniVec described previously, was responsible for air pollution eight times the limit and water pollution thirty-five times the limit established in national law.[31] Other mills were accused of even greater violations, with water pollution levels over 200 times the legal limits.[32]

Whereas SIPROSA lacked teeth, Gómez was all bite; he charged the directors of firms personally with environmental crimes, scaring and embarrassing people of power. Unlike the equilibrium sought by SIPROSA, Gómez had no problem with shutting down entire industries if they could not comply.

---

[26] Tucumán's provincial regulations had specific technology requirements for air pollution mitigation. This made it easier to enforce regulation than in Santa Fe, which just had general ambient air quality standards.

[27] Interview: T20, Federation of Environmental Non-governmental Organizations, Yerba Buena, Tucumán, 11/3/2008

[28] *LGT* "El fallo en contra de los ingenios: 'fue una lucha entre David y Goliat'" 09/15/2008

[29] Interview: T08, Federal Court of Tucumán, Tucumán, 4/14/2009

[30] *La Gaceta de Tucumán* "Investigan 60 causas por daño ambiental" 10/23/2006

[31] Actuación Preliminar N 62 "La Trindad," Ministerio Público Fiscal, San Miguel de Tucumán, 3/13/2007

[32] Actuación Preliminar No 61 "Ingenio Ñuñorco p.s.a. inf. Arts. 55, 56 y 57 de la Ley 24.051," Ministerio Público Fiscal, San Miguel de Tucumán, 3/13/2007

Locally powerful political actors, such as firm owners, were limited in their ability to fight back against Gómez because he was part of the federal, not provincial, judicial system. The pressure was such that the main business association, the Economic Federation of Tucumán (FET), met with politicians looking for help. The firm owners enlisted the National Deputy Beatriz Rojkés de Alperovich (who is also the governor's wife), attempting to convince the national legislature to declare an "environmental emergency" in Tucumán and to suspend the court cases against the firms. The proposal supported by the industry was for the government to give firms ninety days to come up with a plan to clean up their production and five years to comply with legislation. This move failed to gain support in the national legislature, and the legal cases continued. A senior official in the Environment Department described the importance of the national-level involvement: "For many years, the environmental problems, the fines and the rest, they were managed politically. There would not be effective fines, or the fines would be suspended, or they would only collect minimum fines, these kinds of things. Then the Federal prosecutor came into the picture, and ... things began to get complicated because they left the borders of Tucumán."[33]

Gómez was not the only force from outside of Tucumán to become involved in environmental politics. Toward the end of the 1990s, there was an external shock from a neighboring province (Santiago del Estero) that was receiving pollution in the Rio Salí from Tucumán's industry. A series of fish kills in a lake at the border between the provinces made the consequences of water contamination highly visible.[34] The hotel association of the tourist-dependent border town, Termas de Río Hondo, estimated that it lost 17 million dollars of tourism business.[35] Officials in Santiago del Estero took the province of Tucumán to Federal court, hoping to compel it to enforce its own environmental laws.[36] The process was very slow and did not have any immediate impact on firms, but it created uncertainty and raised the specter of industry needing to reduce pollution at some point in the future. With very slow-moving political maneuvering over cross-jurisdictional pollution, conflict that was not contained in institutions spilled out onto the streets. Loosely organized protests on the border increased, and by October of 2006, for a number of days, protesters in Santiago del Estero blocked the roads that link Tucumán to the ports in Buenos Aires and Rosario.[37] There were also protests by Santiagueños in the

---

[33] Interview: T17, Senior Official, Tucumán Environmental Secretariat, Tucumán, 11/3/2008

[34] *LGT* "Hallan una mancha de aceite y peces muertos en El Frontal" 08/10/2005; "El embalse de Río Hondo se llenó de algas y peces muertos" 08/17/2006

[35] *La Gaceta de Tucumán* "Por la contaminación, Las Termas pierde $ 50 millones" 10/18/2003

[36] *LGT* "Grave demanda contra Tucumán" 09/28/2002

[37] *La Gaceta de Tucumán* "Pobladores de Las Termas protestaron cortando la ruta 9" 10/10/2006. "Caos en la ruta 9 por un reclamo en Las Termas" 11/04/2006 and "Termenses afianzan su plan de lucha" 11/04/2006

Mobilization against pollution 199

main square of San Miguel de Tucumán, and, in December 2006, 3000 letters were written to the governor of Tucumán about the contamination, news that made the front pages of the local newspaper.[38]

The protests and road-blocks were seen by businessmen as a genuine threat that could disrupt exports of citrus goods and shipments of sugar.[39] A leader of one of the groups in Santiago said: "Our intention is to call the attention of the entire country. We want the problem to be nationalized. Until we have victory, we do not know how long the blockages will go on."[40] Unrest and road-blocks hit a potential sensitive point in the economy of Tucumán because "... the land routes to Buenos Aires pass through Santiago de Estero. The train passes through Santiago. Therefore, the communities in Santiago started to threaten to block the routes. The sugar would not pass; the citrus exports would not pass. This created a fear among the industries that they wouldn't be able to send their goods to Buenos Aires, to the port."[41]

It is important to note that the increase in pressure to address pollution was not simply due to environmental organizations in Tucumán gaining strength or having greater resources than those in Santa Fe or Córdoba. There were no major changes in environmental organizations from the 1990s to 2000s – only the creation of two relatively modest neighborhood-level groups (UniVec and Pacto Verde). The only established professional environmental organization in Tucumán was the FA. It had only one staff member, but it could draw on the resources of the professional societies. Two medium-size groups were Pro-Eco and Pacto Verde; both included some individuals with professional backgrounds, but were otherwise local community organizations with few members. Neither of these organizations had the staff, international connections, or presence of groups like Taller Ecologista and ECOSur in Santa Fe, or CEDAH in Córdoba. Nor was the absolute number of groups larger in Tucumán than it was in other provinces – of the three provinces, Córdoba had the greatest number of civil society organizations that worked on environmental issues, and Tucumán the least.[42]

In sum, mobilization against pollution in Tucumán took a qualitatively different shape from that of Santa Fe. There were flare-ups of unrest around specific communities and firms, but there was also a series of pressures that threatened all firms in the citrus and sugar industries, including: protests, courts that were willing to hear cases like those of the FA, the efforts of federal

---

[38] *La Gaceta de Tucumán* "Tres mil cartas le enviaron los santiagueños a Alperovich" 12/2/2006
[39] Business leaders were especially concerned because of the blockades of the bridge in Entre Rios over the Botnia paper mill, which was condoned by President Kirchner. Interviews: T17, Senior Official, Tucumán Environmental Secretariat, Tucumán, 11/3/2008; T49, Tucumán Regional Sugar Industry Association (CART), Tucumán, 11/14/2008
[40] *La Gaceta de Tucumán* "Anuncian cortes de ruta en Las Termas" 02/20/2007. "Ambientalistas cortan la ruta 9 durante 24 horas" 2/15/2007
[41] Interview: T17, Senior Official, Tucumán Environmental Secretariat, Tucumán, 11/3/2008
[42] Luna and Cecconi 2004

200   *Pollution in the "Garden of the Republic"*

prosecutor, and the threats of officials in federal bureaucracies. In combination, these developments threatened the entire industry's license to operate, not just that of individual firms unlucky enough to have mobilized neighbors. The implications of this form of mobilization will be explored in detail later in the chapter, but first we will examine the changes in the patterns of enforcement.

SHIFTING PATTERNS OF ENFORCEMENT

In response to the conflict surrounding pollution, the provincial government of Tucumán could have taken several courses of action. Regulators could have put out as many fires as possible, mediating conflicts between individual firms and communities where there were disruptive mobilizations without taking further steps (as happened in Santa Fe and Córdoba). Alternatively, regulators could have stepped back while the courts slowly worked through their process. Court orders could have been met with a pro-forma response that would have simply defended the politically powerful industries (e.g., regulators could have claimed that firms were complying with regulations even if they were not).[43] As one firm owner noted, "delays in our justice system have advantages. … and paradoxically create rationality."[44] Any of these reactions would have been possible without allocating scarce resources to environmental regulators. Tucumán, however, took a different course of action, slowly building up the capabilities to regulate industry. These efforts involved two programs that were layered on top of SIPROSA. The first program was the Provincial Plan for Clean Production (*Plan de Producción Limpia,* or PPL) and the second was the Program for Industrial Reconversion (*Programa de Reconversión Industrial,* PRI). This section describes these programs and the subsequent changes in enforcement.

The Plan for Clean Production was created at the end of 2001 and beginning of 2002.[45] The PPL was born out of a collaboration between the federal environmental secretariat and the province of Tucumán, with money from the national government and support from the United Nations Environment Program and the World Bank.[46] The PPL had two central features. First, firms were offered the opportunity to sign voluntary agreements and commit to introducing pollution reduction in their plants. In total, twenty-eight firms, including eight sugar mills and three citrus plants, signed the agreements. Second, to implement the plan, a Center for PPL was established in a partnership between the provincial government, federal government, and the National

---

[43] A common response by Argentine regulators is to *generar numeros,* meaning to undertake actions that look good in quantitative evaluations but have no real substance.

[44] Interview: T49, Tucumán Regional Sugar Industry Association (CART), Tucumán, 11/14/2008

[45] Interview: B28, Federal Secretariat of Environment and Sustainable Development, Buenos Aires, 9/22/2008

[46] *La Gaceta de Tucumán* "Tratarán en un foro la contaminación del Salí" 10/6/2002

Shifting patterns of enforcement 201

University of Tucumán. The new program and regulatory body did not displace SIPROSA; instead the PPL was a parallel effort layered upon the existing weak institutions.

With the PPL, there was an incremental increase in enforcement, as regulators collected more information about firm performance and responded pedagogically to problems in the industry. The PPL staff audited environmental management in the firms in order to identify changes that would reduce waste generation, water consumption, and energy use. Thus, the state began to collect detailed information on the processes of the most polluting industries in the province, not just on the effluents that were released by industry. In response to this information, the PPL gave free consulting advice to the firms (many of which did not have in-house expertise in environmental management), looking for "win-wins" that immediately made pollution prevention profitable. Regulators also encouraged firms to collaborate with one another, as well as with the state, in search of better technical solutions to the root causes of pollution. In addition, the PPL brought in experts outside of the province to talk about environmental management with industry. In sum, for two critical tasks of enforcement (information collection and crafting a response) officials substantially increased outputs over the previous period.

The PPL did not, however, include penalties for noncompliance. On the contrary, the PPL shielded firms from pressures while industry tried to improve its performance. A senior official who was involved in the PPL described the informal exchange: "There was a verbal commitment that while a firm is in the PPL, it would not be penalized. This was a commitment absolutely outside of the law because the agreements could not modify the law."[47] This function of PPL was to help firms that were struggling to manage increasing demands for compliance, not to create penalties for those that did not comply. A manager at a citrus firm described the importance of the plan:

[The regulators] knew no one could comply with the legislation. It was for that reason that they established the PPL, and that is why we were part of the project ... We could say [to the courts and environmental groups] "well, we are working, we are in the PPL, we are doing things, but we still haven't gotten to the pollution levels, but we are looking for a better technology." With this, the PPL helped us. It was a commitment to really find a solution.[48]

The focus on incremental change contrasted strongly with the all-or-nothing structures of the legal regulations. A PPL official explained:

The law that says what the BOD should be ... was copied from some other law from some other country. Nobody here thinks that industry can get to those levels ... This is an international standard in the academic world. [The firms say:] "I can't get to this level because I am at 60,000 and I can't reduce to 250 [sic], it is impossible." Well, now we

---

[47] Interview: T10, Cleaner Production Center, Tucumán, 11/11/2008
[48] Interview: T02, Environmental Specialist, Citrus Firm, Cevil Pozo, Tucumán, 4/17/2009

*say, "How much can you do?" They say, "OK, I can go from 60,000 down to 30,000."
And we say, "Great, how long will it take you?" [They respond] "Eighteen months."
[We ask them]: "You are willing to sign an agreement?" . . . That's it. The agreement is
signed. That is Cleaner Production.*[49]

To make these extra-legal negotiations possible, SIPROSA's enforcement agents were kept on the outside and did not receive information from the audits.[50] An official involved with PPL described his strategy: "I always tried to make it so the firms did not see us as a bridge to a group of disguised inspectors. To try to separate as much as possible."[51] The objective was for firms to be open with PPL about their difficulties in complying without risking local prosecution. The voluntary nature of the PPL did, of course, limit the program. Some firms "hid, stayed quiet, and no one was going to bother them. And no one visited them or controlled them."[52] And among those that participated, many firms undertook projects that increased environmental efficiency without actually tackling the problems that led to their noncompliance with existing regulations.[53]

Notwithstanding the organization's limitations, increases in enforcement under the PPL contributed to a number of concrete improvements in environmental performance. Through engagement with the PPL, some firms began to introduce environmental management into their processes. As a manager explained, "We started with the problems of order and housekeeping. From there, we started to find lots of things, such as the waste of oils, products, and paper."[54] The PPL not only reduced pollution, but it improved management, which led to real benefits for some firms. For example, the sugar mill, Marapa, increased energy efficiency with a savings of more than $100,000 and invested in better filtration systems that reduced pollution, as well as waste, with a three-year payback. The citrus firm Citrusvil reduced the use of sodium hydroxide in their operations and saved thousands of dollars in the process. And the citrus firm Citromax improved water efficiency to reduce usage, and costs, by 5%.[55]

After the PPL ended in 2005, Tucumán created the Plan of Industrial Reconversion (PRI). The PRI included a new round of voluntary agreements with all citrus firms and sugar mills. The PRI went beyond the PPL in two key ways. First, the PRI was closely linked with the broader regulatory system and

---

[49] Interview: T10, Cleaner Production Center, Tucumán, 11/11/2008

[50] Interview: T18, Environmental Inspector, Tucumán Ministry of Health (SIPROSA), Tucumán, 11/4/2008

[51] Interview: T10, Cleaner Production Center, Tucumán, 11/11/2008

[52] Interview T10, Cleaner Production Center, Tucumán, 11/11/2008

[53] Interview T15, Industrial Engineer, Tucumán Environmental Secretariat, Tucumán, 10/28/2008 and 11/10/2008

[54] Interview: T23, Environmental Specialist, Sugar Mill, Tucumán, 11/12/2008

[55] González, J. (2003). *Producción limpia en tucumán: Primera experiencia demonstrativa en argentina.* Tucumán: Ministerio de la Economía, Gobierno de la Provincia de Tucumán. See also: *LGT* : "La Producción Limpia aumenta las ganancias" 07/17/2002

Shifting patterns of enforcement 203

prescribed real penalties for noncompliance with the agreement. As described here, all three key tasks of enforcement – collecting information, crafting responses, and overcoming political resistance – increased markedly under the PRI. Second, in addition to introducing general improvements in environmental management, the PRI agreements contained specific plans and requirements for reduction of key effluents (e.g., acidity and BOD in wastewater). These agreements also included specific timelines for the construction of controls on effluents, the adoption of management practices, and the attainment of specific pollution levels.[56] For example, the sugar mill Concepción agreed to go from a baseline of dumping 700 tons of cachaza in the canal system per day to stopping all dumping in a two-year period. Pollution reductions retained progressive elements and did not always mean compliance; an official explained "we had to write something in the agreements that the firms could comply with; in other words, we couldn't have a utopian objective."[57] Nevertheless, the PRI agreements were substantially stricter than they were under the PPL.

In order to monitor the progress that firms made in meeting their goals, the PRI regulators collected information through multiple channels. At the start of the program, the province conducted a baseline analysis of all firms in the citrus and sugar industries, noting their effluent levels and their technology for pollution control. Once the agreements were negotiated, every two months firms had to send progress reports on their investments. In addition, regulators conducted three types of inspections.[58] First, inspectors made unannounced visits to the areas around the plants to take samples of pollution concentrations – data that revealed whether or not a sugar mill was dumping *vinaza* into the canals. Second, regulators conducted announced inspections to monitor the progress that firms were making with the plants; these inspections often involved long meetings with managers to discuss options for realizing the program's goals. Third, regulators went on joint inspections with SIPROSA and the water resources agency to identify and penalize the firms when they were out of compliance.

In an additional departure from information gathering in the PPL, regulators gained intelligence about the performance of firms from community and environmental organizations. An official described the process, stating "we are in constant contact with the people from the NGOs. [They say] 'this firm is better, this one is worse,' or 'look, this firm is dumping this filth into the river, go [inspect them].'"[59] For instance, the neighborhood group, UniVec, arranged

---

[56] Source: Analysis of all of the PRI agreements provided by the provincial government.
[57] Interview: T17, Senior Official, Tucumán Environmental Secretariat, Tucumán, 11/3/2008
[58] Interview: T15, Industrial Engineer, Tucumán Environmental Secretariat, Tucumán, 10/28/2008 and 11/10/2008
[59] Interview: T13, Lawyer, Tucumán Environmental Secretariat, Tucumán, 10/28/2008

204   *Pollution in the "Garden of the Republic"*

meetings between residents living near polluted streams and the Secretary of Environment Alfredo Montalván.[60]

Constant monitoring was important because even when firms invested in technological fixes to contamination problems, it was necessary for firms to change their operations and maintain new practices in the long run. For example, large capital investments, such as boilers, had not only to be maintained but used, as one regulator explained.

This mill has a beautiful boiler, new, the latest generation technology, and managers don't open the water circuit [that enables the air filter] ... because it costs money to run the water. Thus, the mill emitted black smoke even though they have everything [technologically].[61]

Similarly, other contamination problems, such as managing semi-solid waste from the sugar mills (*cachaza*), involved putting systems into place to ensure that organic matter was carried into the fields by trucks and not dumped in rivers and canals. Such a process needed constant monitoring, as it was not accepted practice in the industry. With their information gathering, regulators were able to monitor firms in the industry, identify those that were backsliding, and help promote changes within.

Regulators responded to problems with a variety of tools. One mechanism was information diffusion. During factory visits, inspectors not only discussed the implementation of pollution control systems but offered suggestions for improvement based on their expertise and experience. The director of environmental health and safety in a large sugar mill described some of the benefits that come from inspections: "They have more information from a variety of industries and are able to solve concrete problems when I don't have access to the information myself. There is a technology transfer."[62] Moreover, the PRI organized meetings between the state and the firms during which each firm explained what it was doing to solve specific pollution problems. In combination, pedagogical inspections and meetings to share information helped mitigate compliance costs by diffusing practices across the industry in a way the industry associations largely had not.[63]

The PPL also created the conditions for experimentation with practices that could generate novel solutions. Learning was critically important for addressing some of the compliance challenges, such as processing the huge volumes of wastewater since cost-effective technology and management systems were not

---

[60] The author was copied on emails after interviewing one of the representative of a neighborhood association.

[61] Interview: T15, Industrial Engineer, Tucumán Environmental Secretariat, Tucumán, 10/28/2008 and 11/10/2008

[62] Interview: T03, Environmental Specialist, Sugar Mill, La Banda del Rio Salí, Tucumán, 4/21/2009

[63] All interviews indicated that the industry associations in Tucumán were not places where firms could go for help with environmental management.

Shifting patterns of enforcement

locally understood. Some firms began testing new forms of treatment, such as incinerating the pollutant vinasse and using it as a fuel. Effective practices were then picked up by regulators. An environmental manager from a citrus firm described her relationship with the regulators:

They come and do their audits, but more than anything, the regulators visit us to find out what is going on, to soak it in, because our processes are applicable to other citrus plants. Our relationship with the people from the PRI is pretty open. The inspectors don't have the knowledge and neither do we. We are buying technology from abroad, and we are learning, and the regulators come to learn as well.[64]

In addition to learning from firm-level efforts, regulators worked with the provincial agricultural research organization, the Agro-Industrial Research Station Obispo Colombres. Representatives from the industry also went along with regulators to the University of Valparaiso in Chile to examine new technologies for treatment of water effluents.[65] All of these actions helped firms identify solutions to pollution problems and reduce adjustment costs.

Joint-learning between regulators and the industry was supported by actual penalties for firms failing to comply. In May 2007, the San Juan sugar mill had its operations suspended for not meeting its commitments.[66] This was the first time ever that a mill was closed down for a period of time due to pollution. In January 2008, the Environment Department closed another sugar mill, La Corona, for failure to install air filters in its smokestacks.[67] The former closure did not involve any particular mobilization by community members, but the latter closure was supported by protests from UniVec that protested the mill and supported the Environment Department's action. Therefore, immediate mobilization was helpful in some cases but was not a necessary condition for punitive measures, indicating that the pattern of enforcement was *not* society-dependent, as it was in Santa Fe and Córdoba.

This enforcement process created a background threat of penalties that motivated intransigent firms and pressured collaborative firms to work with regulators.[68] A senior official in the Environment Department described the intent of these closures as a signal of the state's seriousness, "The state will close

---

[64] Interview: T02, Environmental Specialist, Citrus Firm, Cevil Pozo, Tucumán, 4/17/2009

[65] Interview: T04, Agro-Industrial Research Station Obispo Colombres, Las Talitas, Tucumán, 4/20/2009

[66] The exact circumstances that led to this particular mill being penalized are unclear. There were rumours that it was due to its owners politically supporting the opponent of the governor and that it was due to the intransigence of management. *LGT* "Por tercera vez en menos de ocho meses clausuran el ingenio San Juan" 01/09/2008. "La clausura del San Juan podría levantarse el lunes" 05/19/2007; "El capítulo local del 'affaire Picolotti'" 07/14/2007

[67] *LGT* "Clausuran el ingenio La Corona por contaminación" 01/06/2008

[68] On the relationship between penalties and problem-solving, see: Kagan and Scholz 1984; Ayres and Braithwaite 1992; Hawkins 2002; Locke, Amengual, and Mangla 2009

206 *Pollution in the "Garden of the Republic"*

you … It was a clear message to the businessmen. 'Don't fuck with me.'"[69] Another official described the move as a way of inducing cooperation.[70] The closures, although temporary, were a significant change in environmental regulation in Tucumán. Firm owners now saw evidence that there was a real possibility they would be shut down for not complying. As result, punitive pressures created the conditions for productive regulator-firm collaboration. The temporary closures also revealed that the regulators did overcome resistance to enforcement by some powerful regulated firms. With these actions, regulators said "air quality is not negotiable. We can negotiate anything else, but not air quality."[71] In sum, there clearly was a notable increase in all of the central tasks of enforcement.

Enforcement did more than put out a few fires; it helped tilt the balance of complete noncompliance in the sugar and citrus industries toward steady investment in pollution reduction. By 2009, tensions reduced substantially; although the head of the FA remained critical of the Secretary of Environment, he noted that "there are fewer problems, fewer complaints, and fewer conflicts than in previous years."[72] This outcome suggests that regulators were able to create some order in a chaotic regulatory environment. In addition, for the first time firms created specialized offices to address environmental concerns. This change could also very well be a key step in firms justifying environmental management in terms of efficiency and competitiveness, a process that has amplified the effect of state regulation in other contexts.[73]

There were also concrete changes in pollution mitigation that coincided with the regulators' efforts. Before 2006, only a third of the sugar mills had a system for managing the pollutant *cachaza*; by 2008, nearly all mills had developed *cachaza* management systems.[74] Similarly, in 2005 very few mills had installed filters to reduce air pollution from burning bagasse. The percentage of air emissions that were filtered increased from 19% in 2006 to 62% in 2007. By August 2009, 96% of emissions were filtered. Firms also invested in experimenting with new practices, and some used short-term methods to reduce water pollution (vinasse) in rivers. Overall, sugar mills reported that they invested nearly 50 million dollars in decreasing pollution in 2008 and 2009.

Improvements in enforcement also coincided with concrete results in the citrus firms, which invested more than ten million dollars in environmental management. A number of firms had installed more advanced pollution treatment systems, and at least two firms gained ISO 14,000 certifications. One firm

---

[69] Interview: Anonymous official, Tucumán, 04/2009
[70] Interview: T17, Senior Official, Tucumán Environmental Secretariat, Tucumán, 11/3/2008
[71] Interview: T17, Senior Official, Tucumán Environmental Secretariat, Tucumán, 11/3/2008
[72] LGT "Ambientalistas aprueban lo realizado, pero piden que les den participación" 10/15/2009
[73] Dobbin and Sutton 1998
[74] Data provided by the Environment Secretariat. These figures are largely supported by interviews with the government critics.

Explaining the shift in Tucumán 207

successfully installed a biogas system to power the plant, thereby reducing greenhouse gas emissions and earning carbon offset credits to gain revenues from treating wastewater.[75] Although the actions of regulators were one of many factors pushing firms to comply, in this case, environmental regulation was clearly successful in helping to induce pollution reduction and bring firms closer to compliance with the laws.

In sum, there was a dramatic shift in enforcement in Tucumán that departed from the general pattern of failed institutions in Argentina. Enforcement reached a high level – with regulators undertaking all of the necessary tasks with greater intensity than had been done in other provinces in both industries. Moreover, the pattern of enforcement was co-produced, as indicated by the heavy involvement of social groups in providing political and operational support as well as a partial decoupling of particular enforcement actions from immediate protests. This outcome was not the only possibility. In response to the threats from courts, federalism, and community mobilization, the provincial government could have taken any number of actions that did not involve investment in resources in the regulatory agency. Regulators could have put out as many fires as possible with the resources they had. In addition, regulators could have simply protected industry by claiming that firms were in compliance when they, in fact, were not, or by dragging their feet in reaction to court demands and federal government pressures. Neither of these courses of action would have required substantial investment of resources in the PPL or the PRI. Yet, the province did not take these paths. Instead, it pushed and enabled firms to improve while beginning to assemble an environmental regulatory agency capable of sustaining this enforcement effort.

The gains in Tucumán were still not cause for a final celebration. The province had some way to go before it gets pollution completely under control. Nevertheless, there were real changes in Tucumán and a substantial departure from the firefighting model of enforcement. Given the weakness of environmental regulation in most of Argentina, these marginal improvements are worthy of close analysis. Moreover, this outcome contrasts strongly with that of the cases discussed in the previous chapter. Whereas in Santa Fe regulators put out fires and made chaotic regulation bearable for industry, in Tucumán regulators systematically took steps to enable entire industries to move toward compliance.

EXPLAINING THE SHIFT IN TUCUMÁN

Why did enforcement change so dramatically in Tucumán? The answer lies, in part, in the shocks created by a combination of factors: social mobilization,

---

[75] *LGT* "Una industria citrícola tucumana es pionera en el proyecto de convertir efluentes en biogas" 12/05/2008

the action of the prosecutor, and the "nationalization" of the issue by virtue of the involvement of Santiago del Estero. Political pressures from outside the province alone, however, are not sufficient for creating enforcement – not only could the bureaucracy lack capabilities for action, but local, politically power-ful actors can block action by provincial regulators. Therefore, an explanation for the changes in Tucumán must first address the question of how regulators for the provincial government were able operationally to undertake the tasks involved in enforcement as well as to identify the mechanisms through which political pressure led to action at the micro-level. Only afterward, can the analysis turn to the way larger forces – from prosecutors and the government – led to the creation of the PPL and PRI.

The central hypothesis from the literature is that, in order to enforce regula-tions, the state should have reformed its bureaucracy to conform to standard organizational designs to improve autonomy. The evidence in this case suggests otherwise; Tucumán's regulatory agencies actually became less Weberian as enforcement increased. There was no meritocratic process for hiring the staff to implement both the PPL and the PRI; officials in both programs were given temporary contracts without civil service protection. Moreover, instead of having career pathways within the state, regulators' careers were tied closely to the very firms that they had to control. After the PPL ended, for example, only one staff member stayed on the side of the regulators; the rest went to work in the private sector. When the PRI was created, key staff came directly from the private sector, where they had been colleagues with the managers that they now needed to regulate. And at least one official working with the PRI was hired away to a sugar mill after the program began. Seen from the point of view of organizational coherence, the PPL and PRI appear to have been a step down both from SIPROSA and from the regulators in Santa Fe (analyzed in the previous chapter). In sum, Tucumán is another case of increasing enforcement without the kinds of reforms that theories of state capacity and policymakers alike argue are necessary.

Even though there was not a reform that improved bureaucratic coherence, there was an expansion of administrative resources that enabled the types of actions described previously in this chapter. When the PPL was launched, the Center for PPL hired a team of twelve young engineers to oversee imple-mentation of voluntary agreements. And when the PPL ended, sixteen new professionals were hired to implement the PRI.[76] Although they lacked civil service protection, all (engineers and a lawyer) had the skills needed to under-take the key tasks of regulation. In addition, the core staff was supported by student interns who could gather simple samples of pollution and extend the reach of the PRI. While operational resources were tight, regulators had better

---

[76] Again, this change was not a move toward a more Weberian bureaucracy. The PRI team had short-term contracts, no clear career path within public administration, and there was no exam to ensure that the hiring was meritocratic.

Explaining the shift in Tucumán 209

access to computers and transportation than did their counterparts in other provinces. Moreover, these staff members were layered on top of SIPROSA, which was incorporated into a newly established Environment Department that consolidated various agencies involved in environmental management into one single agency. Ultimately, these changes overall gave Tucumán a level of staffing, expertise, and resources that was much higher than that in most Argentine environmental agencies. The increases in administrative resources allowed regulators to go beyond firefighting and strategically to plan their enforcement efforts, which help account for the breadth of enforcement. These levels of administrative resources compared favorably with those of Santa Fe and Córdoba, provinces in which regulators had "little margin" for action due to a lack of manpower and budget.

Although close personal ties with industry can promote industry capture, in some ways regulators used these relationships to further enforcement. In order to jointly engage in problem-solving with industry, regulators first needed access. One senior official described how his previous experience with the firms helped:

With the people who manage the firms, there is a relationship of trust, and, with some, of friendship. Everyone knows me because I was classmates of a number of them at the university. ... This relationship that I have with the people who manage the firms has been very valuable because it has opened doors for me.[77]

These types of relationships were key for problem-solving and for collaborating with allies inside firms who wanted to promote change.

Within each firm, there are conflicts with the people who work on environment. And you know what happens? They call us on the phone from their private phones and they say 'Can you come down and do an inspection so they give me money?' In order to get the firm to spend money on the technical team, we have to go and be the bad guys to say 'you have to fix this problem.'[78]

Thus, in this case, the ties that developed between regulators and firms led to greater enforcement compared with that of the earlier period of SIPROSA.

The absence of bureaucratic features to insulate regulators could have been a recipe for blocked enforcement. To understand why it was not, we have to take fuller account of the way the state was porous to different sets of societal organizations – it is insufficient to examine only the potential of business to influence the actions of regulators without also exploring what pro-regulation groups could do. In Tucumán, the ability for regulators to interact with environmental organizations changed substantially. Initially, SIPROSA did not have linkages with environmental organizations and, therefore, there was no

---

[77] Interview: T17, Senior Official, Tucumán Environmental Secretariat, Tucumán, 11/3/2008
[78] Interview: T15, Industrial Engineer, Tucumán Environmental Secretariat, Tucumán, 10/28/2008 and 11/10/2008

210 *Pollution in the "Garden of the Republic"*

countervailing power against businesses that sought to block enforcement. Even during the PPL phase of enforcement, there were few formal or informal openings for participation from environmental groups, and, with no direct pressure on regulators, the agreements lacked teeth.[79]

Barriers to the environmental groups forming linkages, however, gradually broke down. In a process akin to the one described in Santa Fe and Córdoba, officials in the state saw it to their advantage to develop connections with groups that could mobilize protests. As the Secretary of Environment described:

Our experience tells us that it is important to communicate with the NGO, and for that we have a working agreement with various NGOs ... The majority of NGOs have received, from us, all of the information about the commitments of the firms. Many times, the NGOs ... have been able to, in some way, follow them from close by.[80]

This view of the relationship between NGOs and regulators was shared by some of the environmental groups. For example, one community leader said that he "sits down with regulators to discuss problems, and they have never denied [us] access to information."[81] Another commented that when there were conflicts, the Secretary of Environment "personally came" to meet with them and they had "fluid" contacts with regulators.[82] One neighborhood group, for example, sent emails to the Secretary of Environment when they observed pollution coming from a sugar mill. Later, the group brokered meetings between officials and neighbors of the mill, putting regulators into direct contact with those who could closely monitor compliance.[83]

Just as in Santa Fe and Córdoba, these linkages with environmental groups helped regulators undertake steps required for enforcement. Not only did the environmental groups have information about violations (as described earlier), but these groups helped regulators overcome resistance from firms. A regulator described some of the ways environmental groups augmented enforcement.

The pressure is one way [they help us]. It helps push the firms to look for technology, to spend money. ... The NGOs ask us for emails with the reports, to know when we are going to intervene. For example, [the PRI agreement with a firm said] that on September 21, the firm had to install a silencer installed on its boilers. What happens if it isn't there? We say to them, "fine, there is a delay, ... [But] the community is going to go and protest the mill."[84]

---

[79] Multiple interviews with environmental groups, officials from the PPL, and firms that participated in the program.

[80] Interview: T07, Senior Official, Tucumán Environmental Secretariat, Tucumán, 11/4/2008, 11/14/2008 and 04/20/2009

[81] Interview: T21, Environmental Activist, Concepcion, Tucumán, 11/15/2008 and 04/16/2009

[82] Interview: T29, Pro Eco, Tafí Viejo, Tucumán, 11/1/2008

[83] The author was copied on emails after interviewing one of the representative of a neighborhood association.

[84] Interview: T43, Engineer, Tucumán Environmental Secretariat, Tucumán, 10/28/2008 and 04/20/2008

Explaining the shift in Tucumán 211

Thus, the use of community pressure was important, in this regulator's account, even in the context of judiciary action and federal pressure from neighboring provinces. Overall, informal connections that enabled information sharing with the societal organizations and political pressure were one element that helped regulators (who themselves lacked insulation from politically powerful actors) respond forcefully to recalcitrant firms.

Developing these linkages was possible because ties created political advantages for regulators who were tasked with preventing conflicts. Building a relationship without mobilized groups could, as one environmentalist put it, "domesticate" the community organizations.[85] Senior officials took steps to encourage environmental organizations to channel their complaints to regulatory officials instead of to the streets. This strategy, not surprisingly, created some strain between regulators and environmental groups. On the one hand, many groups were wary about legitimizing programs that could protect firms from judicial claims.[86] Organizations also did not want to end up being controlled by the state by signing formal agreements of collaboration with regulators. On the other hand, the regulators wanted to maintain control over enforcement while bringing environmental groups out of the street and into structured forms of conflict. Regulators favored neighborhood organizations, as one senior official notes. "As a policy principle this Environment Department goes to where the neighbors are, to understand the problem from the neighbor, not from the interpretation of an NGO."[87] Ultimately, the porous nature of the state fluidly admitted neighborhood organizations and NGOs that could directly access officials with few barriers.

Beyond linkages – the politics of providing resources to regulators for co-production

In some ways, such a dynamic was similar to the one observed in Córdoba and Santa Fe – mobilization opened up space for linkages that, in turn, enable regulators to enforce. Unlike those cases, however, regulators in Tucumán were not completely dependent operationally on social organizations – using their own administrative resources, regulators could collect information even when there was no neighborhood group. These operational capabilities allowed regulators to extend their actions, leading to higher, and broader, levels of enforcement. While in Santa Fe and Córdoba mobilization created immediate responses without triggering any broader change, a senior official explained

---

[85] Interview: T25, Pro Eco, Tafí Viejo, Tucumán, 11/1/2008
[86] Interview: T21, Environmental Activist, Concepcion, Tucumán, 11/15/2008 and 04/16/2009. *LGT* "Ambientalistas aprueban lo realizado, pero piden que les den participación" 10/15/2009
[87] Interview: T07, Senior Official, Tucumán Environmental Secretariat, Tucumán, 11/4/2008 and 11/14/2008 and 04/20/2009

that in Tucumán, "All of the actions of the NGOs I see as opportunities to grow institutionally ... to gain more resources."[88] The question remains, therefore, what about Tucumán resulted in investment in administrative resources?

One key difference between the case of Tucumán and those of Santa Fe and Córdoba was the fact that an exchange for support (or at least acquiescence) by particular social groups for access to the state apparatus was not a viable strategy for responding to political pressures generated by pollution. Crucially, mobilization by individual community groups was combined with broader threats on firms and with added pressure on political leaders. For one, complaints by the government of Santiago del Estero drew the attention of federal officials. The Secretary of Environment, Romina Picolotti, visited Tucumán a number of times and met with the governor to try to work out a solution. When the federal government was drawn into the dispute, it could offer resources, but it could not take direct enforcement actions. As the Secretary of Environment Picolotti explained: "The power [to regulate] is exercised by the province of Tucumán, but the federal government offered assistance to [Governor] Alperovich, and he accepted."[89] Thus, conflict that went well beyond the community level created the conditions for resources to be allocated to regulators in Tucumán.

In addition to the province of Santiago del Estero, the federal prosecutor directly threatened firms in an arena that created uncertainty for all businesses. This threat led to businesses supporting the governor's acceptance of funds to enlarge the regulatory apparatus. While the prosecutor had not yet put anyone in jail or shut down firms, business leaders could not be sure this situation would last. Blocked from changing the laws,[90] industry saw that its back was against the wall. A leader in the industry summed up the challenge this way: "The idea was that we would have sugar as cheap as in a village in Africa and production methods as clean as the highest level of the first world ... which generated a very difficult situation." Eventually "[we] have to comply or we will be shut down."[91] Although firms had been successful in the past in resisting

---

[88] Interview: T07, Senior Official, Tucumán Environmental Secretariat, Tucumán, 11/4/2008 and 11/14/2008 and 04/20/2009

[89] *LGT*, "'Evidentemente, el Plan de Producción Limpia no es suficiente,' opinó Picolotti" 10/28/2006

[90] When all of the legal battles began heating up in 2006, the main business association, the Economic Federation of Tucumán (FET), met with politicians looking for help. They enlisted the national Deputy Beatriz Rojkés de Alperovich (who is also the governor's wife) to declare an "environmental emergency" in Tucumán and suspend the court cases against the firms. This attempt was unsuccessful and the court cases went forward. *LGT* "Proponen que se declare en emergencia la cuenca del río Salí" 10/24/2006, "Hay voluntad política para sanear la Cuenca" 12/19/2006

[91] Interview: T49, Tucumán Regional Sugar Industry Association (CART), Tucumán, 11/14/2008

Explaining the shift in Tucumán

pressures, there was a perception (whether it was warranted or not) among leading industrialists that the questions were when and how, not whether, they would have to change. Thus, even though the firms did not support stricter regulations, they did support the expansion of the state's ability to act as an intermediary and to assist them in compliance.

Compared with facing the onslaught of social mobilization and prosecution on their own, the prospect of more active state regulators presented substantial advantages to industry. The firms needed help figuring out how to deal with the new demands. For some issues, such as air pollution from boilers in the sugar mills, the technical solution was fairly clear, only requiring investment in new technologies and their associated operating costs. For other issues, such as treatment of water pollutants, even leaders in the industry did not know what solution might work in a cost-effective way. At the beginning of the 2000s, most firms did not have environmental managers or engineers with training in pollution mitigation. In addition, firms also wanted regulators to provide them with protection from the coming social pressure (exercised through the courts and in the street) while they looked for a solution. All the firms in the citrus and sugar industries (not just those located next to mobilized communities) were threatened. Anything that could buy the firms time to upgrade progressively instead of forcing changes upon them all at once would help firms survive. For example, when the PPL ended, "firms were desperate to continue to have a refuge," and they recognized that the regulators "gave them the ability to introduce environmental issues in their factories."[92] Ultimately, the expansion of administrative resources was created with the backing of industry and the fiscal support of the federal government.

In sum, the key to explaining change lies in the increase of administrative resources and the shift in the way the state was porous to societal groups, which, combined, paved the way for co-produced enforcement. First, investments in administrative resources augmented the operational capacity of the regulators. Through the PPL and PRI, regulators were able to gather more information and take more actions to encourage, as well as enable, firms to improve performance. Second, officials worked to channel the continued actions of environmental groups into regulatory institutions, thereby developing ties with community organizations; these linkages expanded regulators' ability to monitor firms and allowed them to exercise political pressure at the base of the bureaucracy. Third, direct pressures placed on firms by the courts prevented linkage formation from being a sufficient response to conflict, thus creating the political conditions necessary for investments in administrative resources. Ultimately, this process led to the co-produced enforcement at a high level.

---

[92] Interview: T07, Senior Official, Tucumán Environmental Secretariat, Tucumán, 11/4/2008 and 11/14/2008 and 04/20/2009

CONCLUSION

Environmental regulations are essential for promoting sustainable and inclusive development. Yet, state responses to noncompliance are highly uneven. This chapter analyzed the province of Tucumán, an unlikely case of a substantial increase in enforcement. The province is mired in poverty, has low levels of political competition, and depends on polluting industries – all factors often attributed to poor environmental performance. Notwithstanding these obstacles, increases in enforcement occurred beyond what we observed in neighboring provinces in the previous chapter. This puzzle has two central implications for the analysis of enforcement in the context of weak institutions.

First, this case demonstrates, once again, that enforcement is possible without the preconditions of creating a traditionally strong bureaucracy. Protecting regulators from political influence was not, in this case, the answer for improving enforcement. By contrast to the expectations of conventional theory, the first-order underpinnings of variation in enforcement could be located in combinations of administrative resources and linkages between regulators and society. The state gained operational capabilities while simultaneously changing the way regulators had informal relationships with organizations in society.

In this way, the eventual outcome of co-produced enforcement in Tucumán closely parallels the case of labor standards enforcement in the garment industry of the Federal Capital. Societal groups in the Federal Capital helped extend the capabilities of regulators and politically influenced them to promote enforcement, but labor inspectors also used their own resources to go beyond punctual societal demands. The similarities in outcomes and in the two primary explanatory factors in the cases of Tucumán environment and Federal Capital labor provide especially strong support to the central argument of this book considering the vast differences in background conditions – Tucumán and the Federal Capital had different political parties in power, different levels of socioeconomic development, and different types of firms being regulated (large heavy industry versus small hidden workshops).

Second, this account focused attention on how politics relates to changes in both administrative resources and in state-society ties. Chapter 7 showed how mobilization did not lead to shifts in administrative resources and, consequently, resulted in continuity in the pattern of enforcement. The outcomes in Santa Fe and Córdoba were similar to those identified in the cases of labor regulation in Peronist provinces – linkages were used to substitute for broader investments in administrative resources. These types of exchanges made society-dependent enforcement appear to be highly robust. Yet, in Tucumán, as in the labor cases of Santa Fe and the Federal Capital, such a dynamic did not occur. Instead, mobilization led to linkages between regulators and social organizations, but not in a way that undermined support for building up administrative resources. In this case, that support was due largely to the

Conclusion

presence of prosecutors and federal pressures. The federal government offered resources and informal pressure, while businesses responded by supporting PPL and PRI. Ultimately, these program augmented the capabilities of regulators to serve as intermediaries and help firms adjust to new demands. This type of political support for administrative resources was, in many ways, distinct from the processes in the labor cases (where partisanship blocked linkage formation, leaving governors exposed to pressure from labor unions). Yet there was a fundamental similarity – linkages alone were not a viable response to political demands. As a result, mounting pressures eventually led to the allocation of resources that enhanced the operational capabilities of the state.

PART III

CONCLUSION

9

Conclusion

This book has developed a framework for explaining regulatory enforcement built around the ways societal groups interact with state bureaucracies that are porous to political influence and have scarce resources. Though the analysis has focused on cases of labor and environmental regulation in Argentina, the argument advanced in this book also sheds light on a larger set of questions about the challenges of weak institutions and states. The idea that institutions matter for a wide range of social, political, and economic outcomes occupies a central place in social science. Formal institutions, however, often fail to effectively structure social behavior; institutional weakness is pervasive in much of the world, and it is common to find substantial differences between the formal rules of the game and actual practices. In these contexts, states can activate institutions through enforcement, and thereby play an important mediating role between formal institutional design and outcomes. The ways states undertake this task, however, are often highly uneven. For developing a fuller account of the way a wide range of institutions function in the world, it is necessary to explain how enforcement occurs and is allocated in society.

A key contribution of this book is showing that enforcement is possible without Weberian reforms to augment autonomy. While such reforms may indeed help enforcement, they are not the only ways to make enforcement possible. In only two cases discussed in this book (Córdoba labor under Angeloz, and Santa Fe labor during the Socialist administration) did a reform of the bureaucracy along conventional lines augment state capacity to increase enforcement. In all other cases, enforcement occurred despite problems of political interference, patronage, and limited resources.

Even in these cases, regulators can, and did, undertake the key steps of enforcement. Organizations in society were able to establish linkages with regulators through different means, including partisan alliances and mobilization. Once organizations established linkages to officials, the porous state was structured in a way that allowed these groups to provide resources as well as political support to regulators. These instances of enforcement were messy and highly imperfect. The allocation of enforcement was politically determined, not programmatic. Moreover, linkages were unstable and dependent on continued mobilization by groups that favored stronger regulation. Nevertheless, this set of political conditions enabled enforcement to occur in various parts of the economy.

Recognition of the unevenness of states and of the various ways in which enforcement levels change creates a substantial number of conceptual challenges for measuring differences across cases. To analyze enforcement, it is necessary but insufficient to categorize enforcement simply as present or absent across a broad geography or industry. Instead, we must unpack qualitative differences in enforcement at a more fine-grain level. A second contribution of this book is the development of a typology of patterns of enforcement. These distinct patterns have real consequences because they determine which individuals and communities gain the protections promised by regulations. The dominant pattern of enforcement known in the literature is the state-driven variant. In this pattern, resources for enforcement are mobilized entirely by the bureaucracy. Groups that mobilize for and against enforcement compete for influence outside of the state apparatus. Technical planners within the bureaucracy (guided by their political principals) allocate enforcement through an organized process. Under this pattern, enforcement is generally broad, and its intensity depends on the resources and organization of the bureaucracy as well as on the support of formal political principals. This pattern of enforcement was most evident in Santa Fe labor regulation, where there was an effort to insulate the health and safety inspectors, provide them with resources, and plan systematic enforcement in the construction industry. The pattern is also mirrored in cases outside of Argentina, like that of Brazil, which involved reforms to professionalize labor inspectorates.[1]

This pattern of enforcement, however, is not the only one. The most prevalent pattern in Argentina approximated the society-dependent ideal. In this pattern, substantial resources for enforcement are mobilized outside of the state apparatus. Officials draw heavily on organized groups for information about where violations occur and for operational resources to undertake the tasks of enforcement. As a result, enforcement is triggered when the groups that have access to the state demand enforcement and have capability to supplement the state. It follows that the distribution of enforcement is highly uneven in the economy, and its intensity is determined by the distribution of mobilized groups with resources and ties to the state. This pattern of enforcement was evident in parts of Córdoba's labor inspectorate, Tucumán's labor regulation, and in Santa Fe's environmental regulation. There were substantial limitations

---

[1] Pires 2008

Conclusion

to enforcement, most importantly in the way its distribution and quality hinged on the qualities of organizations in society, but the state did not drop completely away as a relevant actor; even if regulators from the state cannot act alone, they do have capabilities that are not located in society.

In addition to the extremes of state-driven and society-dependent enforcement, I have identified a third type of co-produced enforcement. In this pattern, substantial resources for enforcement are mobilized both within the state apparatus and in society. As in the society-dependent pattern, organizations outside the state provide information and, in some cases, material support. However, by contrast, in the co-produced pattern, the state also contributes resources toward the operational tasks of enforcement. Such a result occurred in Tucumán's environmental regulation as well as in labor regulation in the garment industry of the Federal Capital. This pattern mirrors the type of positive-sum interaction that Ostrom identified in her original formulation of co-production; nonsubstitutable attributes of the contributions of state and society combine in ways that make them more than the sum of their parts.[2] Enforcement is triggered both by groups making demands and by bureaucratic planning processes that are programmatic in nature. The combination of triggers and greater mobilization of resources results in enforcement that is broad and intense.

A third contribution of this book is the identification of specific conditions that result in distinct patterns of enforcement. To summarize, when there are substantial resources in the state but few linkages between officials and pro-regulation groups, enforcement approximates the state-driven pattern. By contrast, when officials have strong linkages to pro-regulation groups but there are few resources inside the state, the result is society-dependent enforcement. And when linkages are combined with resources internal to the state, enforcement can be co-produced. Identifying the interactions of these two key variables allows for a more complete theory of the politics of enforcement. In addition, by doing so, we are able to explain how differences in partisan alliances, ideology, and social mobilization lead to linkage formation and the allocation of administrative resources. Specifically, the interests that appointed officials have in allowing linkages to form are central to understanding differences in state-society relations. Partisan alliances in labor regulation created the conditions for robust linkages to form between unions and officials. It was possible to trace the processes by which partisan alliances led to the appointment of union leaders to heads of inspectorates who, in turn, supported the creation of linkages. When the partisan allies of unions did not gain power, appointments differed systematically, and the leaders of the bureaucracies took steps to curb linkages between inspectors and unions. In addition to the processes identified in the case studies, quantitative evidence from the cross-sectional

---

[2] Ostrom 1996

survey of inspectors in six provinces also revealed a relationship between partisanship and linkages structures.

Mobilization of societal groups, under certain conditions, also resulted in the formation of linkages. Linkages did not automatically occur due to the presence of a group in society with resources that could further enforcement. Many professional environmental organizations, for example, did not form close ties with regulators. Rather, linkages formed when groups gained power by taking to the streets and the courts (for example, by threatening to blockade factories). Moreover, linkage formation was prevented by alliances between political leaders and competing organizations and by ideological differences. The interplay between linkages and administrative resources reveals ways by which political support for enforcement only sometimes translated into the allocation of greater administrative resources. When linkage formation can satisfy the demands of mobilized groups, political leaders can choose not to allocate scarce resources to augment the operational capabilities of the state. Investments in administrative resources are much more likely when linkage formation is not a sufficient response to political demands. The case studies identified two sets of conditions under which this can occur – preexisting partisan alliances can block linkage formation, and ties with a specific group might not be able to quell a broad conflict.

PROBING THE LIMITS IN COMPARATIVE CONTEXT

All of the cases studied in this book took place in a democratic, middle-income, country with a history of highly mobilized societal organizations and a reputation for extremely porous bureaucracies. In the introduction, I laid out a set of scope conditions for the argument. Specifically, I expect the theory to explain variation in enforcement in contexts in which there are some societal organizations that have capabilities and interests broadly aligned with policy goals. Thus, there needs to be the availability of groups that can form linkages. In addition, there have to be some resources inside the state to enforce policies – otherwise only societal action can play a role and the state should have little importance. These scope conditions are very expansive and include a broad range of countries. Indeed, as recounted above, broadening the set of cases in which enforcement can be identified and explained beyond restrictive dominant approaches is one of the objectives of this book. How far can the theory travel outside of Argentina? Are the patterns of enforcement identified in Argentina evident in other countries? Or, are the particular features of Argentina – mobilized society, highly politicized state apparatus, middle-income – the only context in which these patterns obtain?

This book relies on detailed, subnational evidence about the nature of state-society relations, the organization of the state apparatus, and the uneven actions of the state to uncover the dynamics of enforcement. Cross-national datasets of state capacity, rule of law, and the density of civil society organization

Probing the limits in comparative context 223

cannot be used to test the theory on a wide sample of cases. Yet, there is a growing body of studies of subnational variation in regulatory enforcement that suggests that the patterns of enforcement evident in Argentina do exist broadly, albeit with different distributions. To probe these questions more deeply, the following sections employ research on subnational variation in enforcement, in a necessarily preliminary fashion, of environmental regulation in Vietnam and labor regulation in the United States and Indonesia. While the policy areas are directly comparable to those empirically analyzed in this book, the contexts differ from those of Argentina across a number of important dimensions.

Society-dependent environmental regulation in Vietnam[3]

Environmental regulation in Vietnam comes with a number of economic and political challenges beyond what was apparent in Argentina. Vietnam overall has lower levels of economic development,[4] and its economy has a greater reliance on exports than does Argentina.[5] According to conventional wisdom, these economic conditions should increase pressures against enforcement of environmental regulations that may impose a cost on firms.[6] In addition, Vietnam is an authoritarian state, and many of the largest polluters were state-owned enterprises. Therefore, we would expect substantially more constraints on social mobilization than we would in a democratic context. For instance, in Vietnam there are severe restrictions on independent and formal organizations outside of the state apparatus. One factor that Vietnam and Argentina do converge on is their reputations for low-quality government bureaucracies.[7] Corruption, patronage, and institutional weaknesses abound. In fact, descriptions of the environmental regulatory agencies in Vietnam mirror those of Argentina; regulatory bureaucracies in Vietnam suffer from "inadequate human and financial resources" and their staff lack training.[8] In addition to the lack of administrative resources, regulatory agencies are rife with political influence (especially by other parts of the state responsible for industrial development), and there is widespread corruption. In sum, according to the priors from dominant theory, Vietnam should have similar challenges in

---

[3] This account draws heavily on O'Rourke 2004a
[4] In 2009, per capita income was approximately $7,600 in Argentina, compared with $1,230 in Vietnam. Source: World Bank
[5] Exports as a percentage of GDP were Vietnam approximately 50% (in 1999), compared with 24% in Argentina (in 2008). I used data from the 1990s in Vietnam Source: World Bank.
[6] Cao and Prakash 2012
[7] According to the World Bank's Governance Indicators (2009) Argentina and Vietnam are, respectively, in the 37th and 36th percentile in control of corruption, 45th and 48th in government effectiveness, 23rd and 29th in regulatory quality, and 29th and 39th in rule of law.
[8] World Bank 2006. p 136

224   *Conclusion*

terms of quality of bureaucracies, but more serious economic and political barriers to enforcing environmental regulation.

Even under these conditions, environmental regulations are, at times, enforced in Vietnam. Consider the case of the Dona Bochang Textile factory, a joint-venture between foreign capital and the state; this plant released air pollution directly into a community church located near the factory. Neighbors of the factory mobilized against pollution for years, complaining to state officials and to management. At first, both the state and the firm ignored the community demands. Community members were able to "build linkages to the state" through their use of the media and by pressuring local officials and national government agencies.[9] Once this occurred, regulators began taking actions to enforce pollution standards. However, the state did not act alone, and community members played a key role monitoring pollution from the factory, including taking videos and collecting health records of the people impacted by pollution. The factory responded with a series of steps aimed at reducing pollution, installing a scrubber and changing some of the procedures so as to minimize clouds of soot raining on the communities. These steps reduced pollution substantially, although not completely. Enforcement in this episode was triggered by community mobilization, but "the community alone was not able to change the company;" instead, the community needed to draw on support from the state to achieve change.[10]

Viet Tri Chemicals also provides another example of enforcement dynamics in Vietnam. In the early 1990s, Viet Tri had a reputation of being one of the worst polluters in the country, rendering the city around it unlivable. As in the previous case, community members mobilized against pollution, complaining to officials and managers. One triggering event was a fish kill due to a chemical spill that led to protests in front of the factory. For years, community demands did not amount to much, but eventually the community was able to find allies in the state. Once they did, they were able to generate sufficient pressure to elicit a change in the actions of both regulators and the enterprise. In response to community demands, local officials developed a program to give community members access to the factory to monitor pollution directly by regularly touring the facility. This interaction between communities and the officials augmented the information that was gathered about pollution. Because Viet Tri was a state-owned enterprise, local officials and the community had to take on the central government that owned the facility to push for change. Eventually, the factory took a series of steps to improve its environmental performance, including upgrading its production process and starting a monitoring program. The factory also trained its workers to improve their environmental practices and gave monetary rewards to those who came up with ideas for reducing

[9] O'Rourke 2004   [10] O'Rourke 2004

Probing the limits in comparative context 225

pollution. Community members who mobilized against the factory observed real improvements in the environment as a result.

Finally, the case of the Tan Mai paper mill demonstrates that community mobilization does not unconditionally result in enforcement. The mill polluted the surrounding communities, killing fish and polluting drinking water. Farmers were particularly affected by the pollution; their crops were damaged and their rice was inedible. As in the other cases, members of the community mobilized against the state-owned enterprise. They wrote letters to government officials, factory management, and the news media. Despite these efforts, mobilized members of the community failed to gain allies in the state. Divisions within the community among those who worked for the factory limited the willingness of local authorities to take up the claims of those who fought pollution. In addition, community members did not circumvent local authorities successfully by going to the media or to other state agencies. Ultimately, the factory did not reduce pollution, and enforcement never occurred.

Enforcement in Vietnam often failed, but it clearly occurred at times, even without the preconditions of a coherent, regulatory bureaucracy. Importantly, the uneven nature of enforcement was not haphazard or random; instead, in certain places it closely resembled the society-dependent pattern. First, enforcement occurred only when community members mobilized and gained access to the state. Mobilized communities were not always successful; instead, their influence depended on their ability to gain allies with the state. Second, mobilized groups served as key sources of information about pollution and provided crucial political support to officials who were conflicted between economic priorities and environmental protection. Thus, mobilized groups not only pressured the state but also augmented the operational ability of regulators to implement policies. Third, although community mobilization was a necessary condition for enforcement, the state was not absent. Regulators did conduct inspections, gathering samples of pollution that were used as evidence of violations. They also mediated between mobilized communities and factories and, at times, even relocated factories.

There are, of course, a series of differences between the dynamics of enforcement in Vietnam and those in Argentina. Notably, some of the communities in Vietnam that O'Rourke analyzes mobilized against state-owned enterprises that pitted one part of the state directly against regulatory agencies. In addition, the degree of confrontation between communities and factories was much more modest than it was in Argentina, where road blockades are a tolerated and powerful tool used by some activists. Notwithstanding these differences, O'Rourke's work identifies a pattern of society-dependent enforcement similar to that of environmental regulation in Santa Fe and Córdoba. What O'Rourke does not identify in Vietnam, however, is a transition to broader enforcement of the co-produced type observed in Tucumán. We do not have enough evidence to know which the dominant pattern in Vietnam is, but it

226   *Conclusion*

is clear that society-dependent enforcement is possible even in an extremely different context from Argentina.

State-driven and co-produced enforcement in United States labor regulation[11]

Labor politics in the United States differs in many dimensions from that of Argentina. Two of these differences are particularly helpful assessing the ability of the argument developed on the basis of Argentine cases to travel. First, unions in the United States are structured differently and are comparatively much weaker, both in terms of membership and in terms of organizational resources. Trade union density in the United States was approximately 11% compared with 38% in Argentina.[12] Moreover, Argentine unions have many organizational advantages stemming from centralized structures and sector-level collective bargaining. In the United States, 13% of workers are covered by collective bargaining agreements, compared with 60% of Argentine workers.[13] Second, unlike the openly politicized context of Argentina, the United States has a reputation for substantially lower levels of corruption and stronger rule of law.[14] In labor politics, there is strong pressure for law enforcement to appear "neutral" and avoid any appearance of favoring one group.[15] Organizationally, regulatory agencies have many of the attributes of internal coherence that the literature suggests are crucial. For example, career staff in regulatory agencies are given extensive training and civil service protection. Thus, key differences in the organization of labor in the United States and politicized nature of the state provide an opportunity to assess whether or not the patterns found in Argentina are confined to corporatist, labor-mobilized, contexts with weak institutions.

As one would expect, the vast majority of enforcement in the United States follows the state-driven pattern. For example, inspection targeting in the Occupational Health and Safety Administration (OSHA) illustrates the way US regulatory agencies seek to approximate administrative rationality.[16] OSHA is required by law to "create an objective and documented basis for targeting inspections" that uses "specific neutral criteria."[17] Thus, officials select firms based on rules that are related to programmatic objectives, such as reducing accidents in a particular industry. Within these bounds, there are substantial

---

[11] This section is based in part on a collaboration with Janice Fine comparing enforcement in Argentina and the United States. I also thank David Weil for his comments and suggestions.

[12] Hayter and Stoevska 2011. Both numbers are the proportion of wage and salaried earners.

[13] Hayter and Stoevska 2011

[14] To use comparable data, the World Bank's Governance Indicators rank the United States at or near the 90th percentile in control of corruption, government effectiveness, regulatory quality, and rule of law.

[15] Huber 2007   [16] Huber 2007 p. 114   [17] Weil 2008 p. 366

Probing the limits in comparative context 227

differences in enforcement that depend on the strategies officials choose. In some cases, regulators have pursued strategies that have been highly effective. For example, one particularly successful effort was a campaign by the Wage and Hour Division of the US Department of Labor to reduce violations in the apparel industries of New York and Los Angeles. Enforcement in these two cities leveraged supply chain relationships to address the particular nature of the apparel industry and, as a result, reduced violations substantially.[18] In such instances of high levels of enforcement, officials attempt to target workplaces with frequent violations, to create effective levels of deterrence, and to create systematic changes in industries.[19] Not all efforts have these elements and, naturally, there is real variance in enforcement. Unlike the Argentine cases, however, this variance is determined by strategic decisions made by regulatory agencies. In these ways, enforcement in the United States approximates what I have been calling state-driven enforcement.

Yet, even within the context of the United States, there are elements of direct influence by societal organizations on enforcement that signify substantial departures from the ideal of state-driven enforcement. To begin, officials, especially appointed ones, are certainly influenced by interest groups, including unions, both in the setting of enforcement policy and in the act implementation. A series of studies has shown that in the US compliance and enforcement is stronger in unionized workplaces. For example, under OSHA, workers have a number of rights to be involved in enforcement, including the right to participate in "pre- and post-inspection meetings between the inspectors and the employer," as well as "to actively participate in the inspection itself."[20] As unions can help workers exercise these rights, analyses find a strong influence of unions on enforcement. Specifically, studies have shown that unionized establishments have an increased probability of being inspected, and that these inspections have longer durations resulting in a greater number of detected violations.[21] Similarly, research on safety in coal mines also has found a union-effect on enforcement, with unionization being associated with increased "frequency, duration, and intensity" of inspections by the Mining Safety and Health Administration, as well as a decrease in fatalities.[22] Thus, even in a country where unionization rates are low and the state less politicized, there are still a variety of ways in which labor groups directly affect enforcement.

Recent research by Janice Fine and Jennifer Gordon has revealed that, in some places, these interactions scale up and approximate the co-produced ideal-type.[23] For example, regulators enforcing labor law in California's janitorial industry had a particularly strong response to widespread violations. Workers recovered more than 38 million dollars in back pay for workers,

---

[18] Weil 2005   [19] Weil 2008 and 2014   [20] Weil 1991. p 21   [21] Weil 1991
[22] Morantz 2011, p 700. Morantz 2013. Note that Morantz stops short of arguing that improved safety is due to increased enforcement, as unions directly affect working conditions.
[23] This section draws heavily on Fine and Gordon 2010

228   *Conclusion*

and regulators took a large number of civil and criminal actions against violators. This effort also brought 3,000 janitorial jobs into the formal sector. As a
result, close observers noticed increased attention to the compliance of their
contractors among companies that hire janitorial services (such as hotels and
supermarkets), indicating a real shift in the norms around labor standards.

Enforcement did not come about through improvements in state capacity or
simply through political pressure on the government. There was political pressure for enforcement from the advocates of low-wage workers, including an
organization called the Maintenance Cooperation Trust Fund (MCTF), established in part by the Service Employees International Union (SEIU). But the
MCTF did not stay on the sidelines. Instead, to enable enforcement, the MCTF
developed linkages with a Janitorial Enforcement Team (JET) established
to focus on enforcement in the industry. The MCTF had a team of twelve
inspectors who gathered information and then passed it on to JET to use for
enforcement. As part of this effort, the MCTF inspectors visited janitorial sites
at night hours when janitors are working most intensely (and state regulators
are not), interviewed the workers, and helped the workers put together information that JET regulators would need to prosecute violators. Many of the
MCTF's inspectors had been janitorial workers, which gave them a strong
understanding of how the industry functions and where to find violations.
MCTF's role was not just operational, but also political. When there was
reluctance to prosecute, the organization pressured regulators to take stronger
actions and held them accountable.

Another case in Los Angeles went even further toward co-production.
The Los Angeles United School District (LAUSD) and Board of Public Works
(LABPW) give out more than a billion dollars of contracts for variety of
projects, including construction. These two public organizations signed agreements with labor organizations, after which unions committed not to go on
strike if a stronger enforcement regime was created to ensure labor law compliance in the contracted work. Thus, instead of only pressuring government
to ensure compliance in its contractors with labor laws, unions pushed to get
involved in the process of enforcement. This agreement involved training and
"deputizing" union-volunteers, called compliance group representatives
(CGR), to take part in enforcement. These volunteers had the ability to enter
worksites, gather information, and interview workers about compliance; they
served, as a union leader put it, as the "eyes, ears, and foot soldiers" of public
officials.[24] The CGRs expanded the internal resources of the state substantially,
increasing the total number of people monitoring worksites by 30%. According
to the officials, the partnership also drastically increased enforcement.

In sum, labor regulation in the United States most often approximates
the state-driven pattern of enforcement. This is not surprising given the

---

[24] Fine and Gordon 2010 p. 563

Probing the limits in comparative context 229

(comparatively strong) tradition of administrative rationality and relatively weak labor unions. Yet, even in this context, unions play an important role and patterns of co-produced enforcement emerged. Many elements of these examples of co-production from the United States are quite similar to the Argentine cases. First, and most importantly, enforcement was made possible by regulators drawing heavily on organizations in society for operational and political support. Linkages were formed in response to mobilization by workers under circumstances in which there was an alignment between the political goals of top officials and of those organizations. Second, there were formal as well as informal elements of the linkages that were dependent on continued political support. In the case of MCTF, there was no formal institutional structure that underpinned the linkages, and eventually the ties were dismantled when political circumstances shifted. Third, there were concerns about the influence of worker organizations. As one regulator told Fine and Gordon, "Many times these organizations are quite adamant about what they want you to do with your cases ... You don't want to end up working for them."[25] This statement directly mirrors those by officials in Córdoba's labor inspectorate, as well as Tucumán environmental regulators, who worried about the loss of independence. Similarly, in the LAUSD/LABPW case, there were concerns about unions targeting enforcement at nonunion workshops, and formal language was put into the agreement to prohibit such actions. While these are only two cases of co-production (they are not alone – there were similar developments in other parts of the United States), they show that co-produced enforcement is possible in a broad range of cases.

Society-dependent enforcement of labor regulation in Indonesia[26]

Indonesian labor politics offers another helpful comparison. As does Argentina, Indonesia faces similar challenges of rule of law and corruption.[27] Research on the Indonesian state strongly suggests it is porous to political influence and far from autonomous. Labor politics in the two countries, however, contrast sharply. One central difference of importance for analyzing enforcement

---

[25] Fine and Gordon 2010 p. 567
[26] This section is based on joint research with Laura Chirot and Mollie Eunjoo Chung conducted in 2014 on labor institutions and Better Work in Indonesia. As part of the project, we conducted interviews with more than 150 government officials, factory managers, union leaders, employer associations, and global buyers.
[27] Indonesia's percentile ranking in the World Bank's Governance Indicators was broadly similar to that of Argentina: 29th in control of corruption, 44th in government effectiveness, 43rd in regulatory quality, and 34th in rule of law. One difference at a structural level is that in levels of economic development. GDP per capita in Indonesia was $2,178 in 2008, compared with $7,600 in Argentina for that year. Source: World Bank data 2012 (the closest year to the time of this research).

politics is the strength of union organizations and the role of unions in partisan politics. For one, union density in Indonesia is extremely low; estimates suggest that unionization is on the order of 2% of the workforce, compared with 38% in Argentina.[28] In addition, unions in Indonesia are highly fractured, pluralistic, and lacking in central coordination.[29] Collective bargaining agreements do not extend to entire industries, and, even at the plant level, factories can have more than one union. Finally, Indonesian unions have not aligned with any particular party, differing quite substantially from the relationship between the Peronists and the labor movement.[30] In sum, Indonesian union strength, structure, and political alignments all differ substantially from those in Argentina.

Notwithstanding contrasts in the labor movements and politics, there were a number of similarities between regulations and administration in the two countries. Both countries have relatively protective labor laws for formal sector workers; these laws were inherited from a previous period and were strengthened in the early 2000s.[31] Yet, there were substantial levels of noncompliance, and many workers were left out. Approximately 54% of workers in Indonesia were in the informal sector; this number is greater than that of unregistered workers in Argentina at the peak of the crisis.[32] Even in the formal sector, violations of basic laws have been widespread. For example, officials from the ILO's Better Work program, which assesses compliance with regulations in the garment industry, found that 60% of factories did not pay workers correctly for overtime, and 85% of factories had violations related to subcontracting and worker contracts.[33] These were just a subset of the violations identified in factories that were operating in the formal sector and that opted into the ILO program. Therefore, these figures likely understate the overall levels of noncompliance in Indonesia. Thus, as does Argentina, Indonesia exhibits relatively strong laws on the book and weak compliance in practice.

The labor inspectorate charged with responding to these violations was, by all means, extremely weak and uneven. Labor inspection is highly decentralized and spread out over 357 local offices and (with few exceptions) is formally controlled by the local (district) government. The number of labor inspectors per capita were similar to those in Argentina – there were 2,160 inspectors, or 0.09 per 10,000 people (compared with 0.09 in Santa Fe, and 0.33 in the Federal Capital).[34] These officials conducted approximately 0.5 inspections per 1,000 residents; this number is very low by international standards and is an order of magnitude below the rates for the Argentine cases analyzed in this

---

[28] Caraway 2004
[29] For an explicit comparison of the two union movements, see: Caraway 2006
[30] Caraway and Ford 2014   [31] Caraway 2004   [32] ILO 2013b
[33] ILO, "Better Work Indonesia: Garment Industry 2nd Compliance Synthesis Report," 2013
[34] Data from the ILO

Probing the limits in comparative context 231

book (e.g., eight per thousand in Córdoba capital).[35] Even though inspectors were taking some actions, the Indonesian inspectorate is far from the Weberian and autonomous ideal. The inspectorates suffered from basic organizational weaknesses, described by the ILO as "uneven distribution of labor inspection, weak supervisory structures, and high turnover impact the capacity of the labor inspectorate."[36] Moreover, by all accounts, the inspectors were subject to constant political interference by the district heads (or mayors). Labor inspectors generally did not have employment protection and could be transferred at any time for political reasons. By some reports, every time there was a new election, the district head replaced all of the labor inspectors with loyal officials.[37]

On top of everything, corruption was widespread in the inspectorate. A survey by the Corruption Eradication Commission of Indonesia of more than 3,000 people in the greater Jakarta area found that the Ministry of Manpower (that includes labor inspection) ranked 26th out of 30 government agencies in corruption and low-quality service.[38] As one factory manager complained, the difficulty of working with regulators is that "you have to pay a certain amount of money" of "illegal payments" each time you need a document approved; another complained that if "I have to go to the labor office, and then I have to pay ... everybody knows."[39] This sentiment was echoed in interviews with dozens of employers, union leaders, and government officials. In sum, the Indonesian labor inspection system shares a number of broad features with that of Argentina (protective labor laws that exclude many workers due to noncompliance, decentralization, limited numbers of inspectors, and political influence/corruption prevailing the bureaucracy), but in Indonesia these features tend to be amplified.

Once again, standard theoretical expectations that emphasize bureaucratic quality suggest there should not be enforcement. Similarly, if the argument advanced in this book applied only in contexts with unions as strong as those in Argentina, enforcement would appears unlikely due to low union density and fragmentation in Indonesia. Yet, a closer look at Indonesian inspection at the local level reveals examples of thick interaction between mobilized unions and inspectors that resulted in pockets of enforcement. For example, in the garment industry, one key area of violations involves the use of short-term contracts by factories to avoid severance pay and other workplace protections. In many cases, regulators can easily be persuaded to allow factories, in the words of one factory manager, to "manipulate the regulation" and to keep

---

[35] Some of the differences may be accounted for by the fact that Indonesian inspectors do not have competency over individual disputes that other labor inspectors do (there is another division in Indonesia, called Industrial Relations that handles these disputes).

[36] ILO 2013b p. 49   [37] Interview U3, Jakarta, 6/2014

[38] Jakarta Post "Shamed ministries pledge to provide better public service," 3/31/2008

[39] Interviews conducted with garment factory managers in West Java and Jakarta in 6/2014

renewing workers on temporary contracts instead of transferring them to permanent contracts when regulations require.[40] These practices were pervasive across the industry, and this particular aspect of labor market institutions was weak.

In the West Java district of Subang, however, a union mobilized and pushed the regulators to change their practice and enforce this law in the garment sector, thus activating the labor market institutions that apply to contracting. The union put direct pressure on employers to convert all workers to permanent contracts, but the factory managers refused. In response to this problem, the union approached the state and put pressure on local officials to enforce the regulations with a strict interpretation of limits on short-term contracts. Backroom meetings between union leaders and regulators were combined with protests and strikes over other issues (such as minimum wage increase) to target the head of the local government. These protests (which occurred broadly in many industrial districts in Indonesia) were a show of force for the unions and created a political opening. In addition, in Subang, there was a shift in the head of the local regulatory office, and the newly appointed official became sensitive to union demands.

According to both labor leaders and employers, political pressure was key in getting the unions' interests heard inside the regulatory bureaucracy.[41] Yet, in contrast with simple principal-agent views of the state, in this case the process was not just a matter of political pressure on elected officials; the process also involved labor leaders going directly to officials in the regulatory bureaucracy when it came to matters of enforcement.[42] Eventually, union leaders developed a thick, yet informal, relationship with the local labor administration.[43] The attributes of the linkages between unions and officials are familiar by now – direct interaction between societal groups and officials through informal channels that mix political pressure and information sharing (thereby extending the operational reach of the state). In the above case, once these ties were established, union leaders reported labor practices that they thought were in violation of the law to local officials. In response, the inspectors investigated the claims and made a decision about the use of temporary contract workers that was more in line with the unions' strict interpretation than the interpretation favored by employers.

In this district, inspectors investigated the use of short-term contracts throughout the garment industry. Eventually, regulators decided not to allow factories to use such contracts in core production positions. In other words, the

---

[40] Interview F7, factory manager, West Java, 6/2014. There were some debates about what is generally the correct interpretation of contracting laws, but even within the bounds of these debates, clear violations were widespread.

[41] Interview G30, government official, West Java, 7/2014

[42] Interview E12, employer, West Java, 7/2014

[43] Interview: U21, union leader, West Java, 7/2014, 5/2015

Probing the limits in comparative context

regulators stopped "manipulating" the rule, as the garment factory manager had put it. Importantly, the officials gave a letter to the union leaders describing the regulatory decisions about the legality of these practices, keeping the unions as political actors involved in the process.[44] After the mobilization, the unions in a handful of factories continually monitored compliance, informing the inspectors when there were extensions of contracts that violated the law, and pressured the front-line officials to enforce regulations with a strict interpretation of contracting rules. Employers, naturally, countered with pressure and a campaign to "educate" the inspectors about the economic and operational realities of garment production that favored the use of temporary workers.[45] The regulators eventually made some concessions to employers and allowed for some flexibility under certain conditions (e.g., temporary increases in orders that required adding additional lines of production). Restrictions were relaxed in most factories, but in ones where the union was active, regulators remained firm and limited the use of short-term contract workers.[46] Thus, enforcement was not programmatic in the district, but rather was focused only on the places where unions made strong demands. The actions by the inspectors lasted for well over a year, opened the door for the union to take factories to the provincial industrial relations court.

Enforcement in this example was, of course, limited – it involved only one specific issue in a small set of factories. Regulators were clearly not programmatic in their efforts and likely would have not undertaken any actions if not for union pressure. Nevertheless, this example demonstrates how the combinations of labor inspectors and mobilized unions (not just unions mobilizing directly against the factory, or inspectors autonomously deciding to strictly interpret the law) resulted in enforcement that activated particular labor market institutions. Moreover, this instance of enforcement occurred in an exporting industry that is notorious for extensive workplace violations and imperviousness to domestic regulation. This was not the only example in Indonesia where unions were able to form ties with inspectors. For example, a leader from a district union in Bogor stated that he had "good communication with even the head of the Dinas ... The inspectors respond to complaints, but they can be quite slow, so we have to push them."[47] Inspectors in the district of Bogor (kabupaten) stated that unions "use inspectors as a point of leverage, very often" and that their first priorities for inspections are areas where there is a crisis or a complaint in order to avoid conflicts.[48] While union leaders often do not win in

---

[44] Interview: U21, union leader, West Java, 7/2014, 5/2015

[45] Interview: F25, factory manager, West Java, 7/2014

[46] At the time of this writing, the conflict is still not resolved even after well over a year of conflict.

[47] Interview U36, FSPMI leader in Bogor, West Java, 4/13/15

[48] Interview G20, labor inspector, West Java, 6/2014 and 4/13/15; G40, labor inspector, West Java, 4/13/15. Inspectors in Jakarta triangulated these finding: Interview G36, labor inspector, Jakarta, 4/2/15

Bogor and many laws go unenforced, their chosen pathway to state action for many violations is through direct contact with state regulators.

Ultimately, in parts of Indonesia where there were union mobilizations, linkages were formed, and the inspectors were able to draw upon the support of unions to enforce. The Indonesian inspectorate was certainly awash with political influence through informal channels that often undermined state action, but these informal channels allowed worker advocates in to push enforcement. The result was a pattern of society-dependent enforcement, one that was highly uneven, but consequential. There were, of course, substantial differences between union-regulator relations in Indonesia and Argentina. In the former, union leaders could not gain appointed positions within state that generated the strong alliances apparent in Córdoba and Tucumán. Instead, the ties more mirrored those apparent in environmental regulation in Argentina. They were more adversarial than collaborative, with social movements putting continual pressure to open up flows of information and influence.

Notwithstanding these differences, the evidence from Indonesia shows that countries do not need the strong, centralized, partisan unions of Argentina in order to develop patterns of society-dependent enforcement. The theory developed in this book suggests that as labor unions gain strength in Indonesia, they should be able to augment enforcement, even without a reform of the inspectorate. Compared with the standard theories that emphasize Weberian reforms and autonomous regulatory bureaucracies, our analysis indicates that there are many more possibilities for state responses to poor labor standards in Indonesia. While reform would certainly be welcome for strengthening institutions, it is highly unlikely, especially given the decentralization of labor inspection.[49] On the contrary, mobilizations in the last few years show that labor unions have become capable of placing pressure on local politicians.[50] If these trends continue, we can expect an increasing number of cases of society-dependent enforcement. Such an outcome would be beneficial for formal sector workers in industries with mobilized unions, but would do little for those in the informal sector. It would also require nearly constant union mobilization in order to create the disruptions necessary to trigger state action. Despite these limitations, enforcement in the labor-intensive light manufacturing sector would be a substantial feat for a country that has struggled to improve labor standards.

BROADER CONTRIBUTIONS

This book has used the study of one particular set of policies as a window into a much larger set of issues related to how states function in much of the world.

---

[49] At the time of this writing, there has been a partial recentralization of labor inspection to the provincial level. It has not been implemented yet and it will only address a small portion of the problems of organizational weakness and politicization.

[50] Caraway and Ford 2014

Broader contributions 235

Our interest is not just in regulatory politics, but in a broad range of tasks that the state has with which to strengthen institutions. The point of departure at the beginning of this book was the particular ways states, and state capacity, are studied in political science. The statist and state-building literatures have focused on the antecedents and the impacts of highly stable, long-run, equilibria of strongly institutionalized structures. This approach has deep roots, going back at least to Weber, and there are good reasons for these efforts to occupy a central place in the debates. Autonomous states and capable bureaucracies have been attributed to a wide range of outcomes, including economic development, social justice, and security.[51] Moreover, autonomous bureaucrats are political actors in their own right; they establish policy agendas and even alter the preferences of organized interests.[52] Thus, to understand fully the functioning of political systems, it became necessary to take into account the interests and actions of states. Long-term processes of state-building are also crucial; once in place, the institutional foundations of strong states have incredible stability.[53] Change normally occurs either in very small increments or in rare moments of critical junctures that result in new structures.

For all of their merits, the emphasis on autonomous states and the formation of state capacity has pushed scholars away from the study of how intermediary states function. Yet, the salient attribute of most states is neither universally strength nor universally weakness. Detailed studies of states often reveal islands of capabilities surrounded by seas of weakness and substantial unevenness. For example, Abers and Keck describe the Brazilian state as "a tangle of fragmented, inconsistently competent, [and] erratically permeable" organizations.[54] Abers and Keck's assessment is very much in line with the state described in this book; most states, in fact, share these features. Understanding the possibilities for these states requires an analysis of how these states are, not of how they might become.

One of the central contributions of this book has been to show that there are indeed many consequential differences across states that are equally politicized. Thus, important variation is not reducible to a state's approximation to the autonomous, strong, ideal-types. Rather than simply conceptualizing differences among bureaucracies in terms of more or less porous (or with officials that have more or less of a role in crafting policy), we need tools to identify the qualitatively different ways in which bureaucracies are porous. Sometimes, porosity provides access to groups that favor action, and sometimes it does not. Although the bureaucracies studied in this book are certainly on a "path," that path allows for more than a little wiggle room. The differences in the ways politicized states function are highly fluid. The changes identified in this study did not occur through reforms of formalized institutions. Instead, as groups

---

[51] Johnson 1982; Geddes 1990; Evans 1995   [52] Skocpol 1985; Carpenter 2001
[53] Kurtz 2013b   [54] Abers and Keck 2013 p. 32

mobilize, contest, and create alliances, ties between state and society can be built or disassembled. Much can be learned across a wide range of policy areas by identifying the consequences of qualitatively different forms of politicization as well as the conditions under which they obtain.

A second implication of this work is to reaffirm the need to break down the distinction between politics and administration. Operational and political aspects of policy implementation are entwined.[55] While this statement is largely uncontroversial, its implications have not been fully realized in the literature. For one, researchers still tend to study the adoption of laws, regulations, and treaties without being attentive to politics occurring after those policies are adopted. In addition, as described above, much of the work on states focuses on how to push politics out of bureaucracies and enhance technocratic nature of implementation. Even in theories of state-society relations, scholars are inclined to divide connections between state and society into two mutually exclusive categories: politically motivated (rent-seeking, patronage, or capture) and cooperative (public good generating).[56] This commitment not only obscures important differences within the category of patronage-based systems, but it also effectively closes off the possibility of politics explaining linkage formation in the cases of "productive" state-society ties. Instead, this book has shown how much can be learned by breaking down that sharp distinction. I have introduced a third category of ties that involve both political expediency and a real extension of capabilities of the state to implement specific policies. By doing so, we can begin not only to account for the formation and disintegration of state-society ties in the short term, but we can also illuminate important elements of policy implementation, such as unions pushing for enforcement, which have been obscured.

Finally, institutions, even weak ones, matter. Political scientists are just beginning to address the politics of institutional weakness,[57] reminding us of how enforcement plays a key role in "activating" institutions. In this study, we have seen how labor market and environmental institutions in Argentina were, in many cases, too weak to effectively to structure social and economic relations. Yet, at times, enforcement activated these institutions. We can expect the same type of process to occur in a wide variety of policy areas (e.g., property rights, access to public services, etc.). One contribution of this book is to show that under weak institutions, we cannot expect enforcement always, or even primarily, to be a matter of administrative and rational policy. Rather, enforcement can be deeply political and can still be consistent with weakly institutionalized rules. Thus, the activation of weak institutions depends not

---

[55] This argument is somewhat congruent with Huber, who similarly argued that one cannot understand bureaucracies as being completely political or Weberian. It departs from this argument because in highly politicized contexts, the appearance of neutrality is difficult to attain and less available as a strategy for agencies to further political ends. Huber 2007

[56] See: Montero 2001   [57] Levitsky and Murillo 2009; Levitsky and Murillo 2013

Conclusion

only on groups solving the collective action problems related to institutional breakdown, but also on groups contesting the ways in which institutions are used to favor their interests.[58]

CONCLUSION – EXPANDING POSSIBILITIES FOR JUST AND SUSTAINED DEVELOPMENT

Although this book speaks to a set of larger theoretical questions, it grows out of an interest in the challenges of balancing economic development with the goals of social and environmental protection. Therefore, I conclude by considering the possibilities for regulatory institutions to contribute to just and inclusive development. The point of departure for this book is the view that regulations can play a key role in embedding the market in society.[59] Regulatory solutions to labor and environmental problems, however, have been controversial and, in many ways, deeply disappointing. Countries around the world have strong laws on their books, but they bear little resemblance to practices. Many scholars and policymakers have given up on state regulation, in part, due to a theory of state capacity that emphasizes features of the state that are absent in most places. States simply seem incapable of enforcing their laws and the prospects for radical bureaucratic reform appeared dim in much of the world.

As a result, policymakers, as well as advocates for workers and the environment, looked for other solutions apart from state regulation to protect workers and the environment. Alternatives have been many, but attention turned to circumventing states and using nonstate substitutes.[60] Experiments with private regulation in the past fifteen years have, however, been not resulted in the improvements that their designers intended.[61] It has become clear that private regulation cannot substitute for the state or transcend local contexts.[62] As a result, calls for a return to state regulation, often in combination with transnational efforts, have grown.[63] Yet, our understanding of what options might exist is still very much rooted in the view of an ideal-typical state that is beyond the reach of most countries. This perspective leaves us with few indications for how to increase the likelihood that states will enforce their regulations.

This book has suggested that the prevailing theory of the necessary conditions for enforcement is, at best, incomplete.[64] This conclusion stands in

---

[58] See also: Markus 2012 for a similar finding in property rights   [59] Polanyi 2001
[60] Bartley 2007; Vogel 2008   [61] Locke 2013   [62] Bartley 2011
[63] Seidman 2007; Amengual 2010; Locke, Rissing, and Pal 2012; Coslovsky and Locke 2013; Locke 2013
[64] This argument aligns with a theoretical tradition of studying the state that still remains submerged in much the dominant discourse around regulatory politics. See: Mann 1993; Soifer 2008

contrast to the widespread pessimism about the possibilities for state regulation that permeates the academic literature and policy debates. Limited resources and organizational flaws within state bureaucracies are problematic, but these features do not completely preclude the state from enforcing regulations in ways that improve standards; rather, such limitations constrain only the range of possible enforcement patterns, not enforcement itself. The Argentine provinces studied in this book had poorly trained staffs with few resources and low salaries – exactly the characteristics that the conventional wisdom predicts should lead to failure. Yet even these constrained regulators can, and did, take far-reaching steps to enforce regulations when they had linkages with civil society organizations. Therefore, statements regarding the impossibility of protecting workers or preventing environmental damage through regulation due to limited budgets are false excuses.

With this view, we can begin to see the challenge of making state regulation of labor and environment standards relevant in much of the world as a political problem that involves choices among different pathways to enforcement. This recognition has both theoretical and policy implications. Theoretically, we can expect that mobilization by pro-enforcement groups in ways that target the state apparatus will lead to changes, even when mobilization falls short of creating a capable state and programmatic policy implementation. This theoretical finding suggests that political efforts to improve standards can go beyond ignoring the state or advocating for Weberian reforms. A choice can be made to pursue political strategies that support the building of linkages and, essentially, to delegate some state authority to civil society organizations. Mobilization by pro-regulation groups that targets regulatory agencies can create quick increases in enforcement by augmenting the operational capabilities of the state while, simultaneously, exercising political power over how policies are implemented. When this occurs, the distribution of enforcement will not follow programmatic criteria; some deserving groups and individuals will be left out. Nevertheless, enforcement will occur in a way that would otherwise be impossible. As a result, people will get paid when they would have previously had their wages stolen; they will gain protections in the event of downsizing; they will be exposed to fewer safety risks; and they will be able to live in cleaner environments. Even if state actions do not tip the equilibrium toward strong institutions, such actions will solve punctual problems for people and deliver, however partially, on the promises of policies.

With alternative pathways to enforcement, however, come many challenges. It has been clear in these analyses that enforcement that relies heavily on organizations outside of the state can have serious limitations in responding to certain labor and environmental injustices. When the state is highly dependent on society for enforcement, inequalities in social organization become exacerbated. Responses to social demands can crowd out programmatic state action, leaving some of the most vulnerable workers and communities unprotected. Perhaps even more troubling is the possibility that under certain

Conclusion

conditions linkages can create opportunities for politicians to avoid making investments in the bureaucracy. We have seen in the Argentine cases how such linkages can undermine the political support for reforms that could possibly lead to the broad actions necessary for solving systematic labor and environmental challenges. A similar dynamic may occur in other parts of the world where regulators put out fires that diffuse social demands, but do not build up state capabilities. In short, society-dependent enforcement has its own politics that differs from the voids that are often assumed – the challenge is not to strengthen institutions from a blank slate, but rather to do so on the basis of what is already in existence. Being aware of how difficult fostering transitions between patterns of state action might be is an important beginning. As future research develops more complete analyses of the politics of state-society relations, state capacity, and enforcement, we can craft strategies that enable states to strengthen regulatory institutions that more effectively harmonize economic development with social and environmental commitments.

Appendix

List of Interviews in Argentina

Identification Code, Position (if available), Organization, Location of Interview, Date

B01   Argentine Construction Association (CAC), Buenos Aires, 10/7/2008

B02   Environment and Natural Resources Foundation, Buenos Aires, 4/7/2009

B03   Technical Evaluation, Federal Capital Environmental Protection Agency, Buenos Aires, 9/18/2008

B04   Operations, Federal Capital Environmental Protection Agency, Buenos Aires, 9/25/2008

B05   Senior Official, Federal Capital Labor Sub-Secretariat, Buenos Aires, 10/7/2008

B06   Senior Official, Department of Labor Inspection, Ministry of Labor, Employment and Social Security, Buenos Aires, 3/13/08 and 2/26/09

B07   Federal Capital Labor Sub-Secretariat, Buenos Aires, 10/1/2008

B08   Senior Official, Federal Capital Labor Sub-Secretariat, Buenos Aires, 9/23/2008

B09   Enforcement Department, Federal Capital Environmental Protection Agency, Buenos Aires, 10/17/2008

B10   Enforcement Department, Federal Capital Environmental Protection Agency, Buenos Aires, 10/6/2008

B11   Senior Official, Federal Capital Labor Sub-Secretariat, Buenos Aires, 02/12/09 and 02/17/09

B12   Senior Official, Santa Fe Ministry of Labor and Social Security, Buenos Aires, 5/26/2009

B13   Defensor del Pueblo, Buenos Aires, 2/26/2009

B14   Argentine Sausage Industry Association, Buenos Aires, 9/30/2008

B15	Inspector, Federal Capital Labor Sub-Secretariat, Buenos Aires, 10/14/2008
B16	Inspector, Federal Capital Labor Sub-Secretariat, Buenos Aires, 10/14/2008
B17	Metal Plating Association of Argentina (ASADAM), Buenos Aires, 10/8/2008
B18	Federal Secretariat of Environment and Sustainable Development, Buenos Aires, 10/1/2008
B19	Metal Workers' Union (UOM), Buenos Aires, 2/12/2009
B20	Lawyer, Argentine Human Rights League, Buenos Aires, 3/25/2009
B21	Legal Department, Federal Capital Environmental Protection Agency, Buenos Aires, 9/22/2008
B22	Federal Capital Labor Sub-Secretariat, Buenos Aires, 9/15/2008
B23	Inspector, Federal Capital Labor Sub-Secretariat, Buenos Aires, 10/14/2008
B24	La Boca Neighborhood Association, Buenos Aires, 10/4/2008
B25	Federal Capital Environmental Protection Agency, Buenos Aires, 10/20/2008
B26	Federal Secretariat of Environment and Sustainable Development, Buenos Aires, 9/18/2008
B27	Argentine Sustainable Business Council, Buenos Aires, 10/15/2008
B28	Federal Secretariat of Environment and Sustainable Development, Buenos Aires, 9/22/2008
B29	Federal Capital Labor Sub-Secretariat, Buenos Aires, 6/30/2008
B30	Legal Department, Federal Capital Environmental Protection Agency, Buenos Aires, 9/23/2008
B31	Federal Capital Labor Sub-Secretariat, Buenos Aires, 10/1/2008
B32	Environmental Specialist, Metal Industry Association of Argentina (ADMIRA), Buenos Aires, 2/18/2009
B33	City Foundation, Buenos Aires, 10/16/2008
B34	Metal Plating Association of Argentina (ASADAM), Buenos Aires, 10/8/2008
B35	Argentine Meat Industrial Union (UNICA), Buenos Aires, 10/17/2008
B36	Inspector, Federal Capital Labor Sub-Secretariat, Buenos Aires, 10/21/2008
B37	Inspector, Federal Capital Environmental Protection Agency, Buenos Aires, 9/29/2008
B38	Metal Plating Association of Argentina (ASADAM), Buenos Aires, 10/8/2008
B39	Former Senior Official, Federal Capital Labor Sub-Secretariat, Buenos Aires, 2/6/2009
B40	Enforcement Department, Federal Capital Environmental Protection Agency, Buenos Aires, 10/1/2008

List of interviews in Argentina 243

B41   Lawyer, Metal Industry Association of Argentina (ADMIRA), Buenos Aires, 2/18/2009

B42   Environmental Commission, Federal Capital Legislature, Buenos Aires, 9/24/2008

B43   Public Relations, Federal Capital Environmental Protection Agency, Buenos Aires, 2/18/2009

B44   Green Party, Buenos Aires, 10/9/2008

B45   Department of Planning, Ministry of Labor, Employment and Social Security, Buenos Aires, 9/17/2008

B46   La Alameda Foundation, Buenos Aires, 2/23/2009

B47   Tannery Workers' Union, Avellaneda, Province of Buenos Aires, 2/18/2009

B48   Superintendent of Workplace Risks, Buenos Aires, 3/13/2008

B49   Laundry Workers' Union (UOETSYLRA), Buenos Aires, 6/30/08 and 10/20/08

B50   Inspector, Federal Capital Labor Sub-Secretariat, Buenos Aires, 10/14/2008

B51   Senior Official Department of Labor Inspection, Ministry of Labor, Employment and Social Security, Buenos Aires, 4/8/2008

B52   Inspector, Ministry of Labor, Employment and Social Security, Buenos Aires, 4/23/2008

B53   Senior Official, Ministry of Labor, Employment and Social Security, Buenos Aires, 9/4/2008

B54   Institute of Economic and Social Development, Buenos Aires, 3/19/2008

B55   Inspector, Ministry of Labor, Employment and Social Security, Buenos Aires, 5/5/2009

B56   Environment and Natural Resources Foundation, Buenos Aires, 3/6/2008

B57   Complaints Department, Ministry of Labor, Employment and Social Security, Buenos Aires, 4/29/2008

B58   Political and Social Department, Argentine Industrial Union, Buenos Aires, 4/9/2008

B59   Labor Lawyer, Buenos Aires, 4/4/2008

B60   Director of a Regional Office, Ministry of Labor, Employment and Social Security, Buenos Aires, 6/17/2008

B61   Superintendent of Workplace Risks, Buenos Aires, 4/23/2008

B62   Former Secretary of Labor, Federal Ministry of Labor, Buenos Aires, 2/28/2008

B63   Department of Human Resources, Ministry of Labor, Employment and Social Security, Buenos Aires, 4/22/2009

B64   Department of Labor Inspection, Province of Buenos Aires Ministry of Labor, Buenos Aires, 3/4/2008

B65	Federal Capital Labor Sub-Secretariat, Buenos Aires, 7/4/2008
B66	Former Senior Official, Federal Capital Labor Sub-Secretariat, Buenos Aires, 2/24/2009
B67	Inspector, Ministry of Labor, Employment and Social Security, Buenos Aires, 4/23/2008
B68	Superintendent of Workplace Risks, Buenos Aires, 3/18/2008
B69	Inspector, Ministry of Labor, Employment and Social Security, Buenos Aires, 4/23/2008
B70	Department of Planning, Ministry of Labor, Employment and Social Security, Buenos Aires, 4/23/2008
B71	Research Department, Ministry of Labor, Employment and Social Security, Buenos Aires, 3/18/2008
B72	Inspector, Ministry of Labor, Employment and Social Security, Buenos Aires, 5/5/2008
B73	Research Department, Ministry of Labor, Employment and Social Security, Buenos Aires, 2/27/2008
B74	Construction Workers' Union of Argentina (UOCRA), Buenos Aires, 10/16/2008
B75	Federation of Energy Workers and CTA, Buenos Aires, 7/2/2008
B76	Minister of Labor, Santa Fe Ministry of Labor and Social Security, Buenos Aires, 3/15/2008
B77	Inspector, Ministry of Labor, Employment and Social Security, Buenos Aires, 4/8/08 and 4/25/08
B78	Department of Planning, Ministry of Labor, Employment and Social Security, Buenos Aires, 4/11/2008
B79	Superintendent of Workplace Risks, Buenos Aires, 4/3/2008
B80	Auto Workers' Union (SMATA), Buenos Aires, 2/16/2009
B81	Public Workers Union Delegate, Ministry of Labor, Employment and Social Security, Buenos Aires, 7/29/2008
B82	Senior Official Department of Labor Inspection, Ministry of Labor, Employment and Social Security, Buenos Aires, 7/4/2008
B83	Labor Lawyer, Buenos Aires, 6/30/2008
B84	Federation of Pastry, Pizza, Ice-cream, and Alfajor Unions, Buenos Aires, 9/24/2008
B85	Commercial Workers' Union, Buenos Aires, 9/16/2008
B86	Department of Special Activities, Federal Capital Environmental Protection Agency, Buenos Aires, 10/1/2008
B87	Inspector, Federal Capital Environmental Protection Agency, Buenos Aires, 9/19/2008
C01	Former Senior Official, Córdoba Labor Secretariat, Córdoba, 06/18/08 and 03/10/09
C02	Industrial Union of Córdoba, Córdoba, 3/17/2009
C03	Union of Pastry, Pizza, and Alfajor Workers, Córdoba, 7/16/2008

List of interviews in Argentina

C04	Former Senior Official, Córdoba Labor Secretariat, Córdoba, 3/11/2009
C05	Tourism, Hotel, and Restaurant Workers' Union (UTHGRA), Córdoba, 7/15/2008
C06	Inspector, Ministry of Labor, Employment and Social Security, Córdoba, 3/12/2009
C07	Metal Workers' Union (UOM), Córdoba, 3/18/2009
C08	Inspector, Ministry of Labor, Employment and Social Security, Córdoba, 6/18/2008
C09	Provincial Legislator (PJ), Córdoba, Córdoba, 3/4/2009
C10	Inspector, Ministry of Labor, Employment and Social Security, Córdoba, 7/17/2008
C11	Senior Official, Regional Office of Córdoba, Ministry of Labor, Employment and Social Security, Córdoba, 6/18/2008
C12	Córdoba Leather Industry Association, Córdoba, 3/5/2009
C13	Industrial Union of Córdoba, Córdoba, 6/19/2008
C14	Shoe Workers' Union, Córdoba, 7/16/2008
C15	Argentine Construction Association (CAC), Córdoba, 3/3/2009
C16	Enforcement Department, Córdoba Environmental Secretariat, Córdoba, 3/18/2009
C17	Construction Workers' Union of Argentina (UOCRA), Córdoba, 7/15/2008
C18	Meat Packing Association, Córdoba, 3/6/2009
C19	Hazardous Waste Department, Córdoba Environmental Secretariat, Córdoba, 3/12/2009
C20	Córdoba Environmental Forum, Córdoba, 3/2/2009
C21	Center for Human Rights and the Environmental (CEDAH), Córdoba, 3/20/2009
C22	Senior Official, City of Córdoba Environmental Department, Córdoba, 3/12/2009
C23	Senior Official, Córdoba Labor Secretariat, Córdoba, 06/23/08 and 03/05/09 and 03/07/09
C24	Former Official, Córdoba Environmental Protection Agency, Córdoba, 6/3/2009
C25	Environmental Defense Foundation, Córdoba, 3/5/2009
C26	Senior Official, City of Córdoba Environmental Department, Córdoba, 3/12/2009
C27	Inspectors, Córdoba Environmental Secretariat, Córdoba, 3/17/2009
C28	Center for Human Rights and the Environmental (CEDAH), Córdoba, 3/16/2009
C29	Enforcement Department, Córdoba Environmental Secretariat, Córdoba, 3/19/2009
C30	Enforcement Department, Córdoba Environmental Secretariat, Córdoba, 3/19/2009

C31	Auto Workers' Union (SMATA), Córdoba, 7/16/2008
C32	Senior Official, Córdoba Labor Secretariat, Córdoba, 7/17/2008
C33	Health and Safety Specialist, Construction Workers' Union of Argentina (UOCRA), Córdoba, 06/20/08 and 03/09/09
C34	Garment Workers' Union (SOIVA), Córdoba, 6/25/2008
C35	Shoe Workers' Union, Córdoba, 7/16/2008
C36	Health and Safety Inspector, Córdoba Labor Secretariat, Córdoba, 6/24/2008
C37	Córdoba Labor Secretariat, Córdoba, 7/14/2008
C38	Córdoba Metal Components Industry Association, Córdoba, 7/15/2008
C39	Inspector, Córdoba Labor Secretariat, Córdoba, 7/18/2008
C40	Provincial Legislator (Opposition), Córdoba, Córdoba, 7/14/2008
C41	Health and Safety Inspector, Córdoba Labor Secretariat, Córdoba, 6/24/2008
C42	Union of Agricultural and Rural Workers (UATRE), Córdoba, 6/26/2008
C43	Senior Official, Córdoba Labor Secretariat, Córdoba, 3/9/2009
C44	Inspector, Córdoba Labor Secretariat, Córdoba, 6/25/2008
C45	Senior Official, Córdoba Labor Secretariat, Córdoba, 6/26/2008
C46	Senior Official, Córdoba Labor Secretariat, Córdoba, 6/19/2008
C47	Metal Workers' Union (UOM), Córdoba, 3/18/2009
C48	Construction Workers' Union of Argentina (UOCRA), Córdoba, 6/26/2008
CH01	Inspector, Chaco Labor Sub-Secretariat, Resistencia, Chaco, 9/10/2008
CH02	Inspector, Chaco Labor Sub-Secretariat, Resistencia, Chaco, 9/10/2008
CH03	Chaco Labor Sub-Secretariat, Resistencia, Chaco, 9/10/2008
CH04	Chaco Labor Sub-Secretariat, Chaco, 9/10/2008
CH05	Chaco Labor Sub-Secretariat, Resistencia, Chaco, 9/10/2008
CR01	Corrientes Labor Sub-Secretariat, Corrientes, 9/8/2008
CR02	Senior Official, Corrientes labor Sub-Secretariat, Corrientes, 9/11/2008
CR03	Tourism, Hotel, and Restaurant Workers' Union (UTHGRA), Corrientes, 9/12/2008
CR04	Inspector, Corrientes Labor Sub-Secretariat, Corrientes, 9/9/2008
CR05	Construction Workers' Union of Argentina (UOCRA), Corrientes, 9/8/2008
CR06	Inspector, Corrientes Labor Sub-Secretariat, Corrientes, 9/8/2008
CR07	Corrientes Labor Sub-Secretariat, Corrientes, 9/11/2008
CR08	Inspector, Corrientes Labor Sub-Secretariat, Corrientes, 9/8/2008
CR09	Corrientes Water and Environmental Agency, Corrientes, 9/12/2008

List of interviews in Argentina   247

CR10	Senior Official, Corrientes labor Sub-Secretariat, Corrientes, 9/11/2008
CR11	Inspector, Corrientes Labor Sub-Secretariat, Corrientes, 9/9/2008
CR12	Corrientes Labor Sub-Secretariat, Corrientes, 9/12/2008
S01	Inspector, Santa Fe Environmental Secretariat, Rosario, 4/30/2009
S02	Senior Official, Santa Fe Ministry of Labor and Social Security, Rosario, 5/5/2009
S03	Health and Safety Inspector, Santa Fe Ministry of Labor and Social Security, Rosario, 5/12/2009
S04	Taller Ecologista, Rosario, 6/3/2009
S05	Inspector, Santa Fe Ministry of Labor and Social Security, Santa Fe, 12/11/2008
S06	Senior Official, Santa Fe Ministry of Labor and Social Security, Santa Fe, 12/10/2008
S07	Metal Plating Association of Rosario, Firm Owner, Rosario, 5/14/2009
S08	Argentine Construction Association (CAC), Rosario, 4/29/2009
S09	Health and Safety Inspector, Santa Fe Ministry of Labor and Social Security, Rosario, 5/12/2009
S10	Senior Official, Santa Fe Environmental Secretariat, Santa Fe, 12/15/2008
S11	Former Senior Official, Santa Fe Labor Secretariat, Reconquista, Santa Fe, 12/16/2008
S12	Senior Official, Santa Fe Ministry of Labor and Social Security, Santa Fe, 12/12/2008
S13	Inspector, Santa Fe Environmental Secretariat, Rosario, 4/30/2009
S14	Senior Official, Santa Fe Environmental Secretariat, Santa Fe, 12/9/2008
S15	Inspector, Santa Fe Ministry of Labor and Social Security, Santa Fe, 12/11/2008
S16	Senior Official, Santa Fe Ministry of Labor and Social Security, Santa Fe, 12/15/2008
S17	Senior Official, Santa Fe Environmental Secretariat, Santa Fe, 12/10/2008
S18	Taller Ecologista, Rosario, 5/14/2009
S19	Senior Official, Inspection Department, Santa Fe Ministry of Labor and Social Security, Rosario, 5/7/2009
S20	Health and Safety Inspector, Santa Fe Ministry of Labor and Social Security, Rosario, 5/12/2009
S21	Metal Industry Association of Rosario, Firm Owner, Rosario, 5/7/2009
S22	Technological Center José Censabella, Alvear, Santa Fe, 4/30/2009
S23	Manos a la Obra, Rosario, 5/7/2009
S24	Industrial Federation of Santa Fe, Rosario, 5/13/2009

S25	Vecinal Santa Teresita, Rosario, 5/8/2009
S26	Health and Safety Inspector, Santa Fe Ministry of Labor and Social Security, Rosario, 5/13/2009
S27	Labor Lawyer and advisor to CGT, Rosario, 5/13/2009
S28	Inspector, Santa Fe Environmental Secretariat, Santa Fe, 12/10/2008
S29	Inspector, Santa Fe Environmental Secretariat, Santa Fe, 12/10/2008
S30	Inspector, Santa Fe Environmental Secretariat, Santa Fe, 12/10/2008
S31	Senior Official, Santa Fe Ministry of Labor and Social Security, Santa Fe, 12/9/2008
S32	Former Senior Official, Santa Fe Labor Secretariat, Santa Fe, 12/15/2008
S33	Senior Official, Santa Fe Ministry of Labor and Social Security, Santa Fe, 12/11/2008
S34	Inspector, Santa Fe Ministry of Labor and Social Security, Rosario, 5/5/2009
S35	CGT Rosario, Rosario, 5/4/2009
S36	Manager, Cereal Industry Firm, Rosario, 5/13/2009
S37	Metal Workers' Union (UOM), Rosario, 6/1/2009
S38	Labor Lawyer and advisor to CGT, Rosario, 5/5/2009
S39	Deputy, Santa Fe Chamber of Deputies, Rosario, 5/6/2009
S40	Metal Workers' Union (UOM), Rosario, 6/1/2009
S41	Construction Workers' Union of Argentina (UOCRA), Rosario, 5/13/2009
S42	Inspector, Santa Fe Ministry of Labor and Social Security, Rosario, 5/5/2009
S43	Construction Workers' Union of Argentina (UOCRA), Rosario, 5/13/2009
S44	Laundry Workers' Union (UOETSYLRA), Rosario, 5/8/2009
S45	Senior Official, Santa Fe Environmental Secretariat, Santa Fe, 12/9/2008
S46	Inspector, Santa Fe Environmental Secretariat, Rosario, 4/30/2009
S47	Vecinal Santa Teresita, Rosario, 5/8/2009
S48	Inspector, Santa Fe Environmental Secretariat, Santa Fe, 12/10/2008
S49	Inspector, Santa Fe Environmental Secretariat, Santa Fe, 12/10/2008
S50	Inspector, Santa Fe Environmental Secretariat, Santa Fe, 12/10/2008
T01	Meat Packing Association of Tucumán and Firm Owner, Alderetes, Tucumán, 4/20/2009
T02	Environmental Specialist, Citrus Firm, Cevil Pozo, Tucumán, 4/17/2009
T03	Environmental Specialist, Sugar Mill, La Banda del Rio Salí, Tucumán, 4/21/2009
T04	Agro-Industrial Research Station Obispo Colombres, Las Talitas, Tucumán, 4/20/2009

List of interviews in Argentina — 249

T05	Environmental Specialist, Citrus Firm, Tafí Viejo, Tucumán, 4/17/2009
T06	Construction Workers' Union of Argentina (UOCRA), Tucumán, 4/14/2009
T07	Senior Official, Tucumán Environmental Secretariat, Tucumán, 11/4/08 and 11/14/08 and 04/20/09
T08	Federal Court of Tucumán, Tucumán, 4/14/2009
T09	Tucumán Citrus Association, Tucumán, 10/28/2008
T10	Cleaner Production Center, Tucumán, 11/11/2008
T11	Province of Tucumán Tax Department, Tucumán, 4/17/2009
T12	Senior Official, Tucumán Labor Secretariat, Tucumán, 10/27/2008 and 11/12/2008
T13	Lawyer, Tucumán Environmental Secretariat, Tucumán, 10/28/2008
T14	Environmental Inspector, Tucumán Ministry of Health (SIPROSA), Tucumán, 11/6/2008
T15	Industrial Engineer, Tucumán Environmental Secretariat, Tucumán, 10/28/2008 and 11/10/2008
T16	Industrial Union of Tucumán, Tucumán, 4/15/2009
T17	Senior Official, Tucumán Environmental Secretariat, Tucumán, 11/3/2008
T18	Environmental Inspector, Tucumán Ministry of Health (SIPROSA), Tucumán, 11/4/2008
T20	Federation of Environmental Non-governmental Organizations, Yerba Buena, Tucumán, 11/3/2008
T21	Environmental Activist, Concepcion, Tucumán, 11/15/08 and 04/16/09
T23	Environmental Specialist, Sugar Mill, Tucumán, 11/12/2008
T24	Environmental Specialist, Sugar Mill, Tucumán, 11/12/2008
T25	Pro Eco, Tafí Viejo, Tucumán, 11/1/2008
T29	Pro Eco, Tafí Viejo, Tucumán, 11/1/2008
T30	Pro Eco, Tafí Viejo, Tucumán, 11/1/2008
T31	Pro Eco, Tafí Viejo, Tucumán, 11/1/2008
T32	Inspector, Tucumán Labor Secretariat, Tucumán, 4/16/2009
T33	Inspector, Ministry of Labor, Employment and Social Security, Tucumán, 11/12/2008
T34	Inspector, Ministry of Labor, Employment and Social Security, Tucumán, 11/12/2008
T35	Deputy, Province of Tucumán, Tucumán, 10/29/2008
T36	Green Pact, Tucumán, 11/4/2008
T37	Former Senior Official, Tucumán Labor Secretariat, Tucumán, 4/14/2009
T38	Senior Official, Regional Office of Tucumán, Ministry of Labor, Employment and Social Security, Tucumán, 11/5/2008
T39	Senior Official, Tucumán Labor Secretariat, Tucumán, 4/17/2009

T40	Inspector, Ministry of Labor, Employment and Social Security, Tucumán, 11/12/2008
T41	Industrial Union of Tucumán, Tucumán, 4/15/2009
T42	Senior Official, Regional Office of Tucumán, Ministry of Labor, Employment and Social Security, Tucumán, 11/5/2008
T43	Engineer, Tucumán Environmental Secretariat, Tucumán, 10/28/08 and 04/20/08
T44	Senior Official, Tucumán Environmental Secretariat, Tucumán, 11/6/2008
T45	Inspector, Tucumán Labor Secretariat, Tucumán, 10/31/2008
T46	Senior Official, Tucumán Environmental Secretariat, Tucumán, 11/6/2008
T47	Tucumán Regional Sugar Industry Association (CART), Tucumán, 11/14/2008
T48	Argentine Construction Association (CAC), Tucumán, 10/29/2008
T49	Tucumán Regional Sugar Industry Association (CART), Tucumán, 11/14/2008
T50	Federation of Sugar Industry Workers in Tucumán, Tucumán, 10/28/2008
T51	Union of Agricultural and Rural Workers (UATRE), Tucumán, 4/15/2009
T52	Construction Workers' Union of Argentina (UOCRA), Tucumán, 10/31/2008
T53	Tucumán Construction Association, Tucumán, 11/4/2008
T54	Inspector, Tucumán Labor Secretariat, Tucumán, 11/11/2008
T55	Inspector, Tucumán Labor Secretariat, Tucumán, 11/11/2008
T56	Inspector, Tucumán Labor Secretariat, Tucumán, 11/6/2008
T57	Metal Workers' Union (UOM), Tucumán, 4/21/2009
T58	Inspector, Tucumán Labor Secretariat, Tucumán, 11/11/2008
T59	Tucumán Labor Secretariat, Tucumán, 11/6/2008
T60	Tucumán Regional Sugar Industry Association (CART), Tucumán, 11/14/2008
T61	Federation of Sugar Industry Workers in Tucumán, Tucumán, 10/28/2008

Works Cited

Abernathy, Frederick H, John Dunlop, Janice Hammond, and David Weil. *A Stitch in Time*. New York, Oxford University Press, 1999.

Abers, Rebecca and Margaret Keck. *Practical Authority: Agency and Institutional Change in Brazilian Water Politics*. Oxford, Oxford University Press, 2013.

Acuña, Guillermo. *Marcos Regulatorios e Institucionales Ambientales de América Latina y el Caribe en el Contexto del Proceso de Reformas Macroeconómicas: 1980–1990*. CEPAL, División de Medio Ambiente y Asentamientos Humanos, Santiago de Chile, 1999.

Adcock, Robert and David Collier. "Measurement Validity: A Shared Standard for Qualitative and Quantitative Research." *American Political Science Review* 95, 3, 2001.

Aguilar, Soledad. "Environmental Non-Government Organizations in Argentina." *Review of European Community International Environmental Law* 11, 2, 2002.

Ahlquist, John S and Margaret Levi. *In the Interest of Others: Organizations and Social Activism*. Princeton, Princeton University Press, 2013.

Almeida, Rita and Lucas Ronconi. *"The Enforcement of Labor Law in the Developing World: Some Stylized Facts From Labor Inspections."* Seventh IZA/World Bank Conference on Employment and Developing. New Delhi, 2012.

Almeida, Rita and Pedro Carneiero. "Enforcement of Labor Regulation, Informal Labor and Firm Performance." *World Bank Policy Research Working Paper*. 2005.

Amengual, Matthew. "Complementary Labor Regulation: The Uncoordinated Combination of State and Private Regulators in the Dominican Republic." *World Development* 38, 3, 2010.

"Cambios en la capacidad del Estado para enfrentar las violaciones de las normas laborales: los talleres de confección de prendas de vestir en Buenos Aires." *Desarrollo Económico* 51, 202–203, 2011.

"Enforcement Without Autonomy: The Politics of Labor and Environmental Regulation in Argentina." *MIT Department of Political Science Dissertation*, 2011.

"Pollution in the Garden of the Argentine Republic: Building State Capacity to Escape from Chaotic Regulation." *Politics & Society* 41, 4, 2013.

"Pathways to Enforcement: Labor Inspectors Leveraging Linkages with Society in Argentina." *Industrial and Labor Relations Review* 67, 1, 2014.

"Linkages and Labour Inspectors: Enforcement in the Garment Workshops of Buenos Aires." *Creative Labour Regulation: Indeterminacy and Protection in an Uncertain World*. Eds. Dierdre McCan, Sangheon Lee, Patrick Belser, Colin Fenwick, John Howe, and Malte Luebker. Geneva, ILO, 2014.

Anker, Richard, Igor Chernyshev, Philippe Egger, Farhead Mehran, and Joseph Ritter. *Measuring Decent Work with Statistical Indicators*. International Labor Organization, Geneva, 2002.

Anner, Mark. "Meeting the Challenges of Industrial Restructuring: Labor Reform and Enforcement in Latin America." *Latin American Politics and Society* 50, 2, 2008.

Solidarity Transformed: Labor Responses to Globalization and Crisis in Latin America. Ithaca, Cornell University Press, 2011.

Aparicio, Susana, Sutti Ortiz, and Nidia Tadeo. "Have Private Supermarket Norms Benefited Laborers? Lemon and Sweet Citrus Production in Argentina." *Globalizations* 5, 2, 2008.

Auditoria General la Ciudad Buenos Aires. *Informe Final: Dirección General De Protección del Trabajo*. 2006.

Ayres, Ian and John Braithwaite. *Responsive Regulation: Transcending the Deregulation Debate*. Oxford, Oxford University Press, 1992.

Bartley, Tim. "Institutional Emergence in an Era of Globalization: The Rise of Transnational Private Regulation of Labor and Environmental Conditions." *American Journal of Sociology* 113, 2, 2007.

"Transnational Governance as the Layering of Rules: Intersections of Public and Private Standards." *Theoretical Inquiries in Law* 12, 2, 2011.

Becker, Gary. "Crime and Punishment: An Economic Approach." *The Journal of Political Economy* 76, 2, 1968.

Bensusán, Graciela. *Diseno Legal y Desempeno Real: Instituciones Laborales en America Latina*. Mexico City, Universidad Autonoma Metropolitana and Miguel Angel Porrua, 2006.

La Efectividad de la Legislación Laboral en América Latina. Geneva, ILO, August 15, 2007.

Berenson, Marc P. "Serving Citizens: How Comparable Are Polish and Russian 'Street-Level' Bureaucrats?" *Comparative Political Studies* 43, 5, 2010.

Berliner, Daniel, Anne Greenleaf, Milli Lake, and Jennifer Noveck. "Building Capacity, Building Rights? State Capacity and Labor Rights in Developing Countries." *World Development* 72, 2015.

Berman, Sheri. "Civil Society and the Collapse of the Weimar Republic." *World Politics* 49, 3, 1997.

Bernhardt, Annette, Siobhán McGrath, and James DeFilippis. "The State of Worker Protections in the United States: Unregulated Work in New York City." *International Labour Review* 147, 2–3, 2008.

Bernhardt, Annette et al. *Broken Laws, Unprotected Workers: Violations of Employment and Labor Laws in America's Cities*. New York, National Employment Law Project, 2010.

Bertonatti, Claudio and Javier Corcuera. *Situación Ambiental Argentina 2000*. Buenos Aires, Argentina, Fundacion Vida Silvestre Argentina, 2000.

Works cited

Brailovsky, Antonio Elio and Dina Foguelman. *Memoria Verde: Historia Ecológica de la Argentina*. Buenos Aires, Sudamerica, 1991.

Brehm, John and Scott Gates. "Donut Shops and Speed Traps: Evaluating Models of Supervision on Police Behavior." *American Journal of Political Science* 37, 2, 1993.

Working, Shirking, and Sabotage: Bureaucratic Response to a Democratic Public Michigan Studies in Political Analysis. Ann Arbor, University of Michigan Press, 1997.

Brennan, James P. *The Labor Wars in Córdoba, 1955–1976: Ideology, Work, and Labor Politics in An Argentine Industrial City*. Cambridge, Mass., Harvard University Press, 1994.

Brinks, Daniel. *The Judicial Response to Police Killings in Latin America*. Cambridge; New York, Cambridge University Press, 2008.

Buchanan, Paul. "State Corporatism in Argentina: Labor Administration Under Peron and Ongania." *Latin American Research Review* 20, 1, 1985.

Burgess, K. "Global Pressures, National Policies, and Labor Rights in Latin America." *Studies in Comparative International Development* 45, 2, 2010.

Cao, Xun and Aseem Prakash. "Trade Competition and Environmental Regulations: Domestic Political Constraints and Issue Visibility." *The Journal of Politics* 74, 01, 2012.

Caraway, Teri. "Protective Repression, International Pressure, and Institutional Design: Explaining Labor Reform in Indonesia." *Studies in Comparative International Development* 39, 3, 2004.

"Freedom of Association: Battering Ram or Trojan Horse?" *Review of International Political Economy* 13, 2, 2006.

Caraway, Teri and Michele Ford "Labor and Politics Under Oligarchy." *Beyond Oligarchy: Wealth, Power, and Contemporary Indonesian Politics*. Eds. Michele Ford and Thomas Pepinsky. Ithaca Southeast Asia Program, Cornell University, 2014.

Carpenter, Daniel P. "Adaptive Signal Processing, Hierarchy, and Budgetary Control in Federal Regulation." *The American Political Science Review* 90, 2, 1996.

The Forging of Bureaucratic Autonomy: Reputations, Networks, and Policy Innovation in Executive Agencies, 1862–1928. Princeton, NJ, Princeton University Press, 2001.

Reputation and Power: Organizational Image and Pharmaceutical Regulation at the FDA. Princeton, Princeton University Press, 2010.

Carpenter, Daniel and David A Moss. *Preventing Regulatory Capture: Special Interest Influence and How to Limit It*. New York: Cambridge University Press, 2013.

Carpenter, Daniel and Gisela Sin. "Policy Tragedy and the Emergence of Regulation: The Food, Drug, and Cosmetic Act of 1938." *Studies in American Political Development* 21, 02, 2007.

Carruthers, David. "Environmental Politics in Chile: Legacies of Dictatorship and Democracy." *Third World Quarterly* 22, 3, 2001.

Carruthers, David and Patricia Rodriguez. "Mapuche Protest, Environmental Conflict and Social Movement Linkage in Chile." *Third World Quarterly* 30, 4, 2009.

Castillo, Carlos Reynoso. "Situación de Trabajo y Protección de los Trabajadores: Estudio del Caso de México." International Labor Organization, 1999.

Chalmers, Douglas "The Politicized State in Latin America." *Authoritarianism and Corporatism in Latin America.* Ed. James Malloy. Pittsburgh, University of Pittsburgh Press, 1977.

Chan, Anita and Robert Ross. "Racing to the Bottom: International Trade Without a Social Clause." *Third World Quarterly* 24, 6, 2003.

Chen, Yuyu, Avraham Ebenstein, Michael Greenstone, and Hongbin Li. "Evidence on the Impact of Sustained Exposure to Air Pollution on Life Expectancy from China's Huai River Policy." *Proceedings of the National Academy of Sciences* 110, 32, 2013.

Christen, Catherine, Selene Herculano, Kathryn Hochstetler, Renae Prell, Marie Price, and J. Timmons Robberts. "Latin American Environmentalism: Comparative Views." *Studies in Comparative International Development* 33, 2, 1998.

Collier, Ruth Berins and David Collier. "Inducements Versus Constraints: Disaggregating 'Corporatism'." *The American Political Science Review* 73, 4, 1979.
Shaping the Political Arena: Critical Junctures, the Labor Movement, and Regime Dynamics in Latin America. Second edn. Notre Dame, University of Notre Dame Press, [1991] 2002.

Cook, María Lorena. "Toward Flexible Industrial Relations? Neo-Liberalism, Democracy, and Labor Reform in Latin America." *Industrial Relations* 37, 3, 1998.
The Politics of Labor Reform in Latin America: Between Flexibility and Rights. University Park, Pa., Pennsylvania State University Press, 2007.

Cooney, Sean. "China's Labour Law, Compliance and Flaws in Implementing Institutions." *Journal of Industrial Relations* 49, 5, 2007.

Coria, Silvia, Leila Devia, Ana Lamas, Silvia Nonna, and Claudia Villanueva. *El Rumbo Ambiental en la Argentina.* Buenos Aires, Ediciones Ciudad Argentina, 1998.

Coslovsky, Salo. "*Compliance and Competitiveness: How Prosecutors Enforce Labor and Environmental Laws and Promote Economic Development in Brazil.*" PhD Dissertation, MIT Department of Urban Studies and Planning, 2009.
"Relational Regulation in the Brazilian Ministério Publico: The Organizational Basis of Regulatory Responsiveness." *Regulation & Governance* 5, 1, 2011.

Coslovsky, Salo V and Richard Locke. "Parallel Paths to Enforcement: Private Compliance, Public Regulation, and Labor Standards in the Brazilian Sugar Sector." *Politics & Society* 41, 4, 2013.

Coslovsky, Salo, Roberto Pires, and Renato Bignami. "Labor Relations in Contemporary Brazil: Stable Regulations, Dynamic Enforcement." 2013.

Coslovsky, Salo, Roberto Pires, and Susan Silbey "The Pragmatic Politics of Regulatory Enforcement." *Handbook on the Politics of Regulation: VII – Towards Better Regulation?.* Ed. David Levi-Faur. London, Edward Elgar Publishers, 2011.

Culpepper, Pepper D. *Quiet Politics and Business Power: Corporate Control in Europe and Japan.* New York, Cambridge University Press, 2011.

Darden, Keith. "The Integrity of Corrupt States: Graft as an Informal State Institution." *Politics & Society* 36, 1, 2008.

Dasgupta, Nandini. "Environmental Enforcement and Small Industries in India: Reworking the Problem in the Poverty Context." *World Development* 28, 5, 2000.

Devia, Leila, Silvia Coria, Marcela Flores, Ana Lamas, Silvia Nonna, and Claudia Villanueva. *Nuevo Rumbo Ambiental.* Buenos Aires, Ciudad Argentina, 2008.

Works cited

DiLulio, John D. "Principled Agents: The Cultural Bases of Behavior in a Federal Government Bureaucracy." *Journal of Public Administration Research and Theory* 4, 5, 1994.

Dimitrov, Martin. *Piracy and the State: The Politics of Intellectual Property Rights in China*. New York, Cambridge University Press, 2009.

Di Paola, Maria. "Government Coordination and Hazardous Waste Enforcement in Argentina." *Sixth International Conference on Environmental Compliance and Enforcement*, 2002.

Indicadores de Aplicación y Cumplimiento de la Normativa Ambiental en la República Argentina. Buenos Aires, Fundación Ambiente y Recursos Naturales, 2002.

"Presupuestos Mínimos de Protección Ambiental II." *Presupuestos Mínimos de Protección Ambiental II*, 2006.

Díaz, Myriam del Valle. *Política Ambiental en Argentina: Un Acercamiento a su Génesis y Devenir en las Tres Últimas Décadas*. San Juan, República Argentina, EFU, Editorial Fundación Universidad Nacional de San Juan, 2009.

Dobbin, Frank and John Sutton. "The Strength of a Weak State: The Rights Revolution and the Rise of Human Resource Management Divisions." *American Journal of Sociology* 104, 2, 1998.

Doyon, Louise M. "El Crecimiento Sindical Bajo el Peronismo." *Desarrollo Económico* 15, 57, 1975.

Dwivedi, O P and Dhirendra K Vajpeyi. *Environmental Policies in the Third World: A Comparative Analysis*. Westport, Conn., Greenwood Press, 1995.

Eaton, Kent. "Can Politicians Control Bureaucrats? Applying Theories of Political Control to Argentina's Democracy." *Latin American Politics and Society* 45, 4, 2003.

Politics Beyond the Capital: The Design of Subnational Institutions in South America. Stanford, Calif. : Stanford University Press, 2004.

Ellermann, Antje. *States Against Migrants: Deportation in Germany and the United States*. New York, Cambridge University Press, 2009.

Espach, Ralph. *Private Environmental Regimes in Developing Countries: Globally Sown, Locally Grown*. New York, NY, Palgrave Macmillan, 2009.

Estlund, Cynthia L. "The Ossification of American Labor Law." *Columbia Law Review* 102, 6, 2002.

Etchemendy, Sebastián. "Constructing Reform Coalitions: The Politics of Compensations in Argentina's Economic Liberalization." *Latin American Politics and Society* 43, 3, 2001.

"Repression, Exclusion and Inclusion: Government-Union Relations and Patterns of Labor Reform in Liberalizing Economies." *Comparative Politics* 36, 3, 2004.

Models of Economic Liberalization: Business, Workers, and Compensation in Latin America, Spain, and Portugal. New York, Cambridge University Press, 2011.

Etchemendy, Sebastián and Ruth Berins Collier. "Down but Not Out: Union Resurgence and Segmented Neocroporatism in Argentina." *Politics & Society* 35, 3, 2007.

Etchemendy, Sebastián and Vicente Palermo. "Conflicto y Concertación. Gobierno, Congreso y Organizaciones ee Interés en la Reforma Laboral del Primer Gobierno De Menem (1989–1995)." *Desarrollo Económico* 37, 148, 1998.

Evans, Peter. *Embedded Autonomy: States and Industrial Transformation*. Princeton, NJ, Princeton University Press, 1995.

"Introduction: Development Strategies Across the Public-Private Divide." *World Development* 24, 6, 1996.

Evans, Peter and James Rauch. "Bureaucracy and Growth: A Cross-National Analaysis of the Effects of 'Weberian' State Structures on Economic Growth." *American Sociological Review* 64, 5, 1999.

Fairfield, Tasha. "Business Power and Tax Reform: Taxing Income and Profits in Chile and Argentina." *Latin American Politics and Society.* 52, 2, 2010.

Figuera Valenzuela, Rodrigo. "Vigilancia y Fiscalización de la Normativa Laboral en Chile: Tendencias y Procesos en la Inspeción del Trabajo." May 9, 2005. Presented at: "Labour Standards Application: A Compared Perspective," Buenos Aries, Argentina. Ministry of Labor.

Fine, Janice. "Solving the Problem From Hell: Tripartism As a Strategy for Addressing Labour Standards Non-Compliance in the United States." *Osgoode Hall Law Journal* 50, 4, 2014.

Fine, Janice and Jennifer Gordon. "Strengthening Labor Standards Enforcement through Partnerships with Workers Organizations." *Politics and Society* 38, 4, 2010.

Fiorino, Daniel J. *The New Environmental Regulation.* Cambridge, Mass., MIT Press, 2006.

Frank, D J, A Hironaka, and E Schofer. "The Nation-State and the Natural Environment Over the Twentieth Century." *American Sociological Review* 2000.

French, John D. *Drowning in Laws: Labor Law and Brazilian Political Culture.* Chapel Hill, University of North Carolina Press, 2004.

Frundt, Henry J. *Trade Conditions and Labor Rights: US Initiatives, Dominican and Central American Responses.* Gainesville, University Press of Florida, 1998.

Fundación el Otro. *Quién es Quién en la Cadena de Valor del Sector de Indumentaria Textil.* Buenos Aires, May 15, 2007.

Gallagher, K P. "Economic Globalization and the Environment." *Annual Review of Environment and Resources* 34, 2009.

Garay, Candelaria. "Social Policy and Collective Action: Unemployed Worker Associ-ations, and Protest in Argentina." *Politics & Society* 52, 3, 2007.

Garcia-Johnson, Ronie. *Exporting Environmentalism: US Multinational Chemical Cor-porations in Brazil and Mexico.* Cambridge, Mass. London: MIT Press, 2000.

Geddes, Barbara. "Building 'State' Autonomy in Brazil, 1930–1964." *Comparative Politics* 22, 2, 1990.

  Politician's Dilemma: Building State Capacity in Latin America. Berkeley, University of California Press, 1994.

Gerth, Hans Heinrich and C Wright Mills. *From Max Weber: Essays in Sociology.* New York, Oxford University Press, 1946.

Gibson, Edward. "Boundary Control: Subnational Authoritarianism in Democratic Countries." *World Politics* 58, 2005.

Gingerich, Daniel W. "Governance Indicators and the Level of Analysis Problem: Empirical Findings From South America." *British Journal of Political Science* 42, 3, 2012.

Goertz, Gary and James Mahoney. *A Tale of Two Cultures: Qualitative and Quantita-tive Research in the Social Sciences.* Princeton, Princeton University Press, 2012.

Goldemberg, José, Suani Teixeira Coelho, and Patricia Guardabassi. "The Sustainability of Ethanol Production From Sugarcane." *Energy Policy* 36, 6, 2008.

Works cited

Grzymala-Busse, Anna. "Political Competition and the Politicization of the State in East Central Europe." *Comparative Political Studies* 36, 10, 2003.

Rebuilding Leviathan: Party Competition and State Exploitation in Post-Communist Democracies. Cambridge, Cambridge University Press, 2007.

Gunningham, Neil, Dorothy Thorton, and Robert Kagan. "Motivating Management: Corporate Compliance in Environmental Protection." *Law & Policy* 27, 2, 2005.

Gutiérrez, Ricardo. "Federalismo y Políticas Ambientales en la Región Metropolitana de Buenos Aires, Argentina." *EURE (Santiago)* 38, 114, 2012.

Gutiérrez, Ricardo A and Fernando J Isuani. "La Emergencia del Ambientalismo estatal y Social en Argentina." *RAP: Revista Brasileira de Administração Pública* 48, 2, 2014.

Ha, Yong-Chool and Myung-koo Kang. "Creating a Capable Bureaucracy with Loyalists: The Internal Dynamics of the South Korean Developmental State, 1948–1979." *Comparative Political Studies* 44, 1, 2011.

Haggard, S. *"The Reform of the State in Latin America." The Challenges of Reform: Proceedings of an Annual World Bank Conference*. Washington DC, World Bank, 1997.

Hawkins, Keith. *Environment and Enforcement: Regulation and Social Definition of Pollution*. Oxford, Clarendon Press, 1984.

Law As Last Resort: Prosecution Decision-Making in a Regulatory Agency Oxford Socio-Legal Studies. Oxford, New York, Oxford University Press, 2002.

Hayter, Susan and Heyter Stoevska. *Social Dialogue Indicators: International Statistical Inquiry 2008–2009*. International Labor Organization, Industrial and Employment Relations Department, Geneva, 2011.

Heller, Patrick. *The Labor of Development: Workers and the Transformation of Capitalism in Kerala*, India, Cornell University Press, 1999.

Henderson, Jeffrey, David Hulme, Hossein Jalilian, and Richard Phillips. "Bureaucratic Effects: 'Weberian' State Agencies and Poverty Reduction." *Sociology* 41, 3, 2007.

Henry, Laura. *Red to Green: Environmental Activism in Post-Soviet Russia*. Ithaca, Cornell University Press, 2010.

Herring, Ronald J. "Embedded Particularism: India's Failed Developmental State." *The Developmental State*. Ed. Meredith Woo-Cumings. Ithaca, Cornell University Press, 1999.

Hettige, Hemamala, Mainul Huq, Sheoli Pargal, and David Wheeler. "Determinants of Pollution Abatement in Developing Countries: Evidence From South and Southeast Asia." *World Development* 24, 12, 1996.

Hochstetler, Kathryn. "After the Boomerang: Environmental Movements and Politics in the La Plata River Basin." *Global Environmental Politics* 2, 4, 2002.

"Fading Green? Environmental Politics in the Mercosur Free Trade Agreement." *Latin American Politics and Society* 45, 4, 2003.

Hochstetler, Kathryn and Margaret E Keck. *Greening Brazil: Environmental Activism in State and Society*. Durham, Duke University Press, 2007.

Holland, Alisha. "The Distributive Politics of Enforcement." *American Journal of Politics* 59, April 2, 2015.

Hopkins, Jack. *Policymaking for Conservation in Latin America: National Parks, Reserves, and the Environment*. Westport, Conn., Praeger, 1995.

258   *Works cited*

Huber, Gregory Alain. *The Craft of Bureaucratic Neutrality: Interests and Influence in Governmental Regulation of Occupational Safety.* Cambridge, [England]; New York, Cambridge University Press, 2007.

Huber, John and Nolan McCarty. "Bureaucratic Capacity, Delegation, and Political Reform." *American Political Science Review* 98, 3, 2004.

Hunter, Susan and Richard W. Waterman. "Determining an Agency's Regulatory Style: How Does the EPA Water Office Enforce the Law?" *The Western Political Quarterly* 45, 2, 1992.

ILO. *Informe de la Misión Tripartita para Evaluar la Eficacia de la Inspección del Trabajo en la Argentina.* Geneva, 1989.

"CEACR: Individual Observation Concerning Convention No. 81, Labour Inspection, 1947 Argentina (ratification: 1955) Published: 2000." *CEACR: Individual Observation Concerning Convention No. 81, Labour Inspection, 1947 Argentina (ratification: 1955) Published: 2000.* March 4, 2000.

General Survey - Labor Inspection. Geneva, ILO, 2006a.

Panorama Laboral 2006. Lima, Peru: International Labor Organization, Regional Office for Latin American and the Caribbean, 2006b.

Strategies and Practice for Labour Inspection (GB.297/ESP/3). Geneva, 2006c.

Panorama Laboral 2008. February 7, 2008.

Labour and Social Trends in Indonesia 2012. Jakarta, 2013.

Inter-American Development Bank. *Regional Policy Dialogue on Environment: Executive Profile of Environmental Management.* 2002.

"Good Jobs Wanted: Labor Markets in Latin America." Washington, DC, Johns Hopkins University Press, 2004.

James, Daniel. *Resistance and Integration: Peronism and the Argentine Working Class, 1946–1976.* Cambridge; New York, Cambridge University Press, 1988.

Jatobá, Vera. *Labour Inspection Within a Modernized Labour Administration.* Lima, Peru, ILO, 2002.

Johnson, Chalmers. *MITI and the Japanese Miracle: The Growth of Industrial Policy: 1925–1975.* Stanford University Press, 1982.

Jones, Mark, Pablo Sanguinetti, and Mariano Tommasi. "Politics, Institutions, and Fiscal Performance in a Federal System: An Analysis of the Argentine Provinces." *Journal of Development Economics* 61, 2000.

Kagan, Robert and John Scholz. "The 'Criminology of the Corporation' and Regulatory Enforcement Strategies." *Enforcing Regulation.* Eds. Keith Hawkins and John Thomas. Boston, Kluwer-Nijhoff, 1984.

Kaufman, Herbert. *The Forest Ranger: A Study in Administrative Behavior.* Washington, DC, Resources for the Future, [1960] 2006.

Keck, Margaret E and Kathryn, Sikkink. *Activists Beyond Borders: Advocacy Networks in International Politics.* Ithaca, NY, Cornell University Press, 1998.

Kelman, Steven. *Regulating America, Regulating Sweden: A Comparative Study of Occupational Safety and Health Policy.* Cambridge, Mass., MIT Press, 1981.

Kiser, E and J Schneider. "Bureaucracy and Efficiency: An Analysis of Taxation in Early Modern Prussia." *American Sociological Review* 59, 2, 1994.

Kohli, Atul. *State-Directed Development.* New York, Cambridge University Press, 2004.

Konisky, David M. "Inequities in Enforcement? Environmental Justice and Government Performance." *Journal of Policy Analysis and Management* 28, 1, 2009.

Works cited

Kurtz, Marcus. *Latin American State Building in Comparative Perspective: Social Foundations of Institutional Order*. New York, Cambridge University Press, 2013.

Kurtz, Marcus and Andrew Schrank. "Growth and Governance: Models, Measures, and Mechanisms." *The Journal of Politics* 69, 2, 2007.

Kuruvilla, S, C K Lee, and M E Gallagher. *From Iron Rice Bowl to Informalization: Markets, Workers, and the State in a Changing China*. Ithaca, New York, ILR Press, 2011.

Kus, Basak. "Regulatory Governance and the Informal Economy: Cross-National Comparisons." *Socio-Economic Review* 8, 3, 2010.

Lam, Wai Fung. "Institutional Design of Public Agencies and Coproduction: A Study of Irrigation Associations in Taiwan." *World Development* 24, 6, 1996.

Lee, Eungkyoon. "Socio-Political Contexts, Identity Formation, and Regulatory Compliance." *Administration & Society* 40, 7, 2008.

Lemos, Maria Carmen De Mello. "The Politics of Pollution Control in Brazil: State Actors and Social Movements Cleaning Up Cubatão." *World Development* 26, 1, 1998.

Levine, David, Michael Toffel, and Matthew Johnson. "Randomized Government Safety Inspections Reduce Worker Injuries with No Detectable Job Loss." *Science* 336, 6083, 2012.

Levitsky, Steven. *Transforming Labor-Based Parties in Latin America: Argentine Peronism in Comparative Perspective*. Cambridge; New York, Cambridge University Press, 2003.

Levitsky, Steven and Maria Victoria Murillo. "Variation in Institutional Strength." *Annual Review of Political Science* 12, 2009.

"Building Institutions on Weak Foundations." *Journal of Democracy* 24, 2, 2013.

"Introduction." *Argentine Democracy: The Politics of Institutional Weakness*. Eds. Steven Levitsky and María Victoria Murillo. University Park, PA, Pennsylvania State University Press, 2005.

Levitsky, Steven and Lucan Way. "Between a Shock and a Hard Place: The Dynamics of Labor-Backed Adjustment in Poland and Argentina." *Comparative Politics* 30, 2, 1998.

Lieutier, Ariel. *Esclavos: Los Trabajadores Costureros de la Ciudad de Buenos Aires*. Buenos Aires, Retorica Ediciones, 2010.

Locke, Richard. *The Promise and Limits of Private Power: Promoting Labor Standards in a Global Economy*. Cambridge, Cambridge University Press, 2013.

Locke, Richard, Matthew Amengual, and Akshay Mangla. "Virtue Out of Necessity? Compliance, Commitment, and the Improvement of Labor Conditions in Global Supply Chains." *Politics & Society* 37, 2, 2009.

Locke, Richard M, Ben A Rissing, and Timea Pal. "Complements or Substitutes? Private Codes, State Regulation and the Enforcement of Labour Standards in Global Supply Chains." *British Journal of Industrial Relations* 2012.

Lora, Eduardo. *Structural Reforms in Latin America: What Has Been Reformed and How to Measure It*. Washington, DC, Inter-American Development Bank, 2001.

De Luca, Miguel, Mark Jones, and María Inés Tula. "Back Rooms or Ballot Boxes?: Candidate Nomination in Argentina." *Comparative Political Studies* 35, 4, 2002.

Luna, Elba and Elida Cecconi. *Indice de Desarrollo Sociedad Civil de Argentina Total Pais*. Argentina: Published by United National Development Program, Inter-American Development Bank, and the Grupo de Análisis y Desarrollo Institucional y Social, 2004.

Madrid, Raúl. "Labouring Against Neoliberalism: Unions and Patterns of Reform in Latin America." *Journal of Latin American Studies* 35, 2003.

Mahoney, James and Kathleen Thelen. *Explaining Institutional Change: Ambiguity, Agency, and Power*. Cambridge; New York, Cambridge University Press, 2010.

Mann, Michael. *The Sources of Social Power: Volume 2*. New York, Cambridge University Press, 1993.

Markus, Stanislav. "Secure Property as a Bottom-Up Process: Firms, Stakeholders, and Predators in Weak States." *World Politics* 64, 2, 2012.

Marshall, Adriana. "Estructura del Empleo, Desempleo y Orientacion Politica: Efectos Sobre la Afiliacion Sindical." *Desarrollo Económico* 46, 182, 2006.

Explaining Non-compliance with Labour Legislation in Latin America: A Cross-Country Analysis. ILO, 2007.

Marshall, Adriana and Laura Perelman. "Sindicalización: Incentivos en la Normativa Sociolaboral." *Cuadernos del Instituto de Desarrollo Económico y Social* 4, 2004.

May, Peter J. "Compliance Motivations: Affirmative and Negative Bases." *Law & Society Review* 38, 1, 2004.

"Regulation and Compliance Motivations: Examining Different Approaches." *Public Administration Review* 65, 1, 2005.

Mazorra, Ximena and Alejandra Beccaria "Especialización Productiva Y Empleo En Areas Económicas Locales." *Estructura Productiva Y Empleo*. Eds. Marta Novick and Héctor Palomino. Buenos Aires Ministerio de Trabajo, Empleo y Seguridad Social, 2007.

McAllister, Lesley. *Making Law Matter: Environmental Protection and Legal Institutions in Brazil*. Stanford, Calif., Stanford Law Books, 2008.

"Dimensions of Enforcement Style: Factoring in Regulatory Autonomy and Capacity." *Law & Policy* 32, 1, 2010.

McAllister, Lesley, Benjamin Van Rooij, and Robert Kagan. "Reorienting Regulation: Pollution Enforcement in Industrializing Countries." *Law & Policy* 32, 1, 2010.

McCubbins, Mathew D, Roger G Noll, and Barry R Weingast. "Administrative Procedures as Instruments of Political Control." *Journal of Law, Economics, & Organization* 3, 2, 1987.

McCubbins, M D and T Schwartz. "Congressional Oversight Overlooked: Police Patrols Versus Fire Alarms." *American Journal of Political Science* 28, 1, 1984.

McGuire, James. *Peronism Without Perón: Unions, Parties, and Democracy in Argentina*. Stanford, Stanford University Press, 1997.

MERCOSUR. *Normas Del Mercosur Relativas a Cuestiones Laborales Y De La Seguridad Social*. 2006.

Moe, Terry M. "Control and Feedback in Economic Regulation: The Case of the NLRB." *American Political Science Review* 79, 4, 1985.

Montero, Alfred P. *Shifting States in Global Markets: Subnational Industrial Policy in Contemporary Brazil and Spain*. University Park, Pa., Pennsylvania State University Press, 2001.

Works cited

Morantz, Alison. "Coal Mine Safety: Do Unions Make a Difference?" *Industrial and Labor Relations Review* 66, 1, 2013.

"Does Unionization Strengthen Regulatory Enforcement? An Empirical Study of the Mine Safety and Health Administration." *New York University Journal of Legislation and Public Policy* 14 (2011), 697–805.

Mosley, Layna. "Workers' Rights in Open Economies: Global Production and Domestic Institutions in the Developing World." *Comparative Political Studies* 41, 4–5, 2008.

Labor Rights and Multinational Production. Cambridge; New York, Cambridge University Press, 2010.

Murillo, María Victoria. *Labor Unions, Partisan Coalitions, and Market Reforms in Latin America.* New York, Cambridge University Press, 2001.

"Partisanship Amidst Convergence: The Politics of Labor Reform in Latin America." *Comparative Politics* 37, 4, 2005.

Political Competition, Partisanship, and Policymaking in Latin American Public Utilities. New York, Cambridge University Press, 2009.

Murillo, Maria Victoria and Andrew Schrank. "With a Little Help From My Friends: Partisan Politics, Transnational Alliances, and Labor Rights in Latin America." *Comparative Political Studies* 38, 8, 2005.

Nonna, Silvia. "*The Environment and Its Regulation in Argentina.*" Sixth International Conference on Environmental Compliance and Enforcement, 2002.

O'Donnell, Guillermo. "On the State, Democratization and Some Conceptual Problems - A Latin American View with Glances at Some Postcommunist Countries." *World Development* 1993.

O'Dwyer, Conor. "Runaway State Building: How Political Parties Shape States in Postcommunist Eastern Europe." *World Politics* 56, 4, 2004.

Oka, Chikako. "Improving Working Conditions in Garment Supply Chains: The Role of Unions in Cambodia." *British Journal of Industrial Relations.* Early View (Online Version), 2015.

Orihuela, Jose Carlos. "Converging Divergence: The Diffusion of the Green State in Latin America." *Studies in Comparative International Development* 49, 2, 2014.

O'Rourke, Dara. "Motivating a Conflicted Environmental State: Community-Driven Regulation in Vietnam." *The Environmental State Under Pressure* 10, 2002.

Community-Driven Regulation: Balancing Development and the Environment in Vietnam. Cambridge, Mass., MIT Press, 2004.

O'Rourke, Dara and Gregg P Macey. "Community Environmental Policing: Assessing New Strategies of Public Participation in Environmental Regulation." *Journal of Policy Analysis and Management* 22, 3, 2003.

Ortiz, Claudia Isabel. *Los Centros de Residentes de Inmigrantes: Nuevas Articulaciones en la Producción de la Identidad.* Córdoba, Universidad Nacional de Córdoba, 2002.

Ortiz, Sutti and Susana Aparicio. "Contracts, Control and Contestation: The Harvest of Lemons for Export." *Journal of Peasant Studies* 33, 2, 2006.

"Management Response to the Demands of Global Fresh Fruit Markets: Rewarding Harvesters with Financial Incentives." *Journal of Development Studies* 42, 3, 2006.

"How Labourers Fare in Fresh Fruit Export Industries: Lemon Production in Northern Argentina." *Journal of Agrarian Change* 7, 3, 2007.

Ostrom, Elinor. "Crossing the Great Divide: Coproduction, Synergy, and Development." *World Development* 24, 6, 1996.

Palomino, Héctor "Los Cambios en el Mundo del Trabajo y Los Dilemas Sindicales." *Dictadura y Democracia: 1976–2001*. Ed. Juan Suriano. Buenos Aires, Sudamerica, 2005.

Pedriana, Nicholas and Robin Stryker. "The Strength of a Weak Agency: Enforcement of Title VII of the 1964 Civil Rights Act and the Expansion of State Capacity, 1965–1971." *American Journal of Sociology* 110, 3, 2004.

Piore, Michael "Rethinking International Labor Standards." *Labor and the Globalization of Production*. Ed. William Millberg. New York, Palgrave MacMillian, 2004.

Piore, Michael and Andrew Schrank.

"Toward Managed Flexibility: The Revival of Labour Inspection in the Latin World." *International Labour Review* 147, 1, 2008.

Pires, Roberto Rocha Coelho. "Promoting Sustainable Compliance: Styles of Labour Inspection and Compliance Outcomes in Brazil." *International Labour Review* 147, 2–3, 2008.

"Flexible Bureaucracies: Discretion, Creativity, and Accountability in Labor Market Regulation and Public Sector Management." PhD Thesis. MIT Department of Urban Studies and Planning, 2009.

"Beyond the Fear of Discretion: Flexibility, Performance, and Accountability in the Management of Regulatory Bureaucracies." *Regulation & Governance* 5, 1, 2011.

Pizaro, Cynthia. *La Vulnerabilidad De Los Inmigrantes Bolivianos Como Sujetos de Derechos Humanos: Experimentando la Exclusión y la Discriminación en la Región Metropolitana de la Ciudad de Córdoba*. Instituto Nacional contra la Discriminación, la Xenofobia y el Racismo Ministerio de Justicia, Seguridad y Derechos Humanos Gobierno de la República Argentina, 2008.

Poblete-Troncoso, M. "The Enforcement of Labour Legislation in Latin America." *International Labour Review* 32, 5, 1935.

Polanyi, Karl. *The Great Transformation: The Political and Economic Origins of Our Time*. Boston, MA, Beacon Press, (1944) 2001.

Post, Alison. *Foreign and Domestic Investment in Argentina*. New York, Cambridge University Press, 2014.

Pressman, Jeffrey L and Aaron Wildavsky. "Implementation: How Great Expectations in Washington Are Dashed in Oakland." Berkeley, Calif.: University of California Press, 1973.

Pritchett, Lant and Michael Woolcock. "Solutions When the Solution Is the Problem: Arraying the Disarray in Development." *World Development* 32, 2, 2004.

Rauch, James and Peter Evans. "Bureaucratic Structure and Bureaucratic Performance in Less Developed Countries." *Journal of Public Economics* 75, 2000.

Remmer, Karen L. "The Political Economy of Patronage: Expenditure Patterns in the Argentine Provinces, 1983–2003." *Journal of Politics* 69, 2, 2007.

Rinne, Jeffrey. "The Politics of Administrative Reform in Menem's Argentina: The Illusion of Isolation." *Reinventing Leviathan: The Politics of Administrative Reform in Developing Countries*. Eds. Ben Ross Schneider and Blanca Heredia. Miami, North-South Center Press 2003.

Romero Gudiño, Alejandro. "Inspección Federal del Trabajo en México." *Revista Latinoamericana de Derecho Social* 6, 2008.

Works cited

Ronconi, Lucas. "Enforcement and Compliance with Labor Regulations." *Industrial and Labor Relations Review* 64, 4, 2010.

"Globalization, Domestic Institutions, and Enforcement of Labor Law: Evidence From Latin America." *Industrial Relations* 51, 1, 2012.

Rueschemeyer, Dietrich and Peter Evans. "The State and Economic Transformation: Toward an Analysis of the Conditions Underlying Effective Intervention." *Bringing the State Back in*. Eds. Peter Evans, Dietrich Rueschemeyer, and Theda Skocpol. Cambridge, Cambridge University Press, 1985.

Sabsay, Daniel and Maria Di Paola. "El Federalismo y la Nueva Ley General del Ambiente." *La Ley: Anales de Legislación Argentina* 32, 2002.

Schiffrin, Adriana. *Presupuestos Mínimos de Protección Ambiental*. Buenos Aires, Fundación Ambiente y Recursos Naturales, 2005.

Schneider, Ben Ross. *Politics Within the State: Elite Bureaucrats and Industrial Policy in Authoritarian Brazil*. Pittsburgh, University of Pittsburgh Press, 1991.

"Elusive Synergy: Business-Government Relations and Development." *Comparative Politics* 31, 1, 1998.

Business Politics and the State in Twentieth-century Latin America. Cambridge; New York, Cambridge University Press, 2004.

Hierarchical Capitalism in Latin America: Business, Labor, and the Challenges of Equitable Development. Cambridge : Cambridge University Press, 2013.

Schneider, Ben Ross and Blanca, Heredia. *Reinventing Leviathan: The Politics of Administrative Reform in Developing Countries*. Coral Gables, Fla., North-South Center Press, 2003.

Scholz, John. "Cooperative Regulatory Enforcement and the Politics of Administrative Effectiveness." *The American Political Science Review* 85, 1, 1991.

Scholz, John T, Jim Twombly, and Barbara Headrick. "Street-Level Political Controls Over Federal Bureaucracy." *The American Political Science Review* 85, 3, 1991.

Schrank, Andrew. "Professionalization and Probity in a Patrimonial State: Labor Inspectors in the Dominican Republic." *Latin American Politics and Society* 51, 2, 2009.

"From Disguised Protectionism to Rewarding Regulation: The Impact of Trade-related Labor Standards in the Dominican Republic." *Regulation & Governance* 2013.

Seidman, Gay W. *Beyond the Boycott: Labor Rights, Human Rights and Transnational Activism*. American Sociological Association's Rose Series/ Russell Sage Foundation Press, 2007.

"Labouring Under an Illusion? Lesotho's 'sweat-free' Label." *Third World Quarterly* 30, 3, 2009.

Silbey, Susan. "The Consequences of Responsive Regulation." *Enforcing Regulation Law in Social Context Series*. Eds. Keith Hawkins and John Thomas. Boston, Kluwer-Nijhoff, 1984.

Skocpol, Theda. "Bringing the State Back In: Strategies of Analysis in Current Research." *Bringing the State Back in*. Eds. Peter Evans, Dietrich Rueschemeyer, and Theda Skocpol. Cambridge, Cambridge University Press, 1985.

Snyder, Richard. *Politics After Neoliberalism: Reregulation in Mexico Cambridge Studies in Comparative Politics*. Cambridge, UK; New York, NY, Cambridge University Press, 2001.

"Scaling Down: The Subnational Comparative Method." *Studies in Comparative International Development* 36, 1, 2001.

Soifer, Hillel David. "State Infrastructural Power: Approaches to Conceptualization and Measurement." *Studies in Comparative International Development* 43, 3–4, 2008.

Soifer, Hillel David and Matthias vom Hau. "Unpacking the Strength of the State: The Utility of State Infrastructural Power." *Studies in Comparative International Development* 43, 2008.

Spiller, Pablo Tomas and Mariano Tommasi. *The Institutional Foundations of Public Policy in Argentina*. New York, Cambridge University Press, 2007.

Stalley, Phillip. *Foreign Firms, Investment, and Environmental Regulation in the People's Republic of China*. Stanford, Stanford University Press, 2010.

Stallings, B. "Globalization and Labor in Four Developing Regions: An Institutional Approach." *Studies in Comparative International Development* 45, 2, 2010.

Steinberg, Paul. *Environmental Leadership in Developing Countries: Transnational Relations and Biodiversity Policy in Costa Rica and Bolivia*. Cambridge, Mass., MIT Press, 2001.

Stern, Rachel E. *Environmental Litigation in China: A Study in Political Ambivalence*. Cambridge [UK]; New York, Cambridge University Press, 2013.

Superintendencia de Riesgos del Trabajo. "Anuario Estadistico 2006." *Anuario Estadistico 2006* 2007.

Tendler, Judith. *Good Government in the Tropics the Johns Hopkins Studies in Development*. Baltimore, Johns Hopkins University Press, 1997.

Tilly, Charles. *Coercion, Capital, and European States, AD 990–1992*. Cambridge, MA, Blackwell, 1992.

Torre, Juan Carlos. "Interpretando (una Vez Más) los Orígenes del Peronismo." *Desarrollo Económico* 28, 112, 1989.

Tsai, Lily L. "Solidary Groups, Informal Accountability, and Local Public Goods Provision in Rural China." *American Political Science Review* 101, 2, 2007.

VanDeveer, Stacy and Geoffry Dabelko. "It's Capacity, Stupid: International Assistance and National Implementation." *Global Environmental Politics* 2001.

Van Lo Rooij, Benjamin, Carlos Wing-Hung. "Fragile Convergence: Understanding Variation in the Enforcement of China's Industrial Pollution Law." *Law & Policy* 32, 1, 2010.

Van Maanen, John. "Observations on the Making of Policemen." *Human Organization* 32, 4, 1973.

Van Rooij, Benjamin, Gerald E Fryxell, Carlos Wing-Hung Lo, and Wei Wang. "From Support to Pressure: The Dynamics of Social and Governmental Influences on Environmental Law Enforcement in Guangzhou City, China." *Regulation & Governance* 7, 3, 2013.

Vasquez Vialard, A and M. Julio Navarro. *Policía del Trabajo: Controlar de las Relaciones Individuales y de las Colectivas de Trabajo*. Buenos Aires, Astrea, 1990.

Vogel, David. *Trading Up: Consumer and Environmental Regulation in a Global Economy*. Cambridge, Harvard University Press, 1995.

"Private Global Business Regulation." *Annual Review of Political Science* 11, 2008.

Weil, David. "Enforcing OSHA: The Role of Labor Unions." *Industrial Relations* 30, 1, 1991.

Works cited

"If OSHA Is So Bad, Why Is Compliance So Good?" *The RAND Journal of Economic* 27, 3, 1996.

"Public Enforcement/Private Monitoring: Evaluating a New Approach to Regulating the Minimum Wage." *Industrial and Labor Relations Review* 58, 2, 2005.

"A Strategic Approach to Labour Inspection." *International Labour Review* 147, 4, 2008.

The Fissured Workplace: Why Work Became So Bad for So Many and What Can Be Done to Improve It. 2014.

Wilson, James Q. *Varieties of Police Behavior; The Management of Law and Order in Eight Communities.* Cambridge, Mass., Harvard University Press, 1968.

"The Politics of Regulation." *The Politics of Regulation.* Ed. James Wilson. New York, Basic Books, 1980.

Wood, B Dan. "Principals, Bureaucrats, and Responsiveness in Clean Air Enforcements." *The American Political Science Review* 82, 1, 1988.

World Bank. "Argentina Managing Environmental Pollution: Issues and Options." 1995.

Vietnam Aiming High: Vietnam Development Report 2007. 2006.

Zapata, Edgar Antonio. *Historia de los Gobiernos Peronistas de Santa Fe.* Santa Fe, Ediciones Sudamérica Santa Fe, 1994.

Index

agency capture. *See* capture
air pollution
  in China, 3
  by Santa Clara Plant, 173–74
  in Santa Fe, 2, 164
  in Tucumán, 192–93, 196–97, 206
La Alameda, 71, 113, 133
  linkages with inspectors, 136–39
  Macri administration and, 141–43
  STBA and, 136–39
Alfonsín, Raúl, 53
Alperovich, José, 103, 107–8
Angeloz, Eduardo, 93–94
Argentina. *See also* 1994 constitution; *specific cities*; *specific provinces*
  administrative resources in, 40, 61
  Botnia paper mill, 161
  business organizations in, 54–59
  CGT in, 55
  decentralization of labor administration in, 59–67
  economic crises in, 56
  Environmental Law in, 39
  environmental politics in, 45, 152
  environmental regulation in, 13, 39, 147–51
  General Environmental Law in, 150–51
  individual rights in, regulation of, 16
  labor laws in, 52–54
  labor regulation in, 13, 40, 54, 71–72
  labor unions in, 45, 54–59
  Ministry of Labor in, 41, 60
  partisan politics in, 54–59, 61
  PJ in, 45

  political control of bureaucracy in, 28
  regulatory politics in, 39–47
  state-society linkages in, 42
  Supreme Court in, environmental regulation rulings, 159–60
  UIA in, 58, 160
Argentine Construction Association (CAC), 104, 124
ATC. *See* Tucumán Citrus Association
auto workers union. *See* SMATA
autonomy
  administrative resources and, 34–35
  bureaucratic, 10
  state capacity and, 5–6, 26, 34–35
  of states, 5–6

Bielsa, Rafael, 117
Bilboni, Homero, 162
Binner, Hermes, 70, 117–20
La Boca Neighborhood Association, 155–56
Botnia paper mill, 161
Brazil
  environmental regulation in, 21, 24, 151
  labor inspections in, 17
  labor laws in, 54
  labor regulation in, 24
  Ministério Público in, 24
brick-making industry
  in Córdoba, 73, 76–81
  enforcement strategies for, 76–81
  health and safety conditions for, 78
  labor regulation in, 68
  labor violations in, 76–81

267

brick-making industry (cont.)
STC enforcement of, 74–75, 79
UORLA Union, 80
Buenos Aires, City of. *See* Federal Capital
bureaucracies. *See also* Weberian bureaucracy
as porous, 235–36
state-society linkages and, 29
bureaucratic reform
in Córdoba, 93
in Santa Fe, 117–20
in Tucumán, 108, 208–9

CAC. *See* Argentine Construction Association
cachaza pollutant, 206–7
capture, 23–24
CCT. *See* Tucumán Construction Associations
CEDAH. *See* Center for Human Rights and
Environment
Center for Bolivian Residents, 81
Center for Human Rights and Environment
(CEDAH), 161–62, 186
Central de Trabajadores de la Argentina (CTA),
128–29
Centro Azucarero Regional de Tucumán
(CART), 191
CGT. *See* General Labor Confederation
Chile, environmental regulation in, 23–24
China
air pollution in, 3
environmental regulation in, 12, 21
intellectual property in, 4
citrus industry
ATC and, 99
collective bargaining agreements in, 100
concentration of, 191
enforcement patterns in, 200–7
export standards for, 101
labor compliance in, 98–99, 101
pollution by, 165–66, 191–93
PRI for, 202–3
responsive enforcement of, 98–101
SIPROSA enforcement of, 193–95, 197–99
clientelism, 55
collective bargaining agreements
in brick-making industry, 77–78
in citrus industry, 100
in garment industry, 130
in Indonesia, 230
in metal industry, 81–82
compliance, labor
within brick-making industry, 76–81
within citrus industry, 101

within construction industry, 84, 101–2, 121
within garment industry, 130–34
labor infractions, 129
within metal industry, 81–82
at national level, 57
unregistered workers, 40
Condiciones y Medio Ambiente de Trabajo
(CYMAT), 84–88
construction industry
CAC, 104
CCT and, 104
in Córdoba, 84–87
CYMAT enforcement in, 84–88
enforcement strategies in, 70, 84–87, 101–4
health and safety enforcement in, 84, 86
in Rosario, 121
in Santa Fe, 85, 121–25
in Tucumán, 73, 101–4
Construction Workers' Union of Argentina
(UOCRA)
in Córdoba, 84–85
in Santa Fe, 122
in Tucumán, 102–3
coproduced enforcement, 8, 37–38, 92–93,
143–44, 213–14, 221
in US, 226–29
Córdoba Environmental Secretariat (CSMA),
187–88
Córdoba province, 1
brick-making industry in, 73, 76–81
CGT in, 55
construction industry in, 84–87
enforcement of labor regulations in, 68–70,
74–97, 143–44
environmental regulation enforcement in,
163–66, 185–88
labor inspectors in, 1–2, 74–75
metal industry in, 73, 81–83
PJ in, 74, 111
professional environmental organizations in,
185–87
public sector employees in, 94
STC in, 74–75
UOCRA in, 84
CSMA. *See* Córdoba Environmental Secretariat
CTA. *See Central de Trabajadores de la
Argentina*
CYMAT. *See Condiciones y Medio Ambiente
de Trabajo*

De La Rúa, Fernando, 53
De La Soto, José Manuel, 94–95

Index

Defensor del Pueblo, 79, 131, 136
  neighborhood environmental organizations and, 154–55
deterrence, enforcement through, 17
DIPOS, 169
Dominican Republic, labor regulation in, 24

Economic Federation of Tucumán (FET), 104, 191, 212
EIA. *See* environmental impact assessment
embedded autonomy, 26
enforcement
  administrative resources for, 17–18, 33–36, 211–15
  in brick-making industry, 76–81
  in citrus industry, 98–101, 204–6
  conceptualization of, 17
  in construction industry, 70, 84–87, 101–4
  co-produced, 8, 37–38, 165–66, 214, 221, 226–29
  through deterrence, 17
  dominant approaches to, 27–28
  explanations of, 19–38
  in Federal Capital, 70–71, 126–44
  in garment industry, 71
  globalization as influence on, 21
  limitations of, 222–23
  in metal industry, 69, 81–83
  patterns of, 36–38, 69, 112–13, 168–69, 180–85, 200–7, 221–22
  political support for, 9–10, 20–23
  at Santa Clara Plant, 177–80
  in Santa Fe, 70–71, 143–44, 180–85
  society-dependent, 8, 36–37, 97–109, 165, 220–21, 229–34
  state capacity for, 5–6, 23–27, 235
  state-driven, 9, 36, 226–29
  state-society linkages for, 7–8, 29–33
  subnational approach to, 41–46
  trade influences on, 20–21
  in Tucumán, 43, 68–70, 104–6, 143–44
  typology of, 8
Environmental Defense Foundation (FUNAM), 185–86
environmental impact assessment (EIA), 171, 178–80
environmental movement
  activists in, 152
  La Boca Neighborhood Association, 155–56
  CEDAH, 161–62, 186
  early organizations in, 153
  FARN, 154

Federation of Environmental Non-Governmental Organizations, 196–97
  as heterogeneous, 157
  historical development of, 153–57
  labor regulation movement compared to, 156–57
  lack of hierarchical structure in, 156–57
  neighborhood organizations in, 154–56, 167
  as non-partisan, 157
  pluralism in, 156
  professional organizations in, 154, 167
  public involvement in, 153
  Socio-Environmental Agenda, 182
  Taller Ecologista, 182–83
  UniVec, 195–96
environmental politics
  in Argentina, 45, 152
  features of, 162–63
Environmental Protection Agency (EPA), 151
environmental protests
  in Botnia, 161–62
  in Córdoba, 1
  in Tucumán province, 199–200
environmental regulation, 12–14
  administrative resources for, 211–15
  administrative structures in, 167
  in Brazil, 21, 24, 151
  in Chile, 23–24
  in China, 12, 21
  community mobilization of, 225
  co-produced enforcement of, 165–66, 214
  in Córdoba, 163–66, 185–88
  decentralized administration of, 157–63
  enforcement patterns for, 200–7
  in Federal Capital, 159–60
  at federal level, 158
  under General Environmental Law, 150–51
  hazardous waste laws and, 149
  historical development of, 147
  inspection rates for, 170
  international influences on, 151
  through judiciary, 150, 196–97
  Law to Protect Glaciers, 152
  in Matanza-Riachuelo watershed, 159–60
  at municipal level, 158
  Native Forest Law, 152
  under 1994 constitution, 149–50
  through PPL, 160
  through PRI, 202–3
  provincial policies for, 150–51, 160–61, 163–66
  in Santa Fe, 163–66, 169–85

environmental regulation (cont.)
  under Secretariat of Natural Resources and
    Environment, 148, 158–59
  SFSMA enforcement of, 169–72
  SIPROSA enforcement of, 193–95, 197–99
  without social mobilization, 148–52
  society-dependent enforcement of, 165,
    184–85
  as top-down process, 167
  in Tucumán, 2, 40, 163–66, 192–93, 207–11
  UIA support for, 160
  in Vietnam, 223–26
  weaknesses of, 157–63
Evans, Peter, 26

FA. *See* Federation of Environmental Non-
  Governmental Organizations
FARN. *See Fundación Ambiente y Recursos*
  Naturales
fatal accidents, 126, 136
Federación Económica de Tucumán. See
  Economic Federation of Tucumán
Federal Capital
  administrative resources in, 127–29
  autonomy features of, 113
  center-left government in, 128–29
  enforcement of labor regulation in, 70–71,
    126–44
  garment industry in, 71, 130–39
  labor inspectors in, 63, 112
  labor violations in, 130–34
  right governments in, 140–43
  STBA and, 60, 126–27
Federation of Environmental Non-
  Governmental Organizations (FA), 156,
  196–97, 206
Fernández de Kirchner, Cristina, 39, 162, 186
FET. *See* Economic Federation of Tucumán
Fine, Janice, 227–28
FUNAM. *See* Environmental Defense
  Foundation
Fundación Ambiente y Recursos Naturales
  (FARN), 154

garment industry
  La Alameda and, 71, 133, 136–39
  collective bargaining structure for, 130
  Defensor del Pueblo and, 131, 136
  enforcement of, 71
  fatal accidents in, 136
  in Federal Capital, 71, 130–39
  home-based workshops as part of, 130

in Indonesia, 232–33
INTI and, 134–35
labor regulation in, 68
labor violations in, 130–34
linkages between inspectors and labor unions
  in, 136–39
under Macri administration, 141–43
SOHO case, 134
undocumented workers in, 130–31
General Environmental Law, 39, 150
General Labor Confederation (CGT), 55
  in Córdoba, 55
Gómez, Antonio Gustavo, 197
Green Party, 157

hazardous waste laws, 149
health and safety regulations
  in brick-making industry, 78
  in construction industry, 84, 86, 123
  in Córdoba, 78, 84, 86
  CYMAT enforcement in, 84–85
  under MTSF guidelines, 123
  in Tucumán, 101–2
  in US, 16–17
home-based workshops, in garment industry,
  130
hot goods provision, 134

IADB. *See* Inter-American Development Bank
Ibarra, Aníbal, 128
ILO. *See* International Labor Organization
Indonesia
  collective bargaining agreements in, 230
  corruption levels in, 229, 231
  garment industry in, 232–33
  labor inspectors in, 230–31
  labor politics in, 229–30
  labor regulation in, 229–34
  labor unions in, 231–32
  society-dependent enforcement in, 229–34
inspections. *See* labor inspectors and
  inspections
Instituto Nacional de Tecnología Industrial
  (INTI), 134–35
Inter-American Development Bank (IADB),
  150, 158
International Labor Organization (ILO), 23,
  59, 118
INTI. *See Instituto Nacional de Tecnología*
  Industrial

Janitorial Enforcement Team (JET), 228

Index

Kirchner, Néstor, 39, 60, 118, 186
environmental policy under, 161–62
labor policy under, 51, 56

labor compliance. *See* compliance, labor
labor infractions, 129
labor inspectors and inspections
in Brazil, 17
code of ethics for, 119
in Córdoba, 1–2, 74–75, 94
corruption among, in Tucumán, 104
in Dominican Republic, 75
education level of, 62–63
in Federal Capital, 63, 112, 126–27
in Indonesia, 230–31
information management by, 91
inspection campaigns, 91
linkages with labor unions, 64–66, 89–90,
 116, 120, 136–39
per capita, by region, 62
under PJ, 113–15
salaries of, 90–91
in Santa Fe, 112–25
tax collection by, 114
training for, 63
in Tucumán, 63, 98, 104
labor laws
in Argentina, 52–54
in Brazil, 54
compliance with, 53
institutional continuity and, 53
in Mexico, 54
under Perón, 52–53
labor regulation, 12–14
in Argentina, 13, 40, 54, 71–72
in Brazil, 24
in brick-making industry, 68
business organizations and, in Argentina, 54–59
in citrus industry, 68
in construction industry, 68
in Córdoba, 68–70
in Dominican Republic, 24
environmental regulation compared to,
 156–57
in Federal Capital, 70–71, 126–43
in garment industry, 68
under ILO guidelines, 23, 59, 118
in Indonesia, 229–34
linkages with labor unions, 93–97
main cases of, 68
in metal industry, 68
partisan politics and, in Argentina, 54–59, 61

political origins of, 93–97
in Santa Fe, 70–71
STC and, 74–75
in Tucumán, 68–70
in US, 226–29
Labor Secretariat, in Tucumán (TST), 97–98,
 102, 104–6
Labor Secretariat of Córdoba (STC)
brick-making industry under, 74–75, 79
construction industry enforcement by, 88–89
metal industry enforcement by, 82
labor unions
in Argentina, 45, 54–59
in Córdoba, 55, 76
deregulatory reforms and, 22
during economic crises, 56
enforcement regulation influenced by, 21–22
enforcement strategies of, 57–58
in Federal Capital, 128–29, 136–37
in Indonesia, 231–32
linkages with labor inspectors, 64–66, 89–90,
 93–97, 116, 120
Perón and, 55–56
PJ and, 55–56
in Santa Fe, 115–16, 120
on shop floors, 56
STSF and, 115–16
in Tucumán, 68–70, 98
UIA, 58, 160
Law to Protect Glaciers, 152
Lieutier, Ariel, 128–29, 138–39
linkages. *See* state-society linkages

Macri, Mauricio, 140–43
La Alameda and, 141–43
garment industry under, 141–43
STBA and, 141–43
Matanza-Riachuelo watershed, 159–60
Menem, Carlos Saúl, 53, 149, 158–59
Mercado, Rogelio, 107–8
Mestre, Ramón, 94
metal industry
collective bargaining agreements, 81–82
in Córdoba, 73, 81–83
enforcement patterns in, 69, 81–83
labor regulation in, 68
in Rosario, 116
STC enforcement of, 82
UOM and, 82, 116
Mexico, labor law in, 54
Ministério Público, 24
Ministry of Labor (MTESS), 60, 130, 132

272   *Index*

Ministry of Labor of Córdoba (MTC), 16, 41
enforcement strategies for, 60
formation of, 93–94
labor inspections by, 94
Montalván, Alfredo, 203–4
MTC. *See* Ministry of Labor of Córdoba
MTSF. *See* Santa Fe Ministry of Labor and
Social Security

National Network for Ecological Action, 156
National Plan for Regularization of Work
(PNRT), 60
Native Forest Law, 152
neighborhood environmental organizations
La Boca Neighborhood Association, 155–56
opposition to Santa Clara Plant, 174–77
Pro-Eco, 196
SFSMA and, 184
in Tucumán, 195–96, 211
UniVec, 195–97, 203–4
Vecinal Santa Teresita, 174–77
NGOs. *See* La Alameda; neighborhood
environmental organizations; professional
environmental organizations
1994 constitution, in Argentina, 149–50
non-governmental organizations (NGOs). *See*
La Alameda; neighborhood environmental
organizations; professional environmental
organizations

occupational health and safety agency (SRT),
118–19
Ortega, Ramón, 107–8

Partido Justicialista. *See* Peronist Party
partisanship, political
enforcement of regulatory practices and,
9–10, 144
Santa Clara Plant and, 174–76
Pereyra, Alejandro, 128, 138
Perón, Juan
administrative resource investment under,
95–96
labor laws established under, 52–53
labor unions and, 55–56
Secretariat of Natural Resources and the
Human Environment and, 148
Peronist Party (PJ), 45
clientelism and, 55
in Córdoba, 74, 111
labor inspectorate under, 113–15
labor unions and, 55–56

PS as alternative to, 117–20
in Santa Fe, 113–15
in Tucumán, 74, 111
Picolotti, Romina, 152, 161–62, 186, 212
PJ. *See* Peronist Party
Plan of Industrial Reconversion (PRI), 202–3
PNRT. *See* National Plan for Regularization of
Work
political partisanship. *See* partisanship, political
politicized states, 6
pollution. *See also* air pollution; water pollution
by citrus industry, 165–66, 191–93
collateral effect of, 196
mobilization strategies against, 195–200
non-point sources of, 191
point sources of, 191
SIPROSA enforcement of, 193–95, 197–99
by sugar industry, 191–93
porous states, 29. *See also* bureaucracies, as
porous
PPL. *See* Provincial Plan for Clean Production
PRI. *See* Plan of Industrial Reconversion
private regulation, state development of, 14
Pro-Eco, 196
professional environmental organizations, 154,
167
CEDAH, 161–62, 186
in Córdoba, 185–87
Córdoba Environmental Forum, 186–87
FARN, 154
FUNAM, 185–86
SFSMA and, 183–84
Taller Ecologista, 182–83
protests. *See* environmental protests
Provincial Plan for Clean Production (PPL)
development of, 179
environmental regulation through, 160,
179–80, 200–2
experimentation conditions under, 204–5
features of, 200–1
function of, 201–2
PS. *See* Socialist Party

Radical Party (UCR), 61, 93–94, 96–97
Riachuelo watershed. *See* Matanza-Riachuelo
watershed
Rodríguez, Carlos Anibel, 118–19
Rosario, Argentina. *See also* Santa Clara Plant
construction industry in, 121
metal industry in, 116
MTSF in, 123
UOCRA in, 122

Index

Sabsay, Daniel Alberto, 154
Santa Clara Plant
  air pollution created by, 173–74
  EIA for, 178–80
  environmental regulation of, enforcement practices for, 172–85
  expansion of, 173
  fires at, 174
  neighborhood opposition to, 174–77
  political partisanship and, 174–76
  PPL for, 179–80
  SFSMA enforcement in, 173–74, 176–80
  Vecinal Santa Teresita and, 174–77
  water pollution created by, 173–74
Santa Fe Ministry of Labor and Social Security (MTSF), 117–18
  health and safety regulations under, 123
  in Rosario, 123
  UOCRA and, 123–26
Santa Fe province
  air pollution in, 2, 164
  allocation of regulatory resources in, 113
  bureaucratic reform in, 117–20
  construction industry in, 85, 121–25
  enforcement of labor regulation in, 70–71, 143–44
  enforcement patterns in, 180–85
  environmental regulation in, 163–66, 169–85
  expansion of state capacity in, 117–20
  labor inspectors in, 112–25
  linkages with inspectors and unions in, 116, 120
  local labor office in, 60
  MTSF in, 117–18
  PJ in, 113–15
  PS in, 117–20
  SRT in, 118–19
  STSF in, 113–14
  UOCRA in, 122
Santiago del Estero province, 198–99
Sappia, Jorge, 93
Savino, Atilio, 161–62
Schiaretti, Juan, 94–95
Secretaría de Estado de Trabajo de Santa Fe (STSF), 113–14
  construction industry enforcement under, 122
  labor inspections by, 116
  labor unions and, 115–16
Secretaría de Medio Ambiente de Santa Fe (SFSMA), 169–72

civil servants in, 183
  fines, 171
  lack of administrative resources for, 180–85
  neighborhood environmental organizations and, 184
  professional environmental organizations and, 183–84
  resistance to, 171
  Santa Clara Plant regulation of, 173–74, 176–80
Secretariat of Natural Resources and Environment, 148, 158–59
SEIU. *See* Service Employees International Union
Sereno, Omar, 79–80
Service Employees International Union (SEIU), 228
SFSMA. *See Secretaría de Medio Ambiente de Santa Fe*
shop floors, labor union representation on, 56
Sistema Provincial de Salud (SIPROSA), 193–95, 197–99
SMATA (auto workers' union), 140–41
Socialist Party (PS)
  linkages between unions and inspectors, 120
  in Santa Fe, 117–20
society-dependent enforcement, 8, 36–37, 220–21, 229–34
  of environmental regulation, 165, 184–85
  in Indonesia, 234
  of labor regulation, 97–109, 113
Socio-Environmental Agenda, 182
SOHO case, 134
SRT. *See* occupational health and safety agency
state capacity
  autonomy and, 5–6, 26, 34–35
  in Córdoba, 93
  for enforcement, 5–6, 23–27, 235
  expansion of, under Binner, 117–20
  investment in, 96–97
  political control and, 6
  theoretical approaches to, 26
state-driven enforcement, 9, 36, 226–29
states
  internal coherence in, 6
  policy implementation within, 236
  politicized, 6
state-society linkages, 42, 236
  dual role of, 32–33
  enforcement and, 7–8, 29–33

274 *Index*

state-society linkages (cont.)
political coalitions and, 31–32
in porous states, 29
structure of, 30–31
STC. *See* Labor Secretariat of Córdoba
STSF. *See* Secretaría de Estado de Trabajo de
Santa Fe
Sub-Secretariat of Labor of Buenos Aires
(STBA), 126–27
La Alameda and, 136–39
garment industry enforcement by, 132–37
labor inspections under, 126–27
linkages between inspectors and labor unions
under, 136–39
in Macri administration, 141–43
sugar industry, 165–66
administrative resources for enforcement in,
211–15
cachaza pollutant, management of, 206–7
CART, 191
closure of factories in, 205–6
pollution by, 191–93
PRI for, 202–3
SIPROSA enforcement in, 193–95, 197–99
in Tucumán province, 190–91

Tafí Viejo, wastewater pollution in, 196
Taillant, Jorge Daniel, 186
Taller Ecologista, 182–83
Telerman, Jorge, 128–29
Terenzio, Marcelo, 182
Tomada, Carlos, 51, 60
trade, enforcement influenced by, 20–21
training, for labor inspectors, 63
TST. *See* Labor Secretariat, in Tucumán
Tucumán Citrus Association (ATC), 99
Tucumán Construction Associations (CCT),
104
Tucumán province, 2, 40
administrative resources in, 211–15
bureaucratic reform in, 208–9
citrus industry in, 73, 98–101
construction industry in, 73, 101–4
corruption among inspectors in, 104
economic development in, compared to
Córdoba, 73–74
enforcement of labor regulations in, 43,
68–70, 104–6, 143–44
environmental protests in, 199–200
environmental regulation enforcement in, 2,
40, 163–66, 192–93, 207–11

explanations of enforcement in, 104–6
Federation of Environmental Non-
Governmental Organizations in, 156
FET in, 104, 191, 212
governors in, 74
health and safety violations in, 101–2
labor inspections in, 63, 98
labor unions in, 68–70, 98
neighborhood environmental organizations
in, 195–96, 211
PJ in, 74, 111
PPL in, 200–2
PRI in, 202–3
regulatory enforcement in, 43
SIPROSA in, 193–95, 197–99
society-dependent enforcement strategies in,
97–109
sugar industry in, 190–91
TST in, 97–98, 102, 104–6
UniVec and, 195–97, 203–4
UOCRA in, 102–4

UCR. *See* Radical Party
UIA. *See* Union Industrial de Argentina
undocumented workers, in garment industry,
130–31
uneven states
enforcement in, 220
weak institutions and, 3–14
Union Industrial de Argentina (UIA), 58, 160
United States (US)
co-produced enforcement in, 226–29
environmental regulation in, 4
health and safety regulation in, 16–17
labor regulation in, 226–29
state-driven enforcement in, 226–29
UniVec, 195–97, 203–4
UOCRA. *See* Construction Workers' Union of
Argentina
UOM, 82, 116, 142
UORLA Union, 80
Uruguay, Botnia paper mill controversy and,
161

Varela, Florencio, 128
Vecinal Santa Teresita, 174–77
Vera, Gustavo, 143
Vernet, José María, 113–14
Viet Tri Chemicals, 224–25
Vietnam, environmental regulation in, 223–26
community mobilization of, 225

Index

275

water pollution
  by citrus industry, 192
  in Córdoba, 187–88
  in Riachuelo watershed, 155
  by Santa Clara Plant, 173–74

  by sugar industry, 191–92
  in Tafí Viejo, 196
weak institutions, 236–37
  uneven states and, 3–14
Weberian bureaucracy, 24–25, 34–35, 208

For EU product safety concerns, contact us at Calle de José Abascal, 56–1°,
28003 Madrid, Spain or eugpsr@cambridge.org.